THE REFUGEES CONVENTION 50 YEAR

The Refugees Convention 50 Years On

Globalisation and International Law

Edited by
SUSAN KNEEBONE
Associate Professor, Monash University, Australia

Routledge
Taylor & Francis Group

LONDON AND NEW YORK

First published 2003 by Ashgate Publishing

Reissued 2018 by Routledge
2 Park Square, Milton Park, Abingdon, Oxon OX14 4RN
711 Third Avenue, New York, NY 10017, USA

Routledge is an imprint of the Taylor & Francis Group, an informa business

Copyright © Susan Kneebone 2003

A Library of Congress record exists under LC control number: 2002041751

ISBN 13: 978-1-138-71525-7 (hbk)
ISBN 13: 978-1-138-71524-0 (pbk)
ISBN 13: 978-1-315-19766-1 (ebk)

Contents

Contributors – Presenters and Commentators from the 2001 Workshop

Paris Aristotle AM is the Director of the Victorian Foundation for Survivors of Torture, a position he has held since the organisation's establishment in 1987. In 2002, Paris was appointed as a part-time Commissioner of the Victorian Law Reform Commission. Paris has also held several positions on government advisory bodies in the settlement and human services fields. He currently holds positions on the federal government's Refugee Resettlement Advisory Council and the Immigration Detention Advisory Group. Paris has been a member of a number of official delegations to the UNHCR Executive Committee and most recently, a member of the UNHCR Executive Committee on Resettlement and Integration. Paris was recently made a Member of the Order of Australia for his work with refugees, in particular survivors of torture.

Mary Crock is a Senior Lecturer in Law at the University of Sydney, teaching administrative law, refugee and migration law and other public law subjects. She is the author of *Immigration and Refugee Law in Australia* (Sydney, Federation Press, 1998); co-author with Ben Saul of *Future Seekers: Refugees and the Law in Australia* (Sydney, Federation Press, 2002); and editor of *Protection or Punishment: The Detention of Asylum Seekers in Australia* (Sydney, Federation Press, 1993). Mary acted as advisor to Senators involved in the inquiry into Australia's Refugee and Humanitarian Program conducted by the Senate Legal and Constitutional References Committee, which published a report in 2000 entitled, *A Sanctuary Under Review*. In 2000, she assisted in the preparation of a report by the Human Rights and Equal Opportunity Commission on the Immigration Detention Centre at Curtin, WA. As well as holding other positions she is Chair of the Nationality and Residence Committee, International Law Section, Law Council of Australia and trustee of the Australian Sanctuary and Settlement Fund.

Liz Curran lectures in Law at La Trobe University and operates the Clinical Legal Education Program in West Heidelberg. She is a former Executive Director of the Catholic Commission for Justice Development and Peace, and also served as the Co-chair of Justice for Asylum Seekers, providing written and oral commentary on public policy responses in the national media. She has also held a position as a Law Reform Officer and Spokesperson on behalf of the Federation of Community Legal Centres. Liz holds a Masters of Law from the University of Melbourne specialising in human rights.

Donald Galloway is Professor of Law at the University of Victoria, British Columbia. He is the author of *Immigration Law* (Canada, Irwin Law, 1997) in the Essentials of Canadian Law series, and various articles on immigration, citizenship and equality. In 1998 he took three years leave of absence to serve as a member of the refugee division of the Immigration and Refugee Board. In 1999 he coordinated efforts in Prince George, British Columbia, to provide hearings to 600 boat arrivals from China. Currently, he is the Director of the Akitsiraq Law School, a program operated by the University of Victoria, in Iqaluit, Baffin Island in the Canadian Arctic, which provides legal training and education to Inuit students.

Matthew J. Gibney is University Lecturer in Forced Migration at the Refugees Studies Centre, University of Oxford and Official Fellow of Linacre College, Oxford. He has completed a MPhil and PhD at Cambridge University and has taught politics at Monash, Cambridge and Harvard Universities. His research interests focus upon the evolution and future of asylum in Western states, the ethical and political issues raised by deportation, and the relationship between forced migration and the modern state. His books include, *Globalizing Rights* (Oxford, Oxford University Press 2002) and *The Ethics and Politics of Asylum: Liberal Democracy and the Responses to Refugees*, which will be published by Cambridge University in 2003. Other recent publications include: 'Between Control and Humanitarianism: Temporary Protection in Contemporary Europe', *Georgetown Immigration Law Journal* (Spring 2000) and 'Liberal Democratic States and Responsibilities to Refugees', *American Political Science Review* (March 1999).

Jose Alvin C Gonzaga is currently a Legal Officer with the UNHCR, Canberra, Australia. Prior to this he has held numerous positions in the UNHCR, including Legal Consultant in the Philippines (1990) and Indonesia (1991–93), and has been involved in refugee status determination. In 1993, he was posted as a Field/Protection Officer in Tuzla and Brcko, Bosnia and Herzegovina. Between 1998 and 2000 he was sent on missions to Thailand, the Former Yugoslav Republic of Macedonia and East Timor, assisting projects such as the Emergency Evacuation Program of the Kosovar Albanian refugees and the supervision of East Timorese displaced persons until after the popular consultation.

Rodger Haines QC was one of the three original appointees to the New Zealand Refugee Status Appeals Authority when it was set up in 1991. He currently serves as Deputy Chairperson and has written many of its principal decisions. Since 1993 he has lectured in immigration and refugee law at the Faculty of Law, Auckland University. Other teaching appointments include co-teaching a paper in comparative asylum law with Professor James C Hathaway at the University of Michigan Law School, Ann Arbor in the fall term, 2000.

Michael Head is Coordinator of the Community Law Program at the University of Western Sydney where he also teaches immigration and refugee law. He writes for the World Socialist Web Site on international refugee issues. He has published articles on democratic rights, global citizenship and legislation passed to provide Safe Haven visas for Kosovar and Timor refugees.

Robert Illingworth is presently Assistant Secretary to the Onshore Protection Branch of the Refugee and Humanitarian Division, Department of Immigration and Multicultural and Indigenous Affairs. Since the early 1990s, he has been involved with the development of policy relating to refugee issues and refugee status determinations. He was previously a policy advisor in the Prime Minister's Department dealing with immigration issues and has been involved with protection visa arrangements since their introduction in 1993.

Susan Kneebone is an Associate Professor in the Law Faculty, Monash University, where she works closely with the Castan Centre for Human Rights Law. Susan teaches administrative law and international refugee law and practice. She has published several articles on procedures for refugee status determination and on Australian refugee law issues. She has also made submissions to Senate and other enquiries into associated issues and is currently working on a large research project on comparative procedures for refugee status determination. In August 2002 she gave evidence to the Australian Senate's Legal and Constitutional References Committee's inquiry into migration zone excision.

Penelope Mathew is a Senior Lecturer in the Faculty of Law at the Australian National University, where she teaches international law and human rights. She completed her doctorate at Columbia University on refugee law and is the author of several articles on this topic. In 1992, she assisted the Jesuit Refugee Service in Hong Kong as a volunteer lawyer, in the mid-1990s she served as a board member for the Refugee Advice and Casework Service and from mid-1999 to mid-2000 worked as a researcher with the Jesuit Refugee Service. Dr Mathew participated in the expert panel on gender-related persecution, membership of a particular social group and the internal protection alternative which was held as part of UNHCR's Global Consultations, held to coincide with the 50th anniversary of the Refugees Convention. She advised UNHCR concerning the legislation introduced by the Australian government in 2001 to implement the Pacific Solution. In August 2002 she gave evidence to the Australian Senate's Legal and Constitutional References Committee's inquiry into migration zone excision.

Margaret Piper has been the Executive Director of the Refugee Council of Australia since 1991. She is a board member of the UNIYA (the Jesuit social research organisation), the Refugee Advice and Casework Service, and the NSW and International Social Services NSW and also a founding member of the Australian National Consultative Committee on Refugee Women.

Nick Poynder is a barrister practising at the NSW Bar in the areas of immigration, anti-discrimination and human rights. He practised at the Victorian Bar (1990–93) and also worked with asylum seekers in detention centres in Port Hedland and Curtin Air Base, and with Aboriginal people in Central Australia. He has also served for three years as a Senior Legal Officer at the Human Rights and Equal Opportunity Commission. He is the author of the two communications to be upheld by the UN Human Rights Committee against Australia, regarding asylum seekers held in mandatory detention.

Savitri Taylor is a Senior Lecturer in the School of Law and Legal Studies at La Trobe University. She has been researching Australian refugee law, policy and practice from public international law and political science perspectives since 1991 and her research findings have been published in a range of academic journals. She has completed a doctorate, Bachelor of Law (Hons) and Bachelor of Commerce from the University of Melbourne.

Kristen Walker is a Senior Lecturer in Law at the University of Melbourne. She completed her articles with Arthur Robinson and Hedderwicks in Melbourne and has served as Associate to Sir Anthony Mason, then Chief Justice of Australia. She teaches law and sexuality, constitutional law and a graduate subject, principles of public and international law. She has also taught international human rights and legal ethics at Columbia Law School, New York. She is currently completing a JSD at Columbia Law School, focusing on refugee law and sexuality.

Acknowledgements

This project would not have been possible without the assistance and contributions of a number of people. Foremost, I would like to thank Professor David Kinley, Director of the Castan Centre for Human Rights Law, Faculty of Law, Monash University for his support and guidance, from inception to completion of the project, and Alison Creighton for her tireless and expert desktop editorial work. I would also like to thank various other people who have assisted me with the editing process, namely Gail Hubble, Pene Mathew, Kobi Liens, Robyn Sweet, Ania Swicki, Elaine Miller and Eddy Gisconda.

I also thank the following people who helped me with the organisation of the workshop: Kay Magnani, Nicola Paton, Stephanie Gutwick and Jill Bell. I thank the paper presenters for the excellent chapters they produced, which in some cases were substantial redrafts of the original papers due to subsequent developments. In many instances they have incorporated the remarks of the commentators. I would particularly like to thank this latter group, who all produced reflective and incisive comments, which if time and space had permitted, could have been included in the book. They were: Paris Aristotle, Rodger Haines, Michael Head, and Margaret Piper. I especially thank Liz Curran who as the rapporteur of the workshop had the unenviable task of summing up on its conclusion, and valiantly brought together the many strands of our 'brainstorming'. Subsequently she produced a very thoughtful final chapter (chapter 12) and assisted me enormously by producing the first draft of chapter 1.

I must also acknowledge the support of the Law Faculty at Monash University which funded this project through an Australian Research Council Small Grant.

Dr Susan Kneebone
Melbourne

Preface

On 13 December 2001, governments from around the world issued a landmark declaration, renewing their commitment to protecting refugees and reaffirming the central role of the 1951 Refugees Convention as the cornerstone of that effort.

Issued in Geneva at the close of an unprecedented ministerial meeting of signatories to the Refugees Convention, the declaration recognised the Convention's 'enduring importance' and the 'continuing relevance and resilience' of the rights and principles it embodies. The participating governments pledged to uphold these rights and to carry out their obligations under the Refugees Convention. The meeting was convened as part of a process of global consultations, launched by the United Nations High Commissioner for Refugees in 2001 to coincide with the 50th anniversary of the 1951 Convention, to which 143 states have now acceded.

The global consultations were conceived to allow constructive debate about the challenge of protecting refugees in today's increasingly complex international environment, and to strengthen refugee protection in years to come.

This book, and the workshop from which it arose, is part of that process of critically examining the Refugees Convention. The contributors to this book, all with a wide range of backgrounds and opinions, identify gaps and dilemmas in the international protection system, while reinforcing the importance of providing protection to refugees. The work of Dr Susan Kneebone is a part of a vital effort by people and organisations around the world to reinvigorate the Refugees Convention, to reinforce it and to ensure that it remains relevant in the future.

I hope that readers of this book will take the opportunity to reflect on the spirit of the Refugees Convention, the humanitarian principles it upholds, and its importance in ensuring that refugees are given the protection and assistance they need.

Michel Gabaudan
United Nations High Commissioner for Refugees
Regional Representative for Australia, New Zealand, Papua New Guinea
and the South Pacific

1 Overview

LIZ CURRAN AND SUSAN KNEEBONE

Introduction

The papers in this collection arise from a workshop organised by Dr Susan Kneebone of the Castan Centre for Human Rights Law, Faculty of Law, Monash University, Melbourne, Australia in June 2001. Liz Curran of La Trobe University was the rapporteur for the workshop. The participants in the workshop, namely the presenters, commentators (see the list of contributors at p vii) and invitees included members of government and non-governmental organisations (NGOs), academics, and practitioners (both legal and other) from diverse countries. Some participants were themselves from refugee backgrounds. The discussion in the one and a half days ranged enthusiastically over policies and practices in Europe, the United Kingdom, Australia, Canada and New Zealand.

The workshop, held on the eve of the 50th anniversary of the 1951 Convention Relating to the Status of Refugees (the Refugees Convention),[1] addressed the issue of whether the Convention provides an adequate framework of protection in the context of globalisation and a developed international law regime. The title of the workshop and this book, *The Refugees Convention 50 Years On: Globalisation and International Law* reflects that theme. Primarily the workshop was concerned with whether the Convention can provide effective protection as an instrument of international human rights law in a globalised world. That is, in the context of economic globalisation and universally recognised human rights, is the Refugees Convention a relevant and effective international instrument?

Particular issues which the presenters at the workshop were asked to examine included:

---

[1] References to the 1951 Refugees Convention throughout this book are to the 1951 Convention Relating to the Status of Refugees done at Geneva on 28 July 1951 and the 1967 Protocol Relating to the Status of Refugees done at Geneva on 31 January 1967.

- to what extent is the reaction of the western nations to the refugee problem a reflection of economic nationalism, and might the concept of economic globalisation be used to forge new international consensus?
- the Convention and other regimes of international human rights protection – is it being interpreted consistently with other international instruments?
- how and why are other instruments such as the Convention Against Torture being used to complement the Refugees Convention?
- a comparison of alternative internal (national) avenues for the exercise of administrative discretion on humanitarian grounds;
- new uses of the refugee definition – the role of the state and private issues, including abused women and gender issues – are they legitimate or marginal extensions of the Convention?
- an evaluation of the role of the United Nations High Commissioner for Refugees (UNHCR);
- the role of NGOs – are they effective instruments for change?
- nationality and citizenship issues – effective nationality and the non-refoulement obligation – Articles 1C and 1E of the Refugees Convention, 'safe third country' exemptions.

Presenters were asked to engage with a policy paper prepared for the Australian government by Adrienne Millbank.[2] In that paper the author canvasses problems and perceptions associated with the Refugees Convention and concludes that:

> There is a concern in both major political parties that asylum seekers could undermine support for migration programs … It seems likely that Australian governments will take whatever measures are necessary to curtail illegal entry and rising numbers of asylum seekers, including challenging the UNHCR and rethinking our obligations under the Refugee Convention.[3]

In hindsight that conclusion was prophetic. At the time the workshop was held we could not have predicted the dramatic events of the *Tampa*

---

[2] A Millbank, *The Problem with the 1951 Convention* (Canberra, Department of the Parliamentary Library, Research Paper 5 2000–01), http://www.aph.gov.au/library/pubs/rp/2000-01/01RP05.htm.

[3] Id, p 20.

crisis, which took place in waters to the north of Australia, and the subsequent 'Pacific Solution' introduced by the Australian government in response to that incident.[4] This refers to the refusal of the Australian government to allow a Norwegian cargo ship, *MV Tampa*, to enter into Australian waters with 433 asylum seekers rescued at sea. The incident took place in the last weeks of the second term of office of the Howard Liberal government and just prior to the terrorist attacks on the USA on 11 September 2001. The Howard government, which subsequently won a third term of office, created the Pacific Solution by entering into agreements with small Pacific island nations for them to host the asylum seekers and to provide facilities for the processing of their refugee claims, in exchange for money payments.[5] These events have put a spotlight on Australia and the way in which it has implemented its obligations under the Refugees Convention. Rather alarmingly, elements of the Australian 'solutions', including the rhetoric for dealing with the ever-increasing tide of refugees are now being mirrored in Europe.

The overwhelming view held by contributors to this book is that despite problems with its implementation, the Convention is fundamentally relevant 50 years on as a flexible statement of basic human rights and values. That message needs to be delivered even more firmly in the current global situation.

The chapters in the book are arranged around two main sub-themes. The first is the effect of globalisation upon the use of the Convention, and the second being to assess its ability and effectiveness as an instrument of human rights protection.

---

[4] See below and M Crock, 'The Refugees Convention at 50: Mid-life Crisis or Terminal Inadequacy? An Australian Perspective', chapter 3 in this book; P Mathew, 'Safe for Whom? The Safe Third Country Concept Finds a Home in Australia', chapter 6 in this book.

[5] In the May 2002 budget it was reported that the Pacific Solution had cost Australia at least $572 million since last September and that a further $431 million had been allocated for the coming year. This included building a new offshore detention facility on Christmas Island: 'Defiant stand on borders', *The Age*, 15 May 2002, p 6.

The Effect of Globalisation

Globalisation today is an epithet which has both positive and negative connotations. The negative points to the results of global economic and cultural imperialism. The manifestation of this is the continuing and increasing disparity in living standards in the industrialised nations and the developing world. The positive points to the role of universal standards and international law, to international cooperation in environmental matters, intervention in regional conflicts and in relation to war crimes, for example. It suggests a global sense of responsibility for the fate of humanity.

The first cluster of chapters provides us with an overview of what Matthew Gibney calls 'the state of asylum' in our globalised world.[6] That is, the authors reflect upon national or state policies towards asylum seekers in a globalised world of interconnected societies and activities, which both work through and cut across nation states.[7] In popular parlance they look at the battle between state or national sovereignty and the international protection regime provided by the Refugees Convention.

One fact that is often forgotten in this battle is that the problems leading to people seeking asylum,[8] or the 'refugee problem' as we shall call it, are themselves often either a manifestation or a consequence of globalisation.[9] It is no accident that of the estimated 21.8 million people 'of concern' to the UNHCR today,[10] a major concentration occurs in the African countries,[11] with other concentrations occurring in the Middle East[12] and

---

[6] M Gibney, 'The State of Asylum: Democratisation, Judicialisation and Evolution of Refugee Policy', chapter 2 in this book.

[7] See the definition of 'globalisation' by Sir Anthony Mason in C Sampford and T Round (eds), *Beyond the Republic: Meeting the Global Challenges to Constitutionalism* (Australia, Federation Press, 2001), chapter 2. As Sir Anthony points out, it is not the fact of globalisation but the intensity of it which is a modern phenomenon.

[8] That is, displacement caused by persecution leading to flight and the seeking of asylum in another 'safe' country. This can be referred to loosely as the state of 'refugeehood'.

[9] C de Jong, 'The Legal Framework: The Convention relating to the Status of Refugees and the Development of Law a Century Later', *International Journal of Refugee Law* 10 (1998) p 688.

[10] UNHCR, *Refugees by Numbers 2001 Edition* (Geneva, UNHCR, 2001), http://www.unhcr.ch.

[11] Ibid. The figure given is approximately 6 million.

[12] See in particular Mathew, above n 4, for figures on the situation in the Middle East.

Asia. In the case of the African countries in particular, the causes of 'refugeehood' stem from de-colonisation, environmental degradation[13] (sometimes deliberately inflicted as an adjunct to ethnic persecution), famine and civil wars caused by the vacuum of power. These problems are exacerbated by the negative effects of globalisation, as the gap between Africa and the industrialised nations increases.

As Robert Illingworth, the Assistant Secretary for Onshore Protection for the Department of Immigration and Multicultural and Indigenous Affairs (DIMIA)[14] observes in chapter 4,[15] the bulk of the asylum seeking population in these countries has fled to neighbouring countries of first asylum. This leads to what Gibney calls a north–south dichotomy, with the poorer countries in the south hosting the larger number of refugees. The greatest burden is borne by the countries of the developing world who often house refugee camps on their borders next to the countries in turmoil. In a globalised context, and from an Australian geographical perspective, this equates to a dichotomy between the First and Third Worlds. This is the very imbalance which globalisation and global solutions should address.[16] Yet as a number of the contributors to this book point out, often the preferred solution of governments is to contain refugee populations in those poorer countries of first asylum. Or, more recently, as the Pacific Solution demonstrates, asylum seekers are kept at bay in poorer nations which are prepared to host them in exchange for financial reward.

Ironically it is the knowledge and increased ease of communication and transport, themselves manifestations of globalisation, which facilitate the outflows of asylum seekers. These refugee seeking populations are intermingled with 'illegal immigrants' seeking to share the economic fruits of globalisation, thus complicating the 'state of asylum'. Both groups are prey to people smugglers who seek to profit from these populations on the move. As Gibney and other contributors observe, these global indicators of

---

[13] A Dupont, 'Unregulated Population Flows in East Asia: A New Security Dilemma?', *Pacifica Review: Peace, Security and Global Change* **9(1)** (1997) p 16.

[14] Before elections in September 2001, the name of the portfolio was Immigration and Multicultural Affairs (DIMA).

[15] R Illingworth, 'Durable Solutions: Refugee Status Determinations and the Framework of International Protection', chapter 4 in this book.

[16] This situation of the unequal burden borne by some poorer countries by comparison to western nations was highlighted by the recent outpouring of refugees into neighbouring Pakistan.

the refugee problem have led to universal responses in the form of restrictive measures.

Mary Crock perceptively points out that there are two user-groups of the Convention.[17] These are asylum seekers and their advocates on the one hand, and governments on the other. Crock and Illingworth represent those two respective groups. There are many interesting counterpoints in their chapters. In chapter 4, Robert Illingworth, in presenting the Australian government's point of view, devotes much of his paper to the issue of people smuggling. He states that the increase in the total number of unauthorised arrivals:

> has arisen primarily as a result of the influence of people smugglers and recent arrivals have increasingly sought to engage Australia's protection obligations in an effort to be allowed to remain in Australia.[18]

This view considers the refugee problem to be a manifestation of people smugglers rather than of the worldwide phenomena of displacement caused by world conflict and persecution. While people smuggling is a serious issue because it exploits the needs of desperate people, it needs to be put in perspective and should not outweigh the rights of genuine asylum seekers. Matthew Gibney (chapter 2) and Mary Crock (chapter 3) both observe that concentration on the issue of people smugglers has led to the restrictive policies of many western (First World) governments.

The presentation of the refugee problem to the public, as Illingworth does in his paper, as issues of 'people smuggling' and 'illegal immigrants' is, as Gibney points out, a common political response of governments to these issues. Gibney argues that the restrictive attitudes and measures of governments in fact reflect the demos or popular view.[19] This political response indicates that politicians lack the political will to lead on these issues, which as a number of participants in the workshop agreed, are fundamentally moral issues.[20] Gibney refers to this as the 'particularistic understanding of responsibility' by states.[21] He asserts:

---

[17] Crock, above n 4.

[18] Illingworth, above n 15, p 91.

[19] Indeed this is the premise of Millbank, above n 2, who refers in a number of places to the popularity of anti-migration measures with voters in the developed world.

[20] A similar point was made by Margaret Piper, the Executive Director of the Refugee Council of Australia. She cited the use of terms such as 'illegals', which imply criminal

State leaders often do not have the interests and needs of their citizens at heart. And even when they do, there will always be neglected and disenchanted sections of their populations who, quite justifiably, feel that their interests do not receive the attention they deserve. How, then, can a state make this claim credible? At a very minimum, any state must convince a substantial section of its citizenry that even if their interests are not particularly high in the state's calculations, they are at least more important than those of foreigners.[22]

Interestingly, Crock's chapter demonstrates that the demos is itself often divided in its support of government policies on these issues. And as Gibney points out, it is often capricious. But in his presentation of the issues Illingworth lends support to Gibney's argument about the 'particularist understanding of responsibility by states'. On the one hand he addresses himself to the (perceived) popular view, but he also recognises the need to treat the root causes of the refugee problem. He acknowledges that restrictive responses are politically advantageous. But he also accepts the need for well-supported international involvement, both political, economic and social, for early intervention and prevention measures to create greater stability and to ease the causes of global displacement.

As Pene Mathew observes, it is the west or First World that is positioned financially and politically to share the burden and to assist with preventative measures to reduce conflict in the international arena.[23] Mathew says for example, that it is:

> highly questionable whether a state like Australia should be able to send Afghan refugees back to Pakistan ... Adoption of the safe third country notion by Australia inverts and misuses the idea of burden sharing.[24]

She argues persuasively that recent Australian 'safe third country' legislation is both a reaction to and a rejection of globalisation. As she and other contributors point out, globalisation in this context is not yet being used to forge a new international consensus on the protection of refugees.

---

activities by persons who are searching for safety and entitled to seek protection under international law as ill conceived and damaging.

[21] Gibney, above n 6, p 32.

[22] Id, pp 32–3.

[23] P Mathew, 'Safe for Whom? The Safe Third Country Concept Finds a Home in Australia', chapter 6 in this book, p 146.

[24] Id, p 146.

The most obvious effect of globalisation is the uniform state responses that the refugee problem receives. States look to each other for fresh ideas on how to restrict the use of the Refugees Convention. For example, Donald Galloway deals with the criminalisation of the refugee problem.[25] This refers to the linking of asylum seekers with illegal activities, such as 'people smuggling', and to popular perceptions that many asylum seekers have criminal backgrounds or that they are potential terrorists. This criminalisation is endorsed by the use of such terminology as 'forum shoppers' and 'queue jumpers'[26] and 'illegal immigrants' to describe asylum seekers. The irony of this criminalisation of the refugee problem is that it recognises that it is a global issue associated with global terrorism. In the wake of the terrorist attacks of 11 September 2001 upon the USA, this criminalisation of the refugee problem has been intensified with specific links being made between asylum seekers and 'the war against terror'.

In particular, Galloway describes attempts by the Canadian government to extend the scope of Article 1F of the Refugees Convention, which excludes Convention protection for persons who have committed serious non-political crimes or crimes against humanity. In Australia, this has been achieved through post-*Tampa* legislation.[27] Sections 91T and 91U of the Migration Legislation Amendment Act (No 6) 2001 (Cth) purport to clarify the meaning of 'non-political crime' in Article 1F of the Refugees Convention and 'particularly serious crime' under Article 33(2) of the Convention. Article 1F was designed to prevent the Convention applying to persons such as war criminals and individuals who might jeopardise internal security. That is, it needs to be read in its human rights framework. However, section 91U in particular, which includes 'detention' offences in the meaning of 'particularly serious crime', arguably goes beyond the spirit of Article 1F.

In chapter 5, Galloway discusses the new Canadian legislation which came into effect in June 2002. Bill C-11 in Canada introduces more restrictions on asylum seekers by the creation of new hurdles and broader definitions of criminality. The new measures taken to restrict the operation of the Convention in Canada include a denial of access to a country where

---

[25] D Galloway, 'Criminality and State Protection: Structural Tensions in Canadian Refugee Law', chapter 5 in this book.

[26] See Mathew, above n 23.

[27] The *Tampa* incident is discussed above.

a person is believed to be a terrorist or associated with organised crime and where it 'would be contrary to public interest for the claim to be heard'. The dangers of such an ambiguous provision are clear.

The Effectiveness of the Refugees Convention

Turning now to the second sub-theme of the book, being to assess the ability and effectiveness of the Convention as an instrument of human rights protection, the authors reveal that there is a tension or conflict between human rights protection on the one hand, and control of one's borders, sovereignty and economic globalisation, on the other. These next chapters measure how the Convention is applied against human rights standards and checks the Convention for its ability to respond to human rights abuses. The authors illustrate how implementation and interpretation of the Refugees Convention by some governments infringes basic human rights when the will to adhere to the spirit of the Convention is lacking.

As the rapporteur Liz Curran pointed out in her oral summary at the conclusion of the workshop, there is a contradiction and perhaps even hypocrisy in the response of state governments to the refugee problem. Resistance to global human rights is met by arguments about national sovereignty and yet global free trade is often embraced by governments as it will bring economic gains. On the one hand, businesses and companies demand that policies encourage corporations to work without borders and restrictions, while governments clamour to support free trade and deregulation. But on the other hand, the free movement of people and labour is discouraged. This means that asylum seekers and illegal immigrants are considered together in the same category. In this restrictive climate there is a serious risk that the rights of asylum seekers will be overlooked. At times it seems that economic considerations override human rights.

Paris Aristotle in his commentary at the workshop on the papers that have become chapters 2–4 of this book, pointed out the disjunction in this view. As he suggested, we need to think laterally about the fact that the west encourages the free movement of capital but not of people. He argued that the world will need freer movement of people to sustain global capitalism. But governments view asylum seekers as an economic burden rather than a bonus.[28] With those remarks in mind it is interesting to reflect retrospectively upon Illingworth's chapter which predates the *Tampa* incident and the subsequent Pacific Solution. Illingworth suggests that the global refugee situation raises the universal problem of:

> the public perception that nations cannot control their own borders and are subject to the whims of criminals involved in organised people smuggling ...[29]

That was the framework in which the *Tampa* incident evolved. Rather than regarding the *Tampa* asylum seekers as bearers of rights, the government characterised the issue as one of border control. Throughout the election campaign Prime Minister Howard was adamant that none of the 'rescuees' (as they were coined in the subsequent litigation) would set foot on Australian soil.

In the litigation for the release of the *Tampa* asylum seekers to Australian territory, the government successfully argued that various statutory obligations under the Migration Act 1958 (Cth), which suggested that it had a duty to take in the asylum seekers and to process them on Australian soil, had been overridden by the power of the executive arm of government to expel the asylum seekers from Australian borders.[30] The closest analogy for this arguably novel 'gatekeeping' power was the right to defend the border from enemy aliens. As Mathew argues in chapter 6, Australia has historically shown a strong interest in maintaining control over its island coastal borders, and continues to do so today. It is interesting to note that the border control legislation was inspired by measures taken by the USA during the 1990s.[31] Other countries are also concerned with

---

[28] For example, Millbank, above n 2, points out that today's asylum seekers come largely from the poorer nations. She argues that there is a correlation between refugee acceptance rates and the need for unskilled labour. However, the underlying assumption that the bulk of asylum seekers are poor and unskilled can be challenged. The contrary view is that it is in the self-interest of states to open their doors to enterprising asylum seekers: H Adelman, 'Refugee or Asylum: A Philosophical Perspective', *Journal of Refugee Studies* **1** (1988) p 7.

[29] Illingworth, above n 15, p 93.

[30] *Victorian Council for Civil Liberties Inc v Minister for Immigration and Multicultural Affairs (MIMA)* (2001) 110 FCR 452 (North J); *Ruddock v Vadarlis* (2001) 110 FCR 491 (Full Court).

[31] N Hancock, 'Refugee Law – Recent Developments', *Current Issues Brief* **5** (2001–02), http://www.aph.gov.au/library/pubs/cib/2001-02/02cib05.htm. See also Crock, above n 4.

protecting their 'sovereign' borders as recent tension between France and England over the Sangatte refugee camp illustrates.[32] In the context of an international legal system this concern with protecting boundaries and territory can be interpreted as an appeal to the popular political will. Mathew describes this as a symptom of an authoritarian government that does not want to be seen as a 'soft touch'. As Millbank points out, many restrictive measures introduced by western governments are the product of racism and xenophobia.[33] They are the result of an 'us and them' mentality as Galloway expresses it,[34] which is very ready to exclude those outside the community as we define it. This was articulated by French J in the *Tampa* litigation when he said:

> The power to determine who may come into Australia is so central to its sovereignty that it is not to be supposed that the Government of the nation would lack under the power conferred upon it directly by the Constitution, the ability to prevent people not part of the Australia community, from entering.[35]

As many have observed, the Refugees Convention is no longer supported by the ideological consensus that existed post World War II when the vast majority of refugees were Europeans fleeing ideologies hostile to liberal democracies.[36] Illingworth (chapter 4) notes that the vast number of asylum seekers to Australia today are from the Middle East.

This lack of support for the Convention suggests a rejection of an international system of human rights of which the Refugees Convention is a part. This extends to a denial of the status of asylum seekers and the basic right of flight under Article 14 of the Universal Declaration of Human Rights (UDHR). This right was arguably denied to the *Tampa* asylum seekers. The *Tampa* litigation in which the asylum seekers were described as 'rescuees' – neutral language deliberately chosen by the government – illustrates how asylum seekers can be dehumanised[37] and neutralised, and

---

[32] 'Blair drafts plan to get tough on border controls' and 'Pressure on French to close camp', *The Age*, 24 May 2002, p 12.

[33] Millbank, above n 2, p 16.

[34] Galloway, above n 25.

[35] *Ruddock v Vadarlis* (2001) 110 FCR 491 at 543, para 193.

[36] Including Millbank, above n 2.

[37] P Lynch and P O'Brien, 'From Dehumanisation to Demonisation: The MV Tampa and the Denial of Humanity', *Alternative Law Journal* **26(5)** (2001) p 215.

the human rights element forgotten. A description by Beaumont J in the Full Court of the Federal Court of the nature of Australia's international obligations under the Refugees Convention implies a rejection of it as an instrument of an international system of human rights applying to the national legal system.[38] In a postscript to his judgment Beaumont J said:

> Finally, it should be added that this is a municipal, and not an international, court. Even if it were, while customary international law imposes an obligation upon a coastal state to provide *humanitarian assistance* to vessels in distress, international law imposes no obligation upon the coastal state to resettle those rescued in the coastal state's territory. This accords with the principles of the Refugees Convention.[39]

By describing Australia's obligations under the Refugees Convention as concerned with municipal law and humanitarian assistance, the judge arguably overlooks the significance of the Convention as an instrument of human rights protection. Mathew (chapter 6) illustrates how the provision of 'safe third countries' can potentially infringe the non-refoulement obligation in Article 33 of the Convention. Other potential abuses arise through the processing of refugees. As the Convention does not prescribe procedures for processing refugees, it is open to governments to decide how this will be done. Nick Poynder starts from the position that there are 'gaps' in the way that Australia implements the Convention, pointing in particular to the administrative processes.[40] He and Crock (chapter 3) illustrate how government policies in relation to processing, such as mandatory detention, infringe basic human rights. Poynder and Crock each lament the difficulties caused by the isolation of detainees, their frustration due to the lack of information, and access to legal and counselling services. Crock also notes that in recent times there has been an escalation in allegations of inadequate care of those in detention.[41]

---

[38] Compare D Otto, 'From "Reluctance" to "Exceptionalism": The Australian Approach to Domestic Implementation of Human Rights', *Alternative Law Journal* **26**(5) (2001) p 219.

[39] *Ruddock v Vadarlis* (2001) 110 FCR 491 at 521, para 126. (Emphasis in the original.)

[40] N Poynder, '"Mind the Gap": Seeking Alternative Protection Under the Convention Against Torture and International Covenant on Civil and Political Rights', chapter 7 in this book.

[41] In February 2001 Mary Robinson announced her intention to visit the Woomera detention facility in South Australia. This followed a period of hunger strikes and lip-

Crock describes in detail how the processes operate in Australia where refugee status determination is an administrative process. By contrast, in Canada it is an adjudicative process and is arguably much fairer.[42] In discussion at the workshop, New Zealand was cited as an example of a relatively inclusive and fairer model of how asylum seekers are processed and treated in the lead up to the final stage of their refugee claim.[43] There are important lessons that can be learnt from the Australian experience, which is clearly a model other governments should *not* copy. As Poynder explains, the result of gaps in implementation of the Convention is that parties have to resort to appeals to international committees for human rights protection.

The *Tampa* episode is a dramatic example of how governments can decide *not* to process certain classes of refugees, and of how they can legislate to avoid their obligations under the Refugees Convention if they have political support. After the *Tampa* incident, which coincided with the last few weeks of the Howard government's term of office, the government rushed through a raft of legislation which, for the most part, received bipartisan support.[44] This included the:

- Migration Amendment (Excision from Migration Zone) Act 2001 (Cth) to remove parts of the 'migration zone' such as Christmas Island from the ambit of the Migration Act for the purpose of processing refugees;

---

sewing episodes in that and other detention facilities around the country and calls by observers appointed by the Minister for Immigration to close the Woomera detention facility. In the same month the solicitor who initiated the *Tampa* litigation, Mr Eric Vadarlis, announced his intention to launch a class action against the Minister for Immigration in negligence for failure to safeguard the health of asylum seekers detained on Manus Island, Papua New Guinea under the Pacific Solution. It is alleged that a number of people have contracted malaria as a result of failure to provide preventive medication.

[42] S Kneebone, 'Merits Review of Refugee Status Determinations and the Natural Justice Paradigm' in Migrant Resource Centre, *Refugee Law, Policy and Practice in Australia* (Melbourne, Spectrum Publications/Myer Foundation, 2001), pp 117–33.

[43] J Donald, '"We Don't Know How Lucky We Are, Mate": Australian and New Zealand Refugee Law – A Comparison', Paper presented at a seminar by Ryken and Associates and George Lombard Consultancy, 12 April 2002, Sydney, http://www.refugee.org.nz/lucky.html.

[44] Hancock, above n 31.

- Border Protection (Validation and Enforcement Powers) Act 2001 (Cth), which included powers in a new section 185(3A) to move people detained on boats to ships or aircraft. This implements the Pacific Solution and is the third piece of border protection legislation introduced since 1999;[45]
- Migration Legislation Amendment (Judicial Review) Act 2001 (Cth), which imposes a stronger privative or ouster clause upon the Federal Court's judicial review jurisdiction of Refugee Review Tribunal decisions. This removes yet another process available to refugee claimants. It arguably infringes Article 16 of the Refugees Convention (free access to the courts).

Savitri Taylor deals with another end of the process.[46] She highlights some of the holes in Australia's approach to removal of failed applicants for protection both prior to a determination of their claims and afterwards when they are removed. She questions the lack of due process involved in their automatic removal,[47] which is often swift and without explanation. She is also concerned about the use of force and medication. She questions the legality of government action when it makes extra judicial removals and engages in extra jurisdictional detention.

Another government policy for implementation of the Refugees Convention is the creation of temporary protection visas.[48] The concern with this visa is that the conditions infringe many of the basic guarantees under the Refugees Convention, such as Articles 3 (non-discrimination), 28 (provision of travel documents) and 31 (no penalties). In Australia the Migration Amendment (Excision from Migration Zone) (Consequential Provisions) Act 2001, passed in the wake of the *Tampa* episode, increases

---

[45] Border Protection Legislation Amendment Act 1999 (Cth) and Border Protection Bill 2001 introduced 29 August 2001 and subsequently defeated due to lack of Opposition support.

[46] S Taylor, 'The Human Rights of Rejected Asylum Seekers Being Removed From Australia', chapter 8 in this book.

[47] Taylor cites the decision of Sackville J in *Kopiev v MIMA* [2000] FCA 1831 (15 December 2000), where the Minister sought summary dismissal of proceedings by reason of the non-attendance of the applicant at proceedings. The applicant did not appear because he had been removed from Australia under section 198 of the Migration Act 1958 (Cth).

[48] See Crock, above n 4.

the categories of asylum seekers who are precluded from applying for permanent protection.

These examples suggest that if governments choose not to implement their obligations under the Refugees Convention in good faith, there are dangers of serious breaches of human rights. Against this we need to measure the work of the courts in interpreting the Convention. Both Gibney (chapter 2) and Galloway (chapter 5) note that in the United Kingdom and Canada common law protections or safeguards are complemented by the human rights frameworks within which the courts operate. Gibney states that prior to the passage of the Human Rights Act (UK) in 1999 the protection and safeguarding of rights was left to the governments which were often slow to act or less concerned about minority protection than pragmatics of majority votes. He presents the courts as the guardians of rights especially since that Act came into existence. Galloway however is more sanguine about the existence of such a dichotomy. He argues that the picture is more complex with the courts just as likely as the government to take restrictive attitudes.

These views are interesting to contrast with Crock (chapter 3) who discusses the tension that exists between the courts and the executive arm of government in Australia. The clear example of this is the way that the government has frequently responded legislatively to judicial decisions of which it disapproves. The most recent example of this is Migration Legislation Amendment Act (No 6) 2001 (Cth), one of the post *Tampa* measures referred to above. This potentially far-reaching legislation seeks in sections 91R and 91S to amend the refugee definition as well as to alter the scope of Article 1F of the Convention. Additionally, in relation to processing issues, it allows adverse credibility inferences to be drawn from the demeanour of the application.[49] At the workshop, Galloway expressed the view that in Canada there appears not to be such an extreme ideological battle occurring between the courts and governments in relation to the place of human rights as seems to be the case in Australia.

Mathew (chapter 6) demonstrates from the context of her discussion that the legal jurisprudence is often unsatisfactory and inconsistent.[50] But recent

---

[49] In section 91V. See also the Migration Legislation Amendment (Procedural Fairness) Act 2002 (Cth).

[50] See also K Walker, 'New Uses of the Refugees Convention: Sexuality and Refugee Status', chapter 10 in this book, and S Kneebone, 'Moving Beyond the State: Refugees, Accountability and Protection', chapter 11 in this book.

decisions of the High Court of Australia show that it is concerned to harmonise its interpretation with international jurisprudence.[51] As Jose Alvin Gonzaga from the UNHCR explains, it is open to governments and courts to interpret the definition in the Refugees Convention either restrictively or broadly.[52] There are many examples in the chapters in this book of scenarios where vulnerable people 'at risk' of persecution remain so, due to constrained interpretations of the Convention. There is nothing inherently wrong with the definition in Article 1A of the Convention which stands today as a valid statement of a human rights standard as it did 50 years ago. Gonzaga notes that the object and purpose of the Convention is to ensure the protection of the specific rights of refugees and to encourage international cooperation. The fact that the UNHCR's mandate has been extended to include the protection of internally displaced persons (IDPs), the largest growing group of 'persons of concern' to the UNHCR testifies to the Convention's continuing relevance as a basic statement of human rights standards.[53] Gonzaga defends the Convention and the UNHCR against its critics.

It is important to note that the Preamble to the Convention contains strong human rights language which, as many of the chapters in this book highlight, is often watered down to ensure that the pragmatic dictates of the state are the focus of refugee laws. As Paris Aristotle, argued in his commentary on the first papers in the workshop, the obligations which arise in relation to asylum seekers and refugees are not merely legal but are moral in nature and derive from our common humanity. They relate, he argued, to the sort of world we want to create, forge and be a part of. As Kris Walker demonstrates,[54] the refugee definition has been interpreted flexibly and in accordance with universal values to include persecution as a result of sexual orientation and sexuality. Walker compares judicial approaches taken to claims for refugees status by those with lesbian or gay identity in different jurisdictions. This is one example of evidence of globalisation and of the rejection of cultural relativism. In this context the

---

[51] *MIMA v Khawar* discussed by Kneebone, ibid.

[52] J Gonzaga, 'The Role of the United Nations High Commissioner of Refugees and the Refugee Definition', chapter 9 in this book.

[53] It is estimated that there are about 25 million IDPs globally. In recognition of this problem the UN appointed Francis Deng as a Special Representative for IDPs in 1992: UNGA Res 1992/73, 5 March 1992.

[54] Walker, above n 50.

courts have recognised fundamental human dignity and interpreted the Refugees Convention consistently with this.

Susan Kneebone takes up the theme of the interpretation of the refugee definition by concentrating upon the underlying concept of a refugee and the issue of state responsibility in the context of persecution by non-state actors.[55] She illustrates through a discussion of recent academic literature and decisions of the High Court of Australia, how state centred refugee law results in restrictive interpretations of the Convention. As Rodger Haines queried in his commentary upon the paper at the workshop – of what relevance is the state to the Refugees Convention? Is it a distraction from the main purpose of the Convention, namely the provision of protection against persecution? Kneebone argues that the limitations of state centred refugee law need to be recognised in a globalised international law context. She suggests that we must move beyond the state in seeking solutions to the refugee problem. She invites us to reflect again upon the Convention, the role of the UNHCR and whether the main purpose of the Convention is being fulfilled.

But that is not the perspective from which governments assess the Refugees Convention. Contemporaneously with the 50th Anniversary of the Convention, a debate around the relevance and scope of the Convention in the 21st Century has emerged. Many western nations, including Australia and the European Community, are seeking a re-examination of the Convention stating that its scope is wider than ever intended.[56] For example, the Australian Minister for Immigration describes the Refugees Convention as 'essentially a standard that is being imposed on developed countries'.[57] Gibney, notes that at the commencement of the election campaign in Britain in 2001 the Prime Minister, Tony Blair outlined his government's intention to seek reform, 'not of the Convention's values but how it operates'.[58] One could argue that how a policy is put in practice is integrally linked to the values which underpin the Convention. As noted above, human rights abuses arise from government implementation of the Convention.

---

[55] Kneebone, above n 50.

[56] This was the rationale for the Migration Legislation Amendment Act (No 6) 2001 (Cth) discussed above. See the second reading speech by Senator Robert Hill, Parliament of Australia *Hansard* Senate, 24 September 2001, p 27603.

[57] Cited by A Millbank, above n 2, p 8.

[58] Gibney, above n 6.

Conclusion

The chapters in this book suggest that the way in which the Convention is applied shows that it has not been used to find positive solutions to a global problem. While governments are keen to embrace economic globalisation, and are happy in principle to endorse an international regime of human rights, they are reluctant to conceive of the Refugees Convention as an instrument of human rights. They do not see the link between the effects of economic globalisation and global movements of people, many of whom are legal refugees.[59] As the final chapter in this book highlights, comprehensive global approaches and burden sharing arrangements are slow to develop.

Our concern is that, in the effort to ensure policies of deterrence and the protection of borders, governments around the world have become distanced from the humanitarian concerns underpinning the Convention. The west has become desensitised and even cynical about the human experiences of the people who seek protection from displacement. Those in genuine need are often discriminated against by being confused with those who abuse the asylum channel. The genuine asylum seekers find it difficult to voice their position publicly. Moreover as Gibney notes:

> refugee lobby groups are generally weak, poorly funded, short-staffed, and lack concentrated bases of electoral support. Their views and perspectives are thus often brushed aside by political elites with relative ease.[60]

Hence the publication of a book such as this that gathers a range of critiques on refugee law and its operation is an important contribution to such public discourse and awareness.

One way of redirecting and refocusing the debate on the Refugees Convention is, as Gibney argues, through raising public awareness. This is something that should not be restricted to the politicians and judges. It is interesting to note that in another not dissimilar context, one of Australia's indigenous leaders, Lowitja O'Donoghue, has stated in her call for reconciliation amongst Australia's indigenous and non indigenous peoples that, 'It is for the people to lead and the leaders will follow'.

---

[59] De Jong, above, n 9.

[60] Gibney, above n 6, p 30.

2 The State of Asylum: Democratisation, Judicialisation and Evolution of Refugee Policy

MATTHEW J. GIBNEY*

Introduction

In May 2001, at the very start of the UK election campaign, the British Prime Minister Tony Blair wrote an article in *The Times* outlining his government's intention to seek reform of the 1951 Refugees Convention. 'The UK is taking the lead in arguing for reform', he stated, 'not of the Convention's values, but of how it operates'. Reform was necessary, according to Blair, in part to ensure, that 'those who are entitled to benefit from the provisions of the Refugees Convention are dealt with swiftly through quick decisions and an effective system for returns'.[1] For many observers, Blair's statement, which reiterated earlier calls by the British Home Secretary,[2] and controversial proposals mooted by the Austrian government in 1998,[3] represented the inevitable culmination of the restrictive practices towards asylum that had emerged across Europe since the mid 1980s. Reform of the Refugees Convention was widely viewed as

* I am indebted to Chimène Bateman, Randall Hansen, Jim Hathaway, Susan Kneebone, Andrew Shacknove and David Turton for helpful discussions on the issues raised herein. Research for this chapter was assisted by a grant from the Canadian Department of Foreign Affairs and International Trade in association with the Foundation for Canadian Studies in the UK.

[1] T Blair, 'Immigrants are seeking asylum in outdated law', *The Times*, 4 May 2001, p 18.

[2] 'Straw calls for asylum change', *The Times Online*, June 2001, http://www.the-times.co.uk/onlinespecials/britain/asylum.

[3] Austrian Government, *Strategy paper on immigration and asylum policy* (Austrian Government, July 1998).

the end point in a teleology of restriction: a single, common thread ran from visa controls, to carrier sanctions, on to safe third country arrangements, to airport liaison officers and, ultimately, to the emasculation of the Refugees Convention itself.

There is certainly something to this view. Since the late 1970s, all western states[4] have resorted to increasingly restrictive measures in an attempt to reduce the number of asylum claims they receive. In particular, they have used a range of common practices – such as visas, carrier sanctions, airport liaison officers and international zones – to prevent asylum seekers from arriving at frontiers where they could claim the protection of the Refugees Convention. The effective use of these practices has in turn exacerbated disparities in the burdens of individual states, as states of first asylum, particularly in the south, unable to insulate themselves from refugee flows, have attracted a disproportionate number of the world's refugees. Where these measures have been ineffective in reducing asylum claims (as has recently been the case with Britain), even more restrictive and punitive measures have been mooted to prevent and deter claims.[5]

Plausible as the teleological account may appear, however, it provides an incomplete and somewhat misleading picture of recent developments in Europe in relation to asylum. Less than two years before his article in *The Times*, Blair's government had orchestrated another key development: the incorporation into domestic British law of the European Convention on Human Rights (ECHR). The Human Rights Act of 1998 effectively brought to British law a written bill of rights and significantly a duty on the state, under Article 3, to refrain from inhuman or degrading treatment. In practice this duty has created amongst European states a potentially wide-ranging and non-derogative extension of the principle of non-refoulement beyond the obligations of Article 33 of the 1951 Refugees Convention.[6]

---

4 In this chapter I use the terms 'constitutional democratic states' and 'Western states' interchangeably.

5 In the British case this has been evident in the proposal in 2001 by William Hague's Conservative opposition to introduce mandatory detention for all asylum seekers. The opposition subsequently lost the election.

6 Article 33 provides:

   1. No Contracting State shall expel or return ('refouler') a refugee in any manner whatsoever to the frontiers of territories where his life or freedom would be

In 1996 in *Chahal v UK*,[7] the European Court of Human Rights found this obligation constrained the removal of an individual even when they could, under other circumstances, have been excluded from the protection of the Refugees Convention on national security grounds. Here was a new and significant development in limiting the sovereign power of the British state to exclude foreigners, albeit one to which the UK and other European states had freely consented.

It was also a challenge to a teleological account of increasing restriction. For here, in the midst of implementing and reinforcing a range of restrictive measures, the UK committed itself to broader human rights protections against removal and deportation. How might one explain the seeming contradiction between government calls for reform of the Refugees Convention and the flourishing of other measures to restrict asylum on the one hand, and the government's consent to an expanding European human rights regime that extends the legal protections of asylum seekers on the other? To put the issue in more practical terms, how should one respond to the following question recently raised by an official from the Enforcement Section of the UK Immigration Service: why is it that one day the Home Secretary orders the Service to increase the rate of removal of rejected asylum seekers, and the next supports the incorporation into law of human rights legislation that places new legal barriers to the return of these same people?[8]

In this chapter I will examine the relationship between increasing government restrictiveness towards asylum seekers and the growing entanglement of states in human rights law that restrains their activities. The argument I will make about the relationship between the two applies best to European states, encumbered by European and European Union (EU) human rights legislation, especially after the Treaty of Amsterdam.[9] However, much of this chapter is of broader relevance to other

---

      threatened on account of his race, religion, nationality, membership of a particular social group or political opinion.

  2. The benefit of the present provision may not, however, be claimed by a refugee whom there are reasonable grounds for regarding as a danger to the security of the country in which he is, or who, having been convicted by a final judgement of a particularly serious crime, constitutes a danger to the community of that country.

7 (1996) 23 EHRR 413.

8 Interview with an official of the UK Immigration Service conducted in May 2001.

9 The Treaty of Amsterdam was signed on 2 October 1997.

constitutional democratic states, and the examples I use will draw freely from non-European countries, including Canada[10] and Australia.[11]

This chapter has four parts. In the first, I will locate the roots of recent restrictive policies by governments over the last 15 years in the dynamics of electoral politics, and particularly in hostile public attitudes towards asylum seekers. In the second, I will argue that the consequences of restrictive pressures emanating from the political realm have been restrained in important ways by legal developments that begin to acknowledge asylum seekers as rights-bearing subjects and vest them with important new legal protections. Third, I will argue that this contradiction between restrictive politics and inclusive legal developments is best understood as reflecting a tension in the idea of the constitutional democratic state. This tension manifests itself practically in the way that the growth of human rights protections for asylum seekers fuels the use by governments of restrictive and exclusionist measures designed to prevent asylum seekers arriving at their territory to access these protections. In the conclusion of this chapter, I address the implications of this account of the evolution of asylum for the future of the values associated with the Refugees Convention 50 years after its birth.

The Politics of Restriction

In this section I aim to consider what has motivated governments across the EU and beyond to put in place a range of restrictive measures to prevent the entry of asylum seekers to their territory since the mid 1980s. One reason is relatively obvious. Since the 1970s there has been a sharp rise in asylum claims across EU countries. Whereas the total number of asylum claims across western Europe averaged no more than 13 000 annually in the 1970s, the annual totals had grown to 170 000 by 1985, and to 690 000 in 1992. Between 1985 and 1995, more than five million claims for asylum were lodged in western states. By 2000 the number of claims

---

10 Also see D Galloway, 'Criminality and State Protection: Structural Tensions in Canadian Refugee Law', chapter 5 in this book.

11 Also see M Crock, 'The Refugees Convention at 50: Mid-life Crisis or Terminal Inadequacy? An Australian Perspective', chapter 3 in this book; and R Illingworth, 'Durable Solutions: Refugee Status Determination and the Framework of International Protection', chapter 4 in this book.

had dropped off somewhat to 412 700 for the states of western Europe.[12] These rising numbers reflect an expansion in the number of the world's refugees in recent decades, mostly as a result of civil conflicts in the former Yugoslavia, Sri Lanka, Somalia, Central America, and the Great Lakes region of Africa. But the increases are also related to developments in transportation and communication that have lessened the distance between the world's richest and poorest countries. A kind of 'globalisation of asylum seeking' has occurred whereby many victims of conflict and persecution, as well as individuals in pursuit of better economic opportunities, can now travel intercontinentally in pursuit of asylum. The resulting 'mixed flows'[13] of migrants (the intermingling of refugees and economic immigrants) has been used by some states to justify policies preventing the arrival of asylum seekers and even the reconsideration the Refugees Convention.

But rising numbers on their own fall short of providing an adequate explanation for increased restriction. To be sure, rising asylum claims may tell us what governments have been reacting to, but they do not tell us why governments have grasped with such alacrity measures designed to restrict and prevent rather than include and manage those striving for asylum. The emergence of these harsh measures appears even more difficult to understand because they seem to contradict the values by which western societies claim to define themselves. Many scholars have pointed to a large (and growing) gap between constitutional (or liberal) democratic values and the treatment meted out to men, women, and children desperate for entry – a gap so large that it may ultimately prove corrosive of these very values.[14]

Despite its importance, there has, in recent years, been relatively little systematic analysis of the motivations of European (or other western)

---

[12] UNHCR, *State of the World's Refugees 1997–1998* (Oxford, Oxford University Press, 1997), p 145; UNHCR, *State of the World's Refugees 2000* (Oxford, Oxford University Press, 2000), p 325.

[13] G Van Kessell, 'Global Migration and Asylum', *Forced Migration Review* **10** (2001) p 10.

[14] For different examples of this genre, see J H Carens, *The Ethics of Refugee Policy: The Problem of Asylum in Western States* (Unpublished, 1998); H Adelman, 'Refuge or Asylum: A Philosophical Perspective', *Journal of Refugee Studies* **1(1)** (1989) p 7. C Boswell, 'European Values and the Asylum Crisis', *International Affairs* **76(3)** (2000) p 537.

governments in constructing a restrictionist regime. Writings on refugee policy by academics (as well as by advocates) has tended to be more descriptive (and condemnatory) than explicitly analytical.[15] Nonetheless, even this writing has implicitly endorsed a range of reasons for the rise of restrictionism. Typically commentators, particularly in fields of refugee studies and law, have pointed to the *character* of political leaders. Elites have been held to possess racist, conservative or unjustifiably alarmist attitudes towards the social disruption caused by the entrance of asylum seekers. Alternatively, the restrictionist agenda has sometimes been seen not as a direct product of the views held by elites themselves, but of their failure to stand up to pernicious and xenophobic attitudes expressed in the media or the general public. Politicians are thus guilty of a failure of political courage or will.

It would be surprising if some of these factors did not play a role in feeding the development of recent asylum practices. Yet these explanations finding fault in the character of political leaders offer at best a partial explanation of the restrictive regime. Their limitations are revealed by the ubiquity of current restrictive practices. Every western state faced with pressure from asylum seekers for entrance, including countries as diverse as Ireland, Sweden, Australia,[16] Germany and the UK has implemented a common range of measures to reduce asylum claims. If one accepts character-based explanations, one seems committed to the idea that weakness of will is common to the diverse range of political leaders across these countries. This seems highly dubious.

The ubiquity of restrictive practices poses similar problems for the idea that party *ideology* explains the growth of restrictionism. Conservative governments, to be sure, have sometimes implemented harsher policies towards asylum seekers than their liberal, labour or social democratic counterparts. The Kohl government in Germany in the 1980s and 1990s and the current Howard government in Australia both introduced a raft of restrictive measures criticised by their left-wing opponents. But this is hardly the rule. The Labour government in the UK has been at least as restrictive (and some would argue more so) than its Conservative

---

[15] For recent examples of this style, see some of the contributions in A Bloch, T Galvin and L Schuster, 'Special Issue on Changing Asylum Policies in Europe', *Journal of Refugee Studies* 13(1) (2000).

[16] See Illingworth, above n 11.

predecessor[17] and Australia's opposition Labor party felt the need to assure voters during the *Tampa* affair in 2001 that it would basically replicate the conservative government's hard line policies against boat people. The differences between western governments in asylum policy have largely been rhetorical. Governments of all political hues have contributed to the establishment and consolidation of the restrictionist regime.

Explanations for the rise of restriction across the west that draw upon features of the international order offer a more plausible alternative. In a recent article, 'The Geopolitics of Asylum', B S Chimni argues that the growth of restrictionist practices by western states is strongly correlated to the end of the Cold War.[18] Developing arguments previously made by Loescher[19] and Weiner[20] amongst others, he argues that with the demise of superpower conflict in the late 1980s, 'the refugee no longer possessed ideological or geopolitical value' for western states, prompting these states to rethink refugee protection in a way that justified the implementation of the current regime geared to preventing arrival.[21] According to Chimni, in order to justify the movement towards a restrictive regime, states used a number of weak rationalisations for exclusion. In particular, they raised the spectre of huge numbers of southerners making their way to the west in search of a better way of life. Furthermore, western states claimed that refugees in the south were too numerous to be assisted through resettlement schemes and, in any respect, were not fleeing persecution and thus ineligible for protection under the Convention. These arguments were central components in what he calls the 'myth of difference: the idea that great dissimilarities characterised the volume, nature and causes of refugee flows in Europe and in the Third World'.[22]

---

[17] On the consistency in UK asylum policy despite changes in government, see A Bloch, 'A New Era or More of the Same? Asylum Policy in the UK', *Journal of Refugee Studies* **13(1)** (2000) p 29.

[18] B S Chimni, 'The Geopolitics of Refugee Studies: A View from the South', *Journal of Refugee Studies* **11(4)** (1998) p 350.

[19] G Loescher, *Beyond Charity: International Cooperation and the Global Refugee Crisis* (Oxford, Oxford University Press, 1993).

[20] M Weiner, *The Global Migration Crisis: Challenge for States and for Human Rights* (New York, Harper Collins, 1995).

[21] Chimni, above n 18, p 351.

[22] Id, p 356.

Chimni's explanation appeals to a causal factor – the end of superpower conflict – whose impact reached far enough across states to address the ubiquity of restrictive measures. Moreover, he touches an important vein by identifying the end of the Cold War as a key turning point in the history of asylum in the west. But his explanation suffers from some important weaknesses. Notably, the onset of restrictive practices by western states predates the end of the Cold War. Germany, for example, was operating expedited asylum procedures and toughening up its asylum regulations by the beginning of the 1980s; Britain imposed carrier sanctions to prevent what it viewed as a rise in fraudulent asylum claims from Tamils in 1987 – a full two years before the fall of the Berlin Wall. Restrictive policies might have been given extra momentum by the changes in superpower relations, but they clearly had a life independent of these relations. Chimni concedes that restrictive policies began before the Cold War's end. However, he is vague about the effect of this admission on his account of why western states reconceived their interests in the 1980s and early 1990s.

A more important limitation of Chimni's account is that he explains the reconstruction of the regime almost exclusively through the changing interests of state elites.[23] Elites did play a key role in ushering in the new, more restrictive paradigm (if that is indeed an accurate way of describing recent practices). But his account of why their interests changed overlooks a much more significant transformation in the balance of power within western states that occurred in the 1980s as a result of the rise of jet age asylum seekers and the end of the Cold War. This shift made state elites increasingly beholden to domestic political actors, not least the general public, in the construction of asylum policy.

During the Cold War refugee admission was primarily a foreign policy matter for western states. The widespread view that accepting refugees took the glitter off communist regimes made their entrance central to the goal of controlling Soviet expansion. By portraying refugee admission as an issue of raison d'état, western elites were able to carve out a significant degree of autonomy from the domestic politics of their states, effectively depoliticising refugee admissions. Such autonomy was necessary because post-war public opinion in western states was generally xenophobic and favourable to tight entrance restrictions on both refugees and immigrants.

---

[23]   Id, p 357. In a slightly conspiratorial way, Chimni also sees some academics as colluding with elites to propagate the 'myth of difference'.

However, the autonomy won by elites was never complete. Even at the height of the Cold War, elites often struggled to convince their electorates that accepting refugees was truly in the national interest and thus should be consented to. Public support for even the most ideologically favoured entrants became highly precarious when movements of refugees began to be perceived by electorates as 'uncontrolled' or particularly large in volume, and thus a threat to border control. This was evident even in the home of the Cold War refugee, the United States. Cuban refugees were welcomed by successive US administrations from Eisenhower to Carter. Nonetheless, generous admissions policies could not withstand the rising public, media and Congressional discontent that emerged in the 1970s and climaxed with the movement of thousands of Cubans during the controversial Mariel boat lift in 1980. The tightening of Cuban entrance policy in the 1980s and 1990s was driven primarily by a *domestic* political backlash rather than any change in the ideological and strategic interests of the US state.[24]

The Cuban example speaks to a general point. The inclusiveness of western responses to communist refugees during the Cold War period did not only depend on the preferences of state elites. The limited number of escapees from communist regimes and, crucially, the fact that most western states incorporated refugees through resettlement programs, were indispensable features of the inclusive regime. When, in the early 1980s, these states became first asylum countries (by virtue, inter alia, of 'jet age asylum seekers'), domestic discontent became harder for governments to ignore.

Chimni is probably right to stress that after the Cold War ended, western political elites no longer had self-interested reasons for operating inclusive asylum policies. But the end of the Cold War also did something else: it deprived state leaders of the most powerful argument they had for constraining highly restrictionist public attitudes. With the demise of communism, any government supportive of maintaining inclusive

---

[24] J I Dominguez, 'Cooperating with the Enemy? US Immigration Policies Towards Cuba' in C Mitchell (ed), *Western Hemisphere Immigration and United States Foreign Policy* (University Park, Penn State University Press, 1992), pp 66–7. Dominguez offers a superb analysis of the twists and turns in US entrance policy towards Cuba. See also C Joppke, *Immigration and the Nation State: The United States, Germany and Great Britain* (Oxford, Oxford University Press, 1999); M J Gibney, *The Ethics and Politics of Asylum: Liberal Democracy and the Response to Refugees* (Cambridge, Cambridge University Press, 2003).

policies had to rely on humanitarian claims, economic needs or global security considerations to justify the entrance of refugees. None of these arguments had anything like the force for galvanising public opinion or neutralising domestic political opposition that the danger of the worldwide advance of communism did.

The rising numbers of 'jet age' (and other onshore) asylum seekers and the end of the Cold War in the 1980s led to a *democratisation of asylum policy* in western states, with domestic political actors (the public, the media, and opposition parties) increasingly calling the tune. As democratisation occurred, the springs of asylum policy shifted from *high politics* (matters of national security) to what one might call *low politics* (matters of day to day electoral politics, including employment, national identity and the welfare state). The results were not pretty. As asylum became part of the cut and thrust of domestic politics, government leaders found themselves facing more pressure to restrict entry. With little incentive to resist (for reasons I shall explain below), governments implemented an increasingly retrograde set of control measures to prevent and deter the arrival of asylum seekers.

The democratisation of asylum policy also had another effect. As asylum seeking became more salient as an electoral issue, governments sought new means to restrict entrance to their territory. Recognising the benefits of international cooperation, a range of bilateral and regional agreements, including the 1985 Schengen Treaty and the 1990 Dublin Convention, were either initiated or reoriented by western states to serve migration control objectives.[25] Paradoxically, then, asylum's transformation into an issue of domestic politics from the early 1980s was accompanied by an unprecedented level of prominence for this issue in international fora.[26] Consequently, it has become difficult to distinguish between asylum as an issue of domestic politics and one of foreign policy.

---

[25] See P Mathew, 'Safe for Whom? The Safe Third Country Concept Finds a Home in Australia', chapter 6 in this book.

[26] In this respect, asylum has shown a different trajectory from other aspects of immigration that, according to Weiner, have shifted in recent years, from being the sole concern of ministries of labour and immigration to matters of 'high international politics, engaging the attention of heads of states, cabinets, and key ministries involved in defense, internal security and external relations': M Weiner, above n 20, p 131. Asylum has remained a prominent international issue since the early days of the Cold War to the present; what has changed are the reasons for its salience.

This leads to my explanation of restrictive asylum policies across constitutional democratic states in recent years. Most western governments, I suggest, have enacted these policies because they perceive that it is in their interests to control (and to minimise) the number of asylum seekers their country faces. The reason why they see their interests in this way is primarily an electoral matter. Political elites believe that if they fail to control asylum it will contribute to or cause their electoral defeat. They make this presumption because they perceive, often with good reason, that key sections of the electorate are intolerant of lax border control and rising numbers of asylum seekers.[27] The roots of restrictive asylum policies, then, lie in a perception by elites that the conduct of asylum policy risks exacting political costs from them. This risk has increased with the rapid growth in the number of asylum seekers seeking entry to western states (in particular, 'jet age asylum seekers'[28]) since the early 1980s and the demise of a cogent national interest justification for accepting refugees after the end of the Cold War.

This explanation is, admittedly, quite underwhelming.[29] It places the blame (if indeed there is blame to be placed) for the rise in restrictionism overwhelmingly on the incentive structure of electoral politics, thus offering an alternative to elite-based explanations reliant on the character, political party or, à la Chimni, on the ideological interests of elites. But it begs the question of why the pressures from the *demos* favour exclusion to the point of being hostile, indifferent, or only weakly responsive to the

---

[27] It is worth emphasising that it is the *perceptions* of elites and electorates rather than the well-foundedness of these perceptions that counts when it comes to determining action. Governments strive to avoid the appearance of laxity because they fear it will make them look impotent in the area of immigration control. Note, for example, President Carter's reference to the Mariel incident after losing the 1980 US Presidential election: 'The refugee question hurt us badly ... It was a burning issue. It made us look impotent when we received these refugees from Cuba': J I Dominguez, 'Immigration as Foreign Policy in US–Latin American Relations' quoted in R W Tucker, C B Keely and L Wrigley, *Immigration and US Foreign Policy* (Boulder, Westview, 1990).

[28] And 'boat people' in the case of Australia, Canada and, to a lesser extent, the US. See Crock, above n 11, for an analysis of the Australian scenario.

[29] I don't believe that this is the only reason why highly restrictive policies have emerged; simply that it is a sufficient reason for such policies. In this chapter I do not address the issue of how much of a role politicians play in whipping up hostility towards asylum seekers. However, I think that critics of current policies often tend to exaggerate this role, and thus skim over the electoral difficulties of creating more inclusive asylum responses.

needs of refugees and asylum seekers. One answer is obvious. Those seeking asylum cannot vote in the countries they wish to enter or remain in, so their preferences are unlikely to count for much in the calculations of politicians. For the preferences of asylum seekers to be represented, they usually have to be registered indirectly through the votes of citizens or, perhaps what is more common, through the activities of lobby or interest groups. To a limited extent, refugee advocacy groups, such as Pro Asyl in Germany, the British Refugee Council in the UK, the Refugee Council in Australia, and the United Nations High Commissioner for Refugees (UNHCR) globally, do manage to give these interests a voice and representation they would not otherwise have.[30] However, in contrast to immigration lobby groups, who, as Gary Freeman has recently argued, can often, through 'client politics', exercise far greater influence on immigration policy than their numerical support would justify,[31] refugee lobby groups are generally weak, poorly funded, short-staffed, and lack concentrated bases of electoral support. Their views and perspectives are often brushed aside by political elites with relative ease.

Now, if what I'm saying is right, the challenge for a more inclusive politics of asylum is clear, if daunting: it is necessary to reorder citizen preferences so that they take more seriously the needs of asylum seekers and, by doing so, provide governments with an incentive to implement political change. The public response to Kosovo in early to mid 1999 showed that restrictive public attitudes towards refugees are not set in stone, fixed and invariable. Within a few days of the mass exodus of Kosovans in March, a tremendous wave of sympathy of a kind unseen since the crushing of the Hungarian revolt in 1956, emerged across much of the west. The force and immediacy of the public response goaded some reluctant governments into a campaign that enabled the resettlment of over 100 000 refugees from Macedonia. Such was the strength of the public reaction across Europe that many people offered to take Kosovan refugees into their own homes.

But if the case of the Kosovans shows us the contingency of restrictionism, it is unclear what lessons it offers for a more inclusive

---

30   The degree of influence they exert is of course partly determined by the legislative system of the state in which they act, and, in particular, the avenues it provides for the input of advocacy organisations.

31   G Freeman, 'Modes of Immigration Politics in Liberal Democratic States', *International Migration Review* **29(4)** (1995) p 881.

politics. Primarily this is because it is difficult to understand just what led to this outpouring of public support. I have argued elsewhere that a range of factors, including the location of the refugees in Europe, the sense of implication in their plight created by the NATO bombing, and the presence of strong cultural affinities, all played a role in connecting the western public to this particular group of refugees.[32] However, even if we accept this diagnosis of what made Kosovans more popular than Afghans, Bosnians, or Liberians, it remains unclear how the factors enabling this sense of connection – what Richard Rorty has called, 'imaginative identification'[33] – can be replicated for other groups of refugees; or whether it is possible, even in principle, to replicate them.

But there is an even more daunting problem facing more inclusive asylum policies exposed by Kosovo: the fact that public support for refugees often proves to be so fleeting. In the history of European asylum policy, the response to Kosovan Albanian refugees was like a shooting star that lit up the entire the night sky for a few moments then fizzled into nothingness. Within weeks of the end of the bombing, the inclusive attitudes towards refugees had disappeared. Moreover, they had gone without leaving a trace on policy responses to refugees in general. The Kosovan crisis came and went without deep or lasting questions being raised about the adequacy of asylum policies based on restriction and exclusion.

The capriciousness of its response would appear to make the *demos* an unreliable ally in the search for more inclusive policies. And it is not surprising, then, that advocates have looked to the courts rather than the general public to seek reform of (or constraints upon) the harshest aspects of government policies. However, before turning to consider the legal realm, I want to say a little more about why European publics remain such an inhospitable base for undermining the current restrictionist regime. One major reason why inclusive public responses to asylum seekers have proven so difficult to sustain is that these responses conflict with a conception of responsibility deeply rooted in the modern state.

The bulk of the public within and beyond Europe view their state (and, derivatively, the electoral politics in which they participate) as something

---

[32] M J Gibney, 'Kosovo and Beyond: Popular and Unpopular Refugees', *Forced Migration Review* 5 (1999) p 28.

[33] R Rorty, *Contingency, Irony and Solidarity* (Cambridge, Cambridge University Press, 1989), p 190.

that exists (or at least rightly *should* exist) to advance their interests *qua* individuals and citizens rather than those of foreigners. In this account of responsibility, states are perfectly justified in implementing asylum policies that attach more weight to the potential costs to citizens associated with the entrance of refugees than the benefits accruing to those seeking asylum. This is not to say that the interests or needs of asylum seekers are of no consequence for citizens in western states; they normally have some weight in the construction of their preferences. But when these interests or needs are perceived as being in direct conflict with their own, citizens generally believe that the state is justified in giving priority to members.

How might we explain this systematic downgrading of the interests of asylum seekers and or refugees? There is good reason to see it as an essential feature of the modern state as political form. Historically, state leaders have taken an active role in promoting a particularistic understanding of responsibility. In order to win the support of those that they have striven to rule, elites have looked for ways of convincing reluctant, divided and diverse peoples that they have an interest in consenting to their rule. This has been the process of creating the state, in John Dunn's words, as 'ideological fiction' – of constructing a relationship of 'assumed intimacy' to replace the reality of the 'massive social distance' that separates rulers and ruled.[34] There have been many aspects to this process.[35] But all of them involve (in one form or another) attempts by the state to convince its members that it exists to further their interests and goals.

This is a difficult claim for any state to make plausible.[36] State leaders often do not have the interests and needs of their citizens at heart. And even when they do, there will always be neglected and disenchanted sections of their populations who, quite justifiably, feel that their interests do not receive the attention they deserve. How, then, can a state make this claim

---

[34] J Dunn, *Interpreting Political Responsibility* (Cambridge, Polity Press, 1990), p 1.

[35] For example, Roger Smith has recently written insightfully on the 'politics of people building', that is, the way that elites attempt (within the constraints of established identities) to fashion distinct peoples from diversity in order to enable efficient rule. This process, he suggests, is of necessity an exclusive one: 'to embrace one sense of personhood and shared way of life is to reject others': R M Smith, 'Citizenship and the Politics of People-Building', *Citizenship Studies* (Forthcoming).

[36] See J Dunn, *The Cunning of Unreason: Making Sense of Politics* (London, Harper Collins, 2000), p 75.

credible? At a very minimum, any state must convince a substantial section of its citizenry that even if their interests are not particularly high in the state's calculations, they are at least more important than those of foreigners. No less acute an observer of politics than Jean-Jacques Rousseau expressed the dynamics of this insider/outsider relationship succinctly:

> Do we want people to be virtuous? Let them start by making them love their fatherland. But how are they to love it if the fatherland is nothing more for them than for foreigners, and accords them only what it cannot refuse to anyone?[37]

States thus have a constitutive interest in demonstrating partiality to the interests and needs of their citizens and, moreover, encouraging an expectation of this partiality in those they rule over. Until we move beyond the state as the dominant form of political organisation, we can expect the interests of asylum seekers to be at best a secondary consideration for electorates and governments alike.[38]

The Law of Inclusion

The rise of restrictionist measures over the last decades, driven primarily by electoral politics, has occurred in tandem with another development of growing significance for asylum: the advance of a human rights culture. The emergence of this culture represents the instantiation across the west of the liberal ideal that *citizens* have fundamental rights that warrant protection both from the state and from majority preferences and desires. However, the language and law of rights, embodied in domestic practices, human rights organisations, national constitutions, and international declarations and conventions have had important spill over effects for *non-citizens* within the sphere of authority of European states. This is true not least of all in the case of immigrants. As Yasemin Soysal has recently

---

[37] Quoted in M Walzer, 'Response to Chaney and Lichtenberg' in P G Brown and H Shue (eds), *Boundaries: National Autonomy and its Limits* (Totowa, Rowman and Littlefield, 1981), p 102.

[38] An expanded discussion of these issues is contained in Gibney, above n 24. See also S Kneebone, 'Moving Beyond the State: Refugees, Accountability and Protection', chapter 11 in this book.

shown, in most European states permanent residents enjoy a panoply of legal rights and protections that make them difficult to distinguish under law from citizens.[39]

Recent literature from political science and sociology has been divided on the source of these developments. In one corner, Soysal and Jacobsen have argued that international human rights conventions, non-governmental organisations (NGOs), international organisations and the human rights norms that have proliferated since 1945 have imposed overlapping *external* constraints on the behaviour of European states towards immigrants and asylum seekers in their territory.[40] International agreements and conventions provide sources of law that can be drawn upon by domestic courts; the language of human rights employed by NGOs and UN organisations has provided a way of expressing the entitlements and claims of immigrants independent of national citizenship.

Others scholars have been more circumspect. Through detailed examinations of European countries, and in the case of Joppke, the USA, Hansen and Joppke have argued that the most influential sources of rights-based constraint on state activity are *internal* to individual states, emerging particularly from national constitutions, and from international law only when incorporated into domestic law.[41] Accordingly, these rights-based constraints should be understood as self-imposed internal limitations on state activity, rather than as the product of an external diminution of sovereignty. The last few decades, as Hansen argues, have seen a 'transfer among institutions of the state – from the executive towards the judiciary and, to a lesser degree, the bureaucracy' rather than 'a transfer from the state to the transnational arena'.[42]

---

[39] Y Soysal, *Limits of Citizenship: Migrants and Postnational Membership in Europe* (Chicago, University of Chicago Press, 1994). Of course, legal standing is not the same as social standing. Many immigrants in Europe continue to face informal discrimination and racism on a daily basis.

[40] Ibid; D Jacobson, *Rights Across Borders: Immigration and the Decline of Citizenship* (Baltimore, Johns Hopkins UP, 1996).

[41] C Joppke, *Immigration and the Nation State: The United States, Germany and Great Britain* (Oxford, Oxford University Press, 1999); R Hansen, *Citizenship and Immigration in Post-War Britain* (Oxford, Oxford University Press 2000).

[42] R Hansen, 'Migration, Citizenship and Race in Europe: Between Incorporation and Exclusion', *European Journal of Political Research* 35 (1999) p 428.

The differences between these two approaches are important. States without internal constraints, such as the lack of a national constitution or a bill of rights, have a great deal of discretion to engage in egregiously restrictive practices towards asylum seekers and immigrants. Joppke suggests that the UK is a case in point,[43] but one could just as easily point to Australia, where, absent a written bill of rights, governments have faced few legal limitations on their mandatory detention policy for asylum seekers. Nonetheless, both 'externalists' or 'internalists' acknowledge that immigration matters across the west have been increasingly judicialised in the last few decades. As a result, fundamental changes in how liberal democracies conceive of their obligations to foreigners within their territory have occurred.

Asylum seekers have felt the implications of the recent rights revolution more slowly and with much with less force than permanent residents and, a fortiori, citizens. Usually lacking communal ties, they have required, in contrast to permanent residents, 'a triumph of the abstract moral over the concrete communitarian obligations', as Joppke has put it.[44] Yet they have not faced the state completely unarmed. They have been able to point to the Refugees Convention, which obliges states to respect the Article 33 principle of non-refoulement, as well as identifying a range of refugee rights that signatory states are required to recognise. The force of this limitation on state discretion has, moreover, been strongest where it is incorporated into domestic law, as it is in almost all western countries.[45]

The Refugees Convention is only the most obvious barrier that exists to curb the politics of restrictionism in the realm of asylum. I want briefly to outline three other developments that represent important manifestations of the new rights culture on the relationship between constitutional democratic states and asylum seekers. These developments are most fully evident in

---

[43] C Joppke, 'Asylum and State Sovereignty: A Comparison of the United States, Germany and Britain' in C Joppke (ed), *Challenge to the Nation State: Immigration in Western Europe and the United State* (Oxford, Oxford University Press, 1998). Joppke's analysis of the UK has been weakened somewhat by the incorporation of the European Convention of Human Rights into domestic British law in 1998.

[44] Id, p 134.

[45] In Canada, the obligation of non-refoulement was incorporated as section 55 of the old Immigration Act. This obligation is now incorporated into Bill C-11, section 115, and came into effect from June 2002. Bill C-11 also incorporates Canada's obligations under the Convention against Torture and Other Cruel, Inhumane or Degrading Treatment or Punishment (CAT).

Europe, but they have also been on display to some degree in Canada, Australia and the US.

The first is the development and consolidation of due process protections for asylum seekers. Since the early 1980s, across European countries, the process of refugee claims determination has moved gradually out of the realm of state discretion to independent, quasi-judicial bodies. This development has been the product of a number of factors including the extension of administrative law to cover immigration decisions in the post-War period, the incorporation of the 1951 Convention into domestic law in many European countries, and impact of the ECHR which has extended the procedural rights of asylum seekers and responsibilities of European states, as well as placing these rights on a firmer footing. One consequence has been that virtually all constitutional democratic states now offer, at a minimum, a standard set of procedures for assessing asylum claims. These include an initial decision by an independent arbitrator, the opportunity for appeal against a negative initial decision to an immigration or refugee appeals tribunal, and the possibility to appeal on matters of law to the judicial courts.

Due process protections in EU states are set to become a feature of EU law in the next few years. A European Commission proposal on 'minimum standards on procedures in member states for the granting and withdrawing of refugee status' is currently being considered by member states. The proposal aims to establish regional standards on matters including procedural guarantees for asylum applicants; minimum requirements for the decision making process; and common standards for the application of certain concepts and practices (such as 'manifestly unfounded claims'). Due process standards will thus become entrenched at European level.

Much debate surrounds how these processes for decision-making work in practice. Advocates have justifiably pointed to the lack of legal assistance in some countries, the operation of 'manifestly unfounded' case procedures, and the (often) limited opportunities for asylum seekers to present their cases in person. Yet the convergence upon a similar set of standards across states with very different legal systems is a considerable achievement, not least for asylum seekers themselves. The gradual judicialisation of refugee decision-making is even more remarkable because the 1951 Convention itself offers little guidance on how states should determine refugee claims.

A second development is the emergence of what I will call the norm of membership through residence. The twentieth century has seen numerous peacetime occurrences of the forceful return by western states of long-term resident foreigners. Economic recession, the expiration of resident permits, or ethnic or racial hostility led, for example, to the mass repatriation of Poles from France in 1934–35 and the deportation of 'Bracero' labour migrants from the US in 1954.[46] However, in recent years, constitutional democratic states have demonstrated a reluctance forcefully to deport long-term resident foreigners, even those with no legal entitlement to remain. This reluctance has been extremely well documented in the case of guestworker immigrants in western Europe, who remained after the migration stop in the early 1970s.[47] Much less attention has been paid to the consequences of this (often implicit) norm for asylum seekers.[48]

The kinds of due process protections I outlined above, have, in combination with growing asylum claims, outdated bureaucratic processing and inadequate resources, helped to create huge backlogs in the asylum determination systems of European states, most notably in Germany in the mid 1990s and the UK at the current time. Indeed, it is probably fair to say that no country that offers asylum seekers the kind of due process protections outlined above has yet found a way of squaring them with speedy and efficient decision making. The UK, for example, has recently celebrated its achievement of reducing the time period for an initial decision in asylum cases to 14 months; hidden from view, however, are the large percentage of appeals that result from these decisions and extend the period before a definitive decision is reached to months if not years longer. With asylum decisions in Europe often taking between two and eight years to reach, by the time finality is achieved, the lives of asylum seekers have often moved on considerably. They may have married, established a family, attained a permanent job, and generally established deep connections with their host country. In the face of these connections, they have become de facto members and, accordingly, the courts and

---

[46] P Weil, 'The State Matters: Immigration Control in Developed Countries', *Report for the Department of Economic and Social Affairs Population Division* (New York, United Nations, 1998), p 6.

[47] See, for example, Soysal, above n 39; Jacobson, above n 40; and J Hollifield, *Immigrants, Markets and States: The Political Economy of Postwar Europe* (Cambridge, Harvard University Press, 1992).

[48] See M J Gibney and R Hansen, *Deportation and the Liberal State* (Oxford, Unpublished, 2001).

governments are often reluctant to deport them. The result is the reinforcement of a norm of membership through extended residence.[49] Evidence for this norm can be derived from government practices. In the UK, for example, the government recently announced in parliament that asylum seekers with children who had been in the country for more than seven years would not be removed. Most other states have a cut off period that ranges from five to ten years after which the removal of overstayers or illegal entrants is a low priority.[50] However, ad hoc and informal practices protecting long staying asylum seekers (and other immigrants) are increasingly supported by immigration rules and legal jurisprudence. In the Netherlands those whose asylum claims take more than three years to process can claim permanent residence.[51] International human rights law can also reinforce the norm. In Canada, the Supreme Court decided in *Baker v Canada*,[52] that under the Convention on the Rights of the Child, the 'best interests of the child' must be taken into account in deportation and removals proceedings.[53] The presence of a child in school in Canada, and the disruption deportation would cause, might, under such rulings, provide a significant barrier to deportation.[54] Article 3 of the ECHR in Europe could also provide similar constraints on the ability of states to remove those who have been resident in the state for an extended period, if that removal can be shown to constitute 'inhuman or degrading treatment', though jurisprudence has yet to move firmly in this direction. Other articles of the ECHR, such as the right to a family life, may also prove important future sources of jurisprudence. The consequences of this new norm partly explain why most western states have had very low rates of return for rejected asylum seekers in recent years.[55]

---

[49] Ibid.

[50] Interviews with officials from the Immigration and Refugee Board (IRB) and Citizenship and Immigration (CIC) Canada, December 2000.

[51] F Leibaut, *Legal and Social Conditions for Asylum Seekers and Refugees in Western European Countries* (Copenhagen, Danish Refugee Council, 2000), p 203.

[52] [1999] 2 SCR 817.

[53] Interview with an official from the IRB, Canada, December 2000.

[54] Ibid.

[55] Other reasons deriving from political and practical constraints are analysed in Gibney and Hansen, above n 48.

A third significant development is the emergence of new legal protections against refoulement that complement (and, some observers fear, replace) the Refugees Convention. The impact and development of these protections are probably most developed in Europe, where as I mentioned above, the European Convention on Human Rights places legal barriers on the return of foreigners to territories where their human rights would be threatened, even if the foreigners in question are ineligible for refugee status. There have, of course, long been forms of subsidiary status (ELR, Duldung, B-Status) offered by states to individuals and groups of de facto refugees who fail to attain Convention status. But the impact of new conventions like the ECHR, the Convention Against Torture (CAT) and the EU's proposed Charter of Fundamental Rights and Freedoms (which recognises a right of asylum) is that these protections against refoulement become enshrined into international and, in many cases, national law.

Some of the most important jurisprudential developments have come through the European Court of Human Rights, which found in *Ahmed v Austria*[56] in 1996 that a person who loses refugee status because of the commission of a serious crime in their country of asylum is still protected from deportation or return home under Article 3 if they would face a real risk of torture, inhumane or degrading treatment or punishment. In *Soering v UK*[57] in 1989 the extradition of a fugitive to the US was deemed to violate Article 3 because the individual concerned was likely to face many years on 'death row'. The case of *Chahal v UK*[58] added a new dimension to ECHR protection by finding that refoulement is not justifiable even when the person concerned might pose a threat to the national security of the state of asylum.

Many questions are raised by the expansion of protection against refoulement. What entitlements should those protected by the ECHR or the CAT have other than the right not to be removed? Some fear that new forms of protection, if used as a substitute for the Convention refugee status, give states too much discretion in determining the civil, political and economic rights that refugees and other protected peoples will enjoy under subsidiary protection arrangements. This has been a common criticism made of the temporary protection arrangements made for Bosnians and

---

[56] (1997) 24 EHRR 278.

[57] (1989) 11 EHRR 439.

[58] (1996) 23 EHRR 413.

Kosovans in Europe. Others are concerned that the development of regional conventions and agreements (in Europe in particular) risk making the 1951 Convention redundant, thus severing the golden thread (already somewhat frayed to say the least) that currently connects the world's poorest and the world's richest states in their dealings with refugees. For others still, the growing constraints on expulsion and deportation seem to be of most benefit to those guilty of serious crimes rather than those 'deserving' of asylum.[59] These concerns aside, the developments outlined here have not only multiplied the resources that asylum seekers might potentially have to gain protection, they have given trump cards to the courts at national and European level by countering some of the restrictive tendencies that emerge from electoral politics.[60]

Theoretical and Practical Tensions in the Constitutional Democratic State

These are key developments in pruning back and restraining some of the worst effects of restrictive practices in recent years. To be sure, they do not signal that asylum seekers are adequately protected within constitutional democratic states, less still that they have become full rights-bearing subjects. In Europe and beyond, many asylum seekers are still likely to face detention, be denied the right to work for extended periods, and face harsher (and more humiliating) welfare regimes than permanent residents or citizens. Recent legislation in the UK, for example, the Asylum and Immigration Act of 1999, enabled the government to operate a dispersal system for asylum seekers, and introduced vouchers as a substitute for cash payments for welfare support.

---

[59]   The concerns are even greater when one believes that there is a risk that restrictions on removal or deportation might *attract* serious criminals to a country of refuge. Canada is currently wrestling with the ethical, political and legal dimensions of this problem, not least in terms of the question of returning alleged or convicted criminals to face the death penalty in the US. See J Brooke, 'Canada's Haven: For Notorious Fugitives, Too?', *New York Times*, 29 December 2000, p A10.

[60]   A very useful discussion of the expanding legal protections against refoulement (and their practical efficacy) can be found in H Lambert, 'Protection Against Refoulement from Europe: Human Rights Law Comes to the Rescue', *The International and Comparative Law Quarterly* 48 (1999) p 515.

The legal gains of asylum seekers thus have to compete with the strong exclusionary measures and pressures that emanate from the political realm that I have outlined. Moreover, the law is itself hardly an unerring foe of state discretion. European Court of Human Rights decisions, for example, invariably begin by reasserting the international law right of states to control the entry, residence and expulsion of aliens. But the importance of the legal gains should not be underestimated. The changes I have discussed complicate, frustrate, and compete with government attempts to manage asylum in a way that causes the least possible political disturbance. Due process protections make asylum determination an exceedingly expensive affair; extensions in the principle of non-refoulement can allow highly unsavoury individuals to gain protection; and limitations on removal can act as a magnet to asylum seekers and undocumented migrants. All these measures thus increase the political risks of asylum. How, then, are we to explain why governments sign conventions and empower judges and courts that undermine their own attempts to control asylum? What explains this seemingly schizophrenic reaction in European states where increasingly restrictive measures exist side by side with growing inclusive legal practices?

There are many ways that one might seek to answer these questions. In order to understand why states accede to human rights instruments one might consider the particularities prevailing in the case of each individual state. Different states sign human rights conventions for a variety of reasons – both principled and pragmatic – ranging from a real commitment to human rights, to the desire to stabilise democratic governance internally, to the hope of gaining entrance to regional or international bodies, like the EU.[61] But rather than consider what motivates individual states to sign particular treaties, I want now to provide an explanation of a more general character, one that draws upon the kind of entities that these (European) states claim to be.

We can understand the tension between the law of inclusion and the politics of restriction I have outlined by seeing it as reflecting a deeper conflict of values in the constitutional democratic state. Recent legal developments have actualised the *constitutional* or *rights-based* values that

---

[61]   An extremely provocative and compelling argument for why European states acceded to the ECHR in the early post-war period can be found in A Moravcsik, 'The Origins of Human Rights Regimes: Democratic Delegation in Postwar Europe', *International Organization* **54(2)** (2000) p 217.

European states claim to uphold and instantiate. Historically, the protections afforded by constitutional democratic states – such as rights to due process – have been available almost exclusively to citizens. Yet the legitimation of these rights has usually been universalistic: they have been presented (for instance, in national constitutions) as rights that should accrue to individuals on the basis of personhood rather than on the basis of membership in a particular state. This gap between the practical reality of membership-based rights and their universalistic mode of justification has provided a foothold for human rights groups and other NGOs to challenge the state's arbitrary treatment of asylum seekers. Their challenge has been most effective in the courts. Insulated from popular politics and empowered by developments in administrative and human rights law, the courts have been able to expand the responsibilities of states to foreigners, including asylum seekers. In the hands of the judiciary, the universality of liberal principles has provided a basis for undermining legal distinctions between citizens and aliens.

The principle of *democracy*, on the other hand, mandates that 'the people' have the sovereign right to deliberate together to fashion their collective future over time. In its attenuated contemporary version, this means the right to elect representatives of their choice.[62] Given the profound impact that decisions on entrance and membership can have on societies, it is not surprising that the right to deliberate on these decisions is a feature of every democratic community.[63] But who should have the right to have their preferences count? Citizenship is prerequisite in the modern state. In recent years, substantial sections of the citizenry in Europe have tended to see asylum seekers as a threat, as competitors to economic, social and political goods that they possess or to which they aspire. The strength of these negative attitudes is contingent and liable to change; it is the product of a set of empirical factors prevailing at a particular point in time (the focus of media reporting, poor housing or social policies, the dynamics of political competition, rising numbers of entrants, etc). But the fact that governments attach more importance to the anxieties of their citizens than the needs of asylum seekers is anything but contingent. It is a result, as I showed earlier, of a system of democratic citizenship in which there are

---

[62] See B Constant, 'On the Liberty of the Ancients Compared to that of the Moderns', in B Fontana (ed), *Benjamin Constant: Political Writings* (Cambridge, Cambridge University Press, 1988).

[63] M Walzer, *Spheres of Justice* (New York, Martin Robertson, 1983), chapter 2.

structural incentives for political leaders to take heed of their citizen's views. The principle of electoral democracy is thus deeply implicated in the rise and maintenance of restrictive asylum policies.

This account of the politics and law of asylum suggests that the paradox with which I started – the existence of increasingly restrictive asylum policies alongside the incorporation and development of human rights legislation – is rooted in the nature of constitutional democratic state itself. The problem is not, as some observers would have it, simply a matter of states failing to live up to principles they claim to represent. It is that the principles western states claim to represent are failing to live up to challenges posed by asylum, as the current asylum crisis exposes the tense and conflictual relationship between the values that constitutional democracies are supposed to uphold. Embodying the principle of democratic rule, electoral politics pushes policies towards closure and restriction; embodying constitutional principles, the law inches unevenly towards greater respect for the human rights of those seeking asylum.

The conflictual and competitive relationship between the law of inclusion and the politics of restriction gives us an insight into the way current asylum policies are evolving. It is plausible to believe that, as legal developments empowering asylum seekers have come to frustrate government efforts to respond to political pressures for restriction within national territory, other outlets for these pressures have been found. European states increasingly resort to non-arrival measures (such as visa regimes, carrier sanctions, international zones, and airport liaison officers) to insulate themselves from claims by asylum seekers. The practices of states outside of Europe are developing along a similar trajectory; to wit, the Australian government's legislative redefinition of its territory for immigration purposes to limit asylum applications in the aftermath of the *Tampa* incident.[64] By using these extra-border measures states have been able to carve out a realm for themselves free of the legal constraint and scrutiny they would face if asylum seekers arrived on their territory.

As one western government official stated, these measures are needed because, when our state confronts asylum seekers outside our territory, the onus is on the asylum seeker to prove why she should be admitted,

---

[64] For a more detailed description of these legislative changes, see Department for Immigration and Multicultural and Indigenous Affairs (DIMIA), *New Measures to Strengthen Immigration Control* (Canberra, DIMIA, September 2001), http://www.immi.gov.au/facts/71border.htm.

whereas once she arrives the onus is on us to show why she should be removed.[65] Non-arrival policies are thus an example of the demands of electoral politics 'striking back' (albeit in a way that fails to discriminate between Convention refugees and other claimants for entry). In short, I am suggesting that the developments made in human rights protections within European states outlined above, are, paradoxically, fuelling practices by states that prevent refugees from accessing protection in their territory. The cost of increasingly inclusive practices towards asylum seekers *within* the territory of the state is the rapid development of exclusive measures *outside* it.

Conclusion

I have attempted to spell out here what I see as one of the central problems facing the future of asylum in Europe 50 years after the signing of the Refugees Convention. The tension between greater liberalism towards asylum seekers and refugees at home and greater restrictionism towards these individuals abroad may not be resolvable, at least not within the structure of constitutional democratic states that profess simultaneously to uphold the value of human rights and the value of membership. Might this tension at the heart of asylum at least be reduced?

There is one obvious way to respond to the conflict between the law of inclusion and the politics of exclusion: expand the reach of the law, and thus judicial scrutiny, to follow a state's activity outside its territorial boundaries. If immigration control and asylum policy have shifted from Sydney to Jakarta or from London to Bombay, the law ought to reflect this fact. The range of measures used by states needs to be made public and subject to the glare of the media; the legality of the full range of non-arrival measures need to scrutinised, especially in the light of the expanding sphere of human rights law; and ways of ameliorating the worst effects of these policies need to be proposed and considered. This last point is of particular importance. Non-arrival measures are not going to go away. The terrorist attacks of September 11, 2001 in the US have ensured that. For security reasons alone, these measures will become an increasingly important part of the immigration control arsenal of constitutional democratic states. Accordingly, more attention needs to be given to how

---

[65]   Interview with official from Citizenship and Immigration Canada, December 2000.

legal and ethical constraints might be placed on these activities, at the very least to ensure that they do not result in refoulement.

It is important to recognise, however, that a further expansion in the law is only part of what is required. One implication of my argument is that restrictive political pressures will find a way of manifesting themselves if they are not addressed. The current approach of using law to smother this restrictionism is having some perverse and disturbing consequences. Clearly, what is required is a more inclusive politics of asylum, one that goes beyond the law to elicit from the public of western states greater identification with and respect for the claims of refugees and asylum seekers. The creation of such new understandings and identifications would require the coordination of many different actors with different interests. At the very least, a new and positive political bipartisanship within western states on refugee questions would be needed. Furthermore, new global institutions may need to be formed if identities that transcend the boundaries of citizenship are to be sustained over time. These are daunting requirements indeed. We are still a long way off from a world where human rights law reflects our politics rather than constrains it.

3 The Refugees Convention at 50: Mid-life Crisis or Terminal Inadequacy? An Australian Perspective

MARY CROCK

Refugee Status Determination in Australia: A System in Crisis

Australia's love-hate relationship with refugees is well documented. As a nation, Australia was a proud participant in the process[1] that delivered the United Nations Convention Relating to the Status of Refugees (the Refugees Convention) and subsequent Protocol.[2] It has done more than its fair share in offering permanent resettlement to persons *overseas* identified as refugees according to the terms of those instruments.[3] The nation's response has been less generous, however, where asylum seekers have come onto Australian territory and invoked the Refugees Convention so as to demand protection.[4] Asylum seekers who arrive without a visa face mandatory detention.[5] Further, those unauthorised arrivals who gain

---

[1] It was Australia's accession to the Convention in 1954 that brought the Convention into operation. For a recent note on the history of the Convention see M Achiron, 'Cover Story: The Geneva Convention has been the Cornerstone for Protection for 50 Years', *Refugee* 2 (2001) p 6 at p 10.

[2] In this chapter, the terms 'refugee claimant' and 'asylum seeker' are used interchangeably.

[3] Australia has admitted over 650 000 refugees and humanitarian cases since the end of the Second World War: Department of Immigration and Multicultural and Indigenous Affairs (DIMIA) Fact Sheet 40, *Special Eligibility System*, http://www.immi.gov.au/facts/40special.htm.

[4] Since 1996 the government has maintained a Humanitarian Program through the Department of Immigration of 12 000 places. 10 000 places are notionally allocated to offshore applicants and 2000 to onshore claimants.

[5] Migration Act 1958 (Cth) (Migration Act), section 189.

recognition as refugees are now granted no more than a temporary three-year visa, with no rights to family reunion and limited access to social security support.[6]

It is these unauthorised arrivals, the onshore asylum seekers, who represent the greatest challenge for Australia as a signatory to the Refugees Convention. The primary function of the Convention was to establish a substitute protection regime for individuals who have lost the protection of their state of origin. In practice, this can mean that the instrument imposes obligations on state parties that fly in the face of politically sacrosanct notions of sovereignty and prerogative power.

Australia's direct experience of involuntary migration in the form of onshore asylum seekers in any numbers is a relatively recent phenomenon. It was slow to take any formal steps to implement the terms of the Refugees Convention – the first formal procedures for determining refugee status were not established until 1978.[7] Even then, the processing of individual cases did not become an issue of concern until the arrival of boat people from Cambodia and China began to work against Australia's political interests.[8] Over the last decade we have seen a congruence of

---

[6] Temporary Visa subclass 785 was created by amendments to the regulations under the Migration Act in 1999. See the Migration Regulations 1994 (Cth), clause 785.2221 in Part 785 of Schedule 2; H Esmaeili and B Wells, 'The "Temporary" Refugees: Australia's Legal Response to the Arrival of Iraqi and Afghan Boat People', *University of New South Wales Law Review* 23 (2000) p 224; and M Crock and B Saul, *Freedom Seekers: Refugees and the Law in Australia* (Sydney, Federation Press, 2002), chapter 7.

[7] See M Crock, *Immigration and Refugee Law in Australia* (Sydney, Federation Press, 1998), pp 126–30; and S Kneebone, 'The Refugee Review Tribunal and the Assessment of Credibility: an Inquisitorial Role?', *Australian Journal of Administrative Law* 5 (1998) p 78 at p 79.

[8] Australia's involvement in the cooperative arrangements to end the conflict in Cambodia in the late 1980s militated against the acknowledgement that fugitives from that country could be 'Convention' refugees. For a discussion of this period see G Evans, *Cooperating for Peace* (Sydney, Allen & Unwin, 1993); M Crock, 'The Evolution of Australia's Mandatory Detention Policy' in M Crock, *Protection or Punishment: the Detention of Asylum Seekers in Australia* (Sydney, Federation Press, 1993), chapter 5. The later fugitives from the People's Republic of China and from refugee camps in Indonesia included individuals who were covered by the 'Comprehensive Plan of Action', devised to deal with the exodus from Vietnam at the end of the civil war in that country. Again, international political considerations led Australia to block consideration of refugee claims made by these people. See Migration Act, sections 91A–91D, discussed in S Taylor, 'Australia's Safe Third Country

factors leading to refugee policy becoming an increasingly charged issue in Australian politics.[9]

In 2001 Australia's refugee determination system would have to be described as a system in crisis. The crisis is not in the number of people seeking refuge in the country: the total of 8000-odd asylum seekers who arrive each year (with or without visas; by plane and by boat) pale next to the approximately 80 000 asylum applications made in the United Kingdom or the 120 000 claiming refugee status in Germany. In most years over the last decade, Australia has actually received well under 2000 undocumented arrivals seeking protection as refugees.[10] In spite of the relatively modest numbers involved, the arrival of boat people to the north of the country regularly induces a state of near hysteria in Australia's public discourse.

In 2001, the Howard government's tough stance against asylum seekers and the institution of what became known as the 'Pacific Solution' were widely credited as significant factors in the federal electoral victory of the Conservative Liberal–National Party Coalition (the Coalition government). This Pacific Solution, put simply, involves the deflection to other countries of all boat people apprehended en route to Australia. In response to financial incentives offered by Australia, compliant Pacific Island nations have agreed to feed and house the asylum seekers while their refugee claims are processed by personnel from the United Nation High Commissioner for Refugees (UNHCR) and the International Organisation of Migration (IOM).

Within Australia, the plight of asylum seekers in remote and punitive detention centres is rarely far from the front pages of the national papers. A variety of bodies have criticised the way the centres are run and have noted with regret the impact detention has on detainees who are ultimately

---

Provisions: Their Impact on Australia's Fulfilment of its Non-refoulement Obligations', *University of Tasmania Law Review* **15** (1996) p 196.

[9] For a discussion of this phenomenon, see D Corlett, 'Politics, Symbolism and the Asylum Seeker Issue', *University of New South Wales Law Journal* **23** (2000) p 13; and P Mares, *Borderline: Australia's Treatment of Refugees and Asylum Seekers* (Sydney, UNSW Press, 2001).

[10] In the 11 years between 1989 and January 2001, Australia received 8202 undocumented plane arrivals and 10 224 boat arrivals, most of whom applied in due course for refugee status. See generally Crock and Saul, above n 6, chapter 3.

released to start a new life in the Australian community.[11] Indeed, Australia's mandatory detention regime does not come cheaply. A recent medical study details the human costs of detention on those incarcerated for extended periods.[12] In May 2001, the Department of Immigration stated in parliament that the financial cost of detention amounts to $105 per person, per day. It also asserted that $96 million was spent on detention in 1999–2000. This figure does not reflect the actual costs incurred as it excludes capital costs relating to the establishment of facilities as well as the extra costs incurred in processing claims where substantial distances separate the asylum seekers from both the processing officials and the claimant's advisers. Others have put the total cost of the regime at as much as $370 million per annum.[13] The cost of the Pacific Solution is difficult to quantify at this early stage. However, some have suggested that the cost of resolving the *Tampa* affair (see below) was

---

[11] These include the Human Rights and Equal Opportunity Commission (HREOC), the Commonwealth Ombudsman, and sub-committees of the federal parliament itself: http://www.hreoc.gov.au/human_rights/asylum_seekers/; http://www.comb.gov.au/publications_information/Annual_Reports/AR2000-01/DIMA.html; and the collection at http://www.immi.gov.au/detention. The most recent parliamentary report – which is also the most radical in its criticisms of the policies in operation – is that of the Human Rights Sub-Committee of the Joint Standing Committee on Foreign Affairs Defence and Trade, *A Report on Visits to Immigration Detention Centres* (Canberra, Parliament of Australia, June 2001), http://www.aph.gov.au/house/committee/jfadt/IDCVisits/IDCindex.htm.

[12] A Sultan and K O'Sullivan, 'Psychological Disturbances in Asylum Seekers Held in Long Term Detention: A Participant-Observer Account', *Medical Journal of Australia* **175** (2001) p 593. See also the other articles on detention and mental health in this special issue of the *Medical Journal of Australia*: M M Smith, 'Asylum seekers in Australia', *Medical Journal of Australia* **175** (2001) p 587; M F Harris and B L Telfer, 'The Health Needs of Asylum Seekers Living in the Community', *Medical Journal of Australia* **175** (2001) p 589; Z Steel and D M Silove, 'The Mental Health Implications of Detaining Asylum Seekers', *Medical Journal of Australia* **175** (2001) p 596; and K King and P Vodicka, 'Screening For Conditions of Public Health Importance in People Arriving in Australia by Boat Without Authority', *Medical Journal of Australia* **175** (2001) p 600.

[13] A Millbank, *The Problem with the 1951 Convention* (Canberra, Department of the Parliamentary Library, Research Paper 5 2000–01), http://www.aph.gov.au/library/pubs/rp/2000-01/01RP05.htm .

$148 million, with some reports – denied by government – putting the cost at between $400 and $500 million.[14] What does Australia see for the expenditure of such vast sums of money? It sees riots in the centres and refugees who leave the determination process scarred not only by the way they have been treated in their country of origin but also by the way they have been treated after their arrival in Australia. It has also seen civil disobedience campaigns organised within the community, which have not been seen in the country since the days of the war in Vietnam.[15] In August 2001 many groups staged almost daily protests when the Prime Minister, John Howard, stepped in directly to deny admission to 433 asylum seekers picked up at sea from their foundering boat by a Norwegian vessel named the *MV Tampa*.[16] These campaigns have continued and intensified since the federal election in November 2001, leaving the appearance of a country deeply divided over its refugee policies.

The human and fiscal cost of the detention facilities represent only a small problem, however, in comparison with the processing problems within the administrative system itself. Put simply, Australia's system delivers no finality in its decision making and review process, notwithstanding the physical availability of persons held in detention. Refugee cases are clogging up the judicial review processes in both the Federal Court and the High Court of Australia. In June 2001, there were no less than 4000 refugee cases in one class action before the High Court, and literally hundreds of individual applications by asylum seekers to that court in its constitutional jurisdiction.[17] Under section 75(v) of the Australian

---

[14] M Seccombe, 'Pacific Solution May Hit Next Budget', *Sydney Morning Herald*, 13 December 2001, http://old.smh.com.au/news/0112/13/national/national1.html; D Marr and M Wilkinson, '*Tampa* Tantrums', *The Age,* 20 October 2001. DIMIA has suggested that the cost of the Nauru facility for 2001–02 would be $72 million: *The Age*, 9 January 2002, p 1.

[15] See, as an illustration, the work of the Refugee Action Cooperative (RAC) in Sydney who vowed in August 2001 to offer sanctuary to escapees from immigration detention, vowing that its members were prepared to face gaol terms for their actions.

[16] See further, below n 31, and 'Assessing the problem'. Public opinion in Australia was firmly behind the Prime Minister: the protesters were dismissed as a 'noisy minority'.

[17] In 1999–2000, the Federal Court received 684 applications for review of Refugee Review Tribunal (RRT) decisions, representing 16 per cent of all RRT decisions in which the primary decision rejecting refugee status was upheld by the tribunal. The rise in applications has been most marked post-1996: 1993–94, 52; 1994–95, 193; 1995–96,

Constitution, there is an entrenched right to seek judicial review of decisions made by 'officers of the Commonwealth', a phrase that includes most decision makers in the immigration context. As people around the world gather to mark the 50th anniversary of the Refugees Convention, it is timely to reflect on Australia's experience as a signatory to this instrument. In early 2001, the Coalition government through the Minister for Immigration, Philip Ruddock, floated the idea of rewriting the Convention, arguing that the instrument is ill suited to modern-day experiences of refugee movements. At least one commentator in Australian parliamentary circles agrees, going further to advocate that Australia withdraw altogether from the Refugees Convention.[18] Predictably, such calls have invoked expressions of regret, alarm and incredulity from the international community. According to one diplomat from the Indian subcontinent: 'Australia is making such a mess of things and is trying to draw moral weight that it does not pull'. Another is reported to have commented:

> Australia is the only country in the Western world that has so many problems with so few asylum seekers – it is a very good case study of why not to go down the detention path that Australia insists on following.[19]

The purpose of this chapter is not to engage fully with the debate over the changes (if any) that should be made to the Refugees Convention.

283; 1996–97, 420; 1997–98, 477; 1998–99, 635; and 1999–2000, 684. Applications to the High Court increased from 65 applications in 1998–99 to 128 in 1999–2000. As of June 2001 there were 54 applications relating to RRT decisions pending in the High Court: Refugee Review Tribunal, *Monthly Statistics*, June 2001, http://www.rrt.gov.au/2000-2001%20/Statistics.pdf; DIMIA Fact Sheet 86, *Overstayers and People in Breach of Visa Conditions*, http://www.immi.gov.au/facts/86overstayers.htm. Many more refugee cases are pending in the High Court's section 75(v) jurisdiction – as at February 2002 there were 108 (J McMillan, talk to the Victorian Chapter of the Australian Institute of Administrative Law, Melbourne, 19 February 2002).

[18] Millbank, above n 13.

[19] Both quotations from P McGeough, 'Global Scorn for Ruddock Refugee Curbs', *Sydney Morning Herald*, 9 July 2001, p 1; and 'Australia in the Dock Over Its Treatment of Refugees', *Sydney Morning Herald*, 9 July 2001, p 7. See also Editorial, *Sydney Morning Herald*, 9 July 2001, p 10; and for the government's view: P Ruddock, 'Australian Government Measures to Reform UN Refugee Bodies', Media Release MPS 088/2000, 29 August 2000, http://www.minister.immi.gov.au/media_releases/media00/r00088.htm.

My more specific aim is to explore the extent to which Australia's refugee problems can be attributed to inadequacies in the Convention, or, conversely, are home-grown products of Australia's own policy choices. It will be quickly apparent that my sympathies are with the second of these propositions. Even if the Refugees Convention is an imperfect instrument for the protection of refugees, the very fact that Australia's experience is not replicated in other asylum countries suggests that the Convention alone cannot explain the problems encountered in this country. Central to any meaningful reform process will be a realistic assessment of how the Australian situation came about.

The Australian Senate's Committee on Legal and Constitutional References began the process of self-reflection that is the necessary precursor to any significant change with a major inquiry into Australia's refugee and humanitarian program in 2000. The recommendations made in the Senate's report have been described in some detail elsewhere,[20] but nevertheless inform many of the comments made in this chapter in the section titled: 'Australia's Implementation of the Refugees Convention – (i) Decision Making'. It is a matter of some regret that the Coalition government rejected summarily virtually all of the 43 (unanimous) recommendations made by this multi-party committee.

The chapter begins with a brief examination of the Refugees Convention and the complaints that have been made about its operation in practice. While noting the inevitable conflict in opinions about the Convention given the competing interests involved, the arguments in favour of the instrument remain as compelling today as they ever were. I argue that, far from being an anachronistic relic of another age, an international legal regime mandating certain basic protections for refugees remains essential because of the domestic politics involved wherever an outsider seeks admission into a community.

The sections titled: 'Australia's Implementation of the Refugees Convention – (i) Decision making and Australia's Implementation of the Refugees Convention – (ii) The Reach of Australia's Protection Obligations', examine in some detail the ways in which Australia has

---

[20] M Crock, 'A Sanctuary Under Review: Where to From Here for Australia's Refugee and Humanitarian Program', *University of New South Wales Law Journal* **23** (2000) p 246. See Senate Legal and Constitutional References Committee (SLCRC), *A Sanctuary Under Review: An Examination of Australia's Refugee and Humanitarian Processes* (Canberra, Commonwealth of Australia, June 2000).

chosen to implement the obligations it has assumed as signatory to the Refugees Convention. On the one hand I argue that the policy choices have resulted in an unhealthy politicisation of refugee issues in Australia. On the other hand, an analysis of the subtle and not so subtle changes made to the administrative regime forms the basis for some suggestions about why so many refugee claimants emerge radically unhappy from the refugee determination process in Australia. The chapter concludes with a brief sketch of what I consider to be the main reforms that need to be made of the system to restore a sense of balance, equity and respect for international law.

Problems with the Refugees Convention

As Hathaway and Neve have shown, governments charged with fulfilling a country's obligations as signatory to the Refugees Convention have two main complaints.[21] First, they protest that it leads to an abdication of migration control and complain about the social and financial impact of granting asylum to large numbers of refugees. Second, they complain about the costs associated with determining individual refugee claims.[22] Arguments are also made about the role that criminal elements play in conveying asylum seekers to chosen countries of refuge and about the inequity of a system that privileges the (mobile) wealthy over those who are condemned to wait for years in the often inhumane conditions of UN-sponsored refugee camps.[23]

---

[21] J Hathaway and R A Neve, 'Making International Refugee Law Relevant Again: A Proposal for Collectivised and Solution-oriented Protection', *Harvard Human Rights Journal* **10** (1997) p 115.

[22] Concerns are rightly expressed about the amounts expended on processing refugee claims compared with the contributions that signatory countries make to the running of UNHCR operations. On this issue, see the critique offered by J Harding in *The Uninvited: Refugees at the Rich Man's Gate* (London, Profile Books, 2000). See also the comments by Millbank, above n 13, p 4 where she notes that in 1990, western countries were spending ten times as much on refugee determination regimes as they were allocating to the UNHCR to perform its global refugee protection functions. The situation has not improved in the intervening years.

[23] For summary of complaints, see Millbank, above n 13; Harding, ibid; and A Schloenhardt, 'The Business of Migration: Organised Crime and Illegal Migration', *Adelaide Law Review* **21** (1999) p 81.

From the standpoint of the asylum seeker, concerns with the Convention focus on the reach of the definition of refugee contained in Article 1, and the consistency of the interpretation of the definition between jurisdictions and with other human rights instruments.[24] Again, concerns have been raised about the equity of a system that favours individuals who fear harm by reason of their (visible) politics or ethnicity, over persons who may face death for reasons that cannot be accommodated within one of the five narrow grounds.[25] In particular, many persons who are victims of serious human rights breaches may be excluded from the definition.

A universal complaint is that the Refugees Convention provides insufficient guidance as to how the refugee definition should be applied and that the standards implicit in the Convention are not easy to discern. Because there is no central authority that can rule on the interpretation of the instrument, real inconsistencies can develop between the way state parties interpret the instrument. Theorists differ on even the most basic precepts underlying the Convention.[26] At a practical level, the Convention has no mechanism for holding states to account in relation to their compliance with the instrument.[27]

The essential difference between the two perspectives of the state and the asylum seeker is this. Countries of asylum invariably want to take responsibility for fewer refugees, while those in pursuit of sanctuary complain that the doors to freedom are too few and too narrow in their compass.

Without denying the strength of some of the criticisms made of the Convention from both sides of the refugee divide, some of the complaints now being heard underscore elements that are both timeless and universal

---

[24] See D J Steinbock, 'The Refugee Definition as Law: Issues of Interpretation' in F Nicholson and P Twomey, *Refugee Rights and Realities: Evolving International Concepts and Regimes* (Cambridge, Cambridge University Press, 1999), chapter 1.

[25] For example, the critiques made about the gendered nature of the definition, summarised most recently and comprehensively in H Crawley, *Refugees and Gender: Law and Process* (Bristol, Jordan, 2001); K Walker, 'New Uses of the Refugees Convention: Sexuality and Refugee Status', chapter 10 in this book; and S Kneebone, 'Moving Beyond the State: Refugees, Accountability and Protection', chapter 11 in this book.

[26] Compare J Hathaway, *The Law of Refugee Status* (Toronto, Butterworths, 1991), p 124; and T A Aleinikoff, 'State – Centred Refugee Law: From Resettlement to Containment', *Michigan Journal of International Law* **14** (1992) p 121. See generally the discussion of the 'protection' and 'accountability' theories in Kneebone, ibid.

[27] Kneebone, above n 25.

in the refugee experience. People who leave their homes to seek refuge in a foreign country have always presented a challenge, a source of annoyance and discomfort. The Refugees Convention is often described as a product of the Cold War – designed to allow western countries to use international law to trumpet their freedoms to the eastern bloc.[28] It was also a product of a time when humanity came together to express a collective sense of horror at the human rights abuses perpetrated during the Second World War. Central to the creation of a regime for protecting the basic human rights of individuals was (and is) the notion that no person should be returned to a situation where his or her fundamental human rights are threatened. Put another way, the principle of non-refoulement in refugee law was created with the recent memory of refugees being denied protection by countries of first asylum, with catastrophic consequences for those seeking protection.[29] While some may dispute the practicality of using the language of rights in a context that inevitably conflicts with ingrained notions of state sovereignty,[30] without a regime of international obligations the pressure of domestic politics is likely to weigh even more heavily than it does now against the protection of refugees.

Nowhere was this more apparent than in the stand-off that developed in August 2001 when Australia refused to admit 433 asylum seekers collected from their sinking boat by the Norwegian vessel the *MV Tampa*. In that instance the Prime Minister's intervention carried all the hallmarks of what Opposition leader Kim Beazley labelled 'wedge politics'.[31] Public opinion in Australia – if nowhere else in the world – was firmly behind the Prime Minister, prompting Mr Beazley to concur in the initial decision to refuse entry. While the incident could be cited as an example of how little regard sovereign states have for refugee law generally when it does not suit their political objectives, the vehemence of the international response to the incident demonstrates the normative force of having an international

---

[28] Hathaway, above n 26; Hathaway and Neve, above n 21; and G S Goodwin-Gill, *The Refugee in International Law* (Oxford, Clarendon Press, 2nd ed, 1996).

[29] P Bartrop, *Australia and the Holocaust 1933–1945* (Kew, Victoria, Scholarly Publishing, 1994); and I Abella and H Troper, *None is Too Many* (Toronto, Lester & Orpen Dennys, 1986).

[30] Hathaway and Neve, above n 21; C Dauvergne, 'The Dilemma of Rights Discourses for Refugees', *University of New South Wales Law Journal* **23** (2000) p 56.

[31] Parliament of Australia, *Hansard,* House of Representatives, 29 August 2001.

regime based on articulated rights and obligations.[32] Ironically, while the Labor Party in Australia saw their political interests in concurring with the stance taken by the government, the Labour Party in Norway saw political mileage in advocating that Norway assist the asylum seekers. The same is true of the governments in New Zealand and Nauru – and East Timor – all of whom offered to take the fugitives.[33]

The simple truth is that the Jewish and other asylum seekers turned away during the Second World War were not wanted any more than today's asylum seekers are wanted when they arrive in a country without appropriate documentation. It was to deal with just such a situation, however, that the Refugees Convention was created: the Convention was designed to force signatories to provide protection to refugees physically on their territory. This is reflected in Prime Minister Howard's insistence that the *Tampa* refugee claimants not be permitted to land on Australian soil.[34] Some may argue that the concept of protected exile is outdated in this age of international diplomacy.[35] Even so, it is still the case that flight remains the only option for many who are faced with extremist regimes or the uncontrolled violence of civil war.

The basic non-refoulement obligation contained in the Refugees Convention provides the strongest argument for maintaining the instrument. Without it the ambiguity of state practice would provide a shakier foundation for the assertion that non-refoulement has passed into the realm of customary international law. Even the most strident critics of the instrument acknowledge that reopening the instrument for debate would almost certainly result in a lessening of the legal protections available to refugees. In this context it is noteworthy that while the government's Pacific Solution involves a resolute refusal to allow boat people access to Australia's refugee determination mechanisms, it does not constitute a program of direct or indirect refoulement. On the contrary, care has been

---

[32] This incident received wide media coverage around the world, with almost universal condemnation outside Australia of the government's stance. For example, M Gee, 'None is Too Many', *Globe and Mail*, Thursday August 30, p A9, and Editorial, 'Australia Sets Callous Example', *Toronto Star*, 1 September 2001, p K6.

[33] Reuters, 'New Zealand and Nauru Will Take Refugees', *Globe and Mail*, 1 September 2001, p A14; AFP, 'Les refugiés du *Tampa* dirigés vers Nauru et la Nouvelle-Zéalande', *Le Soleil*, 1 September 2001, p A27.

[34] Reuters, ibid.

[35] For example, Millbank, above n 13.

taken to ensure that the UNHCR and the IOM process the refugee claims of the asylum seekers and organise their resettlement, while they are housed on the Pacific Islands participating in the scheme.

Of course, the immediate protection of refugees from refoulement is not the sole function of the Refugees Convention: the mandate of the UNHCR is much wider.[36] It is hardly surprising that countries like Australia are most comfortable with the concept of refugee protection in the context of managing the accommodation and resettlement of refugees located in other countries, in cooperation with the UNHCR. Australia is one of only a handful of countries that accepts refugees for resettlement through such programs.[37] It often boasts of its record in resettling more than 600 000 refugees since the end of World War II.[38] In theory, the establishment of an effective regime for the protection of refugees would remove the need for individuals to seek asylum in other countries. Until a perfect system can be devised, however, a mechanism for the protection of asylum seekers will remain a necessity. The Refugees Convention provides such a base, and should be used as such in building mechanisms for more equitable burden-sharing.[39]

Australia is not unique in its concerns about the loss of control implicit in the principle (and practice) of non-refoulement of refugees. What sets it apart is the length to which Australia has gone in its attempt to assert its control. As the *Tampa* incident illustrates, Australia's response places it at grave risk of itself becoming an international pariah in the domain of human rights protection.

---

[36] V Turk, 'The Role of the UNHCR in the Development of International Refugee Law' in Nicholson and Twomey, above n 24, chapter 8.

[37] Only about 12 countries have resettlement programs and accept annual quotas of refugees. Australia is the third most generous (currently about 6000 of a notional quota of 10 000) behind the USA (72 000) and Canada (13 500); UNHCR, *Refugees by Numbers 2001 Edition* (Geneva, UNHCR, 2001), http://www.unhcr.ch.

[38] DIMIA, Fact Sheet 60 *Australia's Refugee and Humanitarian Program*, http://www.immi.gov.au/statistics/refugee.htm.

[39] Hathaway and Neve, above n 21.

Australia's Implementation of the Refugees Convention – (i) Decision Making

Australia has chosen not to enact domestic legislation implementing all the terms of the Refugees Convention.[40] Instead, it has taken the permissible option of devising laws and policies that are consistent with its obligations under this instrument – at least in most respects. Again, the decision not to replicate the Refugees Convention in its domestic laws is not so unusual. Australia stands out, however, in the extent to which politics has been allowed to intrude into its refugee determination process. If the organisational structures leave the system open to the vagaries of popular politics, there has also been a disturbing tendency to weight the administrative process against the applicant in refugee cases. I will argue that recent changes to the migration legislation evince a pervasive sense of distrust and defensiveness against non-citizens who come to Australia and claim protection as refugees. I explore the extent to which the cumulative effect of the provisions – and their application in practice – might explain why so many asylum seekers leave the process unhappy with their experience. I look in turn at how Australia's defensiveness is reflected in three phases of the refugee determination process: the initial application, administrative appeal and judicial review stages.

Locating the Power to Determine Who Is or Is Not a Refugee: The Politics of Refugee Decision Making

My view is that many of the problems encountered in the administration of migration decision making in this country have their source in the inexorable politicisation of the system, with consequent loss of independence and transparency. Over the last decade of the 1990s, sequential changes were made to the migration legislation that resulted in the gradual concentration of power in one person: the minister responsible for immigration matters (the Minister for Immigration). Although not limited to one administration, it is under the stewardship of the Coalition Party's Minister for Immigration, Philip Ruddock that the transformation has been most marked.

---

[40] In Canada for example, the Immigration Act 1976 directly incorporates most provisions of the Refugees Convention.

At a general level, the decision to codify migration decision making using the device of detailed regulations – made by a Labor government in 1989 – operated to increase the involvement of parliament in the day to day operations of the immigration portfolio. As a matter of practicality, the agenda for determining the content of relevant regulations is set by the Minister for Immigration. In addition to this general role, the regulatory system has also given the Minister specific powers within the overall context of the immigration portfolio. As others have documented,[41] the most striking feature of Australia's immigration laws is that they remove the independent discretion of decision makers to deal with cases that do not fit neatly within the terms of specific regulations. The only 'real' discretions that remain are those conferred on the Minister for Immigration. These are expressed in innovative legislative formulae that empower the Minister to intervene so as to reverse an adverse decision, but only if and when the Minister is minded so to act. He or she cannot be compelled to exercise the relevant power, and decisions relative to the exercise or non-exercise of the power cannot be reviewed by any court or tribunal.[42]

One of the most disturbing aspects of the regime now in place is the extent to which the regulatory regime has been developed in response to administrative and – more problematically – judicial decisions involving migrants and refugees. At each stage, the accretion of power to the Minister has been reflected in a reduced or compromised role given to the courts in determining the legality of migration decisions.[43] In the refugee area, one of the first and most striking examples of this process in action was the response of the legislature to the landmark ruling of the High Court in *Chan Yee Kin v Minister for Immigration and Ethnic Affairs*.[44] This decision is the starting point for Australian jurisprudence on the definition of refugee contained in the Refugees Convention because in it

---

[41] S Cooney, *The Transformation of Immigration Law* (Melbourne, BIPR, 1995).

[42] Crock, above n 7, p 274–6. Also see *Bedlington v Chong* (1998) 87 FCR 75, and the Migration Act, section 48B (power to permit making of further application for a protection visa), sections 351 and 417 (Minister may substitute more favourable decision of tribunal).

[43] For a study of the relationship between developments in the courts and changes to the Migration Act in and after 1989, see M Crock, *Administrative Law and Immigration Control in Australia: Actions and Reactions* (Melbourne, Unpublished, 1994), and D Pearce, 'Executive Versus the Judiciary', *Public Law Review* 2 (1991) p 179.

[44] (1989) 169 CLR 379. This case is discussed in Crock, above n 7, pp 135ff.

the High Court made important statements about the way the Convention definition of refugee should be interpreted. The case established that the reference to 'well founded fear of persecution' in the Convention definition required claimants to have a 'real chance' of persecution upon return to their country of origin. But it was the context of the decision that is significant for the present discussion. The case came before the High Court on an application for judicial review of an adverse decision of a delegate of the Minister, and succeeded on the sole ground of 'unreasonableness' – an ambiguous ground in any context. This decision led to the passage of the initial Part 8 of the Migration Act which limits the grounds of review before the Federal Court.[45] It set in train a pattern of legislative responses to judicial decisions of which the government disapproves.[46] The latest and most far reaching of these is the new section 91R described below.

The government was also most concerned that the High Court should be reading the international standard as though it had been incorporated verbatim into Australian domestic law. Philip Ruddock, then opposition spokesman for immigration, described the ruling as a 'rod for the government's back'.[47] The remedy prescribed by parliament in the migration legislation was to interpose some distance between the interpretative work of the Australian courts and the international definition of refugee.[48] In one stroke, the role of the courts was altered so that the international definition of refugee ceased to be the prime focus of the

---

[45] M Crock, 'Judicial Review and Part 8 of the Migration Act: Necessary Reform or Overkill?', *Sydney Law Review* **18** (1996) p 267.

[46] For instance, clause 2 Migration Legislation Amendment Bill (No 3) 1995 (Cth) was introduced in response to *Minister for Immigration v Applicant A* (1995) 57 FCR 309 ('one child' policy). As a result of the High Court decision (1997) 190 CLR 225 in favour of the government, the Bill did not proceed. The decision in *Human Rights and Equal Opportunity Commissioner v Secretary, Department of Immigration* (1996) 67 FCR 83, in which the applicant successfully sought mandamus to require the delivery of letters about legal advice to asylum seekers, led to Migration Legislation Amendment Bill (No 2) 1996 (Cth) which was not passed. See, however, section 193 which limits the rights of unauthorised arrivals to legal advice. See also P Mathew, 'Safe for Whom? The Safe Third Country Concept Finds a Home in Australia', chapter 6 in this book, for further examples.

[47] Parliament of Australia, *Hansard,* House of Representatives, 5 May 1992, pp 2372–84; 4 November 1992, pp 2620–3; 16 December 1992, p 3935.

[48] Section 22A of the Migration Act was amended to provide that: 'If the Minister is satisfied that a person is a refugee, the Minister may determine, in writing that the person is a refugee'.

decision, becoming instead a precondition or jurisdictional fact for the personal satisfaction or opinion of the Minister. As the High Court acknowledged in the subsequent decision of *Wu Shan Liang v Minister for Immigration and Ethnic Affairs*,[49] the change reduced considerably the scope for judicial supervision of refugee decision making. The legislation now provides for the grant of a protection visa to non-citizens who 'the Minister is satisfied' meet the criteria for the grant of a visa.[50] As the High Court has emphasised in a number of cases, this effectively makes decisions about refugee status in Australia an administrative decision of the Minister.[51]

In September 2001 legislation was enacted[52] that specifically sets out to:

> restore the application of the Convention relating to the Status of Refugees ... in Australia to its proper interpretation; and promote integrity in protection visa application and decision making processes ...[53]

This was a response to perceived expansive judicial interpretation of the refugee definition. The new section 91R(1) introduces the concept of dominant purpose, providing that a refugee claimant will only meet the definition of refugee if she or he fears persecution, the 'essential and significant reason' for which is one of the five Convention grounds (of race, nationality, religion, membership of a particular social group or political opinion). The new provisions specify further that the persecution must involve 'serious harm' and 'systematic and discriminatory conduct'.

---

[49] (1996) 185 CLR 259. The effect of the change is that when a court examines a refugee ruling, its task is no longer simply to assess whether the definition of refugee has been correctly interpreted and applied. Instead, it can only intervene if there was *no evidence* upon which the Minister (acting through his officer or through the appellate body) could reach the decision made or if an egregious error of interpretation was made by the decision maker. In practical terms, the distinction is one that acts as a considerable constraint on the ability of a court to review refugee decisions.

[50] This is the combined effect of section 36 (grant of protection visa to 'non-citizens' to whom Australia has protection obligations under the Refugees Convention) and section 65, which makes the satisfaction of the Minister a precondition to the making of any visa decision.

[51] For example *Minister for Immigration v Eshetu* (1999) 197 CLR 611 at 647.

[52] Migration Legislation Amendment Act No 6 2001 (Cth), introducing sections 91R–91U into the Migration Act. Other aspects of this Act are discussed below.

[53] Migration Legislation Amendment Act (No 6) 2001 (Cth), Explanatory Memorandum.

Although not inconsistent with the original ruling in *Chan* the new provisions do represent a tightening of the definition from the perspective of recent Federal Court jurisprudence.[54]

For his part, Minister Ruddock has come close on occasions to asserting that he alone should have the power to determine the content and application of the Rule of Law in immigration and refugee cases. Where the tribunals or the courts have disagreed with his own interpretation of the law prescribed by Parliament, Minister Ruddock has labelled the reviewers undemocratic – running 'against the will of the people'.[55] Interestingly, in most cases, the battle lines between the Minister and the courts have been drawn in cases where disagreements have arisen over the characterisation of a non-citizen as a refugee. In recent times, the Minister has become more and more explicit in charging that the Australian courts are 'too generous' in their interpretation of the Refugees Convention definition of refugee.[56]

It is my view that as each successive change has been made to toughen the refugee determination system and to increase the powers of the Minister, 'user' satisfaction has declined. People are emerging from the refugee determination experience unhappy with the way they have been treated and not just by the decision as such. The ultimate irony is that the more obstacles that are placed in the way of disgruntled asylum seekers wishing to challenge an adverse refugee determination, the more judicial review applications seem to be made.[57] If this phenomenon were to be explained by the nature of the Refugees Convention, as adopted in a western democracy, one would expect Australia's experience to be typical.

---

[54] Some of this jurisprudence is discussed in Kneebone, above n 25, and Walker, above n 25.

[55] See the address by Philip Ruddock MP to the National Press Club, Canberra, 18 March 1998 where he stated: 'Only two weeks ago a decision to deport a man was overturned by the Federal Court although he had been convicted and served a gaol sentence for possessing heroin with an estimated street value of $3 million. Again, *the courts have reinterpreted and rewritten Australian law – ignoring the sovereignty of parliament and the will of the Australian people. Again, this is simply not on.*' (Emphasis added.)

[56] Ibid; and P Ruddock, 'Narrowing of Judicial Review in the Migration Context' (1997) 15 Australian Institute of Administrative Law Forum 13. See also the Migration Legislation Amendment (Judicial Review) Bill 1997, Second Reading Speech, Parliament of Australia, *Hansard*, Senate, 2 December 1998, p 1027 and the comments of the Honourable Justice Sackville, 'Judicial Review of Migration Decisions: An Institution in Peril', *University of New South Wales Law Journal* 23 (2000) p 190.

[57] See above, n 17.

This is not the case, however. While refugee appeals are a concern in some countries, the rate of curial applications experienced in Australia has no parallel anywhere else in the common law world.

Refugee Status Determinations: The Application Process

To understand why individuals might be emerging from the refugee determination system in Australia feeling disgruntled with their experience, it is necessary to delve in some detail into the laws and practices that have developed in this country. On paper, most of Australia's procedures comply with the little that is demanded as a matter of strict international (refugee) law. The Refugees Convention does not tie signatory countries to particular administrative practices, although the UNHCR has developed some guidelines.[58] But there are some aspects of Australia's laws and some aspects of its procedures that advocates argue are in contravention of various international legal obligations assumed by Australia. The laws mandating the detention of asylum seekers who arrive without papers are an obvious example in point. The differential treatment of 'undocumented' refugees as opposed to refugees who arrive in Australia with valid visas is another.[59] For present purposes, however, my interest is in the cumulative effect of the subtle and not so subtle changes that have been made over the years to the laws and policies governing the way refugee claimants are treated and processed. The choices made are arguably within the realm of the Australian government's discretion about how it implements the Convention, although the fairness of these processes as I demonstrate below can be questioned. The real issue is whether the measures adopted represent an optimal use of resources from the two perspectives of the asylum seeker (as consumer) and the Australian taxpayer who is ultimately at the paying end of the human and fiscal equation that is formed.

One of the most interesting criticisms of Australia's refugee determination process made by the Senate Legal and Constitutional References Committee (SLCRC) in its report in 2000 related to the efficiency of the procedures adopted at an applicant's point of entry into the refugee determination process. Implicit in the SLCRC's criticisms is the understanding that an overly defensive attitude can work against

---

[58] UNHCR, *Handbook on Procedures and Criteria for the Determination of Refugee Status* (Geneva, UNHCR, 2nd ed, 1992).

[59] See above, n 4.

Australia's interests. At a purely legalistic level, it expressed some concern that asylum seekers are often interviewed and assessed at first instance without giving them access to any form of legal advice. The SLCRC noted that this practice carries with it a danger that officials will miss people who should invoke Australia's protection obligations, for the simple reason that the asylum seekers do not use the right 'language' to articulate their claims. For persons with no English and no understanding of how the system operates, misplaced politeness or reticence can have disastrous consequences.[60] In this context, the SLCRC made various recommendations about information that should be made available to prospective refugee claimants, to enable them to understand and participate fully in the application process. For example, the committee suggested that asylum seekers be provided with written material and an informational video explaining the rudimentary elements of the Convention definition of refugee and the processes that are involved in determining refugee status.[61] It also considered in some detail the adequacy of the legal advice that is provided to asylum seekers admitted into the refugee determination process.[62]

The SLCRC could have explored in much greater depth how Australia's migration legislation operates at this vital point of first contact. In fact, an examination of the legislation reveals an extraordinary imbalance between the rights of asylum seekers and the powers of the authorities charged with the determination of refugee claims. Applicants have no right to legal advice even after they are admitted to the process, unless they are in detention and unless they request access to such advice in respect of their detention.[63] If detained after the initial screening process, they are allowed an advisor, but under the government sponsored scheme, claimants are

---

[60] HREOC, *Human Rights Violations at Port Hedland Immigration Detention Centre*, http://www.hreoc.gov.au/human_rights/asylum_seekers/index.html. The Commission also comments on this practice in other reports available at this site. See also the criticisms of this practice in SLCRC, above n 20, pp 76–85.

[61] SLCRC, above n 20, pp 76–85, recommendation 3.1.

[62] Id, chapter 3.

[63] Migration Act, section 256. Unauthorised arrivals are put through a screening process without being given access to any advice. When challenged by refugee advocates, the immigration authorities generally allege that the detainees have not requested legal advice. In the more remote detention facilities, this screening process can sometimes take weeks to complete.

given no choice but are allocated lawyers or agents who operate under contract with the immigration authorities.[64] Refugee claimants also have no legislative right to an oral hearing of their claims at first instance, but must submit their applications in writing, in English. Indeed, the SLCRC heard that only about 10 per cent of all those who claim asylum are interviewed before a decision is made on their case.[65] While a heavy onus is placed on claimants to supply all information available to them at the time of lodging their application, there is no mutuality in this duty.[66] Decision makers are obliged by law only to reveal to an applicant information relevant to a claim that is personal to an applicant's claim and that is obtained from a source apart from the applicant. There is no duty on the decision maker to seek comment from an applicant where an adverse inference is drawn from material supplied by the applicant.[67] Indeed, once a valid application is received, the Act specifies that 'a decision to grant or refuse a visa may be made without giving the applicant an opportunity to make oral or written submissions'.[68]

These provisions operate together in a way that engenders a sense of secrecy and defensiveness in the all-important first stage of the refugee determination process. Some advocates argue that this is an inevitable result of giving the task of implementing Australia's protection obligations towards refugees to a bureaucracy whose avowed function is to protect the

---

[64] These contracts are awarded after a tender process. Before the Senate inquiry in 2000, concerns were expressed about the quality of the work performed by some contractors, while some contractors complained that the funding arrangements do not permit adequate preparation of claims, especially where translation and medical examination costs were incurred. See SLCRC, above n 20, p 94ff.

[65] For a critique of this practice, see SLCRC, above n 20, pp 72–4.

[66] Migration Act, section 54 provides that the Minister (vis the decision maker) is only obliged to consider information included in an application. Material submitted after the application must be considered if it is received before a decision to grant a visa has been made, or where the information has been sought by the decision maker. However, decision makers have no obligation to delay making a decision so as to allow for the lodging of further material: section 55.

[67] Migration Act, section 54. This particular provision was introduced in response to the decision by the Federal Court in the two cases of *Somaghi v Minister for Immigration and Ethnic Affairs* (1991) 31 FCR 100 and *Heshmati v Minister for Immigration and Ethnic Affairs* (1991) 31 FCR 123.

[68] Migration Act, section 54(3).

integrity of Australia's borders by controlling immigration.[69] A preferable arrangement, in the view of these people, would be to place the entire process of determining refugee claims in the hands of the country's first law office – the Attorney General. In my view, however, it is not the site of the decision making process that is at fault in this aspect of Australia's refugee procedures. Rather, it is the defensive culture implicit in the provisions that is regrettable and that needs to be addressed as a matter of urgency.

The tenor and detail of Australia's initial processing provisions stand in sharp contrast with, to take one comparative example, the laws of Australia's near neighbour, New Zealand. Although New Zealand receives fewer refugee claims than does Australia, it has not been immune from the phenomenon of mobile asylum seekers, with between 1500 and 2000 applications made each year.[70] In New Zealand undocumented arrivals wishing to claim refugee status are interviewed at point of arrival. More often than not they are issued with a work permit or other temporary permit on the spot and given direction to an open reception centre or hostel. The asylum seeker is also given instructions regarding the choice of a lawyer who is authorised in turn to provide 16 hours of legally aided assistance in preparing and presenting the refugee claim. Under the New Zealand laws, applicants must be given copies of all documents relevant to their claim collected and held by the immigration authorities.[71] As will be pursued in greater detail below, the institution of quite generous provisions for asylum seekers does not appear to have resulted in abuse of the system, or in an increased tendency to contest negative assessments. If anything, the reverse is true.

---

[69] SLCRC, above n 20, pp 129–30.

[70] New Zealand Refugee Law, *Statistics*, table 34, http://www.refugee.org.nz. This compares with an annual intake of around 10 000 each year in Australia. Relative to population size, the per capita intake is not too disparate. New Zealand has a population of four million, compared with Australia's 18.5 million.

[71] The author is indebted to Rodger Haines QC and to legal practitioners Deborah Manning and Jeanne Donald for their accounts of the New Zealand procedures in action. See New Zealand Immigration Service, *Operational Manual, Border Policy* (Wellington, New Zealand Immigration Service, 1995), http://www.immigration.govt.nz/operations_manual/, part 5 'Border Policy', paras Y7.1 and Y7.5. See also *E v Attorney General* [2000] 3 NZLR 257 (CA) which confirms that the power to issue permits at the airport is discretionary and that there is no presumption in favour of grant.

In its report, the SLCRC proffered a range of criticisms about the quality of refugee decision making at departmental level. The SLCRC noted complaints about the Country Information Service, the government body charged with gathering information about the countries from which asylum seekers have fled.[72] It also noted and accepted criticisms about the skills, knowledge and ability of the primary decision makers, recommending that officials be given further specialist training both before and during their tenure. It added:

> The Committee is concerned that the overall trend in the primary decision making stage may be for decision making along the line of least resistance, that is, a tendency to reject an application in the knowledge that a person can appeal and to leave the real decision making to the RRT.[73]

Unfortunately, the politicisation of refugee decision making in the lead up to the federal election in 2001 did nothing to alleviate this situation. On the contrary, legislation was enacted that further entrenches the culture of institutional distrust of the asylum seeker. The Migration Legislation Amendment Act (No 6) of 2001 (Act No 6) includes provisions that allow interviewing officers to force asylum seekers interviewed in 'immigration clearance' (or point of arrival) to swear or affirm a statement that their claims were true in fact. The legislation then provides that where an applicant changes his or her story or where 'the Minister' (that is, the immigration officer) has 'reason to believe' that a sworn statement is 'not sincere', the Minister 'may draw any reasonable inference unfavourable to the applicant's credibility'. The provision spells out that the Minister may form his or her opinion on the basis of 'the manner in which the applicant complied with the request' for a sworn statement, or 'the applicant's demeanour in relation to compliance with the request'.[74]

Leaving aside the inherent uncertainty in the formula prescribed in these provisions,[75] their lack of sensitivity to the situation of the refugee claimant

---

[72] SLCRC, above n 20, pp 130–3, 153–5. One critic described the country information supplied by the Department of Foreign Affairs and Trade as 'views from the cocktail bar of the Tehran Hilton': p 132, n 100.

[73] SLCRC, above n 20, recommendation 4.3 and p 128.

[74] Migration Legislation Amendment Bill (No 6) 2001 (Cth), Schedule 1, section 5, inserting section 91V into the Migration Act.

[75] It is my view that a legal challenge could be mounted as to their constitutionality because of the uncertain operation of a formula based on personal assessments of a

at point of first contact with the government authority of a country of asylum is breathtaking. That refugees will lie or give the appearance of being flustered in situations where they are unsure of themselves and of the motives of their interrogators is so common as to be a fact of life in asylum claims.[76] The likelihood that individual's lie is heightened in situations where they are interviewed without the aid of a lawyer or any other trusted advisor who can tell them what to expect and what is expected of them. Refugees are by definition people who are desperate and in fear of their lives. Those who come with the assistance of people smugglers and without a valid visa start from a base where the asylum seeker's focus has been on the end to be achieved rather than on the (legal) means to that end.[77] Given Australia's avowed commitment to refugee protection, the credibility provisions of Act No 6 themselves beggar belief. The provisions will almost certainly increase the risk that Australian officials will fail in their international legal obligations to identify and offer protection from refoulement to persons who meet the Refugees Convention definition of refugee.

Credibility is already cited by many decision makers as the basis for rejecting refugee claims.[78] Because of the personal nature of such assessments and the legal requirement that decision makers be 'satisfied' that an individual meets the definition of refugee, rulings made on this basis are notoriously difficult to challenge on legal grounds. In such circumstances, it seems neither necessary nor equitable to further bolster

---

person's demeanour, which carries with it the penalties implicit in a finding of adverse credibility. See for example, *King Gee Clothing Co Pty Ltd v Commonwealth* (1945) 71 CLR 184; *Communist Party of Australia v Commonwealth* (1950) 83 CLR 1.

[76] J Cohen, 'Questions of Credibility: Omissions, Discrepancies and Errors of Recall in the Testimony of Asylum Seekers', *International Journal of Refugee Law* 13 (2001) p 293; W Kalin, 'Troubled Communication: Cross-Cultural Misunderstanding in the Asylum Hearing', *International Migration Review* 20 (1986) p 230; S Legomsky, 'The New Techniques for Dealing with High Volume Asylum Systems', *Iowa Law Review* 81 (1996) p 671.

[77] See comments by Gummow and Hayne JJ in *Abebe v Minister for Immigration and Multicultural Affairs (MIMA)* (1999) 197 CLR 510, at 577 (para 191):

the fact that an applicant for refugee status may yield to temptation to embroider an account of his or her history is hardly surprising. It is necessary always to bear in mind that an applicant for refugee status is, on one view of events, engaged in an often desperate battle for freedom, if not life itself.

[78] Kneebone, above n 7, p 78.

the powers of the decision makers at the expense of the asylum seeker – and at the expense of the courts to intervene to correct individual injustices.

Administrative Appeals: The Refugee Review Tribunal

The contrast between the Australian system and those of most other western refugee receiving countries – including New Zealand – is also apparent at the administrative review phase of the refugee determination process. In this area, Australia is clearly compliant with its international legal obligations, having created a quite elaborate regime for the review of adverse refugee determinations by an independent administrative review authority. Once again, however, in practice the system does not seem to engender satisfaction in those who submit to its processes: of those whose claims are rejected by this tribunal, nearly 16 per cent lodge applications for judicial review, claiming that the decision made was flawed in law.[79]

Here too, comparisons with the system in New Zealand are instructive, if somewhat alarming. The overall rate at which onshore asylum seekers gain recognition as refugees in both Australia and New Zealand is modest in world terms. Over the ten years before 1999, 'western' refugee receiving countries (as a group) have admitted as refugees an average of 26 per cent of those seeking asylum. In contrast, Australia has recognised an average of 13 per cent of claims and New Zealand 17.6 per cent of claims.[80] The real contrast, however, is in the rate at which failed asylum seekers seek judicial review of the decisions made in their cases. According to Rodger Haines QC, only 46 judicial review applications involving decisions of the Refugee Status Appeals Authority were filed in the New Zealand High Court between 1992 and 1999. Of these only 17 cases resulted in a remittal and rehearing of the application either by consent or by court order.[81]

---

[79]   Above n 17.

[80]   UNHCR, *Refugees and Others of Concern to UNHCR, 1999 Statistical Overview* (Geneva, UNHCR, July 2000), http://www.unhcr.ch. This is the most recent statistical overview available at the UNHCR website. The acceptance rate in Australia has climbed dramatically since 1999, when the first Afghani and Iraqi refugees began arriving. Amongst the boat people from these countries and from the Middle East generally, recognition rates have been between 75 per cent and 95 per cent.

[81]   R Haines, 'An Overview of Refugee Law in New Zealand: Background and Current Issues', Paper presented to the Inaugural Meeting of International Association of Refugee Law Judges, 10 March 2000,

As noted earlier, there were well over one thousand applications made for the judicial review of migration cases in Australia over this same period.[82] The real reasons why so many failed refugee applicants seek judicial review of decisions made by Australia's Refugee Review Tribunal (RRT) cannot be known without detailed empirical research. At an impressionistic level, however, it is possible to identify features in the set-up and operation of the tribunal that may be undermining its general efficacy. As is the case in the initial processing of refugee claims, the Australian system is once again characterised by provisions that speak of defensiveness, distrust and constraint. Before the RRT, refugee applicants do have a right to an oral hearing before their claims are rejected, and they have a right to an interpreter, should one be required. However, while advisors may attend hearings, claimants have no right to legal or other forms of representation. Appeals are heard by single members and are closed to the public.[83] The quasi-inquisitorial procedures prescribed for the tribunal are said to compensate for any need in claimants to have such assistance. The theory is that RRT members are neutral arbiters of whether individual asylum seekers have a claim sufficient to invoke Australia's 'protection obligations'.[84] Their task is to solicit the relevant information through a process of questions and answers, in dialogue with the claimant.

The absence of legal advisers from the administrative review process is a feature of the system, reflecting the distrust of lawyers that seems to have developed in Parliamentary circles since the late 1980s. There is no acknowledgement that lawyer advocates can provide guidance for RRT members in what has become a very complex area of law. RRT members themselves are not required to have legal training: in 2000, only 29 out of 52 members had such qualifications.[85]

---

http://www.refugee.org.nz/IARLJ3-00Haines.html. Mr Haines is Deputy Chair of New Zealand's Refugee Status Appeals Authority.

[82] See above n 17.

[83] For the protection of claimants, the tribunal is required to take various measures to ensure that the identity of individual asylum seekers is not made public: Migration Act, sections 429 and 439. These restrictions do not apply to the Federal Court or the High Court, where litigants must request the suppression of their name if they are concerned to maintain their anonymity.

[84] SLCRC, above n 20, pp 148–50.

[85] Id, pp 173, 176–79. Compare this with recommendation 5.8 of the SLCRC.

Unfortunately, the supposed neutrality of the RRT appears to be lost on some refugee claimants who find it difficult to distinguish between the RRT, sitting as a single member in camera, and a government official acting as interrogator. This is particularly so in cases where claimants have not been interviewed at all at first instance and yet have had their refugee claims rejected. In these circumstances, the tribunal is the asylum seeker's first human contact with Australia's immigration authorities, and represents the first opportunity that the claimant has to tell his or her story.

The defensiveness of the system is apparent at other levels, too. As at first instance, the procedural obligations placed on the RRT are carefully crafted to minimise the scope for arguments about denial of procedural fairness. Even where the legislation envisages a flow of information between the primary decision makers, the RRT and the applicant, in practice the exchange of information is questionable. There would appear to be no parallel in Australia to the New Zealand practice of reproducing and giving to applicants the entirety of the file held by the immigration authorities.[86]

In its inquiry in 2000, the SLCRC heard a considerable amount of evidence about the RRT from former asylum seekers, tribunal members and practitioners. Its report documents complaints made about the tribunal that range from the adequacy of the training given to tribunal members to the wisdom of appointments made to the tribunal from within the ranks of the government bureaucracy.[87] The SLCRC also recommended that the Law Reform Commission be requested to make a detailed study of why failed asylum seekers are seeking curial review of their decisions in such numbers. For present purposes, it suffices to note that the statistics for the RRT to a certain extent speak for themselves. It is clear that failed asylum seekers in Australia are emerging from the totality of the determination process unhappy with their experience. If Australia cares to lift its gaze to observe what is happening in other countries, there may be a greater acceptance that its own experience is not inherent in the asylum process. Rather, it is a product of the particular way in which Australians have crafted their laws and policies.

---

[86] This comment about New Zealand is based on statements made by R Haines, Deputy President of the New Zealand Refugee Status Appeals Authority. Australian practice is the subject of a class action in *Herijanto v Refugee Review Tribunal* High Court, No S97/1998, 17 August 2000, http://www.austlii.edu.au.

[87] SLCRC, above n 20, chapter 5.

Judicial Review

Nowhere is the defensiveness of Australia's approach to refugees and to migrants generally more apparent than in the special regime it has established for the review of immigration decisions. As noted earlier, Australia's immigration laws have been defined by the battles that have been enjoined between the immigration Ministers and the courts. The most striking feature of these battles has been the amazing tendency of the Ministers to personalise particular decisions to the point where rulings on the legality of particular decisions by the judiciary seem to be taken as personal attacks on the Minister in question. Under the administration of Minister Ruddock, Ministerial statements or press releases about particular cases or about alleged improper activism on the part of the courts have become almost commonplace. It is in these statements that the politicisation of Australian immigration law is most apparent.

The form and operation of Part 8 of the Migration Act 1958 as it was until September 2001 has been described elsewhere. In essence the regime operated to reduce the power of the Federal Court of Australia to review the legality of migration decisions, removing the traditional broad grounds of review relating to natural justice or procedural fairness, relevancy and reasonableness.[88] The grounds that remained enabled the Federal Court to do little more than to check that the terms of the migration legislation have been complied with on their face. The legislation became the source of an ever-expanding body of jurisprudence. For present purposes it suffices to note that the seven years following the introduction of Part 8 in 1994 have seen the legislation achieve none of the aims envisaged by its drafters. Instead of reducing the number of applications for judicial review, immigration cases have come to dominate and overwhelm both the Federal Court of Australia and, more problematically, the High Court. The dilemma facing the High Court stems from its own rulings in two cases in which the court upheld the constitutionality of Part 8[89] and struck down an attempt by

---

[88] Migration Act, section 476(2) and (3). For an analysis of these provisions, see M Crock, 'Necessary Reform or Overkill?: Part 8 of the Migration Act and the Judicial Review of Migration Decisions', *Sydney Law Review* 18 (1996) p 267.

[89] *Abebe*, above n 77.

the Federal Court to circumvent the effect of the provisions through the creative interpretation of other parts of the legislation.[90]

On 26 September 2001 Part 8 was repealed and replaced with what is referred to as either a 'privative clause' regime, or (in American parlance), 'court-stripping' provisions.[91] On the face of Australia's new laws, most migration and refugee related decisions would be 'privative clause decisions'. Where a privative clause decision is reviewable by the Migration Review Tribunal (MRT) or the RRT, or is subject to the exercise of one of the Minister's residual discretions, judicial review is now excluded. The central privative clause reads as follows:[92]

Section 474: A privative clause decision:

(a) is final and conclusive; and

(b) shall not be challenged, appealed against, reviewed, quashed or called in question in any court; and

(c) is not subject to prohibition, mandamus, injunction, declaration or certiorari in any court on any account.

The privative clause limits the powers of all Australian courts to intervene – including the High Court of Australia to the extent that such constraint is possible under the Australian Constitution.[93] To restrict access to the High Court entirely a constitutional amendment would be required.[94]

---

[90] *Eshetu*, above n 51; M Crock, 'Of Fortress Australia and Castles in the Air: The High Court and the Judicial Review of Migration Decisions' *Melbourne University Law Review* 24 (2000) p 190.

[91] For an account of the emerging jurisprudence on provisions in US law limiting access to the courts in migration cases, see G Neuman, 'Jurisdiction and the Rule of Law After the 1996 Immigration Act', *Harvard Law Review* 113 (2000) p 1963.

[92] The new provisions amending the Migration Act were inserted by the Migration (Judicial Review) Act 2001 (Cth).

[93] P Ruddock, Second Reading Speech, Parliament of Australia, *Hansard*, House of Representatives, 25 June 1997.

[94] This is because section 75(v) of the Constitution invests the High Court with original jurisdiction whenever a remedy is sought against an officer of the Commonwealth. This would include a tribunal member. The High Court also has original jurisdiction where any issue is raised that involves an international treaty to which Australia is a party: section 75(i). For a recent case on point, see *Re East; Ex parte Nguyen* (1998) 196 CLR 354. As paragraphs 75(i) and (v) are constitutional grants of jurisdiction, it is beyond the power of the parliament to withdraw any matter from the grant of

Nevertheless, High Court authority suggests that such clauses can be effective to narrow the scope of judicial review provided that three criteria are met. The protected decision must constitute a bona fide attempt to exercise the power conferred on the decision maker; it must relate to the subject matter of the legislation, and it must be reasonably capable of reference to the power given to the body. This is known as the *Hickman* principle.[95]

In practice the provisions operate as rules of statutory construction.[96] It is said that they operate to expand the validity of acts done by a repository of power by deeming everything that they do to be within the law, provided that the three *Hickman* criteria are satisfied.[97] However, recently the High Court set the scene for another battle between the courts and the government. In *Minister for Immigration v Yusuf*,[98] it suggested that the concept of jurisdictional error is broad. This may lead to findings that the *Hickman* criteria are not satisfied.

Under the old Part 8 provisions, the restrictive legislation saw an interesting discourse develop between the Federal Court and the superior High Court. In spite of the restrictions of Part 8 some judges of the lower court continued to make every effort to find ways to rule against the legality of adverse refugee decisions.[99] By and large, the High Court struck down the creative efforts of the Federal Court, forcing the judges to find new grounds to critique the decisions being made. It will be interesting to see whether a similar pattern emerges with the new judicial review regime, especially after *Yusuf*. Importantly also, the Federal Court may no longer be

---

jurisdiction or to abrogate or qualify the grant: *Waterside Workers' Federation of Australia v Gilchrist, Watt and Sanderson Ltd* (1924) 34 CLR 482; *Australian Coal and Shale Employees' Federation v Aberfield Coal Mining Co Ltd* (1942) 66 CLR 161; *Deputy Commissioner of Taxation v Richard Walter Pty Ltd* (1995) 183 CLR 168 per Mason CJ.

[95]　*R v Hickman; Ex parte Fox and Clinton* (1945) 70 CLR 598 at 615. The *Hickman* principle has been cited with approval time and time again. For example: *R v Coldham; Ex parte Australian Workers' Union* (1983) 153 CLR 415.

[96]　*Deputy Commissioner of Taxation v Richard Walter Pty Ltd* (1995) 183 CLR 168; *R v Coldham* id, p 418 per Mason ACJ and Brennan J.

[97]　*O'Toole v Charles David Pty Ltd* (1991) 171 CLR 232 at 275.

[98]　(2001) 180 ALR 1.

[99]　For a critical review of the emerging jurisprudence, see J McMillan, 'Federal Court v Minister for Immigration', *AIAL Forum* 22 (1999) p 1.

precluded from examining legal issues involving the procedural fairness of an administrative process.[100]

Contrary to the prevailing governmental view, the Australian courts have been relatively conservative in their interpretation of the Refugees Convention. There have been a number of key instances where the High Court has chosen to restrict the reach of Convention protection in Australia. One involved the characterisation of couples fleeing forced sterilisation or even forced abortion under China's 'One Child' Policy.[101] Another involved the non-recognition of asylum seekers from countries in the grip of civil wars, where it is not possible to identify any form of civil government or formal 'state'.[102] In the High Court, the judges who have attempted to shape their interpretation of the Refugees Convention so as to conform to the human rights spirit of the instrument have been in the minority.[103]

Having said this, there has been a series of decisions in recent times in which the judges of the High Court appear to be drawing a judicial line in the sand, taking a more robust stance in cases involving perceived error of law. This trend will be encouraged by *Yusuf's* case. Some have involved the interpretation of the Refugees Convention definition of refugee.[104] Others have involved instances of alleged bad decision making where the

---

[100] In *Re MIMA; Ex parte Miah* (2001) 179 ALR 238 the High Court decided that the procedural code in the Migration Act which governs primary decision makers did not exclude the rules of natural justice. See the discussion below at n 104–106 (text and notes). It is interesting that the government seems to have recognised the potential for continued judicial activity in this area. One day after the passage of the Migration (Judicial Review) Act 2001, it introduced the Migration Legislation (Procedural Fairness) Bill 2001 (Cth) – legislation that limits judicial scrutiny of procedural fairness matters to checking compliance with the procedural provisions of the migration legislation.

[101] *Applicant A v Minister for Immigration and Ethnic Affairs* (1997) 190 CLR 225. For critiques of the decision, see P Mathew, 'Conformity or Persecution: China's One Child Policy and Refugee Status', *University New South Wales Law Journal* 23 (2000) p 103; C Dauvergne, 'Chinese Fleeing Sterilisation: Australia's Response Against a Canadian Backdrop', *International Journal of Refugee Law* 10 (1998) p 77.

[102] *MIMA v Ibrahim* (2000) 175 ALR 585 and Kneebone, above n 25. Mr Ibrahim was one of nearly 50 detainees who escaped from the immigration detention centre at Villawood in Sydney in July 2001. His whereabouts remained uncertain at time of writing.

[103] M Crock, 'Apart from Us or a Part of Us? Immigrants' Rights, Public Opinion and the Rule of Law', *International Journal of Refugee Law* 10 (1998) p 49.

[104] *Applicant A*, above n 101; *Chen Shi Hai v MIMA* (2000) 201 CLR 293.

High Court has overruled the procedures followed by either the primary decision maker[105] or the RRT.[106] In both instances, the High Court has confirmed that a gross breach of the rules of procedural fairness can constitute a 'jurisdictional error'. By implication, the High Court in such cases may be prepared to rule that the decisions fail the *Hickman* test by failing to constitute a bona fide attempt to exercise a legislative power.

Whether or not one agrees with the way the courts have been dealing with the applications made for the judicial review of refugee decisions, there can be little doubt that the judges handling these cases are angered by the surge in judicial review cases involving failed refugee claimants. Even before September 2001, many Federal Court judges expressed their frustration at the constraints placed on their own powers.[107] Justices of the High Court made repeated statements about the impropriety and irrationality of a system[108] that saw the highest court in the land reviewing first instance decisions,[109] sometimes at the behest of an applicant who

---

[105] *Miah*, above n 100.

[106] *Re Refugee Review Tribunal; Ex parte Aala* (2000) 176 ALR 219; *Re Refugee Review Tribunal; Ex parte H* (2001) 179 ALR 425.

[107] On this issue generally, see Sackville, above n 56.

[108] See the long tirade of McHugh J in *Re MIMA; Ex parte Durairajasingham* (2000) 168 ALR 407 at 411 where his Honour made the following points (references are to paragraph numbers):

> 13 ... I find it difficult to see the rationale for the amendments to the Migration Act 1958 (Cth) ("the Act") which now prevent this Court from remitting to the Federal Court all issues arising under that Act which fall within this Court's original jurisdiction. No other constitutional or ultimate appellate court of any nation of which I am aware is called on to perform trial work of the nature that these amendments to the Act have now forced upon the Court.

> 14 There is no ground whatever for thinking that the judges of the Federal Court are not capable of dealing with all issues arising under the Act which fall within this Court's jurisdiction ...

> 15 The reforms brought about by the amendments are plainly in need of reform themselves if this Court is to have adequate time for the research and reflection necessary to fulfil its role as "the keystone of the federal arch" and the ultimate appellate court of the nation. I hope that in the near future the Parliament will reconsider the jurisdictional issues involved.

See generally, Crock, above n 7, chapter 13.

[109] *Miah*, above n 100. This case came before the High Court in its original jurisdiction because the 28 day time limit for appealing the original decision to the RRT had expired. The 28 day time limit for appeals to the Federal Court under Part 8 runs

comes before it without legal representation.[110] It remains to be seen whether the new Part 8 improves this situation

The government's response to the crisis in judicial review has been to introduce ever more extreme measures aimed at restricting access to the courts. In addition to the new Part 8 provisions, other amendments removed the right of asylum seekers and migrants generally to bring class actions challenging the way decisions are made.[111] Once again, the primary function of all of these provisions would appear to be the 'judge-proofing' of adverse refugee decisions.

In my view, the explosion in the number of judicial review applications by failed asylum seekers is not a matter that can be addressed by simple proscriptive measures. The problem must be seen and treated in an holistic sense. The present statistics suggest that applications for judicial review result in a remittal and reconsideration of cases in 25 to 30 per cent of all applications lodged. That is, a fault of some kind in the decision made by the RRT, is found by the courts (or acknowledged by consent) in almost one-third of all appeals. Even if the remittal rarely results in a different substantive ruling, these figures suggest that more can be done to improve decision making at the administrative review level.

A survey of the recent case law does suggest a mood of discontent amongst the judges who are sitting on refugee cases.[112] The criticisms expressed by the Federal Court judges are often targeted at the harshness of the legislative regime governing refugee decision making, and at the unfairness of the processes that are followed pursuant to the relevant provisions.[113] Here again, it is not enough to dismiss the many curial expressions of concern and even pity as 'typical' of the judicial review

---

from the date a decision is made and can only be suspended by the lodgement of an appeal to the RRT. This meant that redress in the Federal Court was impossible, leaving the High Court the only avenue for redress.

[110] *Re Refugee Review Tribunal; Ex parte HB* (2001) 179 ALR 513.

[111] Migration Legislation Amendment Act (No 2) 2000 (Cth), discussed in S Harris, 'Another Salvo Across the Bow: Migration Legislation Amendment Bill (No 2) 2000 (Cth)', *University of New South Wales Law Journal* 23 (2000) p 208.

[112] See the cases discussed by McMillan, above n 99.

[113] See the comments by Mansfield J who had the task of adjudicating a series of 17 applications for judicial review lodged outside the strict 28 day time limit by asylum seekers detained at the Woomera Detention Centre in South Australia: *Salehi v MIMA* [2001] FCA 995.

process in refugee cases. These have no parallels in judgments in other refugee receiving countries. It is interesting to ponder whether Australian judges would show more deference towards the decisions made by the RRT and by the Minister, if they truly believed that refugee claimants in this country were being treated fairly in accordance with the Rule of Law.

The government's desire to restrict the power of the courts to review refugee decisions has not diminished with the passage of time. In August 2001, it acted to address the problem of Federal Court applications by introducing legislation that would expand the role of the newly established Federal Magistrates Service.[114] This measure may alleviate to some extent the burden of refugee cases in the Federal Court. However, it remains to be seen whether the change will have any impact on judicial review applications generally, given the lesser status of magistrates and the complexity of many of the cases now before the Federal Court.

Australia's Implementation of the Refugees Convention – (ii) The Reach of Australia's Protection Obligations

The meanness of Australia's response to the challenge of implementing obligations assumed as a signatory to the Refugees Convention is also apparent in other aspects of Australia's migration laws. Barriers are raised at virtually every point to restrict the ability of refugees to reach Australian territory. Australia's visa system, together with the physical placement of its embassies overseas, are arguably the most effective barriers for asylum seekers. We have also borrowed liberally from Europe in the construction of mechanisms for the deflection of refugee claims where an asylum seeker has any sort of right to enter or reside in a 'third' country.[115] Refugee appeals involving the legislation passed in 1999 suggest that these restrictive provisions are beginning to impact quite heavily on asylum seekers who come to Australia via one or more (safe or relatively safe) countries of transit.[116]

---

[114] Jurisdiction of the Federal Magistrates Service Legislation Amendment Bill 2001 (Cth), introduced into parliament in late August 2001.

[115] See the detailed consideration of these laws in Mathew, above n 46.

[116] *Applicant C v MIMA* [2001] FCA 229 (12 March 2001); *V856/00A v MIMA* [2001] FCA 1018 (14 August 2001). These cases are discussed in Mathew, above n 46.

In recent times, the Australian government has taken more radical steps to prevent asylum seekers from landing in Australia. Reference has been made already to the *Tampa* affair and to the Pacific Solution. The relevant events and the legislative response on 26 September 2001 are considered elsewhere in this book.[117] Other proactive measures taken include the establishment of refugee determination centres in Indonesia for the processing of persons apprehended in that country who would otherwise have ended their journey in Australia. According to media reports about the operation, Australia is funding the UNHCR to process the asylum claims of the apprehended asylum seekers.[118] While most of those processed are being found to be refugees, the arrangements are based on the agreement that persons recognised as refugees will be eligible for resettlement in any safe country except Australia. In August 2001, few of those determined to be refugees in this context had achieved resettlement. The balance allegedly languished in Australian-funded camps in Indonesia.[119]

For present purposes it suffices to note that real doubts exist as to whether Australia's current practices are in accordance with its international legal obligations. First, Australia's ability to board foreign vessels outside of its maritime territory is limited at international law. Put simply, the sweeping new powers conferred on Australian officials under the new border protection legislation raise serious questions of compliance with international law.[120] Second, the Refugees Convention prohibits the return or refoulement of refugees either directly or indirectly to a place where they will face persecution. The simple excision from Australia's migration zone of Australia's offshore territories may not be sufficient to

---

[117] L Curran and S Kneebone, 'Overview', chapter 1 in this book. See also M Crock, 'Echoes of the Old Countries or Brave New Worlds? Legal Responses to Refugees and Asylum Seekers in Australia and New Zealand', *Revue Québécoise de Droit International* 14 (2001) pp 55–89.

[118] P Mares, 'Moving the Barriers Offshore: Cooperation with Indonesia Reduces the Number of "Boat People" Arriving in Australia', *Asia Pacific Features*, 6 August 2001, para 15.32, http://www.abc.net.au/ra/asiapac/features/AsiaPacFeatures–341432.htm.

[119] See the discussion of the *Tampa* incident in 'The Future of Refugee Protection in Australia', below.

[120] Border Protection (Validation and Enforcement Powers) Act 2001(Cth). See also Mathew, above n 46.

release it from its international obligations.[121] While the initial arrangements with UNHCR and IOM may be sufficient to meet this requirement, the countries receiving the boat people are not all signatories to the Refugees Convention. If the international organisations refuse to extend their involvement, real concerns could arise about the long-term safety of the deflected boat people.

The worst aspect of the Pacific Solution, however, is the precedent it sets. It is common knowledge that the vast majority of the Afghani and Iraqi asylum seekers are refugees in dire need of protection.[122] There is no doubt that Australia is better equipped to offer protection than is Indonesia, the most recent transit country of most of the asylum seekers. The same is true with respect to transit countries such as Pakistan. Australia is not the only state to engage in the practice of deflecting asylum seekers. Indeed, there are disturbing parallels between its recent policy change and moves by the United States to interdict would-be asylum seekers and migrants from Haiti and Cuba. With over 60 000 such boat people interdicted in the mid 1990s, the United States has also established offshore holding and processing centres at Guantanamo Bay, the US-leased enclave in Cuba. The importance of these US precedents was not lost on those involved in the flurry of legislative changes made by the Australian parliament on 26 September 2001.[123] Little reference appears to have been made, however, either to the many criticisms made of this program, or to the dreadful impact the interdictions had on the asylum seekers from Haiti, in particular.[124] Uncomfortable parallels can be found between Australia's

---

[121] Migration Amendment (Excision from Migration Zone) Act 2001, and the Migration Amendment (Excision from Migration Zone Consequential Provisions) Act 2001.

[122] 'UN deems many from *Tampa* refugees', *The Age*, 5 January 2002, pp 1–2.

[123] N Hancock, 'Border Protection (Validation and Enforcement Powers) Bill 2001 (Austl)', *Bills Digest* 62 (2001–02) p 3, at n 55 and 56, http://www.aph.gov.au/library/pubs/bd/2001-02/02bd062.htm. See also N Hancock, 'Refugee Law – Recent Legislative Developments', *Current Issues Brief* 5 (2001–02), http://www.aph.gov.au/library/pubs/cib/2001-02/02cib05.htm.

[124] 'Symposium: Refusing Refugees: Political and Legal Barriers to Asylum: Haitian Asylum Seekers: Interdiction and Immigrants' Rights', *Cornell International Law Journal* 26 (1993) p 695. Note that the US Supreme Court upheld the legality of the interdiction program on the basis that neither US domestic law, nor the tenets of the Refugees Convention applied to extraterritorial actions taken by US marines: *Sale v Haitian Centers Council* 113 S Ct 2549 (1993). Justice Blackmun delivered a powerful dissent, following up with an article: H A Blackmun, 'The Supreme Court and the Law

behaviour in repelling the boat people and what many western countries did in refouling Jewish refugees before World War II.[125]

For those who pass the threshold and are admitted to Australia's refugee protection regime, Australia's compliance with its international legal obligations only approaches generosity in cases where individuals enter Australia on valid visas. Unauthorised arrivals who gain recognition as refugees receive second rate protection, whichever way you look at the regime now in place. Instead of permanent residence, they are given three-year visas with work rights but limited access to social security benefits. Where other refugees have an immediate right to sponsor family members to join them in Australia, this new breed of refugee has no such entitlement but must wait out their three years in the hope of gaining permanency thereafter.[126] Amendments to the migration legislation in September 2001 extended the reach of these temporary visas to asylum seekers recognised as refugees overseas pursuant to the arrangements adherent to the Pacific Solution.[127] Given that the key factor determining the characterisation of onshore refugees as temporary protection cases is the manner of their entry into the country, it is difficult to see how the Temporary Protection Visa regime can be consistent with Australia's obligations under the Refugees Convention. This instrument provides very explicitly in Article 31(1):

---

of Nations', *Yale Law Journal* **104** (1994) p 39. See also the decision of the Inter-American Commission on Human Rights ordering the US to make reparations for breach of its international legal obligations: *The Haitian Centre for Human Rights v United States*, (Case 10.675, Report 51/96, Inter-Am.C.H.R.,OEA/Ser.L/V/II.95 Doc 7 rev at 550, 1997), http://www1.umn.edu/humanrts/cases/1996/unitedstates51-96.htm.

[125] Abella and Troper, above n 29.

[126] Temporary Protection Visa holders are also denied access to education and English language training: see above n 4.

[127] The Migration Regulations (Cth) 1994 were amended as follows: Subclass 447 Secondary Movement Offshore Entry (Temporary) allows for the admission for three years of refugees processed offshore who are in continuing need of protection and who have connections with Australia. A longer stay of five years is available under the Subclass 451 Secondary Movement Relocation (Temporary) Visa. In both cases the visas are available to people fearing persecution or abuse of human rights who may or may not meet the UN Convention definition of refugee. However, the extra criteria relating to alternative resettlement prospects, visa 'caps' and connections with Australia narrow the range of eligible applicants considerably. The five-year visas appear to be designed for persons processed by the UNHCR overseas who have not been intercepted by Australian officials, while the shorter visas apply to those intercepted at sea and processed under the new arrangements.

A Contracting State shall not impose penalties, on account of their illegal entry or presence, on refugees who, coming directly from a territory where their life or freedom was threatened in the sense of Article 1, enter or are present in their territory without authorisation, provided they present themselves without delay to the authorities and show good cause for their illegal entry or presence.

Although the Australian government professes vehemently to the contrary, the ban on family sponsorship for temporary visa holders is regarded by many as a penalty because of the differential application of the law.

With the rise in the number of refugees in Australia's geographical region and in response to the refugee crisis in Kosovo, Australia has also introduced special temporary protection regimes to accommodate specific groups of refugees evacuated to Australia under the auspices of the United Nations. Again, these schemes have features that have been criticised as mean-spirited and needlessly costly.[128]

One final point can be made about the reach of Australia's refugee and humanitarian protection program. It goes to the protection Australia is prepared to afford to asylum seekers who do not meet the Convention definition of refugee, but who are nevertheless in need of protection. Australia has had no generalised mechanism for granting protection to 'near-miss' refugee cases since 1989, when provisions allowing for the grant of visas in 'compassionate and humanitarian circumstances' were removed from the migration legislation. As noted earlier, the only avenue now available for the grant of protection to such cases in Australia is recourse to the Minister, who has a residual discretion to intervene so as to grant a visa.[129] Put another way, Australia recognises no 'Refugee B' class. The omission was a matter of some concern to the Senate Legal and Constitutional References Committee in 2000, which recommended that remedial measures be considered. As the Committee acknowledged, the present system is one that encourages an unhealthy reliance on deal-making and fosters political favouritism. It is also one that provides few guarantees that Australia will act in accordance with obligations it has

---

[128] S Taylor, 'Protection or Prevention? A Close Look at the Temporary Safe Haven Visa Class', *University of New South Wales Law Journal* 23 (2000) p 75.

[129] By means of the discretion vested by section 417, see above n 42.

assumed as a signatory to human rights instruments other than the Refugees Convention.[130]

The Future of Refugee Protection in Australia

Assessing the Problem

In spite of the complaints made about the instrument, renouncing the Refugees Convention is not an option that has been considered with any seriousness in Australia. Leaving aside the opprobrium that would be heaped on the country in international circles, it is difficult to see what would be gained by such action. As noted earlier, the primary obligation under the Convention not to refoule refugees is now thought to be an obligation of customary international law. If denunciation is not a realistic option, and reform of the Convention is academic, the real question must be what can be done to make Australia's refugee determination system fairer and more efficient.

Unfortunately, while renunciation of the Convention is not seriously on the agenda, the Australian government has remained steadfast in the pursuit of a policy that would see Australia assume fewer and fewer protection obligations towards refugees. The most egregious example of Australian reluctance to take in asylum seekers was still an unfolding story at the time of writing this chapter. As noted in the course of this chapter, the government took advantage of the storm of concern raised by the *Tampa* incident to push a series of seven Bills through, each of which impacts negatively on the rights of refugees in Australia. Initiatives such as these provide little hope of any amelioration of Australia's refugee protection regime under a Conservative Liberal–National Party Coalition administration.

If any lesson is to be learned from the unfortunate incident involving the *Tampa* and the ongoing saga that is the Pacific Solution, it must involve an acknowledgement of the evils of allowing politics to intrude into the duty of refugee protection. While public opinion polls are an expression of the

---

[130] For example, the non-refoulement obligation in the Convention Against All Forms of Torture and Cruel and Degrading Treatment or Punishment (CAT); N Poynder, '"Mind the Gap": Seeking Alternative Protection Under the Convention Against Torture and the International Covenant on Civil and Political Rights', chapter 7 in this book.

democratic process, it is well to remember that public opinion is formed by what people read and hear: it is not 'born' out of nowhere. Presented week in and week out with statements from those in elected office expressing concern about the security of Australia's borders and about the evils of asylum seekers 'stealing the places' of 'real' refugees, it is hardly surprising that the general public would react as they did in August 2001.[131] Again, what stands out so much in the Australian context is the extent to which the politicians have both inflamed public fear of asylum seekers and then played to that fear with more and more draconian legislation.

Towards Some Solutions

My personal prescription for reform of Australia's refugee laws would involve first and foremost a cessation of hostilities – with asylum seekers generally and with the courts in particular. One of the most significant and endemic problems with the refugee determination system as it now operates in Australia is that there is no sense of common enterprise between those charged with making refugee decisions at first instance and those whose task it is to review either the merits or the legality of decisions. Compliance with Australia's protection obligations is not vested in any one authority. Rather, it is a matter that requires cooperation and tiered decision making that facilitates the protection of individuals who may slip through the system at first or even second instance.

As many in the Australian community are now affirming in a variety of ways, Australia has no reason to fear the phenomenon that it has been experiencing in recent years. Control of immigration into the country has never been tighter. Australia is not being swamped either with illegal migrants or with asylum seekers by any standards. Its experience is part of a worldwide phenomenon and should not be a cause for great concern. Australia's political elites have chosen to make the issue part of Australia's political discourse, playing to protectionist and racist elements in the community that could be but sad vestiges of the long gone White Australia Policy.

---

[131] Opinion polls taken at the outset of the *Tampa* incident showed overwhelming support for the Prime Minister's stand at the outset, although the public's response became more ambivalent as the days wore on and the actions of the Australian authorities became more extreme.

From a practical perspective, there is also little evidence that the current policies work to 'protect' Australia, anyway. In spite of all the hype both in Australia and overseas, the harsh measures adopted to discourage refugee claims do not appear to be acting as an effective deterrent to genuine refugees. All they have achieved in Australia is a modification of asylum seeker behaviour. For example, within a very short period after the introduction of legislation reducing the family reunion rights of undocumented refugees, the number of children arriving by boat jumped from around 6 per cent to over 30 per cent. The problems generated by a policy mandating the detention of these young asylum seekers has been magnified by the fact that an increasing number arrive unaccompanied, that is, without the protection of an adult relative or guardian. The fact that we are forcing refugee parents to make these choices for their children is hardly a situation that can invoke pride in the average Australian.[132]

There are a number of changes that must be made to Australia's refugee and humanitarian program, some of which present a challenge, but others of which could be done easily and which could make the system less politically explosive. I will begin my prescription for reform with the changes that should be easiest to achieve in political terms, bearing in mind the mood of the electorate (and the extent of public agitation that has occurred), and the complexity of the changes involved.

The first is to replace the policy of mandatory detention with laws that provide for the detention of only those asylum seekers who represent a threat of some kind to Australia. Few dispute the need to take new arrivals into custody for the purposes of ascertaining identity, health and security status or where there is a risk that a person will abscond. In the vast majority of cases, however, undocumented arrivals represent no greater risk than any of the other refugee claimants and migration applicants who wait out the processing times for their visas in the Australian community. By reducing the incidence of immigration detention, the government could quite plainly save itself a lot of money and reduce the public profile of asylum seekers.[133]

---

[132] See the comments of Andrew Theophanous, MP, speaking on the *Tampa* incident and the Border Protection Bill 2001: Parliament of Australia, *Hansard,* House of Representatives, 29 August 2001, pp 30574–5.

[133] See the alternative detention model proposed by community groups and HREOC, 'Time to Examine Alternatives to Detention', Media Release, 28 November 2000, http://www.hreoc.gov.au/media_releases/2000/00_43.html.

An end to the current detention policy is an absolute prerequisite to Australia winning back a basic sense of compassion and humanity in its dealing with refugees. If the present laws are hurting both those in custody and those charged with the detention of asylum seekers, they are also harming the country both in economic terms and in the eyes of the world. The second series of changes that need to be made are more problematic but critical nonetheless. They relate to the deflection of boat people and to the differential treatment meted out to refugees according to their mode of entry into Australia. The current system was created in haste. Unless changes are made in short measure, the regime is truly one that Australia will repent at leisure. Australia cannot afford to maintain its policy of sending asylum seekers to Pacific Islands: the policy is expensive in human terms and prohibitively expensive in financial terms.[134] It is causing incalculable damage to Australia's reputation overseas, even though Australia's alliance with America means that it will be tolerated on the surface.[135] The climate of fear and distrust of refugees engendered by the policy is also very damaging to the multicultural fabric of Australian society. In August the boat people were reviled as 'queue jumpers' or as manipulative and therefore less worthy refugees. After the attacks in America on 11 September they became potential terrorists.[136] There is some evidence that the fury of the campaign to protect Australia's borders spilled into more incipient and ugly actions against visible minority groups within the Australian community. In the last weeks of 2001, reports emerged of an arson attack on a mosque in suburban Brisbane; and of Muslim Australians establishing vigilante groups to enable their womenfolk to go about their daily lives without harassment and racist attacks.[137] While both the government and the opposition stand united in the assertion that boat

---

[134] See above n 14 and accompanying text.

[135] V Marsh, 'Canberra in Hot Water Over Refugee "Crisis": The Government Has Been Accused of Using the Boat People Issue to Win Election Votes', *Financial Times* (UK), 12 December 2001, http://globalarchive.ft.com/globalarchive/article.html?id=011212001183.

[136] In a poll taken by MSN Nine on 12 September a resounding majority answered yes to the question 'Do boat people increase the risk of terrorist attack?': http://www.ninemsn.com.au.

[137] Australian Associated Press, 'Police Crack Down On Anti-Muslim Crime', 17 September 2001, http://www.news.com.au.

people must be repelled because of the risk they represent,[138] the fears expressed by the Australian public are easily explained. Well may Labor politicians lament that the government's policy is effective only in its ability to bring out the very worst in Australians. What is needed is some reassurance from the politicians that the country will not be ruined by taking in refugees today – any more than it has been ruined by the admission of boat people over the last 30 or so years.

Some comment is merited also in relation to those refugees admitted into the Australian community on three or even five year visas who either came to the country by boat or who were apprehended attempting to do so. These people will generally cease to be refugees at the end of their temporary visas. Most will go on to become permanent residents and Australian citizens. Putting aside the bitterness engendered by the current temporary protection regime, it cannot be in Australia's interest to delay the process of healing and re-education that is so important to making the transition from refugee to citizen. Permanent residence can be granted to temporary permit holders with the stroke of the regulatory pen. This should be done as a matter of priority and in a way that does not require the current visa holders (and the immigration authorities) to revisit the stories and the traumas that grounded the original visa grant.

The third change that is needed also involves the undoing of measures introduced in recent years and relates to the basic human rights of asylum seekers in Australia. Under the regime now in place, there has been a steady erosion of the social welfare rights of refugee claimants of all descriptions. One by-product has been a leap in the number of claimants in the community living in the most dire poverty. The re-establishment of basic income support, together with more equitable access to legal aid services would do much to improve the efficiency as a whole. Not only would claimants come into the determination system better able to make their claims; they would also leave the system with a greater sense that they had been treated fairly.

These three series of steps represent only a starting point for reform. Implicit in the criticisms made throughout this chapter is the view that Australia can achieve much by dropping its defensive attitude to refugee claims and by embracing a more proudly compassionate persona. One

---

[138] Australian Associated Press, 'Ruddock Says Serious Security Concerns Over Boat People', *The Age* 17 September 2001.

aspect of such a change would be to return the immigration process to the mainstream of Australian administrative law. The old Part 8 of the Migration Act 1958 was a failure, but the answer is not to place further restrictions on judicial review. The courts have an important role to play in establishing and upholding the Rule of Law in Australia's democracy. That judges are not elected, and that they hold life tenured appointments, are critical features of the system as it means that our courts are less susceptible to the vagaries of popular opinion and of politics. Rather than restricting access to the courts, judicial review should be reintegrated into the process in the context of a holistic regime allowing for the open and accountable determination of refugee status.

The most difficult aspect of affecting the changes that are needed will be in persuading the politicians in general, and the Minister for Immigration in particular, to reduce some of their involvement in the refugee determination process. The current safety net – the ubiquitous Ministerial discretion – must be either replaced or supplemented with a regime that widens the scope for compassionate and humanitarian decision making within the bureaucracy. The culture of defensiveness within the system also needs to be addressed both by training and by changes in the procedures adopted by decision makers. Most importantly, some recognition needs to be made of both the positive role that lawyers can play in the refugee determination system and of the absolute futility of adopting measures to try and shut them out of the process. Lawyers are born and bred in the thickets of statutes and legal rules. Attempts to legislate away the involvement of this profession is an open invitation to a legal version of guerrilla warfare. The jurisprudence that has grown up around Part 8 of the Migration Act stands testament to this (almost universal) truth.

Sorting out the problems of Australia's refugee determination system is something that will take time, care and a real sense of vision. Sadly, the administration of the Conservative Liberal–National Party Coalition appears to have its gaze fixed firmly in the wrong direction. For those who believe that a country's treatment of refugees is a measure of its basic belief in the worth and dignity of all human beings, the current state of affairs is a matter of enduring shame.

4 Durable Solutions: Refugee Status Determination and the Framework of International Protection

ROBERT ILLINGWORTH

Introduction

During the financial year 1999–2000 there was a surge in the number of unauthorised arrivals reaching Australia by boat, with 4174 people arriving on 75 boats, compared with 920 on 42 boats in 1998–99. Up to 30 April in the financial year 2001, there were 3309 unauthorised boat arrivals on 45 boats. Unauthorised air arrivals in Australia also continued at a high though declining rate. There were 1234 people refused entry at Australia's airports between July 2000 and April 2001.

The rapid increase in the total number of unauthorised arrivals has served to highlight long-held concerns regarding illegal immigration. In particular, this increase has arisen primarily as a result of the influence of people smugglers and recent arrivals have increasingly sought to engage Australia's protection obligations in an effort to be allowed to remain in Australia.

This recent influx has also raised public awareness of Australia's role and level of contribution to the framework of international protection for refugees – a role which extends far beyond the domestic implementation of Australia's international obligations not to return (refoule) a refugee who is within its borders.[1] Before considering Australia's more recent responses to the influx of unauthorised arrivals, it is important to recognise the size and nature of the refugee problem.

---

[1] Editor's note: contrast the discussion of this concept by P Mathew, 'Safe for Whom? The Safe Third Country Concept Finds a Home in Australia', chapter 6 in this book, at n 51 and accompanying text.

The United Nations High Commissioner for Refugees (UNHCR) estimates that there are some 21.8 million refugees and displaced people of concern. Many of these people are in countries neighbouring their homeland. For most of these people, the preferred solution is return to their homeland in safety and dignity. In the meantime, the efforts of neighbouring countries and the broader international community focus on providing support and on addressing the root causes of the persecution that has created the refugee situation. In some cases, return is not a viable option and integration into the community in the country providing shelter, or resettlement to a third country, will be the preferred solution.

However, of all the durable solutions, resettlement in a third country is potentially the most disruptive for the individuals concerned. In larger numbers, resettlement can actually help persecutory regimes by 'removing' potentially disruptive influences from the region. It can also weaken the intellectual, cultural, political and economic capacity of the source country to improve its human rights record and its quality of life.

At a very practical level, refugee problems of the magnitude which face the international community cannot be solved by the wholesale resettlement of people to countries such as Australia. Resettlement places are a scarce commodity – Australia is one of a very few countries to offer resettlement opportunities and with 12 000 places funded each year for onshore and offshore visas,[2] is one of the most generous refugee resettlement nations per capita of population. Even so, this commitment comes at a significant cost to the Australian Budget. Every thousand Humanitarian Program places cost the Australian people over $21 million in settlement, welfare and medical costs. This equates to over a quarter of a billion dollars each year for the program.

It is clear that no country could cope with the volumes or the financial impacts of large-scale refugee resettlement at anywhere near the levels needed to solve the world's refugee problems. It is important to understand also that settlement impacts on receiving countries are substantial,

---

[2] Editor's note: contrast the discussion of the Humanitarian Program by M Crock, 'The Refugees Convention at 50: Mid-life Crisis or Terminal Inadequacy? An Australian Perspective', chapter 3 in this book, at n 4. Statistics from the UNHCR indicate that of the 10 000 places available to onshore claimants, in the year 2000, 6600 places were allocated: UNHCR, *Refugees by Numbers 2001 Edition* (Geneva, UNHCR, 2001), http://www.unhcr.ch. See also Department of Immigration and Multicultural and Indigenous Affairs (DIMIA), *Humanitarian Program Statistics*, http://www.immi.gov.au/statistics/refugee.htm.

irrespective of whether the person comes through an offshore resettlement intake or is identified as in need of protection after arrival. The counting of both onshore refugee and offshore resettlement places within Australia's capped 12 000 place annual Humanitarian Program reflects this underlying and inescapable connection.

The critical challenge for the UNHCR and for countries such as Australia is to ensure that the available refugee resettlement places are assigned to those who are in greatest relative need of resettlement, recognising that for many refugees there are other viable alternatives. This challenge is made more difficult by the growing use of refugee protection processes in desirable migration destinations by people who would otherwise not qualify for residence in those countries.

The recent Australian experience with large numbers of unauthorised boat arrivals to this country from countries some considerable distance away is a reflection of a worldwide trend. Increasingly, large numbers of people – some refugees and some not – are seeing the domestic refugee protection processes in countries such as Australia as an opportunity to gain a preferred migration outcome. Increasingly, smuggling operations are facilitating and promoting the illegal movement of people over long distances to these 'desirable' destination countries for this purpose.

The growth in numbers of people moving illegally between countries raises a number of serious problems, including:

- the risk of harm to the unauthorised arrival through the method of travel, which frequently involves travel on fraudulent documentation and on unseaworthy vessels;
- the cost to the receiving country of receiving and assessing unauthorised arrivals, processes that are essential if nations are to maintain the integrity of migration and customs controls;
- the encouragement of organised criminal activities which can flow over into other areas of criminal activity in source, transit and destination countries;
- the public perception that nations cannot control their own borders and are subject to the whims of criminals involved in organised people smuggling;
- the undermining of the system developed by the UNHCR and refugee receiving nations for the orderly management of those requiring the support of the international protection system; and

- the very real risk that increasing flows of unauthorised arrivals around the world could draw attention away from the plight of the bulk of refugees displaced worldwide and potentially lead to a reduction of the commitment of many nations to the international protection system.

As a result, the federal government has adopted a comprehensive, integrated strategy to combat the problems of unauthorised arrivals and people smuggling. This is a key element of broader strategies to support durable solutions for refugees. It needs to be highlighted from the outset that Australia remains committed to the provision of protection to those in need and is strongly committed to the international protection system. The changes in 1999 to Australian immigration legislation, particularly those introducing new protection arrangements for unauthorised arrivals found to be refugees, need to be understood as part of this strategy. Their fundamental objective is to ensure that the international system of protection, with Australia as an element of that system, can continue to deliver durable solutions for those in genuine need.

Australia's Recent Experience

The use of boats to enter Australia unlawfully is not a new phenomenon:

- between 1975 and 1980, more than 2000 Indochinese arrived unauthorised by boat in Australia, fleeing oppressive regimes and internal conflict in Vietnam and Cambodia;
- a further 200 Cambodians arrived unauthorised by boat in 1989–90 to escape fighting between the Khmer Rouge and the then new Cambodian government after Vietnamese troops withdrew from Cambodia in 1989; and
- throughout the 1990s there has been a regular flow of unauthorised arrivals by boat from China, with a total of 1867 arriving between 1989 and 2000.

Similarly, Australia has seen a steady growth in the number of people arriving unauthorised by air from 500 in 1994–95 to 1234 in the first ten months of 2000–01, with a peak of 2106 in 1998–99.

There were, however, some notable changes in the pattern of arrivals during 1999–2000 that have been a cause of concern to the government.

First, the sheer number of arrivals was unprecedented in Australia's recent history. Between July 1999 and April 2001, 7484 people arrived unauthorised in Australia by boat. By comparison, the total number of people that arrived by boat without authorisation in the period from 1989–90 to 1998–99 was 4114. In other words, nearly twice as many unauthorised boat arrivals arrived in Australia in the past two years as they did in the previous nine years.

Second, there has been a distinct shift in the nationality profile of unauthorised boat arrivals caseload. Australia's previous experience had been of unauthorised arrivals from various parts of Asia, primarily China, Vietnam and Cambodia. During the first ten months of 2000–01, the bulk of arrivals were from the Middle East, with 52 per cent claiming they had come from Afghanistan, 22 per cent from Iraq and 13 per cent claiming to be from Iran.

Third, there has been an increase in the percentages of these arrivals who present protection claims. For the period 1 July 2000 to 30 April 2001, 85 per cent of unauthorised boat arrivals in Australia made protection visa applications. This compares to 83 per cent for the previous 12 months, and 46 per cent for 1998–99.

The high incidence of document disposal amongst unauthorised arrivals, together with advice from those apprehended, indicates that people smuggling is behind a large proportion of unauthorised arrivals. The disposal of identifying documentation before arrival in Australia obscures the identity of unauthorised arrivals and prevents Australian officials from accessing material, which might help to verify the claims made by those arriving.

Global Experience of People Smuggling

While people smuggling is not a new practice, more people are currently turning to smugglers to facilitate international migration. In part, this reflects the large pool of people now seeking migration and/or protection outcomes. Of the 22.5 million refugees or other displaced persons identified as of concern to the UNHCR, approximately seven million are in Africa, seven million are in Asia (including the Middle East) and six million are in Europe:

- these figures include refugees who have been outside their country of origin for very long periods of time and who can see no prospect of a durable solution for their plight; and
- they also include refugees who are experiencing an erosion of the level of protection that countries of first asylum are now prepared to provide, a percentage of whom have the means to pay people smugglers.

People smuggling is not a trivial industry. The International Organisation for Migration (IOM) estimates that the worldwide proceeds of people smuggling are in the order of US$7 billion per year. The number of countries affected by people smuggling is growing as new routes are created, existing routes are entrenched and as international air travel becomes more accessible and affordable. While it could be argued that people smugglers are merely the conduits for those seeking to access the international protection system, the reality is far more sobering, and less romantic:

- people smugglers are making large amounts of money through exploitation of a largely vulnerable group of people. It is well known that people die during their journey because of the perilous conditions in which they are placed. It can be assumed that others also perish but are not discovered. Many of those that reach their destination safely become dependent on agents and employers and are vulnerable to exploitation in an insecure and unfamiliar environment, particularly when in need of income to pay back the debt incurred to smugglers;
- people smugglers break not only the migration and entry laws of the destination country, but frequently also break the migration, customs and quarantine laws of their country of origin or first asylum, and any transit countries. These acts breach national sovereignty principles of those countries. Nothing in the 1951 Convention and the 1967 Protocol relating to the Status of Refugees (Refugees Convention) gives a person a right to arrive without authority and demand entry to another country;
- people smuggling is increasingly being undertaken by organised criminal elements. These criminals are also associated with drug trafficking and the exploitation of women and children in the context of prostitution and economic slavery. People smugglers

increase the incidence of these crimes in origin, first asylum, transit and destination countries;

- fraudulent documentation is a large part of the people smuggling industry. People smuggling encourages document forgery and identity fraud in, first asylum, transit and destination countries and facilitates greater use of fraudulent documentation in other contexts within those countries; and

- undocumented or fraudulently documented arrivals may also constitute a threat to the national security of the countries they enter. Unauthorised and undocumented arrival makes it extremely difficult for a country accurately to identify a person and undermines the safeguards and security checks that usually assist governments to identify those persons who represent a risk to the community or to national security.

Smuggling of Refugees

The above points apply irrespective of the nature of the person being smuggled. However, additional issues arise when smuggled people also seek refugee status in the destination country. Illegal entry undermines the capacity of states to exercise their sovereign right to decide who can enter and stay. Where illegal entry is accompanied by the attempt to choose their country of protection and achieve a simultaneous migration outcome, it is the single most serious threat to the continued viability of the international protection system and to organised efforts to provide durable and appropriate solutions for the millions of refugees in the world:

- smuggling activity diverts the resources of destination countries away from capacity building, integration and resettlement assistance in source countries or countries of first asylum;

- the supply of planned resettlement places offered by the few countries which, like Australia, offer such places is drying up as these same countries grapple with the problems and costs of smuggled refugees; and

- where effective protection has already been provided within the international protection system, people smuggling results in unnecessary cost duplication in destination countries and diversion of international resources and protection away from refugees those who lack durable solutions.

At a conservative estimate western states are spending, each year, $US10 billion on determining refugee status (with the attendant administrative law review arrangements) for half a million asylum seekers within their borders, of whom only a small percentage are refugees and many of whom already have (or had but abandoned) access to effective protection in alternative jurisdictions.

In contrast, the UNHCR has an annual budget of only $US1 billion with which to respond to the needs of the more than 22 million refugees and people of concern. Savings of just 10 per cent of asylum determination costs could release funds equivalent to double the current budget of the UNHCR.

If we are to ensure that the international protection system continues to work towards providing protection for those who need it, it is essential that the international community addresses the problems of unauthorised arrivals and people smuggling. Unless these threats are addressed, it will be the smugglers who determine who will receive resettlement places and this will be on the basis of who can pay, not greatest relative need. The current international protection system is not perfect. This chapter describes some of Australia's efforts to improve it. However, the practical implications of a breakdown and dismantling of the system for those refugees who do not have protection alternatives are unthinkable and warrant our best efforts to ensure that this does not happen.

Australia's Approach to Unauthorised Arrivals and People Smuggling

Australia has developed a government strategy to address the problem of unauthorised arrivals and organised people smuggling. This strategy relies heavily on efforts to promote international cooperation to address the plight of refugees and also targets the threats posed by the growth in organised people smuggling. It includes three key elements:

- prevention of the problem by minimising the outflows from countries of origin and secondary outflows from countries of first asylum;
- working with other countries to disrupt people smugglers and intercept their clients en route to their destination, while ensuring that those people in need of refugee protection are identified and assisted as early as is possible; and

• developing appropriate reception arrangements for unauthorised arrivals who reach Australia, focusing on the early assessment of the refugee status of the individual, the prompt removal of those who are not refugees, or who are refugees but can access effective protection elsewhere, and the removal of additional benefits not required by the Refugees Convention to minimise the incentive for people to attempt illegal travel to Australia.

A key element of each of these strategies is the development of a broad international consensus on the need for action and strengthened cooperation. Australia is working to this end through our relationships with source, first asylum, donor, destination, and transit countries, in international forums and with the UNHCR and other international organisations.

Resolving Refugee Problems Where They Arise

There is a range of influences at work in source countries to generate refugee outflows, these include conflict, human rights abuses and persecution. Outflows of people may also be attributable to economic or environmental factors or to civil war situations and these people may or may not be refugees. Because the causes of refugee flows are diverse, responses designed to achieve sustainable repatriation also cover a wide range, including security, political, social and economic aspects.

Apart from international efforts to encourage improvements in the human rights records of refugee producing countries, government strategies have focussed on increasing support for sustainable repatriation, and for countries of first asylum, by providing aid and assistance through international agencies operating within the relevant countries. The government has provided the Department of Immigration and Multicultural and Indigenous Affairs (DIMIA) with $20.8 million over four years starting from June 2000 to support responses to the large numbers of displaced Afghans and Iraqis.

In mid-July 2000, $1.7 million of this funding was provided to the World Food Program's drought relief appeal for Afghanistan, which is aimed at alleviating suffering and reducing the likelihood that these people will become displaced. Further opportunities to assist source countries for refugees are being sought out and considered.

Countries of first asylum bear a large responsibility for the immediate humanitarian response to refugee outflows. Further, where the situation within source countries becomes entrenched, as in the case of Iraq and Afghanistan, the ongoing problem for countries of first asylum can be substantial. For example, Iran and Pakistan, as the two countries hosting the largest populations of refugees, have sustained populations of Afghan and Iraqi refugees that have numbered in the millions for the last twenty years. It is estimated that between them they currently host up to 3.5 million Afghan and Iraqi refugees.

The conditions of refugees in countries of first asylum have a significant influence on secondary refugee outflows and the use of people smugglers by these refugees. The level of access to educational and health services, the ability to work and the availability of official opportunities for resettlement all contribute to the decision by asylum seekers to leave countries of first asylum.

Australia has sought to work with countries of first asylum to assist them in providing temporary protection while durable solutions are found. In June 2000, the Ministers for Foreign Affairs and Trade, and Immigration and Multicultural Affairs allocated $1.5 million from the 1999–2000 Aid budget to the UNHCR 2000 southwest Asia Appeal, which was intended to increase the self-reliance of refugees in Iran and Pakistan. An additional $4.5 million has been reallocated from within Australia's broader aid allocations in 2000–01 to support efforts to reduce refugee outflows or promote repatriation, as appropriate opportunities arise.

A further component of Australia's strategy involves the development of an information campaign to highlight to would-be unauthorised arrivals the dangers associated with the services offered by people smugglers.

Intercepting and Protecting Refugees Moving Illegally

From extensive networks of information exchange, it is clear that the operations of people smugglers are highly organised, complex and flexible with links extending worldwide. It is clear also that the people moving illegally will be doing so for a range of reasons. Some may be refugees and some may not. Efforts to disrupt smuggling activity need to be complemented by arrangements by transit countries, in concert with the UNHCR, to identify and protect those in need of protection and enable the quick return home of those who do not need protection. Organisations such as the IOM have a key role to play in the latter regard.

Australia has been strengthening its information gathering efforts in support of this strategy. This work includes:

- arrangements with a range of countries for the exchange of information on routes used by people moving illegally between countries, and the activities and methods of people smugglers;
- the establishment of a joint Australian Federal Police (AFP) and DIMIA team to investigate organised people smuggling;
- the creation of a National Surveillance Centre in Customs to enhance high-level coordination, especially in relation to information sharing between agencies to improve coastal surveillance and the early detection of unauthorised arrivals; and
- emphasising information exchange issues through multilateral fora such as the Inter-Governmental Consultations on Asylum, Refugee and Migration Policies in Europe, North America and Australia (IGC) and the Asia-Pacific Consultations on Refugees, Displaced Persons and Migrants (APC).

Australia has also taken a number of measures to strengthen its border integrity and to build technical capacity within countries along the smuggling routes to Australia. In addition, penalties and fines for those involved in people smuggling have been increased to up to 20 years imprisonment and over $220 000 in fines.

Reception Arrangements for Unauthorised Arrivals

The government's commitment to the maintenance of the international protection system is matched by its commitment to provide protection to those people within Australia who are owed protection obligations under the Refugees Convention – no matter how they have arrived.

That said, Australia has in recent years offered benefits in excess of those required by the Refugees Convention to those people within Australia who are found to need refugee protection. The Convention does not, for example, require that refugees be provided with permanent residence in the first instance, nor family reunion sponsorship rights. It needs to be recognised that offering such generous additional benefits can contribute significantly to the incentives for people to use the services offered by people smugglers.

In the context of an international protection system, it is essential that there be an incentive for those who need protection to seek that protection from the first available source. Those people with adequate protection already should not be encouraged to attempt to trade on their status as refugees in order to gain a more preferable migration outcome in a different country. Accordingly, the government announced in October 1999 that a range of measures designed to reduce Australia's attractiveness to unauthorised arrivals were to be introduced, including:

- excluding unauthorised arrivals from accessing permanent residence in the first instance by granting those who are refugees a three-year temporary protection visa (TPV);
- TPV holders are not eligible for the full range of settlement services and benefits usually provided to refugees permanently resettling in Australia, including DIMIA's Adult Migrant English Program;
- stopping people who have effective protection overseas from gaining refugee protection in Australia; and
- developing stronger identification powers to help to ascertain the identity of asylum seekers.

These measures are built on the existing legislation, which requires that, except in extenuating circumstances, all unauthorised arrivals be held in administrative detention until there are either granted a visa or removed.

The temporary protection visa measures are aimed at unauthorised arrivals who may have bona fide protection needs, but who are seeking to gain a preferred migration outcome by travelling to their preferred country and using the onshore protection avenues to gain residence and family sponsorship rights. Importantly, the TPV changes are consistent with Australia's obligations under the Refugees Convention and guarantee access to Medicare, work rights, appropriate levels of social support and education for minors. Our fundamental obligation not to refoule a refugee is guaranteed by arrangements allowing all TPV holders to apply for and obtain permanent refugee protection after 30 months, if they are still owed protection obligations.

The measures were also aimed at strengthening our capacity to verify the identity of people arriving unlawfully. There is no doubt that this poses a serious challenge to Australia. Obtaining any objective verification of the identity and claims of people arriving without authority can be made very difficult where they arrive without identifying documentation of any provenance or reliability. Domestic refugee determination processes, combined with unauthorised entry provide attractive opportunities for people who may not be refugees to try to use new identities to gain residence in countries such as Australia.

The government has also put in place legislative arrangements to reflect the decision taken by Australian courts that Australia does not owe protection obligations to a person who already has a right to enter and reside in a country where effective protection is available. Under this legislation, the Minister for Immigration and Multicultural Affairs can, after seeking the views of the UNHCR, declare that a particular country:

- provides adequate access to effective procedures for the assessment of the protection needs of asylum seekers;
- honours its protection obligations; and
- meets relevant human rights standards.

Such a declaration has the effect of preventing people from making a valid application for a protection visa, where they have a right to re-enter and reside in a declared country and they have previously resided in that country for at least seven days. A ministerial power is available to enable the Minister to allow an application where he considers this to be in the public interest. As yet no country has been declared under these provisions.

A further component of the strategy is the need to develop arrangements that provide for the speedy return of people found not to be refugees to their country of nationality, an issue the UNHCR itself recognises as necessary to ensure the integrity of the international protection framework. The non-return of such people fundamentally undermines the institution and public support for those accepted as refugees. Prompt return is even more important if the person found not to be a refugee has used unlawful means of entering a country.

Popular Misconceptions – The Domestic Debate

The new protection visa arrangements preserve, for those refugees who entered Australia lawfully on genuine documents, immediate access to permanent residence, family reunion sponsorship, full settlement services and full access to the social welfare system. But contrary to claims from some quarters, there is no Refugee Convention requirement to provide equal benefits to all refugees. Article 31 of the Refugees Convention identifies some very particular circumstances where member states are not to impose penalties upon refugees because of their unlawful entry. However, differentiation in the level of benefits does not constitute a penalty, particularly so when all refugees still receive the level of protection and support owed them under the Convention. Article 31 also only relates to people 'coming directly from a territory where their life or freedom was threatened ...' This is hardly a description fitting large numbers of illegal arrivals to Australia who have travelled through many countries, and have often lived outside their homeland for years or decades, before travelling to Australia.

There have been similar claims repeated in domestic debate that the detention of unauthorised arrivals itself constitutes a penalty and is in breach of international obligations. These claims also do not stand up under scrutiny. The High Court of Australia has in fact affirmed that administrative detention of people without visas while a visa application is processed or removal is arranged is lawful and is not punitive in nature.[3] Similarly, the United Nations Human Rights Committee has indeed looked at Australia's immigration detention arrangements, but it concluded that they 'do not per se constitute a breach of Australia's international obligations'.[4] Yet some commentators in Australia frequently claim – but do not quote – that these authorities have made findings to the contrary.

There is no international treaty that is offended by Australia's legislative arrangements for detaining unauthorised arrivals. Indeed, even the non-binding guidelines issued by the UNHCR on detention of asylum seekers recognise that states may decide to detain unauthorised arrivals seeking refugee protection while their identity is verified and medical issues are resolved. Where, as is the case in Australia, unauthorised arrivals are very well organised and there is a pattern of document disposal before arrival, identification is critical to any protection decision. Detention periods while waiting for a protection decision are largely attributable to verification of basic identification and closely related matters such as checking for past criminal behaviour or for national security issues, which could exclude the person from protection under the Refugees Convention.

---

3   *Chu Kheng Lim v Minister for Immigration, Local Government and Ethnic Affairs* (1992) 176 CLR 1.

4   United Nations Human Rights Committee, *Concluding Observations of the Human Rights Committee: Australia* (Communication 560/1993, A/55/40, 24 July 1997), http://www.unhchr.ch/tbs/doc.nsf, paras 498–528.

What is noteworthy about the recent debate in Australia over domestic refugee protection arrangements is that it has focused attention on the people who have already reached Australia, at the expense of the much larger numbers of refugees overseas for whom international support is in critical need.

This is not to say that the voices of those people who have arrived in Australia and been granted TPVs – their arguments for greater assistance, for earlier entitlements for benefits such as family reunion sponsorship, or indeed any other concerns they express about their treatment here – should be ignored. However, it is important to balance these voices with those of the much larger number of refugees overseas, those people still in need of a durable solution and for whom resettlement is the *only* viable option.

TPV-holders are safe – they are protected from refoulement and are provided with a range of benefits which places them far beyond the standards of existence of many of the worlds refugees who are waiting for resettlement. They are the lucky ones: the ones who could pay the smugglers, who were not hampered by gender, family responsibilities or poor health.

There is no question that refugees in Australia will be protected. The real issue which the TPV arrangements highlights is whether Australia is prepared to continue to provide additional benefits, beyond those required by its Refugee Convention obligations, in circumstances where it is known that this encourages others to place themselves in the hands of people smugglers. Do we really want Australia's finite capacity to resettle those in need to be taken-up on the basis of decisions of organised criminals about who they will ship to Australia? Or would we want to use as many places as possible to resettle those people identified as in greatest need of resettlement through coordinated international efforts under the UNHCR?

Reform of the UNHCR and the International Protection System

Finally, it is useful to turn briefly to the need for the reform of the UNHCR and the international protection system. In the past 50 years the UNHCR has made significant contributions to the protection of refugees and supporting the international system of protection. This system is coming under increasing pressure, not least by those who have access to effective protection but choose to obtain protection elsewhere by paying people smugglers.

Australia is keen for the UNHCR to assist countries providing protection to refugees while combating people smuggling. In particular, in the context of the strategy outlined above, Australia has serious concerns about:

- the lack of an effective mechanism for burden sharing, leaving countries of first asylum with insufficient assistance; and
- pressure from a variety of sectors to expand the Refugees Convention definition of 'refugee' and its coverage, as this pressure is contributing to misuse of asylum systems and diversion of resources from those most in need of protection.

Accordingly, Australia is working, through its bilateral and multilateral engagements, to seek the reform of the UNHCR and its Executive Committee (Ex Com) to ensure:

- a re-exertion of states' control over the direction of the organisation, complemented by enhanced leadership from the High Commissioner;
- greater leadership and direction from a reinvigorated Ex Com;
- improved review, evaluation and accountability frameworks within UNHCR;
- recognition of the interrelationships between people smuggling, unauthorised arrivals and the international protection framework and the critical role of the UNHCR in international efforts to address these matters;
- greater assistance to countries of first asylum so that the protection system delivers equitable outcomes for refugees; and
- strategies to focus the resources and efforts of member states where this will have the greatest positive impact on solving refugee problems, recognising that key destination countries are currently expending ten times more on domestic refugee determination processes than is available to the UNHCR to deliver support to the vast bulk of refugees.

Conclusion

Australia remains committed to the international protection system as the best method for assisting those in genuine need of protection. The flow of unauthorised arrivals targeting Australia has not diminished this commitment. However, it has strengthened resolve to ensure that the protection system works for those for whom it was intended and does not provide opportunities for misuse as a de facto migration avenue by people who are not refugees or who have abandoned or ignored protection provided to them elsewhere.

While much can be done by countries such as Australia acting at the national level, no one country holds the key to solving the problems of the millions of refugees displaced worldwide. Enhanced cooperation between countries at the bilateral, regional and multilateral levels is essential if the framework of international protection is to be effective, and particularly if the serious threat posed by large-scale illegal movements of people and organised people smuggling to desirable migration countries is to be addressed.

Failure to deal with these problems carries a high price for the refugees themselves if the countries feeling the strain of unauthorised arrivals reduce their support for international protection system, and if scarce resettlement places are allowed to become a commodity sold off by people smuggling organisations to those who can pay the price.

5 Criminality and State Protection: Structural Tensions in Canadian Refugee Law

DONALD GALLOWAY

Introduction

After a lengthy phase of relative stability, Canadian refugee law is entering a period of transition and transformation. The changes are occurring on two separate fronts and, on each front, it appears that problems and paradoxes associated with criminality have been the major stimulus for review of the status quo.

First, change is being effected in the Supreme Court of Canada, which is currently considering two appeals that challenge many of the premises of the current law.[1] At the heart of the appeals is the question whether the Canadian Charter of Rights and Freedoms (Charter of Rights)[2] requires that state protection be made available to all individuals who face a substantial risk of torture in their country of origin, even those who are regarded as a danger to the security of Canada because of their connection with terrorist groups or their past criminal acts. The appeals also focus on the proper interpretation of the Convention Against Torture (CAT).[3] The appellants and intervenors have presented the CAT as a document that promotes the dignity of the individual strictly and single-mindedly. It is distinguished

---

[1] The decisions under appeal are *Suresh v Canada (Minister of Citizenship and Immigration)* (2000) 183 DLR (4th) 629 and *Ahani v Canada (Minister of Citizenship and Immigration)* (2000) 73 CRR (2d) 156.

[2] Constitution Act 1982 (Canada), Part I, being Schedule B to the Canada Act 1982 (UK), c 11.

[3] Convention Against Torture and Other Cruel, Inhuman or Degrading Treatment or Punishment, 10 December 1984, UN Doc A/RES/39/46 (entered into force 26 June 1987).

from the Convention relating to the Status of Refugees (Refugees Convention) in that the latter is presented as a flawed document: a political compromise that is diluted by qualifications and riders that operate in a manner that jeopardises fundamental human rights. The CAT, on the other hand, is identified as an important milestone in the development of the international tradition of human rights protection, and the appellants and intervenors argue that its unqualified stance against torture should be reflected in the interpretation of the Canadian Constitution. The Canadian Government is responding vigorously to these appeals, even as it recognises that its interpretation of the CAT runs counter to that promoted by the Committee on Torture and contradicts jurisprudence from the European Court of Human Rights.[4]

The two appeals are the most recent in a series of cases in which the Supreme Court has considered the rights of alleged criminals who are facing an order to return to another country. Until 1998 the Supreme Court had only twice considered substantive issues relating to the protection of refugees. The first occasion was in *Canada (Attorney-General) v Ward*,[5] where La Forest J, for the court, parsed carefully and quite exhaustively the inclusive terms of the definition of the term 'refugee' found in the Refugees Convention and incorporated into Canadian law. The second case was *Chan v Canada (Minister of Employment & Immigration)*,[6] where the majority of the court showed reluctance to make any comment about the law, preferring, instead, to dismiss the appeal on grounds relating to the sufficiency of evidence.

Since 1998, however, the Supreme Court has entered the field directly and indirectly on another two occasions, and in both cases, the rights and status of the 'criminal claimant' have been a focal point of attention. The pivotal case has been *Pushpanathan v Canada (Minister of Citizenship & Immigration)*,[7] where the Supreme Court addressed the meaning of the rule of exclusion found in Article 1(F)(c) of the Refugees Convention and determined that this section did not exclude a person who had conspired to traffic in narcotics. In the course of his majority opinion, Bastarache J

---

[4]   *Chahal v United Kingdom* (1996) 23 EHHR 413.

[5]   [1993] 2 SCR 689.

[6]   [1995] 3 SCR 593.

[7]   [1998] 1 SCR 1222, discussed in D J Mullan, 'Deference Deferred – The Immigration and Refugee Board', *Reid's Administrative Law* **7(5)** (1999) p 97.

offered an unconventional and oblique analysis of all three sections of Article 1F, suggesting a narrow ambit for each. Article 1F(a) excludes those with respect to whom there are serious reasons for considering that they have committed crimes against peace, war crimes or crimes against humanity; Article 1F(b) excludes those with respect to whom there are serious reasons for considering that they have committed serious non-political crimes outside the country of refuge prior to admission; and Article 1F(c) excludes those with respect to whom there are serious reasons for considering they have been guilty of acts contrary to the purposes and principles of the United Nations.

Extrapolating from some of Bastarache J's obiter comments, the Federal Court of Appeal in *Chan*[8] has since held that Article 1F(b) does not exclude from refugee status those who have been found guilty of an offence and have served their sentence. Instead, it has determined that the article excludes only those who are extraditable for serious non-political crimes. It explicitly rejects the government's argument that a prior conviction for a serious non-political offence should operate to automatically deny that person refugee status. Significantly, in *United States of America v Burns*,[9] the Supreme Court also addressed whether the constitutionally protected right to security of the person would be violated where a person is extradited to face the death penalty and has rejected the government's position that the return of a person to a jurisdiction where he would face the death penalty is not unconstitutional.

The second arena of change is parliament, where the federal government has recently tabled a bill, known as Bill C-11,[10] that aims radically to reshape refugee law by wholesale replacement of the current legislation with rules that aim to 'ensure that Canada's immigration and refugee protection system is able to respond to new challenges'.[11] It states that this aim will be achieved by providing:

---

[8] *Chan v Canada (Minister of Citizenship & Immigration)* [2000] 4 FC 390 (FCA).

[9] [2001] 1 SCR 283.

[10] Bill C-11, an Act respecting immigration to Canada and the granting of refugee protection to persons who are displaced, persecuted or in danger, 1st Session, 37th Parl, 2001. This Bill came into force in June 2002 and is now the Immigration and Refugee Protection Act (Canada).

[11] Bill C-11, 'Summary'.

a strong, effective refugee protection program that incorporates the protection grounds of the Refugees Convention and the Convention Against Torture and the grounds of risk to life or of cruel and unusual treatment or punishment[12]

and:

tightened ineligibility provisions for serious criminals, security threats and repeat claimants who seek access to the refugee protection process of the Immigration and Refugee Board.[13]

Given that torture and cruel and unusual treatment are not novel phenomena, and that to some extent there has already been incorporation of all the protection grounds into domestic law,[14] one quickly gets the idea that it is the 'serious criminals, security threats and repeat claimants' who are seen as providing the new challenges to the refugee determination process. The strong rhetorical implication is that members of these groups are not genuine claimants and therefore the primary challenge is first to prevent them from abusing the determination process, which they can do by wasting the time of the Immigration and Refugee Board with their false claims or by enjoying benefits to which they are not entitled, and then to remove them from Canada as illegal migrants. This contrasts starkly with the approach of the Supreme Court, which, in the current appeals, accepts the genuineness of the claims to protection but identifies the challenge as being to determine whether they should be recognised.

Concern with criminality has penetrated deeply into the details of the proposed legislation. While the statements quoted above suggest that the issue arises only at the stage of determining whether a criminal is ineligible to make a refugee claim before the independent Immigration and Refugee Board, this is not the case. At each stage of the determination and post-determination process, new hurdles have been constructed and broader definitions of criminality have been introduced. At this point, it is useful to give a brief overview of the most significant proposed changes.

---

[12] Ibid.

[13] Ibid.

[14] See below n 22.

The Proposed Amendments

First, there are the proposed amendments to the ineligibility criteria. The ineligibility criteria govern access of refugee claimants to the Immigration and Refugee Board. Introduced more than ten years ago, these criteria identify many uncontroversial factors that are clearly consistent with the aims and principles of refugee law. For example, access is denied to individuals who have been identified as Convention refugees in other countries.[15] Denial of access in such a case is easy to defend by reference to the basic principle that refugee law offers surrogate state protection to those to whom it has been denied. Where another country has offered such protection there is no need for Canada to consider the claim.

Some of the ineligibility criteria are more controversial. For example, under current law, where an adjudicator has found that there are serious reasons for believing that the claimant is connected with various forms of criminality and where the Minister is of the opinion that the claimant is a danger to the public, access to the independent Board is denied.[16] More sinister is the denial of access to claimants who are believed to be terrorists or associated with organised crimes or are or were officials of governments that engaged in systematic and gross human rights abuse where the Minister is of the opinion that it would be 'contrary to public interest for the claim to be heard'.[17] Such claimants are diverted from the refugee determination process. Their sole hope to avoid a removal order is to make an application to an immigration officer representing the Minister for humanitarian and compassionate consideration.

Bill C-11 proposes to expand the already broad ineligibility criteria by including individuals who have committed a serious crime in Canada without any determination of their dangerousness being made.[18] A serious crime is defined as a crime punishable by a maximum of ten years and for which a sentence of at least two years was imposed.[19] In fact, the new criteria allow for the suspension of refugee claims already commenced

---

[15] Immigration Act RSC c I-2 (Immigration Act (Canada)), section 46.01(1)(a).

[16] Id, section 46.01(1)(e)(i).

[17] Id, section 46.01(1)(e)(ii).

[18] Bill C-11, section 101.

[19] Id, section 101(2)(a).

where charges in relation to a serious crime have been laid until there has been a judicial determination of the matter.[20]

Second, beyond the ineligibility criteria, Bill C-11 also expands the impact of criminality within the refugee determination process by extending the ambit of the exclusion clauses found in the Refugees Convention. The proposals continue to allow these clauses to operate when the Refugee Division is considering whether a person is a refugee. However, the Bill also permits the Refugee Division to consider other matters, and allows the exclusion clauses to operate there also. The Refugee Division is granted the authority to determine whether a person is a 'person in need of protection'. This is defined as a:

> foreign national in Canada whose removal to their country of nationality ... would subject them personally (a) to a danger, believed on substantial grounds to exist, of torture within the meaning of Article 1 of the Convention Against Torture (CAT) or (b) to a risk to their life or to a risk of cruel and unusual treatment or punishment ...[21]

Those who fit within the exclusion clauses of the Refugees Convention are excluded from this status also. In one sense, this is not an expansion of the denial of claims to criminals since it merely alters the forum where certain matters are heard. Under current law, refugee claimants who are found not to have a well-founded fear of protection are automatically held to have made an application to an immigration officer to be recognised as a member of the Post-Determination Refugee in Canada Class.[22] This application is regarded as part of the immigration process. It allows for the grant of landing to those who have been found not to be refugees but who face a risk in the country of origin. It is not available to, amongst others, those who have been found to fit within the Article 1F exclusion.

However, in the new Bill the government explicitly notes that it is incorporating into domestic law the obligations found in the CAT. Unlike the Refugees Convention, this Convention makes no mention either of a protected status or of individuals who are to be excluded from it. It contains a definition of torture; a requirement that each state party take effective measures to prevent acts of torture in its own territory; explicit recognition

---

[20] Id, section 103.

[21] Id, section 97.

[22] Immigration Regulations, 1978, SOR/78-172, as amended, section 2(1).

that torture cannot be justified by any exceptional circumstances; a prohibition on each state party to return a person to another state where there are substantial grounds for believing that he would be in danger of being subjected to torture; and the requirement that each state party undertake to prevent other acts of cruel, inhuman or degrading treatment in any territory in its jurisdiction.[23] By identifying the new status of protected person, the government makes explicit its view that the CAT has the same structure as the Refugees Convention and that the prospect of torture, even when based on substantial grounds does not by itself vest rights in an individual. Rather than present the Refugees Convention as an atavism or a flawed relic of yesteryear, Bill C-11 presents it as a document with continued vitality that merely requires supplementation.

The concern with criminality also surfaces at a third level. Article 33(1) of the Refugees Convention recognises the right of a refugee not to be returned to a territory where his or her life or freedom would be threatened because of various factors. Article 33(2) however denies the right not to be returned to a country of origin to refugees who are regarded as a security risk or, having committed particularly serious crimes, are regarded as a danger to the community. Currently, the Immigration Act (the Act) specifies a set of criteria to identify those refugees who may be returned to their country of origin that is consistent with Article 33(2).[24] It singles out those who can be connected with particular forms of criminality who are also determined by the Minister either to be 'a danger to the public in Canada' or 'a danger to the security of Canada'. Bill C-11 expands the factors that can be used to justify the return of a person found to be a refugee.[25] It permits the return of a refugee who is inadmissible on grounds of security, violating human or international rights or organised criminality if, in the opinion of the Minister, it would be:

> contrary to the national interest for the foreign national to remain in Canada on the basis of the nature and severity of acts committed or of danger to the security of Canada.

---

[23] See N Poynder, '"Mind the Gap": Seeking Alternative Protection under the Convention Against Torture and the International Covenant on Civil and Political Rights', chapter 7 in this book.

[24] Immigration Act (Canada), section 53.

[25] Bill C-11, section 115(2).

By referring to the nature and severity of acts committed, the section substantially expands the grounds for return listed in Article 33(2) of the Refugees Convention. Moreover, the same provision applies not only to refugees but also to those who are at risk of torture and cruel or unusual treatment or punishment. The provision does not identify what aspects of the national interest are thought to be affected by the continued presence of a person who is not considered dangerous but who has engaged in egregious acts.

Criminality surfaces yet again at a fourth point. Under current law, before a removal order is executed, a person has the opportunity to make an application to an immigration officer representing the Minister to consider compassionate or humanitarian grounds for not executing the order.[26] No restrictions are placed on the Minister's representative when making hearing such an application. Under the terms of Bill C-11, a person who has been found inadmissible for grounds of security, violating human rights serious criminality or organised criminality will if successful in making a plea for humanitarian relief, receive only a stay of the removal order.[27] Others may receive refugee protection. The difference is significant since the latter may apply for landed immigrant status while the former may not. As a result, the former will always remain in a state of limbo.

These measures relating to criminality are bolstered by a set of provisions that increases the penalties to which human smugglers and traffickers are liable. For example, those who have organised the arrival into Canada of ten persons or more who are not in possession of valid papers will be liable to a fine of $1 000 000 and to life imprisonment.[28] As I argue at the end of this chapter, these provisions, while they are unlikely to provoke constitutional challenge are among the most controversial in the Bill.

Competing Philosophies?

This brief introduction reveals that in both parliament and in the courtroom, norms of refugee law are being challenged and reformulated, prompted, it seems, by the difficulties of accommodating the criminal claimant within

---

[26] Immigration Act (Canada), section 114(2).

[27] Bill C-11, sections 112–14.

[28] Ibid, section 117.

the process. A cursory glance suggests that the government's concerns and objectives are quite different from, and antithetical to, those of the Supreme Court. In the past, the government's attempts to defend its 'tough on crime' stance before the Supreme Court have not been successful.

The flurry of activity in both arenas has not escaped public attention. Bill C-11 is not having an easy passage through parliament, as critics, particularly those representing the legal profession, challenge the details of the government's proposals. Moreover, the government's defence before the Supreme Court of its alleged authority to return individuals to a country where there are substantial reasons to believe that they will face torture has attracted a number of interventions in the case from rights groups such as Amnesty International[29] as well as the United Nations High Commissioner for Refugees.[30]

The Supreme Court has also attracted its share of criticism. For example, the decision in *Burns*[31] not to permit the extradition of individuals to the United States without assurances that they will not face the death penalty has provoked the worry that Canada will become a haven for criminals on the run.

The apparent opposition between the government's stance and that of the court has popularised an interpretive account of the current reforms that explains the current dynamic in terms of a conflict between the two branches of government based on two competing philosophies or ideological stances. The thrust of this popular account is that the government's concern with denying access to the refugee process to serious criminals, excluding them from the category of those who have a right to protection, and its eagerness to include them amongst the ranks of those who may be returned to face possible persecution or torture in their country of origin, is based on a harsh form of instrumentalism that is antithetical to the recognition of substantive rights. By way of contrast, the account identifies the Supreme Court as the defender of a rights-based ethic that refuses to look for politically acceptable equilibria among conflicting goals. It is commonplace to hear the criticism that the court has improperly (or even illegitimately) accorded to refugee claimants the same rights that are

---

[29] Amnesty International, *Response to Bill C-11* (Canada, Amnesty International, March 2001), http://www.amnesty.ca/Refugee/Bill_C-11.pdf.

[30] UNHCR, *Comments on Bill C-11* (Geneva, UNHCR, March 2001), http://www.web.net/~ccr/c11hcr.pdf.

[31] *United States of America v Burns* [2001] 1 SCR 283.

accorded to citizens, and that the rights-based ethic on which it relies is improperly impersonal. By appropriating the lexicon of human rights, it is argued that the court ignores the communal ties, social bonds and social values that make it appropriate for a community to prevent the entry of individuals who are regarded as undesirable or to remove them if they have already entered.[32]

The federal government, on the other hand, is charged with recognising rights only insofar as it is useful to do so, ignoring their pull when competing ends demand it. From this point of view, individual rights are respected only insofar as such respect promotes or is consistent with the general well-being of the community. Once conflict appears, support for the recognition of the right diminishes. Moreover, the instrumentalist outlook presents respect for individual rights as one social goal, amongst others, that is worth pursuing. If the basic interests of a particular individual need to be sacrificed in order to achieve this goal, then so be it. Thus, respect for the individual is not regarded as a mandatory constraint on action but as a general aim. The thrust of the instrumentalist critique is that this devalues the tradition of human rights and misconstrues the nature of a right. By construing a right as a reason for action like any other reason for action, the instrumentalist fails to appreciate that its weight is sufficient in itself to place an obligation on another party such as the government. Rather than accept the view that obligations come into play only after a full utilitarian calculation has been made, the rights theorist identifies an obligation of one sort or another once an entitlement has been identified. Critics identify that such an instrumentalist stance underlies Bill C-11.

Moreover, while it recognises that the proposed amendments in Bill C-11 are not insignificant, the instrumentalist critique claims that they do not evince a radical change in philosophy. Under the current Immigration Act criminal claimants risk losing important benefits to which they would be entitled were it not for their criminal conduct. However, the new measures, by expanding the categories of individual who cannot benefit from the state protection scheme, confirm the charge that the government is not according proper weight to individual rights as it is obligated to do by international convention and by the Constitution and that it is tailoring refugee law to ensure that protection is available only to the good immigrant or when the social costs are minimal.

---

[32] For a discussion of these ideas, see D Galloway, 'Liberalism, Globalism and Immigration', *Queens Law Journal* **18** (1993) p 266.

Possibly the strongest bases of support for the instrumentalist critique are the very language of the Immigration Act and the rhetoric used by officials when defending it. The Act lists a series of objectives that it seeks to achieve,[33] while remaining silent on basic principles or substantive rights that demand its respect. Also, reference is made to the need to 'uphold Canada's humanitarian tradition'[34] which implies that the allocation of benefits is regarded as a matter of generosity and largesse rather than being based on entitlement.[35] This gives rise to the impression that hard cases are to be determined by compromising conflicting goals rather than by tracing the meaning of one's principled commitments. Moreover, as noted above, the government's defence of its current position and proposed amendments appears to be aimed solely at quelling the fear that criminals are abusing the refugee determination process. This is understandable in the current political climate where political support is gained by appealing to emotion rather than presenting philosophically sound arguments.

In the following pages I argue that the popular account of a deep ideological rift between the government and the court cannot be maintained as starkly as the above outline suggests. If there were such a rift, then one could confidently predict first of all that the current appeals before the Supreme Court will be granted and that many of the proposed amendments will be ruled unconstitutional. In a showdown between the courts and the federal government it is the courts that have the last word. I believe that such confidence is misplaced.

One can appreciate that this is so by examining the details of the recent decision in *Burns*, the extradition case in which the court recognised that, except in highly exceptional circumstances (which the court refuses to specify) it would be unconstitutional to extradite a person to a jurisdiction where he may face the death penalty. I also suggest that in *Pushpanathan*,[36] one can find argument that supports the proposal in Bill C-11 to extend the exclusion clauses beyond their current ambit and to restrict the right of no return beyond the explicit terms of the Refugee Convention.

---

[33] Immigration Act (Canada), section 3. These objectives include fulfilment of 'Canada's international legal obligations with respect to refugees and to uphold its humanitarian tradition with respect to the displaced and the persecuted'. See section 3(g).

[34] Ibid.

[35] See also C Dauvergne, 'Amorality and Humanitarianism in Immigration Law', *Osgoode Hall Law Journal* **37(3)** (1999) p 597.

[36] *Pushpanathan*, above n 7.

I also argue that the expansion of the ineligibility criteria, while indefensible, will likely not attract judicial attention.

I conclude by arguing that neither the proposed amendments nor the current appeals succeed in addressing adequately some of the central issues of political morality raised by the problem of involuntary migration. In effect, despite the flurry of activity, the important issues are being bypassed.

Individual Rights and the Principles of Fundamental Justice

In *Burns*, the court argues as follows. First, it holds that section 7 of the Charter of Rights, which protects 'the right to life, liberty and security of person and the right not to be deprived thereof except in accordance with the principles of fundamental justice' is the only section engaged by the extradition order. It refuses to hold that the right protected by section 12, namely the right not to be subjected to cruel and unusual treatment or punishment is at stake. The court argues that this is because the Charter of Rights applies only to government action and the cruel and unusual punishment in this case would not be meted out by the Canadian government but by officials in the jurisdiction to which the appellants would be extradited. It reaches its decision despite acknowledging the wording in the French version of the Charter of Rights, which specifies that individuals have the right to protection from cruel and unusual treatment, implying that the right can be infringed by omission as well as by a positive act. Two considerations underlie the court's determination in relation to section 12. First, that it is wise not to apply the Charter of Rights extra-territorially, and second that it is proper to rely on a narrow conception of complicity. These views are quite contentious and I return to consider them below. At this point it is important to point out that the court draws a distinction between engaging in cruel treatment and returning a person to face cruel treatment. This has important bearing for the current appeals in which the appellants argue that the absolute proscription against torture found in the CAT applies equally to the proscription against returning a person to face torture. The willingness of the court in *Burns* to distinguish the act of return from the treatment suggests that this argument will not be successful.

Having restricted consideration to section 7 of the Charter of Rights, the court maintains that the principles of fundamental justice to which reference is made in that section are principles that are 'derived from the basic tenets of the legal system'.[37] In determining the concrete rights of the individual, it is necessary to balance his or her interest in life, liberty and security of the person against these values. The court states adamantly that there is a difference between the values inherent in the principles of fundamental justice and normal public policy considerations. However, it does not articulate with any level of precision wherein the distinction may lie. The court offers the following analysis:

> The distinction between 'general public policy' on the one hand and the 'the inherent domain of the judiciary as guardian of the justice system' is of particular importance in a death penalty case. The broader aspects of the death penalty controversy including the role of retribution and deterrence in society, and the view that capital punishment is inconsistent with the sanctity of human life, are embedded in the basic tenets of our legal system, but they also reflect philosophic positions informed by beliefs and social science evidence outside 'the inherent domain of the judiciary' The narrower aspects of the controversy are concerned with the investigation, prosecution, defence, appeal and sentencing of a person within the framework of the criminal law ... These considerations are central to the preoccupation of the courts, and directly engage the responsibility of the judges 'as guardians of the justice system'. We regard the present controversy as engaging the special responsibility of the judiciary for the protection of the innocent.[38]

This paragraph reveals that the judiciary, although unwilling to consider the full panoply of public policy is nevertheless willing to consider countervailing factors that may limit the ambit of constitutional rights if they are well-entrenched in the law. In the past courts have not been shy to cite the Latin maxim: salus populi est suprema lex.[39] Moreover, in an earlier immigration case decided by the Supreme Court, *Chiarelli v Canada (Minister of Employment and Immigration)*,[40] Sopinka J for the court notes:

> in determining the scope of principles of fundamental justice as they apply to this case, the Court must look to the principles and policies underlying

---

[37] *United States of America v Burns* [2001] 1 SCR 283, at 326.

[38] Ibid.

[39] The safety of the people is the supreme law.

[40] [1992] 1 SCR 711.

immigration law. The most fundamental principle of immigration law is that non-citizens do not have a right to enter or remain in the country.[41]

These comments and the foregoing analysis suggest that it is by no means clear that the court will reject the government's arguments that there are sound reasons relating to danger and national security for returning individuals to jurisdictions where there may face torture. As was noted by the Court of Appeal in *Suresh*,[42] as long as one frames the question to be addressed in terms of whether a law which permits deportation to a country which exposes a person conflicts with fundamental values underlying human rights legislation and international norms, the answer appears obvious. Torture 'contravenes basic and intuitive notions of what is just and fair'.[43] However, if the question is framed: 'in terms of whether it is contrary to the principles of fundamental justice to deport a suspected terrorist to the only country which will accept him, in circumstances where that person represents a danger to Canada's national security [the answer is] not as self-evident'.[44]

The decision in *Burns* was based on the finding that the government had failed to identify any public purpose that would be served by extradition without assurances that is not substantially served by extradition with assurances that no death penalty would be imposed. There is no guarantee that the court will reach the same conclusion in the face of the government's arguments about the dangerousness of a particular activity or the threat that he presents to national security.

One of the factors that distinguishes the current appeals from *Burns* is the fact that the CAT identifies that each state party is under an obligation not to return a person to a territory where he or she may face torture. This suggests that any balancing between individual interests such as the interest in security of the person, and other concerns of fundamental justice, has already been completed. In other words, that Canada has already committed itself to the position that the right to security of the person and the right not to be deprived thereof except in accordance with the principles of fundamental justice can be concretised to embrace a right not to be

---

[41]   Id, p 733. See also *Singh v Canada (Minister for Employment and Immigration)* [1985] 1 SCR 177.

[42]   *Suresh v* Canada, above n 1, p 677–8.

[43]   Id, p 678.

[44]   Ibid.

returned to face the substantial risk of torture. If the court accepts such a position, then another idiosyncrasy of the Canadian Constitution will come into play. Section 1 of the Charter of Rights stipulates that the rights recognised therein are subject only to such reasonable limits prescribed by law as can be demonstrably justified in a free and democratic society. While the Supreme Court has placed a heavy onus on those attempting to justify an infringement of a right, requiring that it be shown that there is a pressing and substantial objective behind the limitation, that there is a rational connection between the objective and the limitation, and that there be minimal impairment of the right,[45] nevertheless the presence of this section reveals a basic premise of Canadian constitutional law – that rights are not given absolute protection.

This discussion reveals that the idea of tracing any dispute between the courts and the government to a philosophical difference between instrumentalism and rights analysis is misplaced. It is clear that the court has been willing to look to social values as factors that limit the ambit of rights, and weigh these against the interest of the individual. Ultimately, its willingness to find for the government in the current appeals will depend on the ability of the latter to show that the values that it is promoting are well entrenched within the legal system, that they directly engage the responsibility of judges and that the negative social consequences of not returning an individual cannot be avoided by other means. This the government may not be able to do if the court is willing, for example, to see detention of those who are regarded as security risks or as dangerous, (which would clearly limit the right to liberty), as an adequate alternative to return.

Not only is it unclear how *Burns* affects the current appeals, it is also unclear how it affects Article 1F(b) of the Refugee Convention, the exclusion clause that denies refugee status to those who are extraditable for serious non-political crimes. One of the consequences of *Burns* is that, if a jurisdiction does not provide assurances that the death penalty would not be sought, the extradition should not proceed. In other words, Canada would be required not to present the individual for trial. The willingness of the court to allow individuals to avoid trial on this basis suggests that the court would also be willing to allow a trial to be foregone in a case where the accused may face persecution on the basis of one of the five grounds. In which case, this ground of exclusion would lose its teeth.

---

[45] See, as an illustration, *R v Oakes* [1986] 1 SCR 103.

Exclusion, Return and Human Rights

Not only has the Supreme Court shown itself to be willing to place restrictions on rights, it has also offered some subtle rights-based reasons for excluding individuals from refugee status, and also, by extension, for excluding individuals from protection under the CAT.

These reasons can be found in the majority opinion of Bastarache J in *Pushpanathan*.[46] In this case, the court focused on the meaning of the Article 1F(c) of the Refugees Convention and determined that a person convicted of conspiring to traffic in narcotics could not be excluded from the definition of a refugee on the ground that his conduct was contrary to the purposes and principles of the United Nations. In the course of articulating his general understanding of the Refugees Convention, Bastarache J cites its preamble to justify an interpretive gloss that it has a 'human rights character'.[47] More specifically, he notes the reference to the General Assembly having 'affirmed the principle that human beings shall enjoy fundamental rights and freedoms without discrimination'.[48] He identifies this phrase as providing the interpretive key that will unlock the puzzles of the Refugees Convention including those found in the exclusion clauses and in Article 33(2). He notes that while Article 33(2) identifies danger to the community as the reason for permitting a state to return a refugee to his country of origin, Article 1(F) makes no mention of such a concern. Bastarache J draws the inference that the exclusion clauses are not founded on a rationale of protecting the community from danger. The challenge is to identify what other values could justify governmental action that could lead indirectly to persecution, and to explain why these values outweigh the need to offer protection to the individual. Bastarache J concludes from the premise that the Refugees Convention promotes a human rights theme that the exclusion clauses apply only to human rights abusers.

There are a number of significant problems with this analysis. First, it ignores the standard account of the Refugees Convention, that regards it as expressing a compromise between concern for human rights and the concern of state parties that they maintain sovereignty over their borders. This is a view promoted by Hathaway, for example, who bases it on an

---

[46]　*Pushpanathan*, above n 7.

[47]　Id, p 1023.

[48]　Ibid.

examination of the historical record, and who, when discussing the meaning of the specific components of the definition, identifies those who are excluded as people who do not deserve protection.[49] In other words, the conventional account identifies the exclusion clauses as embodying values that can qualify the requirement that human rights be protected.

Second, the analysis is not internally consistent. As noted above, in obiter remarks, Bastarache J indicates that Article 1F(b) applies to exclude individuals who are extraditable. In other words, he suggests that a state's interest in trying an individual for serious crimes may outweigh an individual's interest in not being persecuted within that jurisdiction. He offers no account of why the 'human rights character' of the Convention does not inform the meaning of this part of the article. However, as noted above, this part of his judgement may not survive the decision in *Burns*.

Third, and most significant, the conclusion does not seem to follow from the premises. It seems odd to suggest that concern for human rights would allow human rights abusers to suffer persecution. To arrive at this conclusion, it would appear that one would have to rely on an instrumentalist interpretation – by permitting persecutors to face the possibility of persecution, one will deter them from engaging in acts of persecution. Such reliance on persecutors to ensure that this deterrence will have bite does not accord with the human rights tradition to which Bastarache J claims allegiance. Moreover, the idea that there will be less persecution if persecutors are permitted to persecute other persecutors, itself seems suspect.

These flaws in Bastarche J's judgment would be fatal were it not that another more subtle interpretation of his reasoning is possible. Although he does not articulate the idea explicitly, it is possible that he is attempting to express the idea that human rights abusers should not be granted refugee status, because to do so alters the nature of asylum that is offered to others who have fled persecution. A person who has fled persecution and has sought protection elsewhere has an interest in not sharing that sanctuary with his persecutors. While the former persecutor may no longer be dangerous, his presence in the protecting state alters the experience of the refugee. Bastarache J may have as his aim the protection of those who have already been or may one day be recognised as refugees from the psychological impact that could be produced by being required to live alongside one's persecutor, and thereby be condemned to re-live the fear of

---

[49] J Hathaway, *The Law of Refugee Status* (Sydney, Butterworths, 1991), p 217.

persecution. From this point of view, the conclusion that persecutors should be excluded from refugee status is quite consistent with the human rights character of the instrument. It is the human rights of other refugees, not the interest of the general community, that requires the conclusion.

This idea makes sense of the government's willingness to expand the class of refugees who do not have a right of no return beyond those identified in Article 33(2). The 'nature and severity' clause, that allows for the return of refugees who are not dangerous but who are believed to have committed egregious acts should be understood as requiring their return because their continued presence jeopardises the interests of others who have been offered protection.

Second, the idea makes sense of the government's willingness to read the exclusion clauses into the CAT. As long as the Refugees Convention is regarded as being based on a historical compromise, the government's attempt to read the exclusion clauses into the CAT appears suspect, particularly if those excluded are not in any way dangerous. The fact that historical compromises were made in 1951 does not, of course, entail that they were also made in 1987, or that they should continue to be made. However, once the interests of others who have been granted refuge are used as the explanation it makes sense to continue and expand the qualification. Being true to the principle of asylum requires that human rights abusers not be permitted to share the communal space.

Thus, it would appear that in *Pushpanathan*, rather than show itself as an antagonist to the government's aims, the Supreme Court has supplied a novel and defensible way to understand them.

Ineligibility and the Courts

As noted above, under current law, the salient ineligibility criteria focus on, first, the dangerousness of the claimant and second, the public interest in not having a claim determined. The former of these is quite logical in the face of a rule that permits those found to be refugees to be returned to their country of origin if they are found to be dangerous. There is no purpose in going through with a hearing to determine a person's status if the grant of the status to the individual will not provide any benefit whatsoever to this individual. Since the Refugees Convention (and Canadian law) permits the return of refugees considered dangerous, this criterion of eligibility appears to be justifiable by promoting efficiency without any negative impact on the claimant. This criterion of eligibility stands or falls alongside the rule permitting return which will be considered below.

However, the more sinister provision seems to bolster the instrumentalist critique, by implying that access to a hearing is not a matter of right but is subject to an assessment of public interest when an association with certain forms of serious criminality has been identified. Without any account being offered of the factors that would define the public interest, the importance of the claimant's interest in having a hearing is reduced by allowing an indeterminate number of factors to weigh against it. However, if this provision is regarded as anomalous and read strictly, it can be regarded as the expression of the limitation found in section 1 of the Charter of Rights: the individual's right to a hearing is limited when it is demonstrably justifiable to do so.

The provisions in Bill C-11 can also be read as giving insufficient weight to an individual's interest in a hearing. The interest does not, to use Ronald Dworkin's metaphor, appear to have any status as a trump over other interests.

The effect of the proposed amendments would be that a person who has the right not to be returned to his country of origin because he is a refugee, may be denied a hearing to determine whether this is the case merely because of his serious criminal acts. The individual's interest is apparently being weighed against society's interest in expressing disapproval of the criminal wrongdoing or in ensuring that only those who it is eventually willing to accept as immigrants have access to the process that could lead to the grant of permanent resident status. On the scales provided, the individual's interest comes up short.

Perhaps this is an uncharitable view of the proposal. A more generous reading of the ineligibility criteria is possible but it is equally problematic. It is possible to regard the criterion requiring avoidance of serious crime as a requirement for a token of good faith from the claimant rather than an expression of disapproval of the crime. Many similar tokens are required of refugee claimants. Time constraints are placed on their capacity to apply for a hearing. They are required to show respect for the process by showing up on the hearing date and are subject to severe sanction if they do not do so, including deemed abandonment of the claim. Similarly, the requirement that the claimant not commit a serious crime can be interpreted as a requirement that the claimant show respect for the social norms of the community that is offering protection. Such requirements do not deny that there is a right, they merely require that the claimant show respect for the processes and the basic social norms of the community. The argument is not that the claimant must approach with clean hands but rather that the claimant must make some (minimal) efforts to show respect for the community offering protection.

The difficulty with this approach is not that it expresses an instrumentalist stance but that it assumes wrongly in many cases that the ability to steer free of crime requires minimal effort. The government has recognised publicly that many people seeking protection are required to put themselves under the control of unscrupulous and ruthless smugglers who make unreasonable demands and who threaten the claimant and their families in their country of origin with violence unless serious crimes, such as drug trafficking, are perpetrated. To demand that the claimant be crime free is to fail to recognise the constraints under which many claimants operate. The demand that they avoid crime is not an appropriate demand if a show of good faith is what is required.

In the past, the government has been forced to defend its eligibility criteria before the Federal Court, and it has been successful in doing so. It has persuaded the court first, that the Refugees Convention does not require that a hearing before an independent tribunal be held. It merely requires, and this implicitly, that due process be accorded to an individual before he be returned to a country where he may face persecution.[50] Second, the government has persuaded the court that the Charter of Rights has not been engaged by the denial of a hearing before an independent tribunal. Since the rights to life, liberty and security of the person and the right not to be deprived thereof except in accordance with principles of fundamental justice are not put in jeopardy until a deportation order is being executed, these rights are not engaged by the failure to provide access to the Immigration and Refugee Board. They would be engaged at the point of execution, but at that stage the principles of fundamental justice would be met by the usual grant of consideration of an application for humanitarian and compassionate treatment.[51] Third, it has persuaded the Federal Court that reference to 'public interest' is not unconstitutionally vague.[52] Cumulatively these arguments reveal the belief that there is no obligation to provide a refugee claimant with a hearing before an

---

[50]   *Nguyen v Canada (Minister for Employment and Immigration)* [1993] 1 FC 696 (FCA).

[51]   Ibid.

[52]   *McAllister v Canada (Minister for Employment and Immigration)* [1996] 2 FC 190 (TD).

independent board. While the claimant has an interest in such a hearing, it is insufficiently weighty to ground an entitlement.

There is some evidence that the judiciary's views on the constitutional question may be shifting. In a recent extradition case, *United States of America v Cobb*,[53] the Supreme Court of Canada determined that the Charter of Rights did not become engaged only at the point when an extradition order was being executed. On the contrary, it held that a person's rights to life, liberty and security of the person, could be engaged at an earlier committal hearing where due process must be accorded. However, this case will probably not have an impact on the earlier cases decided by the Federal Court of Appeal. While it is true that there would be no need of due process if the right to security of person were not engaged, there is a difference between having an unfair hearing at an early stage of a process and having no hearing at all. Submitting a person to an unfair hearing may itself be a way of infringing their security of the person in a way that not providing a hearing is not.

State Protection and Political Morality

The discussion so far has presented both the federal government and the Supreme Court of Canada as attempting to cope with the paradoxes involved in granting state protection to individuals who are regarded as undesirable, who are regarded as dangerous, who are seen as a threat to state security and whose continued presence within a community may alter the nature of the sanctuary that is offered.

The discussion has focused on the issues of responsibility for returning individuals. It has not focused on measures taken by the government to prevent the arrival of refugee claimants whether desirable or not. Yet in recent years the government has been devoting more resources to achieve this end. The most notable example occurred in April 2000 when the Canadian Minister of Citizenship and Immigration, in response to the arrival in Canada of four barely seaworthy vessels from China carrying about 600 individuals, visited the country of origin in order (in her own words) 'to seek cooperation with my Chinese counterparts ... to prevent

---

[53] *United States of America v Cobb* (2001) SCJ #20, SCC file #27610.

human trafficking operations in the future'.[54] She placed the visit in context by stating:

> Canada has assumed a leading role in working with other nations to develop a United Nations Convention to Combat Transnational Organised Crime, and a related protocol on migrant smuggling.[55]

While the conditions on the boats were quite horrendous and while there is well-documented evidence of the harsh treatment suffered by the victim of smugglers and human traffickers, the visit to China and anti-smuggling proposals can be interpreted as a crass attempt to relieve the pressure – both political and social – created by the unheralded arrival of large numbers of refugee claimants.

The proposals do not distinguish between those who are engaged in the trade of assisting migrants and those who are engaged in the dangerous task of aiding flight from persecution. The distinction does not appear to be significant to the government. Thus it is reasonable to draw the inference that the measures are really about reducing the number of arrivals, rather than being about curtailing ill-treatment. I do not mean to suggest that it is easy to distinguish between the mercenary trafficker and the altruistic smuggler, although one can imagine a due diligence defence being made available. However, I suggest that the government's inability to take responsibility for the international consequences of its acts can lead to unacceptable results.

The idea that the most successful solution to the problem of a large influx of refugee claimants is to staunch the flow from the country of origin is not novel. In the past the arrival of large numbers of claimants, who are believed to be abusing the refugee determination process, has frequently spurred the government to impose visa restrictions on the country of origin. Some governments have gone further. Indeed, the Minister's predecessor, in response to a large number of Roma refugee claimants from the Czech Republic placed visa restrictions on people from that country. In that instance, the Minister appeared to be motivated not by the number of false claims but because the Immigration and Refugee Board accepted an overwhelming number of the claims that had been made and the decisions

---

[54]　Speech to the Canada China Business Council, Beijing, 25 April 2000.

[55]　Ibid. See also A Kirchner and L Schiano di Pepe, 'International Attempts to Conclude a Convention to Combat Illegal Migration', *International Journal of Refugee Law* **10** (1998) p 662.

seemed to be premised on the unequivocal documentary evidence relating to the situation of Roma in that country. The decision seemed to be based on the perceived potential of false claimants being attracted by the magnet provided by the number of successful claims. The decision to seek assistance from the Chinese authorities seems to fit in line with these earlier examples. The visit indicates a willingness to jeopardise the wellbeing of some individuals in the interests of reducing some of the negative externalities associated with the refugee determination process.

However, the visit to China was unique in one way. China is a refugee producing country and the authorities from whom the Minister was seeking cooperation are the same authorities whose conduct has induced many people to flee. While ultimately the independent Immigration and Refugee Board recognised only a small number of the boat arrivals to be Convention refugees, these arrivals accounted for only a small fraction of the refugee claims from China made during the same year. Credible information about official persecution and torture in China has been, and continues to be, accepted by the Board. In fact, the majority of claims from that country have been accepted in recent years.[56] Nevertheless, without any apparent sense of irony, the Minister displayed willingness to collaborate with the authorities from China to prevent people from leaving.

Clearly, the Minister does not conceive of herself as a collaborator in human rights violations, yet she must have realised that, had her visit proved successful, and had smuggling operations been closed down, the end result would be that a large number of individuals would have no means available to escape foreseeable persecution and ill-treatment. Indeed, even by putting a dent in the operations, as she appears to have done, it is foreseeable that she may have caused, albeit indirectly, some individuals to suffer severe costs. It would appear that from the Minister's point of view the activities of the smugglers are of more concern than that of the authorities. Her concept of complicity is apparently insufficiently broad to render her responsible for any of the ensuing foreseeable persecution. In this regard she can muster support from the decision of the Supreme Court of Canada, noted earlier, identifying that section 12 of the Charter of Rights is not engaged by a decision to return claimants. However, there is a major difference and that is that the Minister's acts are extra-territorial in nature. Of course, she is, realistically speaking, immune from constitutional

---

[56] Exact statistics are available from the Immigration and Refugee Board, http://www.irb.gc.ca/index_e.stm.

challenge since it is highly unlikely that a plaintiff could be found. Yet, her acts pose as great a challenge to the human rights tradition as the attempts to qualify or modify the CAT.

Postscript

Since this chapter was written, the Supreme Court of Canada reached decisions in the cases of *Ahani v Canada (Minister of Citizenship and Immigration)*,[57] and *Suresh v Canada (Minister of Citizenship and Immigration)*.[58] It explicitly adopted the approach articulated in *Burns* and held that only in exceptional circumstances could a person be returned to a country where he or she faced a risk of torture. It did not articulate the nature of these circumstances. Further, it held that International Law as found in the CAT absolutely proscribed the return of individuals to face torture.

However, the court also stated that it would show great deference to the Minister's decision relating to whether there was a risk of torture and whether the individual in question posed a security risk to Canada. Suresh's appeal was successful because of a perceived procedural irregularity. Ahani lost his appeal on the ground that the court accepted the Minister's decision that he had provided insufficient evidence that he faced a risk of torture. Ahani's lawyer has taken further measures to prevent his deportation.

---

[57] [2002] SCC 2; (2000) 73 CRR (2d) 156.

[58] [2002] SCC 1. Both cases can be found on the Supreme Court's website: http://www.lexum.umontreal.ca/csc-scc/en/index.html.

6   Safe for Whom? The Safe Third Country Concept Finds a Home in Australia

PENELOPE MATHEW*

Introduction

Their plans were to exploit the limitations of our current laws.

The 'mother ship' was to wait in international waters. Accomplices ... were to travel out to the vessel in high-powered ocean-going speed boats that had been specifically purchased for this purpose.

Those accomplices were to ferry the passengers [here] under cover of darkness.

The mother ship, relieved of its human cargo, would then sail back ... without being detected or arrested.[1]

The passage above may sound like a scene from the American sci-fi TV series Star Trek. In fact, it's an extract from the second reading speech for the Border Protection Legislation Amendment Act (Cth) 1999 (the Act). Passed by the Australian Parliament on 8 December 1999, this Act amended the Migration Act (Cth) 1958 along with customs and fisheries legislation. The Act sought to enable the extra-territorial enforcement of Australian law in order to deal better with illegal entry into Australia,

---

* This chapter draws on a submission to the United Nations High Commissioner for Refugees (UNHCR) written by the author on behalf of the Jesuit Refugee Service and a paper delivered to the 7th International Research and Advisory Panel of the International Association for the Study of Forced Migration, Johannesburg, 2001. The author extends her thanks to Liz Biok and Simon Jeans, NSW Legal Aid, for supplying information about the case RRT N00/31751 (30 June 2000) (see below n 127 and accompanying text), and to Ellen Hansen, UNHCR, and Carolyn Graydon for their insights. I am also grateful for the perceptive editorial suggestions made by Susan Kneebone. The views expressed in the chapter, and any errors, are the author's.

[1] Border Protection Legislation Amendment Bill, Second Reading Speech, Parliament of Australia, Hansard, House of Representatives, 22 September 1999, p 10147.

giving Australian officials new powers of chase, search and arrest in various maritime sectors, including the high seas.[2] The Act also contains a series of amendments entitled 'amendments to prevent forum-shopping' which introduced a comprehensive notion of 'safe third countries' into Australian legislation for the first time.[3]

The limits of the law were tested in the *Tampa* crisis.[4] Indeed, the legislative reaction to the *Tampa* tends to show that the concept of safe third countries as implemented by the Border Protection Legislation Amendment Act is perceived as a failure even by the Australian government. The *MV Tampa* was a Norwegian freighter that rescued a

---

[2] Migration Act 1958 (Cth) (Migration Act), sections 245A–245H.

[3] The courts introduced a variant of the safe third country concept into the case law in *Minister for Immigration and Multicultural Affairs (MIMA) v Thiyagarajah* (1997–1998) 80 FCR 543. Thiyagarajah had been recognised as a refugee in another country and the Federal Court of Australia determined that Australia did not owe such a person protection obligations under the Refugees Convention. Since then the courts have extended the concept: see 'The Extent of Australia's Protection Obligations' below; J Hunyor, '*Warra Warra*: Refugees and Protection Obligations in Relaxed and Comfortable Australia', *Alternative Law Journal* **25** (2000) p 227 at p 228. In addition to developments in the common law there had been piecemeal legislative amendments introducing the concepts of safe third country and first asylum in relation to particular categories of asylum seekers. Sino-Vietnamese asylum seekers fleeing the Bei Hai region of the People's Republic of China were precluded from refugee status in Australia by virtue of section 91G of the Migration Act. The readmission agreement with China has recently been renewed: P Ruddock, 'Australia Renews Agreement with People's Republic of China on Returning Illegal Arrivals', Media Release MPS 051/2000, 15 May 2000, http://www.minister.immi.gov.au/media_releases/media00/r00051.htm. Asylum seekers passing through countries participating in the Comprehensive Plan of Action for Indo-Chinese refugees were similarly precluded by sections 91A–91F of the Migration Act. For analysis, see S Taylor, 'Australia's "safe third country" provisions: their impact on Australia's fulfilment of its *non-refoulement* obligations', *University of Tasmania Law Review* **15** (1996) p 196; N Poynder, 'Australia's Recent Implementation of the Refugees Convention and the Law of Accommodations under International Treaties; Have We Gone Too Far?' *Australian Journal of Human Rights* **2** (1995) p 75.

[4] It is unclear whether the executive relied upon the relevant provisions of the Border Protection Legislation Amendment Act, in particular section 245F, in its efforts to eject the *Tampa*. When the executive's actions were challenged in the Federal Court, an argument to the effect that section 245F required asylum seekers on board the *Tampa* to be brought to Australia failed because it was not clear that the section had been relied on and the requirements for standing were not fulfilled: *Victorian Council for Civil Liberties Incorporated v MIMA* [2001] 182 ALR 619, paras [146]–[150]. The argument was not pursued on appeal to the Full Court of the Federal Court.

boatload of asylum seekers and brought them into Australian waters after the captain decided some of the asylum seekers needed medical attention. The Australian government took the view that the coastal state (Australia) was not responsible for the asylum seekers and refused to let them disembark, even for the purposes of temporary refuge.[5] In the wake of the *Tampa*, the government decided to amend the law again, as it now wished not simply to enforce Australian law extra-territorially and to send asylum seekers back to 'safe third countries', but to keep asylum seekers from arriving in Australia in the first place. After one failed attempt to introduce legislation, the September 11 terrorist attacks on New York and Washington DC secured political support for the suggested changes and parliament passed the Border Protection (Validation and Enforcement Powers) Act 2001 (Cth) in order to ensure that boats headed for Australian shores could be interdicted and ejected from Australian waters,[6] rather than simply chased and boarded.[7] Legislation also excised certain Australian territories from the national 'migration zone',[8] thereby creating a legal fiction whereby persons who entered these territories would not be able to apply for refugee status under the usual Australian refugee status determination procedures.[9] Instead, they may be taken to 'safe third

---

[5] On a number of occasions, the UNHCR has called on coastal states to permit disembarkation at least for the purposes of temporary refuge: see particularly, Executive Committee of the High Commissioner's Programme (Ex Com) Conclusion 23, 'Problems Related to the Rescue of Asylum-Seekers in Distress at Sea', para 3, http://www.unhcr.ch, and Ex Com, Sub-Committee of the Whole on International Protection, *Problems Related to the Rescue of Asylum-seekers in Distress at Sea* (EC/SCP/18, 26 August 1981).

[6] See particularly, Migration Act, sections 7A, 245F(8) and (9).

[7] See above n 2, and accompanying text.

[8] Section 5(1) of the Migration Act, as amended by the Migration Amendment (Excision from the Migration Zone) Act 2001 (Cth), contains a list of 'excised offshore places' which include Christmas Island, Ashmore and Cartier Islands and the Cocos (Keeling) Islands.

[9] Under section 5(1) of the Migration Act people who would be 'unlawful non citizens' if they entered the migration zone and who enter 'excised offshore places' become 'offshore entry persons'. Section 46A of the Migration Act bars 'offshore entry persons' from applying for protection visas (the usual route by which Australia observes its obligations towards refugees) unless the Minister for Immigration exercises a non-compellable discretion on their behalf.

countries' for processing.[10] These 'safe third countries' have agreed only to act as offshore processing centres rather than to accept asylum seekers and accordingly are not the focus of this chapter, although the provisions are very similar to those introduced by the Border Protection Legislation Amendment Act and therefore raise similar questions as to their legality as a matter of international law. A safe third country is supposed to be one in which an asylum seeker either has received or may receive protection consistent with the 1951 Convention relating to the Status of Refugees (the Refugees Convention). However, as this chapter demonstrates, the concept of a safe third country diminishes the protection available under the Refugees Convention.

The long-arm approach to the law reflected in both the Border Protection Legislation Amendment Act and the package of legislation introduced post *Tampa* is a reaction to and rejection of globalisation in the form of refugees and the international law that seeks to regulate their treatment. The legislation aims to protect Australian sovereignty through the unilateral extension of Australia's jurisdiction. The post *Tampa* amendments permit removal of boats from Australian shores,[11] which raises the possibility of refoulement contrary to the Refugees Convention. Both the practices of interdiction and the concept of a safe third country attempt to push the responsibility for refugees back to developing countries close to the source of refugee flows. The Border Protection Legislation Amendment Act also demonises asylum seekers as persons seeking a particular 'migration outcome' rather than protection as refugees. In the year of the 50th anniversary of the Convention, Australia, which has just celebrated its 100th birthday as a federation, has undermined the Convention because of the same fears concerning immigration that prevailed at the time of, and helped to fuel the movement for the federation of the colonies that became Australia.[12] Even the imagery used in the second-reading speech for the

---

[10] See Migration Act, section 198A, inserted by the Migration Amendment (Excision from the Migration Zone) (Consequential Amendments) Act 2001 (Cth).

[11] See Migration Act, sections 7A, 245F(8) and (9). These powers have already been used to return boats to Indonesian waters: P Ruddock, 'Suspected Illegals Turned Back', Media Release MPS 193/2001, 21 December 2001,
http://www.minister.immi.gov.au/media_releases/media01/r01193.htm; I Henderson, 'Navy Tows Away Asylum seekers', *The Weekend Australian*, 20–1 October 2001, p 5.

[12] See M Crock, *Immigration and Refugee Law in Australia* (Sydney, Federation Press, 1998), pp 11–15.

Border Protection Legislation Amendment Act – that of a feminised alien spawning illegal immigrants into Australia – is similar to the racialised imagery of 'Asian hordes' prevailing at the turn of the last century.[13] This chapter will show that just as the isolationism of that period proved unworkable, the concept of a safe third country as a buffer to Australia's immigration system is likewise untenable.

Massive Increases in Illegal Immigration? A Critical Examination of the Statistics

The rationale for the safe third country provisions in the Border Protection Legislation Amendment Act is evident from the reference to 'forum-shopping'. Although introduced late in the legislative history of the Border Protection Legislation Amendment Bill, just days before it was passed, these provisions had been on the government's agenda for some time.[14] As far as the government was concerned, all aspects of the legislation were important to the achievement of its key aim, being to 'respond to a massive increase in the numbers of attempts at illegal entry into Australia'.[15]

It is worth establishing whether there was a 'massive' increase in the number of attempts to enter Australia illegally, and what reasons there might be for the increase. The Minister's statistical analysis was limited to the following statement:

---

[13] On the fear of Asian immigration generally, see D McMaster, *Asylum Seekers: Australia's Response to Refugees* (Melbourne, Melbourne University Press, 2001).

[14] P Ruddock 'Ruddock Announces Tough New Initiatives', Media Release MPS 143/1999, 13 October 1999, http://www.minister.immi.gov.au/media_releases/media99/r99143.htm. One can only speculate as to whether the late addition of these provisions to a Bill that had already been before parliament for some time and had gone through the second-reading stage was a deliberate strategy to keep those provisions under wraps until the last minute, thus avoiding scrutiny by non-government organisations and public debate in the media.

[15] Border Protection Legislation Amendment Bill, Second Reading Speech, above n 1. In a fact sheet on people smuggling, 'stopping people who have effective protection overseas from gaining onshore protection in Australia' is listed as an initiative to combat people smuggling: Department of Immigration and Multicultural and Indigenous Affairs (DIMIA) Fact Sheet 73, *People Smuggling* (Canberra, DIMIA, 16 November 2001), http://www.immi.gov.au/facts/73smuggling.htm.

We have seen a dramatic increase in the number of people from Iraq and Afghanistan who are arriving illegally by boat. Of the 378 people who arrived by boat in July and August this year, 262 were from Iraq and 71 from Afghanistan. That is more than twice the number of Iraqis that arrived in the full financial year 1998–99.

According to the Minister:

[o]ne of the factors behind this dramatic increase may be the perception that past illegal arrivals from those countries had been successful in engaging Australia's protection obligations.

A more plausible reason for the increase is the simple fact that, worldwide, claims by Iraqis and Afghans were extremely high during the relevant period. The United Nations High Commissioner for Refugees (UNHCR) statistical analysis of asylum applications in Europe up to July 2000 lists Iraq as the second most common country of origin for asylum applications behind the Federal Republic of Yugoslavia, accounting for 9 per cent of all new applications.[16] Afghanistan was fourth on the list, accounting for 6.8 per cent of all new applications.[17] During 1999, the period to which the Minister referred, UNHCR's statistical overview showed that Iraq and Afghanistan respectively generated the second and third largest number of asylum applications worldwide, behind Yugoslavia.[18] During the year 2000, Afghanistan generated the largest refugee population while Iraq was third,[19] and for the industrialised countries during January–April 2001, Iraq generated the highest number of asylum claims and Afghanistan the second highest number of claims.[20]

---

[16]   UNHCR, *Asylum Applications in Europe January – July 2000* (Geneva, UNHCR, 15 September 2000), http://www.unhcr.ch/cgi-bin/texis/vtx/home/opendoc.pdf?tbl=MEDIA&id=3b9378e3a&page=PUBL, p 1.

[17]   Ibid.

[18]   UNHCR, 'Asylum Applications and Refugee Status Determinations by Origin' in UNHCR, *Refugees and Others of Concern to UNHCR, 1999 Statistical Overview* (Geneva, UNHCR, July 2000), http://www.unhcr.ch/cgi-bin/texis/vtx/home/opendoc.pdf?tbl=MEDIA&id=3ae6bc834&page=PUBL, table IV.2.

[19]   UNHCR, *Refugees by Numbers 2001 Edition* (Geneva, UNHCR, 2001), http://www.unhcr.ch, p 4.

[20]   UNHCR, *Asylum Applications Lodged in 27 Industrialised Countries, January – April 2001*, (Geneva, UNHCR, 2001), http://www.unhcr.ch/cgi-bin/texis/vtx/home/opendoc.pdf?tbl=MEDIA&id=3b9378e43&page=PUBL, p 1.

Australia is not even mentioned in UNHCR's table relating to asylum applications and refugee status determination by origin and country/territory of asylum for 1999, whether in relation to Iraq, Afghanistan or any other country. Provisional figures for January–November 2001 show that Australia received 1958 Afghan asylum seekers, while the similar-sized Netherlands received 3328.[21] The Australian figures pale into insignificance when compared with countries such as Pakistan through which many Afghan asylum seekers in Australia first transited. UNHCR put the Pakistani figures of '*prima facie* refugee arrivals' from Afghanistan for the relevant period at 92 700,[22] and it is now estimated that around 2.6 million Afghans have fled to Pakistan since 1989. One of the questions we should ask here is whether Australia should be able to tell Pakistan that it must take responsibility for Afghan asylum seekers simply because of geographical proximity.

This is an especially pertinent question, when, relative to the numbers of asylum seekers received by other countries, Australia's intake is small. The Refugee Council of Australia (RCOA), the peak non-governmental representative body in the field of refugee advocacy and support groups, has prepared a statistical picture of Australia's total humanitarian intake over a ten year period.[23] The table compares the figures for Australia, Canada, Denmark, Sweden and the UK. Canada, Denmark and Sweden have similar population sizes to Australia and all four countries have similar political, social and cultural characteristics. In relation to Australia, the table shows a very small shaded area for asylum seekers (signifying less than 10 000 persons) although it has a reasonably generous shaded area for resettled refugees (signifying over 100 000 persons) and persons of humanitarian concern.

---

[21] UNHCR, *Asylum Applications Lodged in Europe, North America, Australia and New Zealand, January – November 2001* (Geneva, UNHCR, 2001), http://www.unhcr.ch/cgi-bin/texis/vtx/home/opendoc.pdf?tbl=MEDIA&id=3c2702d47&page=PUBL, p 3. The figures in relation to Iraqi asylum seekers are similar, with Australia receiving 16 more applications than the Netherlands.

[22] See UNHCR, 'Prima Facie Refugee Arrivals by origin and Country/Territory of Asylum, 1998 and 1999' in UNHCR, *Refugees and Others of Concern to UNHCR, 1999 Statistical Overview*, above n 18, table II.3.

[23] This includes resettlement of refugees and others of concern from abroad and acceptance of asylum seekers who make claims for protection after arrival in Australia: Refugee Council of Australia, http://www.refugeecouncil.org.au/ngraph1.htm.

RCOA has also created a picture of the figures with respect to arrival of asylum seekers (as opposed to persons receiving protection) between 1989 and 1997.[24] Again, the comparison does not show that Australia is overburdened by arrivals and Sweden and Canada have consistently higher numbers of applications. More recent figures available from UNHCR show a similar picture.[25] Most telling, perhaps, is a graph prepared by UNHCR relating to Asylum Applications submitted in Europe, North America, Australia and New Zealand 1980–2000, which shows that even combining Australia and New Zealand, the number of applications received in those countries is both low and relatively flat.[26] Furthermore, although the early figures for 2001 do show an increase in the number of asylum seekers in Australia,[27] it is sobering to compare Australia's total notional humanitarian intake of around 12 000 (the actual intake has been smaller in recent years) with the increases in new arrivals of refugees over the period of January–September 2001 in the Democratic Republic of Congo (48 600); Zambia (27 400); the United Republic of Tanzania (22 800); and Ethiopia (13 600).[28] None of these countries are as well equipped to deal with arrivals of refugees and asylum seekers as Australia.

The position with respect to illegal arrivals is unlikely to be much different to that in relation to intake of refugees and arrival of asylum seekers. The number of apprehended unlawful arrivals in Australia is very small.[29] The problem of visa overstayers is much larger. The total number

---

[24]   Ibid.

[25]   In 1999 Canada had 30 100 applications; Sweden had 11 200. Tiny Switzerland had 46 100 applications. See annex 9, 'Asylum Applications and Refugee Admissions to Industrial States 1990–99', in UNHCR, *The State of the World's Refugees: Fifty Years of Humanitarian Action* (Geneva, UNHCR, 2000). In 2000, the number of asylum applications in Australia was still relatively small at 19 400: UNHCR, *Refugees by Numbers 2001*, above n 19, p 8. Switzerland's figure dropped sharply to 17 610, but Canada's figure increased to 34 250. The Netherlands' figure was 43 900.

[26]   UNHCR, *The State of the World's Refugees*, id, figure 7.1.

[27]   UNHCR *Asylum Applications Lodged in 27 Industrialised Countries*, above n 20, p 1.

[28]   UNHCR, *Global Refugee Trends: January – September 2001* (Geneva, UNHCR, 14 December 2001), http://www.unhcr.ch/cgi-bin/texis/vtx/home/opendoc.pdf?tbl=MEDIA&id=3c1f22417&page=PUBL, p 2.

[29]   In the period 1 July 2000 to 31 June 2001 there were 1508 unlawful air arrivals and 4141 unlawful arrivals by boat in Australia: DIMIA Fact Sheet 70, *Border Control* (Canberra, DIMIA, 19 November 2001), http://www.immi.gov.au/facts/70border.htm.

of overstayers in Australia is currently estimated to be around 53 000.[30] The author is not aware of any figures for the estimated yearly growth in the illegal immigrant population in Australia, however it is doubtful whether the figures would compare with the estimated growth for the United States (US) of 275 000 each year,[31] or for western Europe which is thought to rival the US figure.[32] The estimated growth in the illegal population in Australia for 1998–99 was 20 000.[33] That suggests Australia experiences a similar yearly increase in illegal population relative to the existing population as experienced by the US. However, even if calculated on a per capita basis relative to the existing Australian population, it may reasonably be expected that Australia would generally receive fewer illegal immigrants each year than the US or western Europe. A look at where the illegal immigrants are coming from gives one a clue as to why Australia might expect fewer illegal immigrants than other countries. Just over half the illegal immigrant population in the US, for example, is from Mexico[34] – a country with which the US shares a land border.

The real rationale for the Border Protection Legislation Amendment Act must be the perception that since other countries have measures in place which attempt to limit the number of asylum seekers, Australia will be seen as a soft touch if it does not follow suit. In addition, or alternatively, there may be a perception that any onshore claims for refugee status, particularly by unauthorised arrivals, are problematic. Both themes are evident in the current governmental rhetoric about asylum seekers. Recently, the Minister stated that places in the offshore humanitarian program had been 'stolen' by onshore claimants for refugee status.[35] This statement reflects a long-standing governmental view that onshore claimants are illegitimate recipients of Australia's protection. That attitude is evidenced by measures

---

[30] A Millbank, 'Boat People, Illegal Migration and Asylum Seekers: In Perspective', *Current Issues Brief* 13 (14 December 1999), http://www.aph.gov.au/library/pubs/CIB/1999-2000/2000cib13.htm.

[31] Immigration and Naturalization Service (INS), *Triennial Comprehensive Report on Immigration* (Washington, INS, 1996), http://www.ins.usdoj.gov/graphics/aboutins/repsstudies/addition.htm, p 58.

[32] Millbank, above n 30.

[33] Millbank, ibid.

[34] INS, above n 31, p 57.

[35] M Saunders, 'Court System Too Generous to Boat People, says Ruddock', *The Australian*, 26 April 2001, p 5.

such as the introduction of temporary protection visas for unauthorised arrivals[36] and the new rolling temporary visa regime for unauthorised arrivals in the 'excised' Australian territories of Christmas Island, Ashmore and Cartier Islands and the Cocos (Keeling Islands).[37] As for being a soft touch, the Minister expressly voiced that very fear in the second reading speech for the Border Protection Legislation Amendment Act:

> [I]f we are not at the forefront in dealing with these issues through legislation of the sort that I am proposing, and other measures, we will be seen as a more attractive destination to the people smugglers who are arranging this sort of trafficking.[38]

Dubious 'Convention' Categories: 'Safe Third Countries' and 'Forum-Shopping'

Rather than being at the forefront, Australia is in fact copying measures adopted by Europe and in some other western countries.[39] The concept of safe third countries, also known as 'protection elsewhere', has received increasing acceptance in state practice over the last 15 years.

The leading example of state practice is that of the member states of the European Union. The original European arrangements regarding the state responsible for determining claims to refugee status were contained in the Convention Applying the Schengen Agreement of 14 June 1985 between the Governments of the States of the Benelux Economic Union, the Federal Republic of Germany and the French Republic, on the Gradual Abolition of

---

[36]   See Migration Amendment Regulations 1999 (No 12) (Cth).

[37]   Unless the bar on visa applications in section 46A is lifted by the Minister for Immigration, 'offshore entry persons' removed to safe third countries under section 198A are eligible to a series of rolling temporary visas: see Migration Regulations 1994 (Cth), schedule 2, Part 447.

[38]   Border Protection Legislation Amendment Bill, Second Reading Speech, above n 1.

[39]   An example of the application of the principle of safe third countries outside Europe is the Canadian Immigration and Refugee Act 2001, section 102, by which regulations may prescribe safe third countries to which applicants for refugee status may be returned. No list of countries was adopted under the equivalent provisions in the former Immigration Act: M Young and J Sinha, (Law and Government Division), *Bill C-11: The Immigration and Refugee Protection Act*, (Canada, revised 13 June 2001), http://www.parl.gc.ca/common/bills_ls.asp?lang+E&ls=c11&source=library_prb&Parl= 37&Ses=1, n 36 and accompanying text.

Checks at their Common Borders of 1990 (the Schengen Convention).[40] Chapter 7 of the Schengen Convention dealt with responsibility for processing applications for asylum. This chapter has since been replaced by the Convention Determining the State Responsible for Examining Applications for Asylum Lodged in One of the Member States of the European Communities (the Dublin Convention)[41] which was signed five days after the Schengen Convention and came into force in 1997. Responsibility generally rests either upon the issuance of a visa or residence permit, or the fact of an asylum seeker's first entry to the EU being to a particular state's territory.[42] The Dublin Convention provides for contracting parties to opt out of its provisions, taking responsibility for an asylum seeker even when another country would be responsible under the Dublin Convention,[43] and to take into account humanitarian grounds concerning family or cultural factors.[44] The Dublin Convention also gives priority to the principle of family unity, or at least, a limited conception of that principle. Article 4 provides that if an applicant for asylum has a spouse, an unmarried child under the age of 18 or – if the applicant is an unmarried minor – a parent legally resident in the territory of a state party, and that family member has been recognised as a refugee, that state will be the responsible state. Of great concern is the fact that it is possible for a state party to return the asylum seeker to a third country (that is, a non EU member).[45]

Whether this development should be viewed as a permissible interpretation of the Refugees Convention is controversial.[46] On the one

---

[40] Convention Applying the Schengen Agreement of June 14, 1985 between the Governments of the States of the Benelux Economic Union, the Federal Republic of Germany and the French Republic, on the Gradual Abolition of Checks at their Common Borders, June 19, 1990, 30 ILM 84 (1991) (Schengen Convention).

[41] Convention Determining the State Responsible for Examining Applications for Asylum Lodged in One of the Member States of the European Communities, 15 June 1990, 30 ILM 425 (1991) (Dublin Convention).

[42] Dublin Convention, Articles 5 and 6; see also Schengen Convention, Article 30.

[43] Dublin Convention, Article 3(4); see also Schengen Convention, Article 29(4).

[44] Dublin Convention, Article 9; see also Schengen Convention, Article 36.

[45] Dublin Convention, Article 3(5); see also Schengen Convention, Article 29(2).

[46] N A Abell, 'The Compatibility of Readmission Agreements with the 1951 Convention Relating to the Status of Refugees' *International Journal of Refugee Law* 11 (1999) p 60 at p 68.

hand, it may be argued that the Refugees Convention does not guarantee a right of entry to particular states, only the right of non-refoulement. Consequently, all that matters is that one country takes responsibility for a particular refugee. Indeed, the Refugees Convention is often said to exist only for those who have nowhere else to go. The second paragraph of the definition of a refugee excludes persons with multiple nationalities from refugee status unless they have a well-founded fear of persecution in both countries.[47] Similarly, Article 1E excludes from refugee status persons who are:

> recognised by the competent authorities of the country in which [they have] taken residence as having the rights and obligations which are attached to the possession of the nationality of that country.

Refugee status also ceases where the person has acquired a new nationality and he or she 'enjoys the protection of the country of his [or her] new nationality'. Why not extend this idea and ask a preliminary question as to which state should bear responsibility for determining a person's claim to refugee status in the first place? Arguably, the Refugees Convention does not outlaw the concept of safe third countries *per se*.

It is also arguable that there is some express textual basis for the safe third country concept in relation to unauthorised entrants. Article 31 of the Refugees Convention provides that penalties shall not be imposed for illegal entry on refugees '*coming directly* from a territory where their life or freedom was threatened ...' Article 31 goes on to state that restrictions on the movement of such refugees shall only be applied if necessary and 'until their status in the country is regularised *or they obtain admission into another country*' (emphasis supplied). This appears to envisage the possibility of safe third countries for unauthorised asylum seekers, although the matter of finding such a country appears to be at the initiative of the asylum seeker and the third country. As Article 31 puts it:

> [t]he Contracting States shall allow such refugees a reasonable period and all the necessary facilities to obtain admission into another country.

There are policy considerations in favour of the notion of safe third countries, too. Cooperative arrangements between states to accept responsibility as 'countries of first asylum' or 'safe third countries' could,

---

[47] See Refugees Convention, Article 1A(2), second paragraph.

in theory, provide a mechanism for responsibility sharing among potential countries of refuge.[48]

On the other hand, what matters is whether any country does take responsibility for a particular refugee *in practice*.[49] Both direct and indirect refoulement are prohibited by Article 33 of the Refugees Convention.[50] Yet, there is evidence that in practice the adoption of the safe third country notion has resulted in refoulement and refugees in orbit.[51] (This evidence is often anecdotal given the difficulties of monitoring deportations which may occur at the border in circumstances where the asylum seeker has no contact with the outside world or even with higher immigration authorities.) Unilateral adoption of the concept of safe third countries as with Australia's legislative provisions raises the distinct possibility that countries nominated as 'safe' will not *in fact* accept responsibility for asylum seekers. There may be some consonance between Article 1E and

---

[48]   Germany has been particularly interested in the Dublin Convention system because it has been the European country receiving the highest numbers of asylum seekers in recent years. For a debate concerning the merits of a 'common but differentiated' responsibility for refugees, whereby developed countries pay for the burden imposed on southern states on the basis that those states continue to shelter most of the world's refugees, and indeed increase the numbers they shelter, see J Hathaway and A Neve, 'Making International Refugee Law Relevant Again: a Proposal for Collectivized and Solution-Oriented Protection', *Harvard Human Rights Journal* 10 (1997) p 115 (pro) and D Anker, J Fitzpatrick, A Shacknove, 'Crisis and Cure: a Reply to Hathaway/Neve and Schuck', *Harvard Human Rights Journal* 11 (1998) p 295.

[49]   As Agnes Hurwitz writes in her assessment of the Dublin Convention:

[t]he fundamental issue ... is not the incompatibility *per se* of the Dublin Convention with the [Refugee] Convention, but rather the potential indirect breach of the *non-refoulement* obligations in each case of transfer of an applicant for asylum to the responsible State. Any application of the Dublin Convention which would lead to violating or even to 'avoiding' the obligation of *non-refoulement* constitutes a violation of good faith in the performance of treaty obligations.

A Hurwitz, 'The 1990 Dublin Convention: a Comprehensive Assessment', *International Journal of Refugee Law* 11 (1999) p 646 at p 676.

[50]   See J Crawford and P Hyndman, 'Three Heresies in the Application of the Refugees Convention', *International Journal of Refugee Law* 1 (1989) p 155 at p 171.

[51]   See, R Dunstan, 'Playing Human Pinball: The Amnesty International United Kingdom Section Report on UK Home Office "Safe Third Country' Practice"', *International Journal of Refugee Law* 7 (1995) p 648; European Council on Refugees and Exiles, *Safe Third Countries: Myths and Realities* (London, ECRE, 1995), http://www.ecre.org/positions/safe.html, summary.

the protection that should be offered by a safe third country.[52] Article 1E recognises that a national or person assimilated to a national has an enforceable right to enter a particular country and it is clearly important that there be some right of entry in relation to a safe third country. In the absence of such a right of entry, there is the risk of refoulement, or, at the very least, refugees in orbit, if Australia goes ahead with returns to so-called safe third countries. Alternatively, it may be impossible to fully implement the legislation.

Furthermore, the idea that the safe third country notion is a mechanism for responsibility sharing is questionable. In the context of the European Union, the argument that Germany should not have to take in refugees who have first been to France may have merit. As mentioned, however, it is highly questionable whether a state like Australia should be able to send Afghan refugees back to Pakistan. The adoption of the safe third country notion by Australia inverts and misuses the idea of responsibility sharing. Developing countries that are geographically proximate to refugee flows are forced to continue to host refugees.[53]

As for the textual basis of the safe third country notion, Byrne and Shacknove have argued that the wording of Article 31 of the Convention relating to illegal entrants should not distract from the primary function of that article. The primary function of Article 31 is to protect against penalties rather than to permit returns to 'safe' third countries.[54] Furthermore, a proposal to amend Article 31 so that it provided immunity

---

[52] See, for example, the statement to this effect by Carr J in *Applicant C v MIMA* [2001] FCA 229 (12 March 2001), para 28.

[53] For a general critique of the notion of burden-sharing in Europe along these lines, see R Byrne and A Shacknove, 'The Safe Third Country Notion in European Asylum Law', *Harvard Human Rights Journal* 9 (1996) p 185 at p 215. According to Byrne and Shacknove:

> [t]he return of asylum seekers to reputed safe countries of asylum stresses the random geographic proximity of host States to the country of origin, runs counter to the intended universal scope of the Refugees Convention and Protocol, and undermines the principle of burden-sharing.

Professor Hathaway makes a similar point: J Hathaway, *The Law of Refugee Status*, (Toronto, Butterworths, 1991), at p 47 citing D Hull, 'Displaced Persons: the New Refugees', *Georgia Journal of International and Comparative Law* 13 (1983) p 755. But see his views on a 'common but differentiated' responsibility between developing and developed states: Hathaway and Neve, above n 48.

[54] See Byrne and Shacknove, above n 53, p 190.

from penalties only to refugees who were able to prove they were unable to find even temporary asylum in another country was dropped.[55] Apart from the dual nationality clause in the second paragraph of the definition of a refugee,[56] there is nothing in the Refugees Convention that clearly excludes a choice by an asylum seeker as to the country of refuge.

Indeed, many support the view that there is some choice concerning the country of asylum by the asylum seeker. In *Adimi's* case, Simon Brown LJ stated that:

> I am persuaded by the [refugee] applicants' ... submission, drawing as it does on the travaux preparatoires, various conclusions adopted by the UNHCR's executive committee (Ex Com), and the writings of well-respected academics and commentators (most notably Professor Guy Goodwin-Gill, Atle Grahl-Madsen, Professor James Hathaway and Dr Paul Weis), that some element of choice is indeed open to refugees as to where they may properly claim asylum. I conclude that any merely short term stopover en route to [an] intended sanctuary cannot forfeit the protection of [Article 31], and that the main touchstones by which exclusion from protection should be judged are the length of stay in the intermediate country, the reasons for delaying there (even a substantial delay in an unsafe third country would be reasonable were the time spent trying to acquire the means of travelling on), and whether or not the refugee sought or found there protection de jure or de facto from the persecution they were fleeing.[57]

There are in fact, many legitimate reasons for an asylum seeker to wish to gain refuge in a particular country, some of which have been recognised by the UNHCR.[58] Australia may be the best place to provide shelter for

---

[55] See Abell, above n 46, p 78; G S Goodwin-Gill, 'Article 31 of the 1951 Convention Relating to the Status of Refugees: Non-penalization, Detention and Protection', Background Paper for the Global Consultations on International Protection, October 2001, http://www.unhcr.ch/cgi-bin/texis/vtx/home/opendoc.pdf?tbl=PROTECTION&page=PROTECT&id=3bcfdf164, para 24.

[56] See Refugees Convention, Article 1A(2).

[57] *R v Uxbridge Magistrates Court; Ex parte Adimi, R v Secretary of State for the Home Department; Ex parte Sorani, R v Crown Prosecution Service; Ex parte Sorani, R v Secretary of State for the Home Department; Ex parte Kaziu* [1999] 4 All ER 520 at 527–8. See also Justice Newman at 537.

[58] See below, 'UNHCR "Soft Law" Standards: Protection, Intention, Connection, and Fairness'.

refugees for reasons other than proximity to the place of origin. These include the presence of relatives and large, flourishing ethnic communities that are able to provide vital support to the refugee. In turn, this support enables the refugee to contribute to Australian society, as have so many other refugees. These factors do not detract from the push factors of persecution that drive the asylum seeker from the country of origin. The terminology 'forum-shopping' is therefore inappropriate.

UNHCR 'Soft Law' Standards: Protection, Intention, Connection, and Fairness

The Executive Committee of the Programme of the United Nations High Commissioner for Refugees (Ex Com) has adopted a number of conclusions relevant to an assessment of Australia's legislation. These conclusions are part of the soft law that can be used to interpret the Refugees Convention,[59] as they are an indication of consensus on particular questions of refugee protection.[60]

In the general conclusion on international protection for 1998, Conclusion 85, Ex Com stated that any country to which an asylum seeker is sent must:

[t]reat the asylum seeker (asylum seekers) in accordance with accepted international standards ... ensure effective protection against *refoulement*, and ... provide the asylum seeker (asylum seekers) with the possibility to seek and enjoy asylum.[61]

Ex Com Conclusion 15 deals with the matter of identifying the state responsible for examining an asylum request as follows:

An effort should be made to resolve the problem of identifying the country responsible for examining an asylum request by the adoption of common

---

[59] J Sztucki, 'The Conclusions on the International Protection of Refugees Adopted by the Executive Committee of the UNHCR Program', *International Journal of Refugee Law* 1 (1989), p 285.

[60] V Turk, 'The role of UNHCR in the development of international refugee law', in F Nicholson and P Twomey (eds), *Refugee Rights and Realities: Evolving International Concepts and Regimes* (New York, Cambridge University Press, 1999), p 153 at p 165.

[61] Ex Com Conclusion 85, 'Conclusion on International Protection', 9 October 1998, para (aa), http://www.unhcr.ch.

criteria. In elaborating such criteria the following principles should be observed:

(i) The criteria should make it possible to identify in a positive manner the country which is responsible for examining an asylum request and to whose authorities the asylum seeker should have the possibility of addressing himself;

(ii) The criteria should be of such a character as to avoid possible disagreement between States as to which of them should be responsible for examining an asylum request and should take into account the duration and nature of any sojourn of the asylum seeker in other countries;

(iii) The intentions of the asylum seeker as regards the country in which he wishes to request asylum should as far as possible be taken into account;

(iv) Regard should be had to the concept that asylum should not be refused solely on the ground that it could be sought from another State. Where, however, it appears that a person, before requesting asylum, already has a connexion or close links with another State, he may if it appears fair and reasonable be called upon first to request asylum from that State.[62]

The situation of countries where asylum seekers have already been granted 'protection', has been dealt with in Conclusion 58.[63] Conclusion 58 states that 'irregular' movement of refugees and asylum seekers from countries where a person has already been given protection from refoulement (though not necessarily a durable solution such as local integration) is undesirable. It provides that return of these persons is permissible if they are:

(i) protected [in the safe third country] against *refoulement* and

(ii) they are permitted to remain there and to be treated in accordance with recognized basic human standards until a durable solution is found there.[64]

Furthermore, 'favourable consideration' should be given to cases where a refugee or asylum seeker 'may justifiably claim that he has reason to fear

---

[62] Ex Com Conclusion 15, 'Refugees Without an Asylum Country', 16 October 1979, para (h), http://www.unhcr.ch.

[63] Ex Com Conclusion 58, 'Problems of Refugees and Asylum-Seekers Who Move in an Irregular Manner from a Country in which they had Already Found Protection', 13 October 1989, http://www.unhcr.ch.

[64] Id, para (f).

persecution or that his physical safety or freedom are endangered in the country where he previously found protection'.[65]

It appears that the relevant conclusions must be read as a package. The terms of Conclusion 85, on the one hand, and Conclusions 15 and 58, on the other, should be read cumulatively. So, for example, in relation to an asylum seeker who has sojourned in another country but has not been recognised as a refugee there, the considerations of intentions, connection and fairness, which are set down in Conclusion 15, must be taken into account first. Then the prerequisites contained in Conclusion 85 concerning protection must be met.

The status of these resolutions in the face of only partially compliant state practice may be a matter for debate.[66] Neither the Australian legislation nor the European arrangements are fully compliant with the terms of these conclusions, particularly Ex Com Conclusion 15.[67] Indeed, the newer version of 'safe third country' provisions introduced after the *Tampa* incident[68] involve safe third countries which the asylum seekers have not even transited and which could not be said to have any legal responsibility independent of the agreements negotiated by them with Australia for assessing the asylum seekers' claims. Nauru, with which Australia reached an agreement concerning the processing of the *Tampa* asylum seekers,[69] is not even a party to the Refugees Convention.

Within certain limits, state practice is an important component of international law. State practice that is not clearly in violation of a treaty may be relevant to its interpretation where the practice evinces agreement

---

[65] Id, para (g).

[66] See Sztucki, above n 59, p 310.

[67] For an early analysis of European developments in light of Ex Com standards, see M Kjaerum, 'The Concept of Country of First Asylum', *International Journal of Refugee Law* **4** (1992) p 514. For other critiques of the European arrangements, see A Achermann and M Gattiker, 'Safe Third Countries: European Developments', *International Journal of Refugee Law* **7** (1995) p 19; N Gamrasni-Ahlen, 'Recent Developments Regarding Refugees: the Dublin Convention and the French Perspective', in G Coll and J Bhabha (eds), *Asylum Law and Practice in Europe and North America* (Washington DC, Federal Publications, 1992), p 109.

[68] See above n 10 and accompanying text.

[69] 'Statement of Principles' signed by the President of Nauru and Australia's Minister for Defence on 10 September 2001.

among the parties.[70] By contrast, state practice conflicting with important norms of customary international law – such as those relating to human rights – will be viewed as a violation of the norm in the face of consistent reiteration of opinio juris.[71] It is not so clear what should happen with conclusions that are essentially statements of opinio juris regarding ambiguous treaty provisions in the face of conflicting state practice.

The weight of the conflicting state practice is itself open to question, however. Relevant state practice is predominantly regional, with the Dublin Convention[72] and various domestic provisions within EU states[73] being the prime examples, although some other states have similar provisions.[74] It is doubtful that this practice on the part of some states really evinces 'agreement' as to the interpretation of the Convention and its Protocol.[75] The two instruments have between them a total of 138 parties.[76] Moreover, the relevant Ex Com resolutions have been recalled and reaffirmed. Conclusions 15 and 58 were recalled by the 1999 general conclusion on international protection (Conclusion 87), and Conclusion 58 was expressly

---

[70] Vienna Convention on the Law of Treaties, Article 31(3)(b).

[71] *Military and Paramilitary Activities In and Against Nicaragua (Nicaragua v USA)* 1986 ICJ Rep 14, paras 202 – 5.

[72] See above n 41.

[73] See below n 117 and accompanying text.

[74] Van Selm writes that 'European States are by no means the only ones which have established "safe third country" rules. As noted above, African states have looked into the concept. Some central Asian states apply the principle also. Belarus defines all neighbouring states as safe; Kazakhstan has denied a number of applications on the grounds of passage through a "safe country". Kyrgyzstan defines Iran, Pakistan and Tajikistan as "safe third countries". Russia uses the concept widely, including for Afghanis transiting Iran or Pakistan. Ukraine likewise uses the concept': J Van Selm, 'Access to Procedures: "Safe Third Countries", "Safe Countries of Origin" and "Time Limits"', Background paper for the Global Consultations on International Protection, June 2001, http://www.unhcr.ch/cgi-bin/texis/vtx/home/opendoc.pdf?tbl=PROTECTION&page=PROTECT&id=3b39a2403, para 47.

[75] G S Goodwin-Gill, *The Refugee in International Law* (Oxford and New York, Clarendon Press, 2nd ed, 1996), pp 341–2.

[76] As of October 1999, 138 states were party to one or both of these instruments: Ex Com Conclusion 87, 'General Conclusion on International Protection', 8 October 1999, para (e), http://www.unhcr.ch.

reaffirmed.[77] Conclusion 87 stated that notions such as that of the safe third country:

> should be appropriately applied so as not to result in improper denial of access to asylum procedures, or to violations of the principle of non-refoulement.[78]

The consensus in terms of opinio juris as expressed by the one body capable of making reasonably authoritative pronouncements concerning refugee status is arguably more evident and significant than such consensus as may be evident in the self-interested and often self-contradictory practice of some states.[79] Consequently, I assess Australia's legislation by reference to these Ex Com conclusions as well as by reference to the obligation of non-refoulement.

Australia's Safe Third Country Provisions

Determination of refugee status in Australia is an administrative procedure. The legislative framework for this decision making process is the Migration Act. As a result of the amendments to the Migration Act made by the Border Protection Legislation Amendment Act, Australia now excludes from refugee status persons deemed to have a safe third country, and it may choose to exclude some persons from the refugee status determination procedure altogether by precluding them from applying for protection visas.

The Extent of Australia's Protection Obligations: Section 36 Before and After the Border Protection Legislation Amendment Act

Until the enactment of the Border Protection Legislation Amendment Act, section 36 of the Migration Act provided simply that a protection visa would be available for:

---

[77] Ex Com Conclusion 87, id, paras 20 (l) and (m). See also Ex Com Conclusion 15, above n 62, and Ex Com Conclusion 58, above n 63.

[78] Ex Com Conclusion 87, above n 76, para (j).

[79] Australia, for example, is a member of Ex Com.

a non-citizen in Australia to whom Australia has protection obligations under the Refugees Convention as amended by the Refugees Protocol.[80]

The extent of Australia's protection obligations pursuant to section 36(2) had been interpreted by the Australian courts, effectively introducing a common law concept of the 'safe third country'. The case law began with the decision in *Minister for Immigration and Multicultural Affairs (MIMA) v Thiyagarajah*.[81] In *Thiyagarajah*, the court considered the case of a person who had been granted refugee status in France. It held that the reference to a person owed protection obligations by Australia in section 36(2) did not extend to a person recognised as a refugee elsewhere, since this meant that the person had 'effective protection', including, 'a right to reside, enter and re-enter that country.'[82] (Problematically, however, there was a suggestion that Thiyagarajah's French visa had expired and that the French authorities would not consent to his return.[83]) Similarly in *Rajendran v MIMA*,[84] the court found that Australia did not owe protection obligations to a person who, though he had not been determined to be a refugee, had permanent residence in New Zealand.

From these fairly unexceptional cases, the case law moved onto more uncertain territory. In *MIMA v Gnanapiragasum*,[85] the court found that 'effective protection' referred not only to situations in which someone had already been granted refugee or permanent residence status elsewhere, but a situation in which it would be possible to claim refugee status, so long as

---

[80]   This definition now appears in slightly modified form, due to amendments introduced by the Migration Legislation Amendment Act (No 6) (Cth) and the Migration Legislation Amendment (Judicial Review) Act 2001 (Cth), as section 36(2)(a) Migration Act. Section 36(2)(a) now provides that '[a] criterion for a protection visa is that the applicant for the visa is ... a non-citizen in Australia to whom the Minister is satisfied Australia has protection obligations under the Refugees Convention as amended by the Refugees Protocol.' The amendments introduced by the Migration Legislation Amendment Act (No 6) also introduced a further limb to this definition ensuring that the family unit is covered by an application for refugee status: section 36(2)(b).

[81]   Above n 3.

[82]   Id, p 562.

[83]   The Full Federal Court remitted the matter back to the RRT with the instruction to consider this new evidence, however, this decision was subsequently overturned by the High Court (Gaudron J dissenting): *MIMA v Thiyagarjah* (2000) 199 CLR 343.

[84]   (1998) 86 FCR 526.

[85]   (1998) 88 FCR 1.

there was a right to leave and re-enter the country, at least temporarily, during determination of status. If the concept of a safe third country is accepted, this finding is not exceptional, although there might be questions concerning compliance with Ex Com Conclusion 15.[86] Moreover, in accordance with the limited role of the court on judicial review, which is not to make decisions on the merits concerning matters of fact, the court did no more than direct the RRT to consider whether the applicant for refugee status would be admitted temporarily to Germany,[87] which is of course a party to the Refugees Convention, and with which the applicant had a 'long established connection'.[88]

In *Al-Zafiry v MIMA*,[89] Emmett J went still further and accepted that a country that was not party to the Refugees Convention could be regarded as a safe third country. He rejected the contention that effective protection as referred to in *Thiyagarajah* encompassed a *legally enforceable* right to enter and reside in a third country. Rather what mattered was that:

> as a matter of practical reality and fact, the applicant is likely to be given effective protection by being permitted to enter and to live in a third country where he will not be under any risk of being *refouled* to his original country.[90]

Emmett J's views were adopted by the Full Federal Court in *MIMA v Al-Sallal*.[91] According to the court, just as a party to the Refugees Convention might not be regarded as a safe third country, it is possible that a non party *could* be regarded as safe because of the fact of 'effective protection' from refoulement.[92] According to Justice French in *Patto v MIMA* there are three situations in which a person can be returned to a third country without breaching the principle of non-refoulement:

1. Return of the person to the third country will not contravene Article 33 where the person has right of residence in that country and is not subject to Convention harms therein.

---

[86] Ex Com Conclusion 15, above n 62.

[87] Id, p 18.

[88] Ibid.

[89] [1999] FCA 443 (25 March 1999); affirmed by the Full Court: (1999) 58 ALD 663.

[90] Id, para 26.

[91] (1999) 94 FCR 549, para 42.

[92] Id, para 47.

2. Return of the person to the third country will not contravene Article 33, whether or not the person has right of residence in that country, if that country is a party to the Convention and can be expected to honour its obligations thereunder.

3. Return of the person to a third country will not contravene Article 33 notwithstanding that the person has no right of residence in that country and that the country is not party to the Convention, provided that it can be expected, nevertheless, to afford the person claiming asylum effective protection against threats to his life or freedom for a Convention reason.[93]

Part 6 of the Border Protection Legislation Amendment Act qualified the extent of Australia's protection obligations as a matter of legislation. Consequently, section 36 of the Migration Act now contains a paragraph entitled 'protection obligations.' Section 36(3) states that:

Australia is taken not to have protection obligations to a non-citizen who has not taken all possible steps to avail himself or herself of a right to enter and reside in, whether temporarily or permanently and however that right arose or is expressed, any country apart from Australia, including countries of which the non-citizen is a national.

There are two exceptions to the safe third country rule established by section 36(3). The first is where the individual concerned has a well-founded fear of persecution within the meaning of the Convention in relation to the putative safe third country: section 36(4). The second is where there is a well-founded fear that the putative safe third country will return the individual to a persecutory country: section 36(5).

One of the first questions to be resolved was how the legislative qualifications concerning the extent of Australia's protection obligations sat with the common law. Did subsections 36(3)–(5) codify, supersede or impose an additional (and different) test to the common law test of 'effective protection'? This question is returned to when the meaning of the words 'enter and reside' is discussed in light of the obligation of non-refoulement, below.[94] The problems with the common law test of 'effective protection' will also be examined at that point.

---

[93] (2000) 106 FCR 119, para 37.

[94] See below, 'Provisions Redefining Australia's Protection Obligations'.

Preclusion of Applications for Visas

In addition to redefining Australia's protection obligations, the Border Protection Legislation Amendment Act seeks to preclude valid applications for refugee status by persons having access to a safe third country. Part 2, Division 3, Subdivision AK of the Migration Act refers to 'non-citizens with access to protection from third countries.' It applies to a non-citizen who:

- is a national of two or more countries (section 91N(1)); or

- has a 'right to enter and reside in, whether temporarily or permanently and however that right arose or is expressed, any country (the *available country*)' and 'has ever resided in the available country for a continuous period of at least 7 days': section 91N(2).

In relation to the second category of persons, the Minister must have made a declaration that the country is safe under section 91N(3).[95]

Persons covered by subdivision AK are precluded from making valid applications for a protection visa: section 91P. Both lawful and unlawful entrants are precluded from applying for visas.[96] If the asylum seeker is an unlawful non-citizen and in immigration detention, he or she must be removed from Australia 'as soon as reasonably practicable' (section 198(9)). The Minister has a 'non-compellable' discretion (that is, the Minister cannot be forced to exercise his discretion) to make exception in individual cases in the public interest. Matters that the Minister 'may'

---

[95] Section 91N(3)(a) empowers the Minister, after considering any advice from the Office of the United Nations High Commissioner for Refugees, to declare in writing that a specified country:

(i) provides access, for persons seeking asylum, to effective procedures for assessing their need for protection; and

(ii) provides protection to persons to whom that country has protection obligations; and

(iii) meets relevant human rights standards for persons to whom that country has protection obligations.

[96] Persons who have not been 'immigration cleared' (which will be due to lack of documentation or suspicion of fraudulent documentation) are precluded from applying for a visa by section 91P(1), while persons who have been immigration cleared (because they entered on a visa of some kind) are precluded by section 91P(2).

consider in relation to the exercise of his discretion 'include information that raises the possibility that ... the non-citizen might not be able to avail himself or herself of protection' from the 'safe' country or alternative country of nationality: sections 91(Q)(1) and (2). As originally enacted, the Minister's exercise of his non-compellable discretion was not judicially reviewable.[97] In any event, the Migration Legislation Amendment (Judicial Review) Act 2001 has introduced a far-reaching 'privative clause' greatly restricting the grounds for judicial review in relation to nearly all migration decisions.[98]

Provisions Ousting Consideration of 'Effective Nationality'

The legislative amendments also exclude the concept of 'effective nationality' from Australian refugee law. Although a persecutory country of nationality should not be a place to which an asylum seeker is returned,[99] determinations of nationality are to be made 'solely by reference to the domestic law' of the country concerned: sections 36(6) and 91N(6). The legislation thus seeks to prevent the future application of two important Federal Court cases and a decision by the Administrative Appeals Tribunal concerning East Timorese asylum seekers. Australia has insisted that East Timorese hold Portuguese nationality and should travel there instead of claiming refugee status in Australia – a move designed to appease Indonesia by avoiding findings that Indonesia persecuted East Timorese. The three cases determined that it was necessary to establish not only what domestic law says, but also whether a person is treated as a national in

---

[97] This was formerly provided for in section 475(2)(e) of the Migration Act.

[98] See Migration Act, section 474. It is almost certain that the scope and effect of the privative clause will be tested before the courts.

[99] The exceptions in subsections 36(4) and (5) of the Migration Act are applicable, although the preclusion of protection visa applications by dual nationals, unless the Minister exercises his or her discretion under section 91Q, creates potential conflict with the criteria for protection visas in section 36. The requirement that there be a declaration of safety by the Minister under section 91(3) does not apply in cases of dual nationality, because an 'available country' for the purposes of section 91(2) is not 'a country of which the non-citizen is a national': section 91N(2)(a)(ii). In theory such a declaration should be redundant because a country of nationality has a duty to receive a national back onto its territory and is also duty-bound to respect the human rights of both its nationals and other persons within territory and jurisdiction. However, while the state of nationality should meet its human rights obligations, this may not always be the case and in some cases, states do not receive back their nationals onto state territory.

practice.[100] In relation to the Portuguese nationality supposedly held by East Timorese asylum seekers, the Federal Court ruled that in effect, Portugal requires East Timorese to make a declaration that they wish to be considered Portuguese.[101] Thus Portuguese nationality is not automatically effective for the purposes of the Refugees Convention.[102]

A Critical Look at the Legislation in Practice

Having looked at the law in the books, it is important to look at the way in which the legislation has been implemented in practice and to examine its conformity with soft law and hard legal obligations.

Non-compliance with Ex Com Conclusion 15[103]

Contrary to Ex Com Conclusion 15 there is no consideration of the intentions of the asylum seeker regarding the country in which he or she wishes to seek asylum. Nor is there any consideration of whether there is a connection with the country of first asylum. The legislation certainly does not require an assessment of whether it 'appears fair and reasonable' to require the asylum seeker to request asylum from that state. The requirement of 'residence' for a period of only seven days for the purposes of precluding a person from applying for a visa may catch someone who was essentially in transit. Factors like the presence of relatives, language skills or other cultural factors like the presence of an ethnic community to which the asylum seeker belongs are all excluded from consideration as to whether the asylum seeker should be returned to the safe third country.[104] Indeed, it is possible that an asylum seeker with relatives in *Australia* –

---

[100] *Jong Kim Koe v MIMA* (1997) 143 ALR 695; *Lay Kon Tji v Minister for Immigration and Ethnic Affairs* (1998) 158 ALR 681; *SSRP v MIMA* [2000] AATA 878. For analysis of the Timorese asylum seekers' situation see P Mathew, 'Lest We Forget: Australia's Policy on East Timorese Asylum Seekers', *International Journal of Refugee Law* 11 (1999), p 7.

[101] See particularly, *Lay Kon Tji*, ibid.

[102] See *Lay Kon Tji* and *SSRP*, above n 100.

[103] Ex Com Conclusion 15, above n 62.

[104] These factors are relevant in Canada: *Charles Kofi OwusuAnsah v Minister for Employment and Immigration* Canadian Federal Court of Appeal Decision A–1265–87, cited in Abell, above n 46, n 80.

even relatives who have been determined to be refugees and in relation to whom UNHCR urges application of the principle of family unity[105] – could be returned to another country under the new legislative provisions. In this regard, the legislation is significantly harsher than the Dublin Convention in so far as that Convention deals with transfer of asylum seekers within member states[106] and may be in violation of Australia's obligations concerning protection of the family under both the International Covenant on Civil and Political Rights and the Convention on the Rights of the Child.[107]

Provisions Precluding Visa Applications: An Impractical 'White List'[108]

The Minister has not yet declared a particular country safe. Presumably, this is due to the need to secure readmission agreements with countries likely to be transited by asylum seekers on their way to Australia. The Minister for Immigration and Multicultural Affairs has had talks with a number of countries in order to promote cooperation between various countries.[109] A 'regional cooperation model' has been concluded with Indonesia, which provides for the 'interception, detention and screening of third country nationals transiting Indonesia en route to Australia'.[110]

---

[105] See UNHCR, *Handbook on Procedures and Criteria for the Determination of Refugee Status* (Geneva, UNHCR, 2nd ed, 1992), http://www.unhcr.ch, para 185.

[106] See Articles 3(4), 4 and 9 relating to opting out of the Convention, family unity and humanitarian factors respectively.

[107] In particular, see ICCPR, Articles 17 and 23 and Convention on the Rights of the Child, Articles 3, 9, 10, 16 and 22. There is not space here to discuss the implications of, and the (relatively sparse) jurisprudence concerning, the relevant rights.

[108] The term 'white list' was first used by refugee scholars in relation to declarations that particular countries of *origin* were safe and could not found claims to refugee status. It is used here for the connotation of a general assessment of a situation in a country that does not account for the safety of particular individuals.

[109] See media releases announcing the commencement and conclusion of a tour to Jordan, Syria, Turkey, Iran and Pakistan: P Ruddock, 'Ruddock leaves on Overseas Anti-People Smuggling Mission', Media Release MPS 001/2000, 7 January 2000; P Ruddock, 'Minister's Anti-People Smuggling Campaign Brings Increased Cooperation', Media Release MPS 008/2000, 26 January 2000. See also media releases announcing a similar tour to Singapore, Malaysia, Thailand, India and France: P Ruddock, 'Minister Begins Five Nation Anti-People Smuggling Tour', MPS 075/2000, 9 July 2000. All available at http://www.minister.immi.gov.au/media_releases/.

[110] UNHCR, *The State of the World's Refugees*, above n 25, p 182.

Such preventative models may work,[111] although the arrival of the *Tampa* asylum seekers, who had come from Indonesia, suggests otherwise. There is also some sort of arrangement with Vietnam to fight people-smuggling and illegal immigration,[112] while the Minister for Immigration has apparently secured agreement on the part of Syrian authorities for returns to Syria of Syrians and some other nationals who have 'no legal basis for remaining in Australia'.[113] On the whole, however, it seems that rapid conclusion of readmission agreements is unlikely. I have heard that when the Pakistani authorities were approached concerning the return of the few hundred Afghan asylum seekers who had made their way to Australia, they replied that they would be happy to help if Australia would only help alleviate the Palestinian refugee problem.

The provisions concerning dual nationality, which preclude the consideration of effective nationality, are problematic for similar reasons. In order to secure return, the agreement of the authorities of the supposed country of nationality is necessary. This should have been the lesson drawn from Portugal's ambivalent response to Australian overtures during the East Timorese litigation.[114] Australian officialdom's reading of another country's nationality law in conformity with perceived Australian national interest is beside the point. What counts is whether the asylum seeker is actually treated as a national and accorded protection on that basis.

Even if readmission agreements are concluded, proof of a particular asylum seeker's transit through a country may become an issue. The European experience is that the country nominated as a safe third country will require documentary proof, which may be missing because asylum seekers have destroyed their documentation.[115] According to a European

---

[111] Indeed, it is apparent that this arrangement is providing the Australian government with confidence that asylum seekers will not be refouled by Indonesia if Australia interdicts them.

[112] P Ruddock, 'Agreement signed with Vietnam on Fighting Illegal Immigration,' Media Release MPS 095/2000, 14 September 2000, http://www.minister.immi.gov.au/media_releases/media00/r00095.htm.

[113] P Ruddock, 'Australia and Syria cooperate on People Smuggling', Media Release MPS 004/2000, 16 January 2000, http://www.minister.immi.gov.au/media_releases/media00/r00004.htm.

[114] See the cases cited above, n 100.

[115] K Hailbronner, 'Fifty Years of German Basic Law – Migration, Citizenship and Asylum', *Southern Methodist University Law Review* 53 (2000) p 519 at p 536.

Commission staff working paper, less than 2 per cent of asylum seekers are actually transferred under the Dublin Convention.[116] As regards returns to non-EU members,[117] the record is also equivocal. Many European countries have adopted lists of safe third countries,[118] and there have been deportations to Turkey, Hungary, Tunisia, Ukraine, Russia, Algeria, Saudi Arabia and Iran.[119] However, in a scathing report on the British provisions in 1993, Amnesty International argued that not only had there been many cases of refugees being 'bounced back' to Britain, but that the special procedures necessary to implement the legislation were lengthier than the ordinary asylum procedures and that the money could have been better spent.[120] Furthermore, where judicial review has been available, political determinations as to the safety of particular countries have sometimes been overturned. For example, in the cases of Javed, Zulfikar Ali and Abid Ali, the English Court of Appeal decided that the decision of the Home Secretary to designate Pakistan as a safe country was reviewable.[121] The court held that the empowering legislation only enabled such a designation when the evidence available enabled him rationally to make that

---

[116] Commission of the European Communities, *Revisiting the Dublin Convention: Developing Community Legislation for Determining which Member State is Responsible for Considering an Application for Asylum Submitted in One of the Member States* (Brussels, SEC, 21 March 2000), para 25.

[117] Dublin Convention, Article 3(5).

[118] See the discussion of the lists in Germany, Finland, the Netherlands, and the United Kingdom in S Weidlich, 'First Instance Asylum Proceedings in Europe: Do Bona Fide Refugees Find Protection?', *Georgetown Immigration Law Journal* 14 (2000) p 643 at p 652.

[119] Id, p 654.

[120] Dunstan, above n 51.

[121] *Secretary of State for the Home Department v Asif Javed, Zulfiqar Ali and Abid Ali* [2001] EWCA Civ 789, 17 May 2001 (Lord Phillips of Worth Matravers MR, Peter Gibson and Latham LJJ), http://www.bailii.org/ew/cases/EWCA/Civ/2001/789.html. The UK Government Statutory Instrument 2000 No 2245 *The Asylum (Designated Safe Third Countries) Order 2000* (London, The Stationery Office Limited, 2000), http://www.hmso.gov.uk/si/si2000/20002245.htm, now lists Canada, Norway, Switzerland, and the United States of America.

conclusion,[122] and that the Home Secretary's conclusions in relation to Pakistan were unreasonable.[123]

Moving from the practical problems with this part of the legislation, the blanket nature of the declarations as to a country's safety under section 91N runs the risk of violating the obligation of non-refoulement. The Minister is to determine that a country has effective procedures for determining claims to refugee status, that refugees are given protection and that the country meets human rights standards. However, the Minister does not make an individualised assessment as to whether a particular asylum seeker will be given access to these procedures and protected in accordance with the Refugees Convention and human rights standards. This appears to be contrary to Ex Com Conclusion 85.[124] Referring to the treatment an asylum seeker must be accorded in the safe third country, Conclusion 85 uses the definite article and thus speaks of particular asylum seekers. This recognises the fact that there are many situations where a country that is safe for most people, is unsafe for some. As the Director of the UNHCR's Department of International Protection, Ms Erika Feller, has noted:

> [i]f the notion of protection elsewhere is to have any currency, its applicability should be determined on an individual basis, not on a country basis ...[125]

One important reason for individual determinations is the problem posed by state parties' inconsistent interpretations of the Refugees Convention. These problems are illustrated by the case of *TI v United Kingdom*.[126] In this case, the European Court of Human Rights was called upon to consider the case of a Sri Lankan who had been refused refugee status by Germany and had then sought asylum from Britain. One of the problems with this man's case was the fact that non state actors had persecuted him. Germany generally will not grant refugee status to such a

---

122 *Javed*, above n 121, para 55.

123 Id, paras 73, 76 and 77.

124 Ex Com Conclusion 85, above n 61.

125 E Feller (Director of the Department of International Protection, Office of the United Nations High Commissioner for Refugees at the Centre for International and Public Law, the Australian National University), 'Refugee Protection: An Unwelcome Responsibility? Emerging Issues in Australia and Globally,' Speech, 6 March 2000, http://law.anu.edu.au/cipl/Conferences/Fellerlecturetext.rtf.

126 [2000] INLR 211.

person unless the conduct can be attributed to the state because the state supports or tolerates the persecution by private groups.

The man travelled to the United Kingdom, which requested that Germany accept responsibility for the applicant's asylum request pursuant to the Dublin Convention. Germany agreed to this request and the UK Home Secretary ordered the asylum seeker's removal. The man applied to the European Court alleging, among other things, a violation by the UK of the implicit non-refoulement obligation in Article 3 of the European Convention for the Protection of Human Rights and Fundamental Freedoms (the European Convention). Article 3 prohibits torture and inhuman or degrading treatment or punishment.

In the end, the court found that the UK was not in violation of Article 3 and declared the case inadmissible. Germany made provision for humanitarian status outside the formal refugee status determination system. Thus there were effective procedural safeguards against removal from Germany. However, the court confirmed that the non-refoulement obligation in Article 3 applied to chain or indirect refoulement and that the Dublin Convention did not alter this position. While the court could not comment on states' obligations under the Refugees Convention, it noted that inconsistent interpretation of the Refugees Convention could render ineffective the provisions of the Dublin Convention.

Australia's legislation ignores the problems presented in the case of *TI*. Australia has adopted a 'white list' approach where particular countries are declared safe in a generic fashion, regardless of the situation of particular asylum seekers. The only provision for a particular asylum seeker's circumstances to be taken into account is the Minister's non-compellable discretion to consider 'information that raises the possibility that ... the non-citizen might not be able to avail himself or herself of protection' of the country concerned. This is not sufficient to meet Australia's obligations. Australia is required by the terms of Article 33 of the Refugees Convention to satisfy itself that a refugee will not be indirectly refouled.

Provisions Redefining Australia's Protection Obligations: How is a 'Right to Enter and Reside' Interpreted Consistently with the Obligation of Non-refoulement?

The provisions in section 36 which redefine Australia's protection obligations may be invoked by decision makers regardless of the fact that no country has been determined by the Minister to be a safe country.

However the amendments to the section raised significant issues of interpretation and it was necessary to determine how the new legislative provisions, sections 36(3)–(5), sat with previous interpretation of subsection 36(2).

What does the 'right to enter and reside' mean? The words 'right to enter and reside' are open to interpretation, as is demonstrated by a decision of the Refugee Review Tribunal (RRT) – the body responsible for merits review of refugee status decisions made by the Department of Immigration and Multicultural Affairs – in mid 2000. The RRT decided that a Colombian family who had transited Argentina for a little over a day should be required to seek protection from Argentina on the basis that Colombian citizens may enter Argentina as tourists for a period of up to 90 days without a visa.[127] Imposing such a requirement seems similar to the rejected version of Article 31 of the Refugees Convention which would have required an asylum seeker unlawfully present in the state of refuge to have demonstrated that he or she was unable to find asylum in another country through which she or he had transited.[128] The RRT went further, commenting that it would not even be necessary for a person to have transited a particular country, placing the onus on refugees to actively scout around for options other than Australia.[129] This could be seen as consistent with the requirement in section 36 (3) that a non-citizen must have 'taken all possible steps' to avail himself or herself of the right to enter and reside in another country.

The decision was appealed by the applicant for refugee status whose adviser placed emphasis on the substantial nature of a stay required by the word 'reside'.[130] The Minister decided not to contest the case, but it highlights the ambiguities and potential reach of the legislation.

These ambiguities were addressed by the Full Federal Court in *MIMA v Applicant C.*[131] At first instance, a single judge of the Federal Court held that the RRT had erred in concluding that the applicant for refugee status

---

[127]   RRT N00/31751 (30 June 2000), cited in Hunyor, above n 3, n 26 and accompanying text.

[128]   Above n 55.

[129]   Above n 127, p 16.

[130]   I am grateful to Liz Biok, NSW Legal Aid, for supplying information about this case.

[131]   (2001) 66 ALD 1 (Gray, Lee and Stone JJ).

had a right to re-enter the putative safe third country. Moreover, the court held that the 'right' to enter and reside in a safe third country had to be a legally enforceable right. The court stated:

> [a] literal construction of the word 'right' in a statute must, in my view, be that it is a legally enforceable right. The extraneous materials to which I have referred above tend to support a literal construction. So does the fact that a literal construction would advance the purposes of the Refugees Convention whereas to construe the word 'right' as meaning something less than a legally enforceable right would place much greater obstacles in a refugee's path.
>
> In the present matter there was no evidence that the applicant had a legally enforceable right to enter Syria. The only evidence was that if he were able to obtain sponsorship from within Syria then he would be permitted to enter Syria and remain there so long as he complied with Syrian laws. There was no evidence that the applicant, who is now in a detention camp in Australia, could obtain the necessary sponsorship. In his supplementary submissions the respondent raised various alternative arguments ... They were all based on the assumption that the applicant had a right to enter Syria. As there was no evidence that such a legal right existed, it is not necessary to consider those submissions.[132]

The Full Federal Court agreed that section 36(3) refers to a legally enforceable right to enter and reside in a particular country,[133] overruling contrary case law.[134] In the lead judgment, Justice Stone also shed light on what such a right may mean:

> It should also be recognised that a right of entry such as I have postulated may arise other than by grant of a visa. A country's entry requirements may be met by proof of identity and citizenship of a nominated country being provided at the border, for example, by production of a valid passport, without the necessity for a visa. This would explain the use in section 36 (3) of the phrase, 'however that right arose or is expressed.'[135]

As the right to enter and reside in the country must be in existence already, however, it appears that her Honour would not expect that an

---

[132] *Applicant C v MIMA*, above n 52, paras 30–1.

[133] Above n 131, para 64, per Stone J.

[134] *V856/00A v MIMA* [2001] FCA 1018 was disapproved.

[135] *MIMA v Applicant C*, above n 131, para 60.

applicant would have to apply for entry to every country which might issue a visa or permit entry upon provision of such proof. Her Honour specifically referred to an exchange in parliament between the Parliamentary Secretary to the Minister for Immigration and Multicultural Affairs, Senator Kay Patterson, and Democrat Senator Andrew Bartlett concerning the meaning of the phrase 'to take all possible steps', and drew the following conclusion:

> This exchange supports [the judge at first instance, Justice Carr's] interpretation of section 36(3). If the term 'right to enter and reside in' had the meaning pressed by the Minister, namely the practical capacity to bring about a lawful permission to enter and reside legally in the relevant country, then, in order for an applicant to take all possible steps to take advantage of such a right, it would be necessary for the applicant to apply at least to all countries where it could be reasonably expected that the applicant would be granted a visa for entry and temporary or permanent residence.[136]

Do subsections 36(3)–(5) codify, supersede or impose a test additional to the common law test of 'effective protection'? This is not simply a question of doctrinal tidiness but of considerable importance given the problematic nature of some of the common law developments. The common law test had been moving onto somewhat dangerous ground from the perspective of compliance with the obligation of non-refoulement. The cases had gradually progressed from returning a person who had found protection as a refugee in another country (*Thiyagarajah*)[137] to the idea that a person could be returned even to a country that is not party to the Refugees Convention (*Al-Zafiry*).[138]

The reasoning in some of the case law is open to criticism for failing to recognise the realities facing refugees. In other cases, while the court cannot necessarily be faulted for its reasoning, the limits of judicial review, particularly the proscription on the courts making decisions on the merits as to matters of fact, has meant that the RRT is left to make decisions about matters of fact with too free a hand and tribunal members may feel encouraged to ignore the realities facing refugees. For example, in

---

[136] Id, para 56.

[137] Above n 3.

[138] Above n 89.

Gnanapiragasum,[139] the court directed the RRT to consider whether the applicant for refugee status would be admitted temporarily to Germany. At that point, one would also hope the RRT would consider the consistent claims by the applicant, which were supported to some degree by the evidence before the court, that the applicants had already been refused refugee status by Germany.[140] The 'long established' connection with Germany may have been somewhat tenuous or, at least, difficult to renew once the applicant had left the country for any length of time. A finding concerning a right to enter a country temporarily for the duration of determination of refugee status becomes meaningless if protection against refoulement in the long term is not forthcoming.

Similarly, in *Al-Zafiry*,[141] the court stated in the abstract that what mattered is what happens as a matter of practical reality and fact, but the country concerned, Jordan, is not party to the Refugees Convention. Though it appeared Jordan was generally tolerant of refugees and permitted many Arabs to remain in Jordan, the position of the applicant could be viewed as somewhat precarious. Refoulement might therefore be a possibility.

Likewise, the reasoning in *Al-Sallal*,[142] that states that are not party to the Refugees Convention, could afford people protection appears logical in the abstract, but not so convincing when practical realities are considered. If the country concerned is not party to the Refugees Convention, a decision maker should surely be looking for an ironclad guarantee of entry and permanent residence in order to ensure non-refoulement. At the very least, consideration of other non-refoulement obligations under the Convention against Torture or Other Cruel, Inhuman or Degrading Treatment or Punishment or under customary international law is required. Decision makers should also acknowledge that even when a country is party to the Refugees Convention or bound by other non-refoulement obligations, if there is no guarantee of entry to a particular individual, the general commitment to non-refoulement is not necessarily going to assure safety for a particular individual. In order to avoid misunderstandings as to

---

[139] Above n 85.

[140] Id, pp 15–16 particularly.

[141] Above n 89.

[142] Above n 91.

why a particular person is being returned to a country it will be essential to secure express agreement concerning the admission of that individual.[143]

Thus, while the emphasis of Australian courts has been on 'facts' as opposed to 'legal rights', the existence of these legal rights is often essential to the factual determination that refoulement will not occur. As stated in a powerful dissenting judgment by Justice Lee in *Al-Rahal v MIMA*:

> [t]he application of 'practical reality and fact' does not alter the relevant questions to be answered, namely, has an obligation to protect the applicant for a protection visa been accepted by a third country and have rights to reside in, leave, and re-enter that country been granted to the applicant by that country. That is, in effect, has a third country undertaken to receive and protect the applicant.[144]

Similarly, as is made clear by the decision of Justice French in *Patto*,[145] mere speculation by a decision maker as to what a particular country might do should be insufficient. In *Patto's case*, French J concluded that the RRT had been wrong to speak of a right to enter and reside in a particular country (Greece) when:

> [t]here [was] nothing in the material to suggest a legal right to return to that country. While it may be that Patto could have remained in Greece indefinitely, his departure [to] Australia and prospective re-entry as a deportee from this country are circumstances which place in the realm of sheer speculation what the attitude of the Greek government might be to his re-entry. This difficulty also confronts the Tribunal's fall-back finding that even in the absence of a legal right he would, as a matter of 'practical reality' be afforded effective protection in Greece.[146]

So, has the introduction of sections 36(3)–(5) made it more difficult for decision makers to return an asylum seeker to a putative safe third country, or does the legislation simply codify, or, alternatively impose an additional

---

[143] See R Marx, 'Non-refoulement, Access to Procedures, and Responsibility for Determining Refugee Claims', *International Journal of Refugee Law* 7 (1994) p 385 at pp 404–5.

[144] [2000] 184 ALR 698, para 55, per Lee J.

[145] Above n 93.

[146] Id, para 38.

test that is different from, but co-exists with, the standard of 'effective protection' established by the common law? In a line of decisions by single judges that followed the decision in *Applicant C* at first instance,[147] the Federal Court decided that the common law test applied pursuant to section 36(2) survived the introduction of sections 36(3)–(5), meaning that there were two situations in which Australia could rely on another state to protect the applicant for refugee status. In *Kola v MIMA*, for example, Justice Mansfield stated that:

> Subsection 36(3) defines circumstances in which Australia is taken not to have protection obligations to an applicant for a protection visa, provided sections 36(4) and (5) do not apply. Its focus is upon the visa applicant, if that person has a 'right to enter and reside on' a third country, having taken all possible steps to have exercised that right. But it does not purport to change the existing operation of section 36(2) of the Act. It has been held in many decisions of the Court that, for the purposes of section 36(2) of the Act, Australia does not have protection obligations to an applicant for a protection visa if that person has 'effective protection' in an intermediate third country. That is because Australia would not be in breach of its obligations under Art 33 of the Convention by refouling the visa applicant to that intermediate third country.[148]

The Full Federal Court in *MIMA v Applicant C*[149] confirmed that the position is that there are now two situations in which Australia may be said not to have protection obligations. Under section 36(2) Australia will not have protection obligations if the common law test of 'effective protection' is met in another country. Under section 36(3), Australia will not have protection obligations where the applicant for refugee status has a legally enforceable right to enter and reside in another country.[150]

Justice Stone also shed some light as to when those different circumstances might arise:

---

147 Above n 52.

148 [2001] FCA 630, 30 May 2001, para 37. This was affirmed by the Full Court: [2002] FCAFC 59. See also *S115/00A v MIMA* (2001) 180 ALR 561; *Bitani v MIMA* [2001] FCA 631 (30 May 2001); *W228 v MIMA* [2001] FCA 860 (5 July 2001); and *V1043/00A v MIMA* (2001) 113 FCR 1.

149 Above n 131.

150 Id, paras 62–3, per Stone J.

The circumstances in which one might be 'satisfied' that effective protection is available in the absence of a right (in the sense in which I have explained ... above) would be rare but not impossible to imagine. For example, if the third country were to give an undertaking to Australia that a certain person would be admitted and allowed to reside in that country, it might be possible to be so satisfied although the person could not be said to have thereby acquired a right.[151]

This statement helpfully, and correctly in light of the purpose of the Refugees Convention, indicates a high threshold before a decision maker may decide that the 'practical realities' are that effective protection will be forthcoming for the purposes of section 36(2).

Problems at the Border?

A final point to make about the Australian legislation is that in the cases reviewed above, the applicants were fortunate enough to enter into the refugee status determination procedure, which is why they had the option of review. What has happened to those unauthorised arrivals detained in remote facilities like Port Hedland and Woomera, who are not provided with lawyers or applications for protection visas unless they request them?[152] (Of course, at present, unauthorised arrivals are likely to be detained in Nauru or Papua New Guinea or interdicted and returned to Indonesia, and should they arrive on the Australian mainland, judicial review may have to be won through a constitutional challenge to the new privative clause.)[153]

The Australian Human Rights and Equal Opportunity Commission has documented at least one case in which an asylum seeker clearly indicated that his rights, and even his life, were threatened should he return to his home country. Yet the Department of Immigration and Multicultural Affairs took the view that the asylum seeker was not seeking to engage Australia's protection obligations and was therefore not to be given information about or assistance applying for a protection visa. The

---

[151] Id, para 64.

[152] See *Wu Yu Fang v Minister for Immigration and Ethnic Affairs* (1996) 135 ALR 583 at 628–35, per Nicholson CJ; Jenkinson J concurring.

[153] See above n 98 regarding the privative clause.

department's record of interview contains the following statement by the asylum seeker:

> If I go back I will die or literally I will be gone. Things are getting worse [in my country], especially in my case because my father had his throat cut out ... I do not know whether the police or terrorists who killed him.[154]

My understanding is that these pre-screening interviews are usually more generous than the one described and that the question of safe third countries is not raised during these interviews. However, it seems possible that just as asylum seekers might be denied access to the refugee status determination system on the basis that they are not claiming protection, asylum seekers could be returned to so-called safe third countries before any questions could be raised as to whether their safety is in fact assured in that country.

Conclusion: All an Illusion?

Australia's legislation regarding safe third countries is an example of Chimni's thesis that a new post Cold War vocabulary has developed which, though superficially humanitarian in tenor, denies the right to seek asylum.[155] The legislation seeks to nominate other countries as safe countries that will offer protection to asylum seekers. Yet, as I think this chapter has shown, the legislation may not sufficiently safeguard against refoulement. The words safety and protection have been abused.

In addition, the legislation picks up on the misuse of language in other countries that have introduced safe third country provisions. Instead of persecuted people deserving of protection, asylum seekers are portrayed as 'forum-shoppers', introducing to the humanitarian scheme of refugee law, non-humanitarian language from another context.[156] This language portrays

---

[154] Human Rights and Equal Opportunity Commission, *Those Who've Come Across the Seas: Detention of Unauthorised Arrivals* (Sydney, AGPS, 1998), http://www.hreoc.gov.au/pdf/human_rights/asylum_seekers/h5_2_2.pdf, p 29.

[155] B S Chimni, 'The Incarceration of Victims: Deconstructing Safety Zones' in N Al-Nauimi and R Meese (eds), *International Legal Issues Arising under the United Nations Decade of International Law* (The Hague; Boston, Martinus Nijhoff, 1995), p 823 at p 824.

[156] Forum-shopping was originally a word applied to litigants seeking the best result by choosing the forum to hear their suit. The Australian Department of Immigration and

asylum seekers as a threat to safety. Instead of the refugee being the victim, the second reading speech to the Border Protection Legislation Amendment Act portrays Australia as the victim of strategic claimants for protection and unscrupulous developing countries who do not do enough to protect Australia from these claimants.

However, available statistics suggest Australia is not really at risk of a massive influx of asylum seekers. Moreover, the prospect of avoiding obligations to refugees may be illusory, as the European experience with the Dublin Convention tends to show. The Border Protection Legislation Amendment Act seems more of an exercise in symbolism than real protection – something, which may well prove true for the post *Tampa* package of legislation as well.[157]

But while refugee advocates may take some comfort from that, Australians in general should not. The symbolism of the legislation demonstrates how little we have grown as a nation. The law shirks international responsibilities. It also fails to acknowledge that Australia is enriched by its acceptance of refugees. In discounting factors that may legitimately attract asylum seekers to Australia – such as family ties or the presence of large ethnic communities – Australia ignores the possibility that these support mechanisms may help refugees to adjust and contribute to Australia. Australia has permitted the safe third country concept to migrate from Europe and find a home, rather than the refugees, because of a fundamental failure to recognise refugees' worth as human beings. In so doing, Australia continues to define itself in negative terms, through exclusion, just as it did at the beginning of the 20th century.[158]

Multicultural and Indigenous Affairs defines forum-shopping as: 'when someone with a *bona fide* protection need seeks to choose a particular migration outcome as well as gain protection': DIMIA, *Illegal Migration Issues, Protecting the Border: Immigration Compliance, Glossary* (Canberra, DIMIA, 1999), http://www.immi.gov.au/illegals/border1999/border-gloss.htm.

[157] The government may have won round one by sending some boats back to Indonesia and by farming out refugees to Pacific islands for processing, but there are serious questions as to how long these strategies can be maintained, especially given the expense involved.

[158] On this theme see generally McMaster, above n 13.

7 'Mind the Gap': Seeking Alternative Protection Under the Convention Against Torture and the International Covenant on Civil and Political Rights

NICK POYNDER

Introduction

It has been stated many times[1] that the Refugees Convention is a document of limited scope, reflecting the historical desire of western states to give primary protection to people whose flight was motivated by persecution rooted in the civil and political ideologies of the Soviet bloc states after the Second World War. Even with the extension of Convention protection to events occurring after 1951, under the 1967 Protocol, the vast majority of persons requiring resettlement today do not come within the terms of the Refugees Convention, since their flight is more often prompted by natural disaster,[2] war, or more broadly based political and economic turmoil, than by 'persecution' grounded in civil and political rights.[3]

---

[1] For example, J Hathaway, *The Law of Refugee Status* (Montreal, Butterworths, 1991), pp 6–10.

[2] Editor's note: changes caused by military or political activity which lead to refugee movements often involve the conscious destruction of the environment. For example, the deforestation of Vietnam and Laos in the 1970s, the draining and poisoning of the Tigris marshes in Iraq: M Hain, *Environmental Refugees* (Melbourne, Unpublished, October 2001).

[3] Hathaway above n 1, pp 10–11.

The restricted nature of the Refugees Convention is exacerbated by the current tendency of western governments to interpret the Convention in a strict and legalistic way, so as to limit the obligation to provide protection to asylum seekers who may, under a more generous approach, have satisfied the requirements for refugee status. At the same time, western governments have imposed penalties and other limitations on the processing of asylum applications which were not originally envisaged by the Refugees Convention. These include time limits on applications, safe third country provisions, and the detention of asylum seekers during the processing of their applications.

In some countries (for example Canada) gaps in the Refugees Convention may be filled by domestic legislation enshrining human rights, such as the right to be free from arbitrary detention, or the right not to be returned to a situation of torture.[4] In other countries (for example the United Kingdom) recourse may be had to regional human rights bodies with the power to make enforceable orders, such as the European Court of Human Rights.[5]

In Australia, however, which is unique among western nations in not having any form of entrenched bill of rights, the protection of human rights is left to the government of the day,[6] which all too often makes decisions based on political expediency and crude majoritarianism that ignores the needs of the most vulnerable people in the community. In recent years, the administration of Australia's refugee program has been debased by a bureaucratic culture of exclusion supported by a government that has so politicised the refugee process[7] that serious questions are being asked about Australia's commitment to provide asylum seekers with a fair hearing of their claims or fair treatment while those claims are being determined.[8] In this climate, it is not surprising that asylum seekers and their advocates have begun to look elsewhere for protection and, in the absence of an

---

[4]   D Galloway, 'Criminality and State Protection: Structural Tensions in Canadian Refugee Law', chapter 5 in this book.

[5]   M Gibney, 'The State of Asylum: Democratisation, Judicialisation and Evolution of Refugee Policy', chapter 2 in this book.

[6]   In particular see the discussion by M Crock, 'The Refugees Convention at 50: Mid-life Crisis or Terminal Inadequacy? An Australian Perspective', chapter 3 in this book.

[7]   Crock, ibid.

[8]   N Poynder, 'The Incommunicado Detention of Boat People: A Recent Development in Australian Refugee Policy', *Australian Journal of Human Rights* **3(2)** (1997) p 53.

effective domestic human rights law, the international sphere is becoming increasingly attractive.

In this chapter I will consider some of the alternative means of assisting asylum seekers where they have failed to establish claims under the Refugees Convention, either because of the inherent limitations in the Convention itself or because of a failure by government to comply with the obligations imposed by the Convention. In particular I consider the scope of the alternative protection provided by the International Covenant on Civil and Political Rights (ICCPR) and the Convention against Torture and Other Cruel, Inhuman or Degrading Treatment or Punishment (CAT). Unlike the Refugees Convention, neither of these instruments is specifically incorporated into Australian domestic legislation.[9] Nevertheless they provide a means of filling gaps in the protection provided by the Refugees Convention, albeit as I shall show, of a fragile nature in light of the attitude of the Australian government.

Identifying the Gaps in the Refugees Convention

The very specific nature of the definition of 'refugee' under Article 1A of the Refugees Convention means that there will be people in need of protection who will not meet the definition and will thereby fall through the gaps.[10] In order to satisfy the definition, an applicant must face persecution *because of* one of the five identified 'Convention reasons', namely: race, religion, nationality, membership of particular social group or political opinion. There must be a *nexus* between the persecution faced and the

---

[9] Editor's note: however the Minister for Immigration can take their provisions into account in exercising discretion under section 417 of the Migration Act: see below n 15. The Senate Legal and Constitutional References Committee (SLCRC), *A Sanctuary Under Review: An Examination of Australia's Refugee and Humanitarian Processes* (Canberra, Commonwealth of Australia, June 2000) concluded (recommendation 2.2) that this was an inadequate safeguard and that the obligations should be expressly incorporated. This has been done in Canada: see Galloway, above n 4. See also J Kinsor, 'Non-Refoulement and Torture: The Adequacy of Australia's Laws and Practices in Safeguarding Fugitives from Torture and Trauma', *Australian Institute of Administrative Law Forum* **25** (2000) p 15.

[10] See also K Walker, 'New Uses of the Refugees Convention: Sexuality and Refugee Status', chapter 10 in this book and S Kneebone, 'Moving Beyond the State: Refugees, Accountability and Protection,' chapter 11 in this book for discussions of the definition.

Convention reason.[11] Without such a nexus, a person may be refused asylum even if it can be proven beyond doubt that he or she will be persecuted upon return to the home country.

One example of a group of needy applicants in Australia who have fallen through a gap in the Convention began with a spate of claims in the early 1990s from women who sought protection from the one-child policy of the People's Republic of China. A series of Federal Court decisions[12] had established that these women – who faced forcible abortion and sterilisation upon return to China – came within the Convention reason of 'particular social group'. In response, the government introduced legislation to overrule the court and deny asylum to this group.[13] However in February 1997 the High Court of Australia stepped in and found that these women did not come within the definition of refugee, since there was no nexus between the persecution faced and the Convention reason.[14] As a result, claims from women fleeing the one-child policy are now immediately rejected by the Department of Immigration, and any possible 'protection' against return to China will depend upon the unenforceable discretion of the Minister to allow them to remain on humanitarian grounds.[15] The unreliability of this discretion was illustrated in July 1997, when a pregnant woman was refused asylum and deported to China, where she was later forcibly aborted.[16]

The protections offered by the Refugees Convention have been further eroded in Australia by recent moves to legislatively restrict the definition of refugee so as to require that the predominant motivation for the persecution

---

[11] *Chen Shi Hai v Minister for Immigration* (2000) 201 CLR 293.

[12] Culminating in the decision of the Full Federal Court in *Minister for Immigration v Respondent 'A'* (1994) 54 FCR 333.

[13] Migration Legislation Amendment Bill (No 4) 1995. See N Poynder, 'Recent Implementation of the Refugee Convention in Australia and the Law of Accommodations to International Human Rights Treaties. Have We Gone Too Far?', *Australian Journal of Human Rights* **2(1)** (1995) p 75; P Mathew, 'Conformity or Persecution: China's One Child Policy and Refugee Status', *UNSW Law Journal* **23(3)** (2000) p 103.

[14] *Applicant A v Minister for Immigration* (1997) 185 CLR 259.

[15] Migration Act 1958 (Cth), section 417. This provision is discussed by Crock, above n 6, at n 42, n 130 and text.

[16] See: SLCRC, above n 9, chapter 9, 'The Case of the Chinese Woman'.

must be for a Convention reason.[17] This is undoubtedly intended to exclude groups such as women fleeing domestic violence[18] and persons fleeing violence from other non-state actors such as criminal gangs.[19] The Minister for Immigration considers that the Refugees Convention was not intended to protect these persons.

Apart from those persons in need who do not come within the Convention definition of refugee, there are other categories of people who are specifically excluded from protection under the Refugees Convention. Article 1F of the Convention prohibits the granting of asylum to persons who have committed crimes against peace and security, serious common law criminals, and individuals who have acted in contravention of the principles and purposes of the United Nations.[20] While these categories may elicit little sympathy, cases have arisen in Australia where persons are convicted of drug offences that may attract relatively minor penalties in Australia, but may lead to the death penalty in their home countries. These people are usually refused asylum either under Article 1F or on the grounds that they face legitimate criminal sanctions rather than persecution.[21]

The other major gap in the Refugees Convention arises from the way it is applied by the state concerned. Many arrivals will be genuine refugees, but may be unfairly denied asylum because of the nature of the refugee determination process under the domestic legal system.[22] There is little doubt that decision makers in Australia are under considerable pressure to reject asylum seekers. Apart from the 'screening out' of applicants from their entitlement to apply for asylum by unaccountable officers in the

---

[17] Migration Legislation Amendment Act (No 6) 2001 (Cth), section 91R. This provision is discussed by Crock, above n 6, at n 53 and text. Section 91S of the same legislation restricts the claims of family members of a 'social group' to Refugees Convention grounds.

[18] *MIMA v Khawar* (2002) 67 ALD 577 (High Court) was decided before these provisions came into effect.

[19] For example, *Giraldo v Minister for Immigration* [2000] FCA 113 (Wilcox J, 23 February 2001). See also P Ruddock, 'Changes to Assist Courts', *Media Release*, 10 May 2001.

[20] Galloway, above n 4. See *MIMA v Singh* (2002) 186 ALR 393 (High Court).

[21] Communication 706/96, *GT v Australia* (UN Doc CCPR/C/61/D/706/1996, 4 December 1997); Communication 692/1996, *ARJ v Australia* (UN Doc CCPR/C/60/D/692/1996, 11 August 1997) discussed in the text below at n 65.

[22] Crock, above n 6, at n 64 and text; Poynder, above n 8.

detention centres, one only has to consider the all too regular examples of irrational, unfair and barely conceivable findings made against applicants by departmental decision makers and the Refugee Review Tribunal (RRT)[23] to see that the system is under great strain in this country.[24]

The scrutiny of primary decisions by the courts is also heavily restricted in Australia, with limitations under the Migration Act which apply to the judicial review of all migration decisions, which attempt to restrict judicial review of such decisions.[25] In addition, the final 'safety net', which is contained in the Minister's section 417 discretion to allow people to remain on humanitarian grounds, is rarely used, and is unenforceable and unreviewable by the courts.[26]

Finally, there is an absence of an effective complaints mechanism under the Refugees Convention itself. Where a person has unfairly been denied asylum, or is otherwise being treated in a way that is incompatible with the Refugees Convention, there is no formalised means of raising these individual concerns at an appropriate international level.[27] The office of the regional representative for the United Nations High Commissioner for Refugees (UNHCR) in Canberra has a difficult task to maintain a good working relationship with the Australian government.[28] While the annual meetings of the Executive Committee of the High Commissioner in Geneva (Ex Com) invariably involve behind-closed-doors criticism of some countries, the public comments by Ex Com are often so generalised as to be of little assistance in promoting specific reform of refugee policies and processes.[29]

---

[23] S Kneebone, 'The Refugee Review Tribunal and the Assessment of Credibility: An Inquisitorial Role?', *Australian Journal of Administrative Law* 5 (1998) p 78.

[24] Crock, above n 6.

[25] Migration (Judicial Review) Act 2001 (Cth) discussed by Crock, above n 6, at n 92 and text.

[26] See above n 15.

[27] J Hathaway, 'Taking Oversight to Refugee Law Seriously', Speech, Global Consultations on International Protection, Ministerial Meeting of States Parties, 12–13 December 2001.

[28] Editor's note: this was evident in the public exchanges between the Australian government and UNHCR in September 2001 during the *Tampa* crisis discussed in L Curran and S Kneebone, 'Overview', chapter 1 in this book.

[29] Editor's note: see the discussion of the role of the UNHCR in L Curran, 'Global Solutions', chapter 12 in this book.

In the light of all the above it is little wonder, therefore, that asylum seekers are looking towards other international mechanisms as an alternative means of protection.

Overview of the International Complaints Mechanisms

The ICCPR and the Convention Against Torture

Apart from the Refugees Convention, the two international treaties which are most relevant to the rights of asylum seekers are the International Covenant on Civil and Political Rights (ICCPR) and the Convention against Torture and Other Cruel, Inhuman or Degrading Treatment or Punishment (CAT). The ICCPR was adopted by the United Nations (UN) General Assembly on 16 December 1966 and it entered into force for Australia on 13 November 1980.[30] As at 21 August 2001 it had been ratified or acceded to by 148 states, Australia having acceded on 13 November 1980.[31] The CAT was adopted by the UN General Assembly on 10 December 1984, and it entered into force in Australia on 7 September 1989.[32] As at 21 August 2001, the CAT had been ratified or acceded to by 130 states.

Each of the conventions contains an optional procedure by which individuals may lodge a complaint (or 'communication') alleging that their rights under the convention are being breached by the state signatory. This procedure is contained in the First Optional Protocol to the ICCPR (OP), and in Article 22 of CAT which provides for recognition by states parties of the communications process. As at 21 August 2001, 102 states had acceded to the OP and 54 states had recognised the complaints process under the CAT.[33] Australia acceded to the OP on 25 December 1991, and it recognised the complaints process under CAT on 29 January 1993.[34]

---

[30] Australian Treaty Series 1980, No 23.

[31] Office of the United Nations High Commissioner for Human Rights, Status of Ratifications of the Principal International Human Rights Treaties as at 21 May 2001, http://www.unhchr.ch. See also the Treaty Bodies Database on the same website.

[32] Australian Treaty Series 1989, No 21.

[33] Ibid.

[34] Ibid. Editor's note: these mechanisms are discussed in the report of the SLCRC, above n 9, at para 2.43–2.65.

The determination of communications is undertaken by specialist committees, which also monitor the general implementation of each convention by the states parties. The ICCPR is supervised by the United Nations Human Rights Committee (HRC), which consists of 18 independent experts 'of high moral character and recognised competence in the field of human rights'.[35] The HRC meets three times a year for sessions of three weeks' duration: in March at the United Nations headquarters in New York and in July and November at the UN Office in Geneva. The CAT is supervised by the Committee Against Torture (UNCAT), which consists of ten experts of similar moral standing and competence.[36] It has two sessions per year. Each committee has rules of procedure which govern the determination of communications.[37]

Requirements for Communications

Communications must not be anonymous, and they should be made by the individual who claims that his or her rights have been violated.[38] Where the individual cannot submit the communication, the Committee may consider a communication from another person who must prove that he or she is acting on behalf of the alleged victim.[39] A third party with no apparent links to the person whose rights have allegedly been violated cannot submit a communication.

Victims do not have to be nationals of the state alleged to be in breach, as long as they are within the jurisdiction and territory of the state.[40] This means that non-citizens within the state will be protected by each treaty.

---

[35] ICCPR, Article 28.

[36] CAT, Article 17.

[37] *Rules of Procedure of the UNHRC* (UN Doc CCPR/C/3/Rev.6, 24 April 2001) and the *Rules of Procedure of the UNCAT* (UN Doc CAT/C/3/Rev.3, 13 July 1998). Each can be accessed via the UN Treaty Bodies Database: http://www.unhchr.ch/tbs/doc.nsf through the links: documents – by treaty – Committee Against Torture/Human Rights Committee – basic reference document (scroll down using 'next').

[38] UNHRC rule 90(a); UNCAT rule 107(a).

[39] UNHRC rule 90(b); UNCAT rule 107(b); see also *Mr Colin McDonald and Mr Nicholas Poynder on behalf of Mr Y v Australia*, (Communication 772/1997, UN Doc CCPR/C/69/D/772/1997, 17 July 2000), reported in *Netherlands Quarterly of Human Rights* **19(1)** (March 2001) p 77.

[40] ICCPR, Article 2(1); OP, Article 1.

The major admissibility requirement for all communications is that the individual must first have 'exhausted' all domestic remedies.[41] This provides the state party with an opportunity to correct the human rights abuse at a domestic level before it is taken to the international sphere. In each case the individual must exhaust all available *judicial* remedies until a final adjudication has been reached, with no possibility of further appeal.[42] In Australia this would usually require the individual to take the matter to the High Court. There is also some suggestion that an individual must exhaust any available *administrative* remedies which offer a reasonable prospect of redress, although non-enforceable administrative and executive remedies tend to be viewed with some suspicion by the committees.[43]

A failure to comply with procedural requirements, such as a failure to meet time limits on the lodgement of an appeal, means that the communication will be inadmissible unless such failure can somehow be attributed to the state party.[44] Lack of funds will not usually absolve an applicant from pursuing domestic remedies unless the state party can be regarded as being responsible in some way, for example by refusing to provide legal aid.[45]

However there is no requirement to exhaust remedies that objectively have no prospect of success. For example, during the 1980s the HRC repeatedly found that individuals lodging communications against the state security forces in Uruguay did not have to pursue all available domestic remedies, as the military regime did not provide a fair and effective system of justice.[46] An applicant will not be required to pursue futile proceedings

---

[41] OP Article 5(2)(b); CAT Article 22(5)(b).

[42] See cases referred to in S Joseph, J Schultz and M Castan, *The International Covenant on Civil and Political Rights: Cases, Materials and Commentary* (Oxford, Oxford University Press, 2000), pp 74–5.

[43] Id, p 75. Note that in the current communication of *C v Australia* (Communication 930/2000) the Australian government has claimed that the alleged victim of prolonged detention should first have made a complaint to the Human Rights and Equal Opportunity Commission, a purely administrative remedy which cannot lead to any enforceable order against the government.

[44] *APA v Spain* (Communication 433/90, UN Doc CCPR/C/50/D/433/1990, 28 March 1994).

[45] *Henry v Jamaica* (Communication 230/1987, UN Doc CCPR/C/43/D/230/1987, 19 November 1991); see also the cases referred to in Joseph et al, above n 42, pp 88–9.

[46] See Joseph et al, above n 42, pp 80–1.

for the purpose of admissibility where the matter has previously been determined by the highest domestic tribunal. For example, since the decision of the High Court of Australia in *Lim v Minister for Immigration*,[47] which established that domestic courts have no power to release asylum seekers lawfully held in detention, applicants alleging arbitrary detention under the ICCPR have not been required by the HRC to pursue the matter to the High Court in order to exhaust domestic remedies.[48]

Finally, there is no requirement to pursue domestic remedies which would be 'unreasonably prolonged'; for example, where a complaint would take several years to make its way through the court system.[49]

Interim Measures

One of the most useful mechanisms for protecting asylum seekers from removal has been the interim measures provision under the Rules of Procedure of each committee. Communications usually take several years to determine. To ensure that the applicant is protected in the meantime the Rules provide that the relevant committee may inform the state party of the desirability of taking interim measures to avoid possible irreparable damage to the person who claims to be a victim of the violation.[50]

In practice in removal cases, a request for interim measures is made at the same time as the communication, and it will be considered urgently by the Special Rapporteur on New Communications. If the rapporteur is satisfied that such measures are required, he or she will contact the relevant state party representative and request that the person not be deported pending a final determination of the communication.

---

[47]　(1992) 176 CLR 1.

[48]　The applicant in the first communication against Australia alleging arbitrary detention, *A (name deleted) v Australia* (Communication 560/1993, UN Doc CCPR/C/59/D/560/1993, 30 April 1997), had also been a party in the High Court proceedings in *Lim* (1992) 176 CLR 1 and there was no question that he had thereby exhausted domestic remedies.

[49]　*Andras Fillastre v Bolivia* (Communication 336/1988, UN Doc CCPR/C/43/D/336/1988, 6 November 1991).

[50]　UNHRC, rule 86; UNCAT, rule 108(9).

Determination of Communications

Once a communication has been received, the committee will request the state party to provide its comments on the admissibility and merits of the matter within six months.[51] This has routinely been ignored by Australia.[52] The applicant is then given an opportunity to comment on the state party's submission, following which the matter is set down at one of the committee sessions for delivery of the final 'views' on the communication.

The committees seek to come to a single view by consensus; however individual members can and often do add their opinions to the views expressed by the committee as a whole.

Views of the committees are not enforceable; however they are widely published[53] and carry significant moral and persuasive authority. There is no doubt, for example, that the HRC's 1994 finding in *Toonen v Australia*,[54] that Tasmania's anti-homosexual laws were in breach of Article 17 of the ICCPR, led directly to the enactment by the Australian parliament of legislation rendering those laws ineffective.[55] Similarly, the finding in *A (name deleted) v Australia* that the detention of a Cambodian asylum seeker was arbitrary and in breach of Article 9 of the ICCPR has meant that the Australian government can no longer credibly claim that its policy of mandatory detention of asylum seekers is not in breach of human rights.

---

[51] UNHRC, rule 91; UNCAT, rule 110.

[52] The Australian submissions are prepared by the well-resourced Office of International Law of the Attorney-General's Department; nevertheless they took some 12 months to be delivered to the UNHRC in the matters of *A (name deleted) v Australia* and *Y v Australia* and 16 months (and three reminders from the UNHRC) in the current communication of *C v Australia*.

[53] Most views can be found in the UN Treaty Bodies Database, above n 37, and are published in the annual reports of each committee to the UN General Assembly. In addition, they are increasingly reported in journals such as the *Netherlands Quarterly of Human Rights, Butterworths Human Rights Cases, International Journal of Refugee Law* and *Interrights Bulletin*, as well as texts such as Joseph et al, above n 42, and M Nowak, *UN Covenant on Civil and Political Rights: CCPR Commentary* (Kehl am Rhein, Engel, 1993).

[54] *Toonen v Australia*, (Communication 488/1992, UN Doc CCPR/C/50/D/488/1992, 4 April 1994), discussed in Walker, above n 10.

[55] Human Rights (Sexual Conduct) Act 1994 (Cth).

As at 29 August 2002, 49 communications had been lodged against Australia under the OP to the ICCPR. Of these, 20 were at pre-admissibility stage, 19 had been determined to be inadmissible, four had been discontinued, two had been determined not to disclose a violation and four had been the subject of findings against Australia.[56] As at 30 May 2002, 18 communications had been lodged against Australia under Article 22 of the Torture Convention. Of these, five were at the pre-admissibility stage, nine had been discontinued, and one had been the subject of a finding against Australia.[57] In three further cases CAT found no violation.

Communications by Asylum Seekers under the ICCPR

The ICCPR contains broad-ranging provisions that protect a number of human rights. It has been used by asylum seekers in Australia to challenge conditions of detention, and to prevent their removal to states where their rights may be violated. Outside the immediate asylum context it has also been used in immigration cases to prevent family breakup, for example, where the forced removal of a non-citizen parent would separate the parent from a child who is a citizen of the state.[58]

The prolonged detention of an asylum seeker was the subject of the second communication under the OP that led to a finding against Australia,

---

[56] United Nations High Commissioner for Human Rights, *Statistical survey of individual complaints considered*, http://www.unhchr.ch/html/menu2/8/stat2.htm. The four findings against Australia were: *Toonen v Australia* (Communication 488/92, UN Doc CCPR/C/50/D/488/1992, 4 April 1994); *A (name deleted) v Australia* (Communication 560/1993, UN Doc CCPR/C/59/D/560/1993, 30 April 1997); *Winata v Australia*, (Communication 930/2000, UN Doc CCPR/C/72/D/930/2000, 16 August 2001) discussed below; *Rogerson v Australia* (Communication 802/98, UN Doc CCPR/C/74/D/802/1998, 20 April 2002).

[57] United Nations High Commissioner for Human Rights, Statistical survey of individual complaints considered, http://www.unhchr.ch/html/menu2/8/stat3.htm. The finding against Australia was in *Elmi v Australia* (Communication 106/98, UN Doc CAT/C/22/D/120/1998, 25 May 1999).

[58] See *Winata v Australia* (Communication 930/2000, UN Doc CCPR/C/72/D/930/2000, 16 August 2001). For the European jurisprudence in this area, see H Lambert, 'The European Court of Human Rights and the Right of Refugees and Other Persons in Need of Protection to Family Reunion', *International Journal of Refugee Law* **11(3)** (1999) p 427.

in *A (name deleted) v Australia.*[59] In that case the HRC found that the detention of a Cambodian national for over four years was in breach of Articles 9(1) and 9(4) of the ICCPR, which prohibit arbitrary detention.[60] A communication is currently under consideration in the matter of *C v Australia,*[61] which involves an Iranian asylum seeker who was incarcerated in immigration detention in Melbourne for so long that he developed a psychiatric disorder.

C v Australia also illustrates the second type of communication which has been pursued before the HRC by asylum seekers. Mr C had actually been recognised as a refugee by the Department of Immigration. However, because of his psychiatric disorder, he formed a delusion about a female employee at the Maribyrnong Detention Centre. Upon release he approached and threatened her on three occasions. The Department of Immigration then sought to deport him to Iran, where it had already found that he faced persecution.[62] For the past five years he has been held in a prison psychiatric ward and, despite the unanimous opinions of no less than four psychiatrists that he has made a full recovery and is no longer a danger to the community, the Minister has refused to release him and is strenuously defending the matter in the HRC.

The usual view taken by the HRC in removal cases is that a state party will be liable where it takes a decision relating to a person within its jurisdiction and the 'necessary and foreseeable consequence' of that decision is that the person's rights will be violated. Thus, if the state party hands over a person to another state, either by extradition[63] or deportation,[64] it would be in violation of the treaty if it is a necessary and foreseeable consequence that the person's rights under the ICCPR will be violated.

---

[59] *A (name deleted) v Australia*, above n 56.

[60] For a general discussion of the decision, see N Poynder, '*A (name deleted) v Australia*: A Milestone for Asylum Seekers', *Australian Journal of Human Rights* **4(1)** (1997) p 155.

[61] Editor's note: in *C v Australia* (Communication 900/2000, UN Doc CCPR/C/76/D/900/1999, 13 November 2002), decided on 13 November 2002, the HRC found against Australia.

[62] *Bektoshabeh v Minister for Immigration* (1998) 157 ALR 95.

[63] *Kindler v Canada* (Communication 470/91, UN Doc CCPR/C/48/D/470/1991, 18 November 1993).

[64] *GT v Australia* (Communication 706/96, UN Doc CCPR/C/61/D/706/1996, 4 December 1997).

Thus far, there have been final views on two communications relating to removal from Australia, each involving persons convicted of drug-related charges who had sought refugee status on the grounds of the treatment they would receive upon return to their home countries.

The case of *ARJ v Australia*[65] involved an Iranian citizen who had been arrested in Western Australia on charges of importing and possessing cannabis resin. He had applied for refugee status and, while the RRT had found that he was likely to face treatment of an extremely harsh nature upon return to Iran, it did not consider that he came within the Convention definition of refugee as his fear arose solely out of his conviction for a criminal act. The applicant had unsuccessfully appealed to the Federal Court, and had been advised by the Legal Aid Commission of Western Australia that any further appeal was futile. He had also been refused humanitarian entry by the Minister for Immigration under section 417 of the Migration Act.[66] In his communication to the HRC he claimed that if he was returned to Iran, which has the death penalty for drug offences, he would face a violation of his right to life under Article 6 of the ICCPR prohibiting the death penalty and Article 7 prohibiting torture. He also claimed that he would have to face the Islamic Revolutionary Tribunals, which would deny him the procedural safeguards guaranteed by Article 14 of the ICCPR.

The HRC issued an interim request that Australia refrain from deporting the applicant pending the determination of his complaint. This was maintained despite a request by Australia that it be withdrawn. The HRC found the communication to be admissible; however it ultimately found against the applicant on the merits of the claim, on the grounds that his offence only carried a five year maximum term of imprisonment in Iran, and there was no evidence that he was likely to be arrested and prosecuted upon return to Iran.

The case of *GT v Australia*[67] involved a Malaysian national who had been convicted of importing heroin into Australia. Following his release on parole, he sought a protection visa on the basis that if he was extradited to Malaysia he would be charged under the Dangerous Drugs Act, which carried a mandatory death penalty. His application for refugee status

---

[65]　*ARJ v Australia*, above n 21.

[66]　See above n 15.

[67]　*GT v Australia*, above n 21.

was rejected and he appealed to the Federal Court and lodged a communication with the UNHRC. Once again the Committee made a request for interim measures and maintained the request despite Australia's submission that it should be lifted. Again, however, the communication was rejected by the Committee on the grounds that nothing in the information before it pointed to any intention on the part of Malaysian authorities to prosecute the applicant.

The way is clearly open, however, to obtain protection under the OP where it can objectively be shown that the removal of the person will lead to a breach of that person's rights under the ICCPR. In the case of *C v Australia*, the Minister has sought to deny that Mr C will be at risk upon return to Iran, despite the finding of his own delegate that he faces persecution in Iran. It will be interesting to see how the HRC weighs up the various items of country information relating to Iran when determining its views on this communication.[68]

Communications by Asylum Seekers under the CAT

Article 3 of the CAT contains an absolute prohibition on states from returning (or refouling) anyone to another state where there are 'substantial grounds for believing she would be in danger of torture'.

'Torture' is defined in Article 1 as:

> any act by which severe pain or suffering, whether physical or mental, is intentionally inflicted on a person for such purposes as obtaining from him or a third person information or a confession, punishing him for an act he or a third person has committed or is suspected of having committed, or intimidating or coercing him or a third person, or for any reason based on discrimination of any kind, when such pain or suffering is inflicted by or at the instigation of or with the consent or acquiescence of a public official or other person acting in an official capacity.

The CAT also prohibits states within their own territories from any acts of 'cruel, inhuman or degrading treatment or punishment',[69] which are

---

[68] Editor's note: the HRC found that Australia had not established any change in the circumstances in Iran which had led to Mr C being granted refugee status as an Assyrian Christian: *C v Australia*, above n 61, para 8.5.

[69] CAT, Article 16.

generally regarded to be lower than torture in the hierarchy of ill-treatment.[70] However the non-refoulement obligation only covers the situation where a person actually faces *torture* upon return. As such, the CAT is more limited in scope than the OP, which covers any breaches of the ICCPR, and indeed it is also more limited in scope than the Refugees Convention, which covers a 'real chance' of persecution not necessarily amounting to torture.

On the other hand, both the CAT and the ICCPR are broader than the Refugees Convention, in that they do not require a nexus between the ill-treatment and one of the five Convention reasons.[71] In addition, the absolute prohibition upon return under the CAT would also cover persons excluded under Article 1F of the Refugees Convention for having committed crimes against humanity.[72]

In determining communications under the CAT, the UNCAT will look afresh at all the facts of the case, including current information as to whether there is a consistent pattern of gross, flagrant or mass violations of human rights in the receiving state.[73] It will also give considerable weight to findings of fact made by the state authorities. Thus, in its views in *NP (name withheld) v Australia*[74] the Committee rejected the applicant's contention that he would be at risk upon return to Sri Lanka, noting the important inconsistencies in his statements before the RRT and observing that he had not provided the Committee with any arguments, including medical evidence, which could have explained such inconsistencies. On the other hand, the UNCAT will not be bound by such findings, and it considers itself free to assess the facts based upon the full set of circumstances in every case.

---

[70] D Anker, *Law of Asylum in the United States* (Boston, Refugee Law Centre, 3rd ed, 1999), p 482.

[71] B Gorlick, 'The Convention and the Committee against Torture: A Complementary Protection Regime for Refugees', *International Journal of Refugee Law* 11 (1999) p 479 at p 484 summarises the jurisprudence of the UNCAT which does require a causal link to be established between the risk of torture and the applicant's background.

[72] Galloway, above n 4.

[73] CAT, General Comment No 1, *Implementation of Article 3 of the Convention in the Context of Article 22* (UN Doc A53/44, annex IX, 21 November 1997), para 6(a); Gorlick above n 71.

[74] *NP (name withheld) v Australia* (Communication 120/98, UN Doc CAT/C/22/D/106/1998, 3 June 1999).

Thus far, all 18 communications lodged against Australia under the CAT have been from failed asylum seekers.[75] Perhaps the most well-known of these communications is the case of *Elmi v Australia*.[76] This involved a Somali asylum seeker who had a strong claim for refugee status, based on his membership of a minority clan which had a well-documented history of persecution from the dominant clan in Mogadishu. His claim was rejected by the RRT on the grounds that any harm he faced upon return to Somalia would be because of the generalised situation of civil war rather than any Convention reason. He had unsuccessfully sought review of his case by the High Court, and he had been refused humanitarian entry by the Minister for Immigration. An attempt was then made to remove him by the Department of Immigration, but this failed when the captain of the airline refused to carry him. By then Mr Elmi had lodged a communication with the UNCAT, which made a request for interim measures to the Australian mission in Geneva. At the same time Amnesty International initiated an 'Urgent Action' against the Minister, which led to a flood of letters of protest to the Minister's office. When the Department finally managed to get Mr Elmi on a plane from Melbourne to Perth, it was held up at Perth Airport by picketing trade unionists. It was only then that the Minister agreed to comply with the interim measure and undertook not to remove Mr Elmi.[77]

When Mr Elmi's case was finally considered by UNCAT, it rejected Australia's argument that the CAT did not apply to a situation of generalised violence, since the majority clan which held Mogadishu could be regarded as exercising de facto control and was therefore responsible for any acts of torture for the purposes of the Convention.[78] The Committee determined that Australia had an obligation to refrain from forcibly

---

[75] See UN Committee Against Torture *Summary Record of the First Part (Public) of the 444th Meeting: Australia* (UN Doc CAT/C/SR.444, 25th Session, 21 November 2000), accessed via the UN Treaty Bodies Database, above n 37.

[76] *Elmi v Australia* (Communication No 106/98, UN Doc No CAT/C/22/D/120/1998, 25 May 1999).

[77] For an account of the failed attempt to deport Mr Elmi, see M Crock, 'A Sanctuary Under Review: Where to from here for Australia's Refugee and Humanitarian Program?', *UNSW Law Journal* **23(3)** (2000) p 246 at pp 261–4. See also SLCRC, above n 9, chapter 7, 'The Case of Mr SE'.

[78] Contrast the discussion of *Ibrahim v Minister for Immigration* in Kneebone, above n 10.

returning Mr Elmi to Somalia or to any other country where he runs a risk of being expelled or returned to Somalia.

Australia's response to the views of the UNCAT in *Elmi* is an illustration of the contempt that it has recently shown to international human rights bodies and their norms.[79] The Department of Immigration's first reaction to the interim measures undertaking was to transfer Mr Elmi to the Port Hedland Detention Centre, where he was completely isolated from his advisers in Melbourne. He was only moved back to Melbourne when an application was lodged by his advisers in the Federal Court. Then, instead of granting Mr Elmi a protection visa in response to the Committee's final views, the Minister determined that he would have to re-apply for asylum from the beginning, and remain in detention during the entire period that his case was being re-processed. Unsurprisingly, his case was rejected by the Minister's delegate and the RRT. Eventually, rather than spend any longer in detention awaiting court appeals, Mr Elmi chose to get on an aircraft heading in the general direction of Somalia, and his current whereabouts are unknown.

Conclusion: The Future of the International Complaints Procedure in Australia

The case of Mr Elmi was undoubtedly one of the issues that brought Australia's grievances against the international communications procedures to a head. It was not only highly embarrassing to the department and the Minister being 'caught out' trying to remove Mr Elmi before his lawyers could protect him; it also illustrated the way in which the international mechanisms could be used to strike at the very heart of the department's and the Minister's culture of control over the refugee determination process. Here was a situation where non-citizens could gain some sort of a migration outcome by appealing to an international body that was not subject to the political and administrative control exercised over the tribunals and courts in Australia.

Accordingly, in a Joint News Release issued on 29 August 2000, ironically entitled 'Improving the Effectiveness of United Nations Committees' Minister Ruddock, along with Foreign Affairs Minister

---

[79] D Otto, 'From "reluctance" to "exceptionalism": The Australian approach to domestic implementation of human rights', *Alternative Law Journal* **26(5)** (2001) p 219.

Alexander Downer and Attorney-General Daryl Williams announced that the government would take 'strong measures' to improve the effectiveness of the UN human rights treaty bodies, including the implementation of a package of measures to 'improve' interaction with UN human rights treaty committees, and the rejection of 'unwarranted requests from treaty committees to delay removal of unsuccessful asylum seekers from Australia'. This move was part of a wider agenda by the government to attack the credibility of the UN human rights system in general which, apart from its criticism of Australia's asylum procedures, had been strongly critical of its policies on Aboriginal people and women.[80] Nevertheless, the writing was on the wall: democratic countries like Australia will not stand for interference in its asylum procedures from unelected committees consisting largely of foreigners.

Since the joint announcement, Australia has indicated its reluctance to cooperate with requests for interim measures from the committees. Shortly prior to the announcement, in June 2000, the Australian Government Solicitor refused to give an undertaking to the UNCAT that it would not remove a Somali asylum seeker pending determination of his communication, although the undertaking was given later, after the person attempted to commit suicide in the detention centre.[81] In other cases, undertakings not to remove applicants which were given prior to the announcement appear to have been honoured.

It is clear, however, that the Australian authorities are greatly irritated by the 'interference' of the international treaty bodies, and things will not be easy for those who seek to remain in Australia by resorting to the communications process. *Elmi's case* suggests that the only remedy which will be provided by Australia to a successful applicant before a committee will be for the decision making process to be remitted to the start, which could lead to the same result after years of waiting, potentially involving further communications and an endless cycle of international and domestic action.

In the meantime, of course, the applicant will remain in detention or, if not already detained, will be taken into detention because there is no

---

[80] See M Kingston, 'Three Wise Men?', *Sydney Morning Herald Web Diary*, 29 August 2000, http://www.smh.com.au/news/webdiary/0106/01/A35098-2000Aug29.html.

[81] *YHA v Australia* (Communication 162/2000, UN Doc CAT/C/27/D/162/2000, 23 November 2001). This matter was rejected by UNCAT: due to the change in circumstances in Somalia the applicant was no longer at risk upon return.

provision for a bridging visa pending the determination of a complaint of an international body.[82] This is of course a powerful disincentive to prospective applicants, and one which will no doubt be resorted to by the Australian authorities regardless of the HRC's views in *A's case* that such detention would be arbitrary and in breach of the ICCPR.

In the longer term, however, it is unlikely that Australia will be able to avoid its obligations under either the ICCPR, the CAT, or any of the communications processes. The one attempt to withdraw from the ICCPR, by Korea in 1997, was met with such severe criticism that it did not proceed.[83] The only state that has ever denounced a communications process was Jamaica, when it denounced the OP with effect from January 1998; however this is widely seen as a petulant and immature response by a country embarrassed by the enormous number of adverse views by the HRC, primarily relating to the death penalty and the death row phenomenon.

It is unlikely that Australia would further risk its international human rights reputation by seeking to withdraw from its obligations under the ICCPR and CAT. What is more likely is that Australia will continue in its diplomatic efforts to have sympathetic members elected to the committees and to otherwise pressure the committees so as to ensure that Australia receives a more favourable hearing.[84] This will not be in the best interests of asylum seekers in this country.

---

[82]   S Taylor, 'The Human Rights of Rejected Asylum Seekers Being Removed from Australia', chapter 8 in this book.

[83]   See for example, Human Rights Committee *Summary Record of the 1616th Meeting* (UN Doc CCPR/C/SR.1616, 26 November 1997).

[84]   The refusal of the Howard government to re-nominate the highly regarded Justice Elizabeth Evatt to the UNHRC and its nomination instead of Professor Ivan Shearer was widely regarded as an attempt to shift the ideological balance of the Committee in Australia's favour: L Brereton, Shadow Minister for Foreign Affairs, 'UN Human Rights Committee: Howard Government Declines to Renominate Justice Elizabeth Evatt', Media Release, 21 June 2000.

8 The Human Rights of Rejected Asylum Seekers Being Removed From Australia

SAVITRI TAYLOR[*]

Introduction

As other chapters in this book demonstrate, there are many aspects of Australia's asylum seeker law, policy and procedures that could raise legitimate concerns that among the non-citizens removed from Australia are many persons who are, in fact, very much in need of international protection. However, this chapter considers only the situation of persons whose asylum claims are rejected by Australia after consideration of protection visa applications made by them.[1] Further, it is assumed for

[*] I gratefully acknowledge the ARC funding provided for this research through a La Trobe University Faculty of Law and Management Research Grant and the research assistance provided by Francesca Bartlett and Julian Littler. Thanks also to Michael Head for his useful comments. I asked the Department of Immigration and Multicultural Affairs (DIMA) for its input in relation to the matters raised in this chapter. I was informed that DIMA could not, for reasons of privacy, provide information relating to individual cases. I was promised input in relation to other matters, but, despite a great deal of persistence on my part, such input was never provided. Editor's note: from September 2001, the Department became the Department of Immigration and Multicultural and Indigenous Affairs (DIMIA).

[1] On 26 September 2001, the government passed the Migration Amendment (Excision from Migration Zone) Act 2001 (Cth) defining Christmas Island, Ashmore and Cartier Islands, Cocos (Keeling) Islands, any other external territory or island that may in the future be prescribed by regulation and Australian offshore installations to be 'excised offshore places'. The Act defines a person who becomes an unlawful non-citizen by entering an excised offshore place as an 'offshore entry person', and invalidates a purported visa application if it is made by an offshore entry person who is an unlawful non-citizen in Australia: section 46A. The Migration Amendment (Excision from Migration Zone) (Consequential Provisions) Act 2001 (Cth), also passed on

present purposes that, in close to all cases, these rejected asylum seekers (that is, failed protection visa applicants) are 'persons not in need of international protection'.[2] If we start with this assumption there is no getting past the fact that after the final rejection of their asylum claim (and at some point the rejection must be considered final), the rejected asylum seeker has no special immunity against the operation of a state's system of immigration control.[3] This is not to say, however, that rejected asylum seekers do not have any rights at all. They do have rights – human rights. This chapter deals with some of the human rights issues arising from the removal of rejected asylum seekers from Australia.

Automatic Removal Provisions

Community-based Asylum Seekers

Sixty-six per cent of those who applied for a protection visa in 1999–2000, arrived in Australia with some kind of temporary visa.[4] A non-citizen, who is the holder of a substantive visa at the time of making a protection visa application, will be granted a bridging visa upon the expiry of the substantive visa. A visa overstayer,[5] who applies for a protection visa, will also normally be granted a bridging visa.[6] A bridging visa gives its holder

---

26 September 2001, allows offshore entry persons to be taken to declared countries (section 198A) and creates visa classes to which offshore entry persons making asylum claims will be given access. The treatment of offshore entry persons whose asylum claims are rejected will not be considered in this chapter.

[2]   This is the sense in which United Nations High Commissioner for Refugees (UNHCR) uses the term 'rejected asylum seeker': Executive Committee of the High Commissioner's Programme (Ex Com) Standing Committee, *Return of Persons Not in Need of International Protection* (Geneva, UNHCR, UN Doc EC/46/SC/CRP.36, 28 May 1996), para 9.

[3]   G Noll, 'Rejected Asylum Seekers: The Problem of Return', Working Paper 4, UNHCR Centre for Documentation and Research, May 1999, http://www.unhcr.ch.

[4]   DIMA, *Refugee and Humanitarian Issues: Australia's Response*, (Canberra, DIMA, October 2000), p 23.

[5]   This is the term commonly used to describe a non-citizen who has remained in Australia after the expiration of a temporary visa.

[6]   A bridging visa will not be granted if the facts of the particular case suggest that detention is necessary for the purpose of ensuring that the non-citizen will be available for removal from the country.

the status of lawful non-citizen, allowing them to be at liberty and protecting them from removal from Australia for the period of its currency. The bridging visa is granted for the duration of primary and, where applicable, Refugee Review Tribunal (RRT) stages of protection visa application processing, expiring 28 days after notification of the RRT decision. If an application is made for judicial review of the administrative decision making, a bridging visa is granted which expires 28 days after a decision in the proceedings (including any appeals).[7] A non-citizen will also be granted a bridging visa to cover the period during which:

• his or her protection visa application is being assessed by an officer against the Minister's guidelines for section 417 intervention for the first time;[8] or
• 'the Minister is personally considering whether to exercise, or to consider the exercise of,' the Minister's section 417 power.[9]

Community-based asylum seekers, who are unsuccessful in all their attempts to obtain a protection visa, but make 'acceptable arrangements to depart Australia' may be granted a bridging visa to keep their status lawful

---

[7]   See M Crock, 'The Refugees Convention at 50: Mid-life Crisis or Terminal Inadequacy? An Australian Perspective', chapter 3 in this book for a discussion of Part 8 of the Migration Act 1958 (Cth) (Migration Act) and the availability of review of decisions.

[8]   If a protection visa applicant is unsuccessful at the RRT stage, the Minister for Immigration has a non-compellable power under Migration Act, section 417 to 'substitute for a decision of the [RRT] another decision, being a decision that is more favourable to the applicant, whether or not the Tribunal had the power to make that other decision.' See Crock, above n 7, n 42, for a discussion of the Minister's discretions under the Act. The Minister is able to use the power to grant protection visas to non-citizens to whom Australia has protection obligations under the Convention Against Torture (CAT) and/or the International Covenant of Civil and Political Rights (ICCPR) though not the Refugee Convention: DIMA, *Migration Series Instruction (MSI) 225: Ministerial Guidelines for the Identification of Unique or Exceptional Cases where it may be in the Public Interest to Substitute a More Favourable Decision under s 345, 351, 391, 417, 454 of the Migration Act 1958* (Canberra, DIMA, 4 May 1999), paras 4.2.2 and 4.2.4. About two-thirds of people rejected by the RRT request exercise of the section 417 power: Senate Legal and Constitutional References Committee (SLCRC), *A Sanctuary Under Review: An Examination of Australia's Refugee and Humanitarian Processes* (Canberra, Commonwealth of Australia, June 2000), para 8.70. In 1997–98 1.35 per cent were successful in getting a visa under section 147. In 1998–99 the figure was 3.64 per cent.

[9]   Migration Regulations (Cth), schedule 2, para 050.212(6).

pending departure.[10] However, those who do not leave the country voluntarily and at their own expense become unlawful non-citizens by reason of no longer holding a valid bridging visa and become subject to detention and removal in the same manner as all other unlawful non-citizens.[11] Of course, they have to be located first and this is not always possible. According to a recent parliamentary research paper, rejected asylum seekers 'comprise a growing proportion of our illegal visa "overstayer" population'.[12] Most western countries face the same problem.

Asylum Seekers in Mandatory Detention

Law Thirty-four per cent of those who applied for a protection visa in 1999–2000 arrived in Australia without any authorisation.[13] Upon entering Australia's 'migration zone',[14] an unauthorised arrival becomes an unlawful non-citizen and remains so until he or she leaves the migration zone or is granted a visa. An unauthorised arrival who applies for a protection visa is usually kept in immigration detention pending determination of their application, but is safe from removal during primary stage consideration of

---

[10] Id, para 050.212(2).

[11] See further below, p 215.

[12] A Millbank, *The Problem with the 1951 Convention* (Canberra, Department of the Parliamentary Library, Research Paper 5 2000–01), http://www.aph.gov.au/library/pubs/rp/2000-01/01RP05.htm. A preliminary estimate by DIMIA suggests that of 62 332 protection visa applicants rejected in the past six years at least 8500 have gone underground: M Madigan, '8500 on the run in Australia', *Herald Sun*, 28 September 2001.

[13] DIMA, *Refugee and Humanitarian Issues: Australia's Response*, (Canberra, DIMA, October 2000), p 23. In 1999–2000, there were 4175 unauthorised boat arrivals and 1737 unauthorised air arrivals: DIMA, *Background Paper on Unauthorised Arrivals Strategy – Statistics* (Canberra, DIMA, 6 September 2001, http://www.minister.immi.gov.au/media_releases/media01/r01131_tables.htm. The numbers for 2000–01 were similar. As a result of the implementation of the Bills passed in September 2001 (see above n 1, and the Border Protection (Validation and Enforcement Powers) Bill 2001), it is expected that most future unauthorised boat arrivals will be intercepted, prevented from reaching the Australian mainland and, therefore, prevented from making protection visa applications.

[14] The 'migration zone' is defined in the Migration Act, section 5, to mean 'the area consisting of the states, the territories, Australian resource installations and Australian sea installations ...' It is important to note that 'excised offshore places' (see above n 1) continue to fall within the definition of 'migration zone'.

the application by the Department of Immigration and Multicultural and Indigenous Affairs (DIMIA) or review by the RRT.[15] However, the moment that either the time for making an RRT application has passed without the making of such an application, or an RRT rejection has been received, their unlawful status renders them liable to removal 'as soon as reasonably practicable'.[16]

Part 8 of the Migration Act 1958 (Cth) (Migration Act) allows for application for judicial review of an RRT decision to be made to the Australian Federal Court within 28 days of notification of that decision.[17] There is, however, no obligation on the Minister to refrain from removing detained asylum seekers before expiry of this 28-day period. Even where an application for review under Part 8 has actually been made, the Minister is free to remove the applicant unless the Federal Court makes an order pursuant to section 482(2) preventing removal pending the making of a decision on that application.[18]

---

[15] Migration Act, section 198.

[16] Ibid. See also the definition of 'finally determined' in the Migration Act, section 5(9).

[17] Migration Act, section 478.

[18] The case of 'X' and 'Y' was a case in which this entitlement to remove was exercised. X and Y were two Kenyan children who had arrived in Australia unaccompanied as ship stowaways. They made applications for protection visas, but these were rejected at both the primary and the RRT stage. The two boys were notified of the RRT rejections on 21 July 1998. They wished to seek judicial review. However, on 3 August 1998, before they had actually lodged the applications for judicial review, the boys were placed on a Singapore Airlines flight out of Australia. A particularly concerning aspect of the case was that they were placed on that flight by a delegate of the Minister for Immigration, their guardian under section 6 of the Immigration (Guardianship of Children) Act 1946 (Cth). The boys' legal advisers immediately lodged two sets of applications with the Federal Court, one set seeking review of the RRT decisions and the other set seeking injunctions to restrain removal pending the review of the RRT decisions. Injunctions restraining removal were granted against the Minister for Immigration and Singapore Airlines. The injunctions were granted while the aircraft was still on the tarmac. It took off with the applicants, despite the grant of the injunctions. However, the court managed to procure the return of the boys to Australia. After hearing the applications for judicial review, North J made orders setting aside the RRT's decisions in the boys' cases and remitting their protection visa applications back to the RRT for further consideration: *'X' v Minister for Immigration and Multicultural Affairs (MIMA)* [2000] FCA 702 (29 May 2000); *'Y' v MIMA* [2000] FCA 703 (29 May 2000). However, the Minister successfully appealed against North J's decisions to the Full Federal Court: *MIMA v 'X'* [2001] FCA 858 (6 July 2001) and *MIMA v 'Y'* [2001] FCA 859 (6 July 2001).

A rejected asylum seeker also has the option of applying for review by the Australian High Court of the primary or RRT decision pursuant to section 75(v) of the Australian Constitution. The High Court has inherent jurisdiction to grant an injunction restraining removal pending the hearing and determination of such an application. However, in the absence of such an injunction removal is possible and in times past probable.[19]

DIMIA policy It is DIMIA's stated policy to give a removee at least 48 hours notice of removal arrangements by service of a standard form letter.[20] However, it is also policy to give a much lesser period of notice

---

Under the Migration Legislation Amendment (Judicial Review) Act 2001 (Cth) the Federal Court retains the ability to make an order preventing removal pending hearing and determination of any judicial review application made to it by reason of Federal Court of Australia Act 1976 (Cth), section 23: DIMA submission to the Senate Legal and Constitutional Legislation Committee, 'Consideration of Legislation Referred to the Committee: Migration Legislation Amendment (Judicial Review) Bill 1998' (April 1999), para 4.20.

[19]   In the case of Ms Seniet Abebe, an immigration detainee who had received an RRT rejection, DIMA indicated its intention to give effect to arrangements to remove her even after she had invoked the section 75 jurisdiction of the High Court. An urgent application for court order was granted by Kirby J preventing removal until 28 January 1998: *Ex Parte Abebe* (1998) 151 ALR 711. On 28 January 1998, DIMA gave the court an undertaking that, until the determination of the matter or an earlier further order, removal would not take place without 72 hours written notice to the detainee or her solicitors: *Ex Parte Abebe* (1998) 152 ALR 177. Ms Abebe was eventually granted a protection visa by the Minister exercising his section 417 power of intervention: see M Crock, '*Abebe v Cth; MIMA v Eshetu*: Of Fortress Australia and Castles in the Air', *Melbourne University Law Review* 24 (2000) p 193, n 12. In another case, the High Court restrained the attempted removal of an Iranian asylum seeker pending review under Australian Constitution, section 75(v) (see *Ex parte MIP; MIMA* (High Court transcript, M30/1999, 15 March 1999)) but before such review could occur the Minister decided to exercise his power under Migration Act, section 48B to allow the asylum seeker to make a repeat application for a protection visa: Refugee and Immigration Legal Centre Inc (RILC), *Submissions to Joint Standing Committee on Migration Reference: MLAB (No 2) 2000*, Submission No 9, (Melbourne, RILC, 2000), p 38–9. The asylum seeker was granted a protection visa upon primary stage determination of the repeat application.

[20]   DIMA, *MSI 267: Advice of Removal Arrangements* (Canberra, DIMA, 10 May 1999), para 4.1.

where there are 'significant security reasons', the possibility of self-harm or disruptive behaviour, and such like.[21]

Migration Series Instruction (MSI) 267 states that, where the removee has a legal representative, notice of the proposed removal is to be given to that person also.[22] In practice, it is left to the detainee to inform their lawyer about the removal arrangements.[23] In some instances where resistance to enforced departure is expected, the removee in question is placed in separation detention from immediately prior to service of the removal notice on them to the time removal is effected.[24] These individuals are effectively disabled from letting their legal representative know about the proposed removal.[25]

Finally, MSI 267 states that 'officers should be flexible in applying [the notice of removal policy], taking into account for example whether the 48 hours coincides with a weekend and the feasibility of the detainee making arrival arrangements in the country of destination'.[26] However, at the time of the Senate Legal and Constitutional References Committee (SLCRC) Inquiry into the Operation of Australia's Refugee and Humanitarian Program there were claimed instances of removals being conducted without much advance notice at weekends and other times when contacting legal representatives and obtaining injunctions would be particularly difficult.[27] Recent news reports suggest that short (or no notice) weekend removals continue to take place.[28]

In recent times, it has also been DIMIA's stated policy to refrain from removing a rejected asylum seeker (without need for an injunction), if the asylum seeker has initiated proceedings for judicial review of a decision in

---

[21] Ibid; SLCRC, *Official Committee Hansard: Reference Inquiry into the Operation of Australia's Refugee and Humanitarian Program* (Canberra, Commonwealth of Australia, 16 September 1999), p L&C 612–3 (Mr Metcalfe, DIMA).

[22] DIMA, *MSI 267*, above n 20, para 4.3.

[23] Interview with Martin Clutterbuck, Coordinator, RILC, 24 May 2001.

[24] Ibid.

[25] Ibid.

[26] DIMA, *MSI 267*, above n 20, para 4.2.

[27] SLCRC, above n 8, para 10.63.

[28] D Jopson and N O'Malley, 'Centre Escapee's Family Deported to Algeria', *The Age*, 31 July 2001, http://www.theage.com.au/news/national/2001/07/31/FFX1RSW4RPC.html.

relation to a substantive visa application.[29] It is clear from the decision in *Tchoylak v Minister for Immigration and Multicultural Affairs (MIMA)*,[30] that departure from this policy would incur the wrath of the Federal Court. In *Tchoylak* the court dismissed an appeal relating to a protection visa application on the basis that it had been rendered moot by the appellant's removal from Australia through administrative error. However, the court went on to say:

> The respondent must take responsibility for ensuring that no one is removed from this country while there are proceedings pending in this Court challenging the validity of the removal. We do not accept that any of the various subsections of s 198 of the Act, which impose a duty in the circumstances there specified to remove a non-citizen 'as soon as reasonably practicable' can be invoked by the respondent to justify what occurred in the present case.[31]

Lest the Minister be tempted to take his responsibility lightly, the court warned that removal by the Minister of an applicant from Australia, 'in circumstances where it is known that he has an application for review pending before the court challenging the respondent's right to remove him' could, in some circumstances, constitute a contempt of court.[32]

Where a rejected asylum seeker has initiated judicial proceedings in relation to some other matter, it is DIMIA's policy to continue with action to remove the asylum seeker without having regard to the fact that those proceedings are on foot.[33] In *Kopiev v MIMA*,[34] for example, the applicant was seeking review of a Migration Review Tribunal (MRT) decision refusing him a bridging visa and also compensation for unlawful detention. The Minister sought summary dismissal of the proceedings by reason of the applicant's non-appearance. The applicant did not appear because he had been removed from Australia pursuant to section 198 of the Migration Act.

---

[29]   DIMA, *MSI 313: Bridging E Visa (Subclass 050) – Legislative Framework and Further Guidelines* (Canberra, DIMA, 10 April 2001), para 3.2.8.13; Interview with John Taylor, Deputy Commonwealth Ombudsman, 31 May 2001; Interview with Martin Clutterbuck, 24 May 2001.

[30]   (2001) FCR 302.

[31]   Id, p 311, para 53.

[32]   Id, p 309, para 41.

[33]   Interview with John Taylor, Deputy Commonwealth Ombudsman, 31 May 2001.

[34]   [2000] FCA 1831 (15 December 2000).

It was argued on behalf of the Minister that section 198 *required* the Minister to remove an unlawful non-citizen despite that person being a party to legal proceedings. This argument was treated with some scepticism by Sackville J.[35] Moreover, although Sackville J did feel compelled to find that section 198 *entitled* the Minister to remove the applicant notwithstanding that the proceedings were on foot, His Honour made a point of noting that, in the case before him, there was no evidence that removal had been effected in order to frustrate the making of the claim for compensation for unlawful detention. It was, therefore, 'not necessary to consider the position had the removal been for that reason.'[36] In addition, His Honour in dismissing the challenge to the MRT decision did so 'without prejudice to any claim the applicant might bring in respect of his detention during any part of the period from 26 June 2000 until his removal from Australia'.[37]

Kopiev was decided several months before *Tchoylak*. By contrast *Bolea v MIMA*,[38] decided shortly after *Tchoylak*, suggests that DIMIA may have to reconsider its policy of continuing with removals while judicial proceedings other than those relating to substantive visa applications are on foot. Mr Bolea was a Fijian citizen who made a protection visa application after arriving in Australia on a visitor visa. He was allowed to remain at liberty in the community pending determination of the application. The application was unsuccessful and likewise a request for exercise of the Minister's section 417 power,[39] but Mr Bolea disappeared into the community rather than departing Australia. Five years later, on 28 February 2001, Mr Bolea was located and detained as an unlawful non-citizen. On 15 March 2001, Mr Bolea made a second request for exercise of the Minister's section 417 power and, on 28 March 2001, he applied for grant of a bridging visa. DIMA's refusal of the bridging visa application was affirmed by the MRT and an application for judicial review of the MRT decision was dismissed on 22 June 2001. On 18 July 2001, Mr Bolea applied to the Federal Court for an extension of time to appeal the judicial review decision. On 19 July the court advised DIMA of this fact and on

---

[35]   Id, paras 23–5.

[36]   Id, para 27.

[37]   Id, para 34.

[38]   (2001) 113 FCR 387.

[39]   See above n 8.

20 July the fact was brought to the attention of Mr Prescilla, a DIMA officer. Mr Prescilla had already made arrangements for Mr Bolea to be removed on 21 July. Mr Prescilla informed Mr Bolea that he would be removed as arranged unless he sought a court injunction preventing removal. While Mr Bolea expressed a wish to remain in Australia pending the appeal, he did not seek an injunction. He was removed from Australia on 21 July. Subsequently the application for extension of time to appeal came on for hearing before Hill J who dismissed it on the basis that Mr Bolea's removal had made it moot. However, His Honour was not content to let the matter rest there. He said:

> 12 ... Mr Prescilla disarmingly concedes that he was aware that an application to the court had been made. His only comment in mitigation is that he told a person in detention, whose English may or may not be such as to have understood him, that if he went to court and got an injunction he would not be removed until after the proceedings, otherwise he would be removed as arranged. One has only to state that proposition to see the practical stupidity of it. No attempt has been made on behalf of the Minister to apologise to the Court ...
>
> 16 ... Eleven days [after the written judgment in *Tchoylak*], what is effectively the same situation has happened again. Unless within 14 days of today the Minister provides satisfactory evidence of procedures to ensure that this situation is never to be repeated as far as human diligence can ensure and tenders an appropriate apology to the Court, I will consider sending the Court's papers to the Attorney-General with a request that he consider whether to commence proceedings directly against the Minister or those answerable to him for contempt of Court.[40]

A detained asylum seeker, who is the subject of a request for exercise of the Minister's section 417 power[41] or section 48B power[42] is not actually

---

[40] (2001) 113 FCR 387 at 390.

[41] See above n 8 and Crock, above n 7, for a discussion of the exercise of the Minister's discretion under section 417.

[42] The Migration Act, section 48A provides that a non-citizen who, while in the migration zone, has made an unsuccessful application or applications for a protection visa may not make a further application for a protection visa while in the migration zone. However, section 48B confers upon the Minister a non-compellable power to exempt a particular non-citizen from the operation of section 48A, if the Minister thinks that it is in the public interest to do so.

making an application for a substantive visa[43] and is, therefore, removable pursuant to section 198 of the Migration Act. In its June 2000 report entitled *A Sanctuary Under Review*, the SLCRC recommended that the subject of a first request under section 417 should not be removed from Australia before finalisation of the process initiated by that request.[44] The government responded that this was already current practice.[45] According to DIMIA it is also current practice to refrain from removing a person from Australia pending finalisation of the process initiated by a request for exercise of the Minister's section 48B power.[46] Such delay is explained on the basis that it is necessary for the purpose of ensuring that Australia does not breach its protection obligations under the Refugees Convention or any other treaty.[47] While this aspect of current practice is to be applauded, it is indicative of selective latitude in the department's interpretation of 'as soon as reasonably practicable'.

Contrary to the position it sometimes takes in public, the department's internal policy guidelines inform departmental officers that the formulation 'as soon as reasonably practicable' allows room for flexibility in dealing with individual cases. It is suggested in MSI 318, which provides an overview of compliance and enforcement, that the formulation 'allows for postponing of removal where, for example, the health of the removee might be endangered or the removee would be uncomfortable or in pain'.[48]

---

[43] *Masila v MIMA* [2001] FCA 649 (1 June 2001). The appeal against this decision was dismissed: *Matila v MIMA* [2001] FCA 1611 (13 November 2001).

[44] SLCRC, above n 8.

[45] Parliament of Australia, *Hansard*, Senate, 8 February 2001, p 21752 (Senator Ellison). See also DIMA, *MSI 313*, above n 29, para 3.2.12.18 which states:

> A request for the Minister to exercise his intervention powers will not affect the operation of s 198, unless the person is granted a Bridging E visa. Section 198 provides that an unlawful non-citizen must be removed as soon as reasonably practicable, once certain circumstances are met.

MSI 294 issued on 13 October 2000, which MSI 313 replaced, contained an identical statement.

[46] SLCRC, *Official Committee Hansard: Reference Inquiry into the Operation of Australia's Refugee and Humanitarian Program* (Canberra, Commonwealth of Australia, 16 September 1999), p L&C 638 (Ms Bedlington, DIMA).

[47] Ibid.

[48] DIMA, *MSI 318: Compliance and Enforcement Overview* (Canberra, DIMA, 26 April 2001), para 9.1.1.

Thus, for example, the removal of an Iranian Kurd asylum seeker family rejected by the RRT was postponed so that the six-year-old son could continue to be treated for detention-induced anxiety and depression at Westmead Children's Hospital.[49]

MSI 54, which elaborates on the implementation of enforced departures, goes further suggesting that representations from interested parties expressing concern about the means or timing of removal 'may be relevant in considering arrangements for enforced departure'.[50] It is made particularly clear that where representations are made by parties capable of causing the Government a political headache, for example, the Commonwealth Ombudsman, the Human Rights and Equal Opportunity Commission (HREOC) or lawyers pursuing 'sensitive or controversial' matters before the courts, the removal action must be suspended pending receipt of advice from the highest levels.[51]

DIMIA practice Part of the removal process involves the completion of a standard form removal checklist by a DIMIA compliance officer and approval of it by a senior compliance officer. According to MSI 267, the purpose of completing this checklist is 'to ensure that matters that may prevent the removal or affect its timing, are brought to notice'.[52]

In May 1999 it was alleged that an eight-month pregnant Chinese woman, who had been removed from Australia in July 1997 as part of a

---

[49]   C Harvey and M Denney, 'Escapees Elude House Raids', *Australian*, 24 July 2001, p 2. Subsequently, the father agreed to allow the child to be placed in foster care rather than being returned to the detention environment. The Minister for Immigration confirmed that the child would not be returned to Iran while seriously ill. However, the Minister added 'that has no impact on the parents' deportation': K Burke and A Clennell, 'Late bid to keep family together', *Sydney Morning Herald*, 15 August 2001,   http://www.smh.com.au/news/0108/15/national/national11.html. Fifteen minutes before the Federal Court was due to hear an application for an injunction restraining removal, the Minister gave an undertaking that the family would be given 72 hours notice of removal: K Burke, 'Traumatised boy's family wins reprieve from Ruddock', *Sydney Morning Herald*, 16 August 2001, http://www.smh.com.au/news/0108/16/text/national12.html. The undertaking was apparently given to enable the family to apply for an extension of time to appeal an adverse Federal Court decision made on 25 May 2001.

[50]   DIMA, *MSI 54: Implementation of Enforced Departure* (Canberra, DIMA, 23 August 1994), para 3.3.1.

[51]   Id, paras 3.3.3–3.3.4.

[52]   DIMA, *MSI 267*, above n 20, para 5.1.

group removal to the People's Republic of China, had subsequently been subjected to a forced abortion by Chinese authorities. The matter excited much media interest and was the final impetus needed for the Senate to establish the wide-ranging SLCRC inquiry that resulted in its *A Sanctuary Under Review* report. One of the recommendations made by the SLCRC in the chapter of the report devoted to the case of the Chinese woman was that 'policies and practices be developed by DIMA to ensure the Minister is made aware of all relevant facts about detainees prior to their removal from Australia'.[53] The government's response was as follows:

In the case of group removals it is established practice that, before the removal, DIMA convenes a meeting of all involved parties to discuss issues relating to individuals in the group. These issues include medical fitness, whether there are any applications before DIMA, the RRT or courts and whether there is any unanswered correspondence from any person being removed.

There is close liaison with the Minister's office in the lead up to group removals.[54]

The government response then went on to address individual removals, referring to the completion of the removal checklist and to the fact that '[w]here there are issues of particular concern or sensitivity in respect of an individual removal, those issues are drawn to the attention of the Minister's office'. The government's response also stated that a 'national removals reporting system designed to improve advance notice of removal issues has recently been put in place'.[55] However, the national removals reporting system is nothing more than a requirement that:

all Compliance Sections (in each state or territory office) report on all removals by e-mail on a weekly basis to the 'Unauthorised Arrivals and Detention' Section in [DIMA's] Central Office in Canberra.[56]

Questions about the adequacy of DIMA procedures 'to ensure that matters that may prevent the removal or affect its timing, are brought to

---

[53] SLCRC, above n 8, recommendation 9.1.

[54] Parliament of Australia, *Hansard*, Senate, 8 February 2001, p 21752 (Senator Ellison).

[55] Ibid.

[56] Email from Julian Warner, Parliamentary & Public Access Unit, DIMA VIC SHQ, 19 June 2001.

notice' were raised again in the case of Mr Tchoylak. Mr Tchoylak was an unsuccessful protection visa applicant who had pursued his case to the stage of making an appeal to the full bench of the Federal Court.[57] The full bench heard the appeal only to be told the next day that Mr Tchoylak had in fact been removed from Australia on 3 August 2000, that is, three weeks before the hearing.[58] The removal was, of course, contrary to the department's stated policy, which is to refrain from removing a person while judicial proceedings relating to a substantive visa application by that person are on foot. The court was informed that the removal had taken place because the DIMA officer, who considered Mr Tchoylak's eligibility for removal under section 198, had mistakenly believed that litigation involving Mr Tchoylak had concluded on 11 May 2000.[59] The mistaken belief was in part induced by problems being experienced at the time 'in extracting reliable information' from DIMA's main client information database.[60] The court was informed that:

> as a result of the applicant's removal, and to avoid any similar reoccurrence, procedures had been put in place which required an inquiry to be made to the Legal Services and Litigation Branch of the department, prior to removal, to check whether any proceedings were still on foot.[61]

Mr Tchoylak himself had no remedy. As previously mentioned, the court dismissed the appeal on the basis that the remedy issue had been rendered moot. Since Mr Tchoylak was no longer 'in Australia', he failed to meet an essential criterion for the grant of a protection visa.[62] Moreover, the applicant had 'no realistic prospect of being permitted to return to Australia' so as to enable him to again meet the criterion of being a non-citizen 'in Australia'.[63] The only way in which Mr Tchoylak could lawfully re-enter Australia was if the Minister for Immigration chose to declare in writing that Mr Tchoylak was taken to have been granted a temporary visa

---

[57] P Heinrichs, 'Did we send a man home to be shot?', *Sunday Age*, 26 November 2000, pp 1–2.

[58] *Tchoylak*, above n 30, para 17.

[59] Id, paras 19–20.

[60] Ibid.

[61] Id, para 24.

[62] Migration Act, section 36(2).

[63] *Tchoylak*, above n 30, para 44.

known as a 'special purpose visa'.[64] The court was informed, however, that, even if the applicant indicated a desire to re-enter Australia, the Minister would not facilitate it.[65]

The result in *Tchoylak* was not one that the court was particularly pleased to arrive at and in obiter comments it made the following points. Nothing further had been heard from the applicant so the court was not in a position to know whether or not the applicant wished to re-enter the country in order to prosecute his appeal.[66] However, had the applicant indicated such a desire:

> serious consideration would have been given by the court as to whether the respondent should be ordered to permit the applicant to enter Australia for that purpose.[67]

Evaluation

All states, including Australia, claim that it is their sovereign right to expel aliens entering or remaining within their territory unlawfully.[68] Article 13 of the International Covenant on Civil and Political Rights (ICCPR)[69] does not constrain the exercise of this right because in its terms it refers to aliens *lawfully* in the territory of a state party.[70] The exercise of the right is, of

---

[64]   Migration Act, section 33(2)(b)(i).

[65]   *Tchoylak* above n 30, paras 29 and 44. The court agreed with the Minister's submission that the exception to the universal visa requirement set out in the Migration Act, section 42(2A)(e), could not be invoked in Mr Tchoylak's case because there was not in force at the time of removal a court order or Ministerial undertaking that such removal would not be effected: *Tchoylak* above n 30, para 40.

[66]   *Tchoylak*, above n 30, para 39.

[67]   Id, para 44.

[68]   G S Goodwin-Gill, 'The Limits of the Power of Expulsion in Public International Law', *British Year Book of International Law* **47** (1974–75) p 121.

[69]   16 December 1966, 999 UNTS 171. This treaty entered into force generally on 23 March 1976 and for Australia on 13 November 1980.

[70]   Article 13 provides:

> An alien *lawfully* in the territory of a State Party to the present Covenant may be expelled therefrom only in pursuance of a decision reached in accordance with law and shall, except where compelling reasons of national security otherwise require, be allowed to submit the reasons against his expulsion and to have his case reviewed

course, constrained by international protection obligations but this chapter deals with individuals who have received a final determination (as defined in Australian domestic law) rejecting their asylum claims. What rights (if any) do *they* have that can be asserted against the right of the state to expel aliens? For a start, they can claim the right to equal protection of the law. Article 26 of the ICCPR provides:

> All persons are equal before the law and are entitled without any discrimination to the equal protection of the law. In this respect, the law shall prohibit any discrimination and guarantee to all persons equal and effective protection against discrimination on any ground such as race, colour, sex, language, religion, political or other opinion, national or social origin, property, birth or other status.

Article 26 'prohibits discrimination in law or in fact in any field regulated and protected by public authorities'.[71]

The ICCPR itself does not contain a definition of discrimination. However, on the basis of definitions contained in other human rights treaties, the United Nations Human Rights Committee (UNHRC) has expressed the view that:

> the term 'discrimination' as used in the Covenant should be understood to imply any distinction, exclusion, restriction or preference which is based on any ground such as race, colour, sex, language, religion, political or other opinion, national or social origin, property, birth or other status, and which has the purpose or effect of nullifying or impairing the recognition, enjoyment or exercise by all persons, on an equal footing, of all rights and freedoms.[72]

The principle of non-discrimination or equal treatment does not require that all individuals be treated identically.[73] A difference in treatment does not violate the principle of non-discrimination, if there is an 'objective and

---

by, and be represented for the purpose before, the competent authority or a person or persons especially designated by the competent authority.

[71] United Nations Human Rights Committee (UNHRC), *General Comment 18: Non-discrimination* (Geneva, UNHRC, 1989), http://www.austlii.edu.au/au/other/ahric/Primary/hrcomm/gencomm/index.html, para 12.

[72] Id, para 7.

[73] Id, para 8.

reasonable justification' for it.[74] It should be noted, however, that such a justification will not exist if the aim to be achieved by the difference in treatment is not legitimate, or if the effects of the difference in treatment are disproportionate to the aim.[75]

Although Article 26 lists some grounds of differential treatment that are automatically suspect,[76] the use of the words 'such as' and the reference to 'other status' indicate that the list is non-exhaustive. In the present case, asylum seekers are effectively being subjected to differential treatment according to their manner of arrival in Australia. Those asylum seekers who arrived in Australia on some kind of temporary visa are given a secure basis for remaining in Australia pending the determination of judicial review applications and a section 417 request through the mechanism of a bridging visa grant. Those who have arrived here without authorisation, on the other hand, are denied a secure basis on which to remain in Australia for the purpose of availing themselves of the same process rights. All they have to rely on is departmental policy, which the evidence suggests is uncertain in its application.

It is quite clear from the political rhetoric that the aims of the automatic removal provisions are two-fold: to discourage future unauthorised arrivals and to prevent system abuse by unauthorised arrivals already in Australia. Without question, the former aim cannot be regarded as a legitimate aim at international law. This is because it involves treating other human beings as if they are no more than means to our ends and thus offends the moral basis of international human rights law: the premise that all human beings are of inherent and equal worth.

As for the latter aim, even if it is a legitimate one, it could only provide objective justification for the difference in treatment specified above, if unauthorised arrivals (as a group) are far more likely to be making abusive judicial review applications and section 417 requests than are those who arrived in Australia on a valid temporary visa. The fact of the matter is that the reverse is true, if the much higher success rate of unauthorised arrivals

---

[74] *Belgian Linguistics case* (European Court of Human Rights, 23 July 1968) (summarised in V Berger, *Case Law of the European Court of Human Rights 1960–1987* (Dublin, Round Hall Press, Vol 1, 1989), p 18) in relation to Article 14 of the European Convention on Human Rights; UNHRC, above n 71, para 13.

[75] *Belgian Linguistics case*, ibid.

[76] E W Vierdag, *The Concept of Discrimination in International Law with Special Reference to Human Rights* (The Hague, Nijhoff, 1973), pp 82, 130–2.

in obtaining protection visas is a valid indicator. Moreover, as long as the policy of mandatory detention of unauthorised arrivals continues, what possible extraneous incentive could such persons have for seeking to delay their removal? All they are buying themselves is a few more traumatising months or years in an immigration detention centre or state prison.

Unfortunately, the jurisprudence of the UNHRC suggests that a state in breach of Article 26 can choose to rectify the breach by 'equalising down'.[77] In the present context, therefore, Australia could choose to make asylum seekers, who arrived in Australia on a valid temporary visa, as vulnerable to removal as unauthorised arrivals presently are.

Another ICCPR provision that is relevant in the context of evaluating Australia's automatic removal provisions is Article 2(3) of the ICCPR:

Each State Party to the present Covenant undertakes:

(a) To ensure that any person whose rights or freedoms as herein recognized are violated shall have an effective remedy, notwithstanding that the violation has been committed by persons acting in an official capacity;

(b) To ensure that any person claiming such a remedy shall have his right thereto determined by competent judicial, administrative or legislative authorities, or by any other competent authority provided for by the legal system of the State, and to develop the possibilities of judicial remedy;

(c) To ensure that the competent authorities shall enforce such remedies when granted.

Two issues arise here. The first is that Australia is presently failing to provide an effective remedy for those claiming that their removal from Australia will result in a violation of Australia's protection obligations under the ICCPR.[78] Australia has set up a protection visa application procedure that prevents primary and merits review decision makers from considering protection claims made under the ICCPR (or any other treaty save the Refugees Convention and Protocol). The only person who can actually decide that a protection visa should be granted on the basis of such claims is the Minister for Immigration acting under section 417 of the

---

[77] This phrase refers to the concept of redressing state Members' violations of international human rights obligations by lowering the rights of others to the level of the victim: S Joseph, J Schultz and M Castan, *The International Covenant on Civil and Political Rights: Cases, Materials and Commentary* (Oxford, Oxford University Press, 2000), para 23.89.

Migration Act. However, the Minister's power of intervention is non-compellable. In these circumstances it would surely defy common sense to assert that persons making protection claims under ICCPR have an effective remedy.

The second issue is raised by *Kopiev*. It is also raised by a more recent case in which seven immigration detainees sued Australasian Correctional Management (ACM) and the Minister for Immigration in the Federal Court seeking damages for breach of a duty of care owed to them.[79] These detainees alleged that on 27 April 2001 they had been assaulted by ACM employees when they protested to an attempt to move them from one part of Villawood Immigration Detention Centre to another, and that they were subsequently denied proper medical attention.[80] At a directions hearing held on 27 July 2001, Justice Wilcox was informed that two of the detainees had already been removed from Australia.[81] His Honour wished to know why removal had occurred while a police investigation and civil proceedings were on foot.[82] On 1 August 2001, the Minister for Immigration responded publicly to this query asserting that the police had investigated the allegations, had decided that there was insufficient evidence on which to prosecute and, therefore, had not sought the grant of criminal justice stay visas[83] to prevent removal.[84] Yet, almost one month later, the Parliamentary Secretary to the Minister, Senator Patterson, referred to the police investigation into the alleged assaults not as long since concluded but as 'close to being finalised'.[85] The civil proceedings were settled out of court in October 2001.[86] Many questions have been asked in the meantime which

[78] UNHRC, *Concluding Observations of the Human Rights Committee: Australia* (Geneva, UNHRC, UN Doc CCPR/A/55/40, 28 July 2000), paras 498–528.

[79] M Videnieks, 'Ruddock to Face Contempt Charge', *The Weekend Australian*, 4–5 August 2001, p 9.

[80] C O'Rourke, 'Video nasty reveals "bashing" of detainees', *Sydney Morning Herald*, 2 August 2001, http://www.smh.com.au/news/0108/02/text/national5.html.

[81] M Videnieks and M Denney, 'Judge Questions Bashing Inquiry', *The Weekend Australian*, 28–29 July 2001, p 7.

[82] Ibid.

[83] See Migration Act, Part 2, division 4.

[84] 'Ruddock clashes with judge over bashing claims', *The Australian*, 2 August 2001, p 5.

[85] Parliament of Australia, *Hansard*, Senate, 29 August 2001, p 26857 (Senator Patterson).

[86] M Spencer, 'Ruddock Bill Set for Taxpayers', *The Australian*, 24 October 2001, p 3.

remain unanswered. For example, on 29 August 2001, Senator Bartlett referred to the fact that 'a few' of the detainees had already been sent back to China and asked in parliament:

> whether it was in each case the fact that people were willingly removed and made a request to be sent back or whether the department removed them despite this ongoing court case and the ongoing investigations, and in such cases whether the department satisfied itself that all investigations – particularly the police investigations – had been fully completed in relation to the persons involved.[87]

As Senator Bartlett pointed out, in a context where Immigration Detention Centre staff are being given more powers over detainees[88] there is increased need for assurance that adequate processes are in place to ensure that detainees complaining about misuse of those powers 'are not shunted out of the country as quickly as possible before they can be properly investigated'.[89] At present, there is no such assurance.

In seeking compensation for wrongful detention, Kopiev was, in fact, claiming that his right not to be subjected to arbitrary detention (Article 9 ICCPR) had been violated by Australia and seeking a remedy for that violation. In a similar vein, those detainees making allegations of assault were in effect claiming that their right not to be subjected to cruel, inhuman or degrading treatment (Article 7 ICCPR) had been violated and were seeking a remedy for that violation. By removing these persons from the jurisdiction before the determination of their claims, Australia was denying them all practical means of placing their claims before the court and obtaining a remedy if those claims were found to be valid. This may not have been the purpose of the removal, but it was the result. These two cases demonstrate that application of the departmental policy of disregarding judicial proceedings that do not relate to substantive visa applications will, on occasions, place Australia in breach of its obligation under Article 2(3) to *ensure* that any person whose ICCPR rights are violated has an effective remedy.

---

87 Parliament of Australia, *Hansard*, Senate, 29 August 2001, p 26856 (Senator Bartlett).

88 See Migration Legislation Amendment (Immigration Detainees) Act 2001 (Cth), which received assent on 18 July 2001, and Migration Legislation Amendment (Immigration Detainees) (No 2) Act 2001 (Cth), which received assent on 17 September 2001.

89 Parliament of Australia, *Hansard*, Senate, 29 August 2001, p 26856 (Senator Bartlett).

Removal Process

Community-based Asylum Seekers

Some rejected community-based asylum seekers depart the country voluntarily without any DIMIA involvement. Some others overstay their bridging visas, but upon coming to DIMIA's attention, seem both willing and able to depart at their own expense and are, therefore, allowed the option of monitored departure or supervised departure. Persons subject to monitored departure or supervised departure are granted bridging visas which allow them to remain at liberty pending departure, though those in the latter category are escorted to the airport to ensure departure.[90]

Rejected community-based asylum seekers, who are either unwilling or unable to depart at their own expense, are subject to the enforced departure process described in the Migration Act as 'removal'. These individuals must, of course, first be made to become unlawful non-citizens who as such are subject to detention and then removal. In the case of those unwilling to depart and judged likely to abscond, this may mean a period in detention while departure arrangements are made.[91] However, those who are simply unable or unwilling to depart at their own expense may well be made unlawful non-citizens and detained just prior to departure.[92]

Asylum Seekers in Mandatory Detention

Agency responsible for executing removal In the case of those rejected asylum seekers who arrived in Australia without authorisation, the Secretary of DIMIA has the power under section 217 of the Migration Act to require the carrier on which the person entered Australia to transport the person from Australia. DIMIA makes use of this power in relation to most unauthorised air arrivals. It also makes use of this power in relation to the small number of ship deserters and stowaways who attempt to enter

---

[90] DIMA, *Protecting the Border* (Canberra, DIMA, 2000), http://dimia.gov.au/illegals/, chapter 8. Persons subject to supervised departure are detained as unlawful non-citizens just prior to departure but are granted another bridging visa at the point of departure so that they depart as lawful non-citizens: DIMA, *MSI 313*, above n 29, paras 3.2.6.7–3.2.6.9.

[91] DIMA, *Protecting the Border*, ibid.

[92] DIMA, *MSI 267*, above n 20, para 2.4; DIMA, *MSI 318*, above n 48, para 7.2; DIMA, *MSI 313*, above n 29, para 3.2.6.6.

Australia each year.[93] However, the power is of no practical use in the case of a few unauthorised air arrivals and most unauthorised sea arrivals, for example, because the vessel on which the person entered cannot be identified or has been destroyed. The responsibility, therefore, falls to DIMIA to remove these unauthorised arrivals and also, of course, those visa overstayers who are unwilling or unable to depart at their own expense.[94] DIMIA usually effects such removals through use of air transport. When removing small numbers, DIMIA uses regularly scheduled commercial flights. When removing a large group, it charters a flight.[95]

DIMIA-contracted escort services Where DIMIA is responsible for executing removal it contracts an escort to carry it out. Each escorted removal takes place under a separate 'agreement for escort service', which specifies exactly the services to be provided by the escort, including a requirement to report in writing on the execution of the removal.[96] The escorts contracted include off-duty police officers, Australasian Correctional Services, which subcontracts service delivery to ACM and, most controversially, a private South African firm called Protection and Indemnity Associates (P & I).[97] When questioned by the SLCRC in July 1999 DIMA explained it had directly engaged the services of P & I in six cases in the preceding year and had done so because, in the case of rejected asylum seekers of African origin, P & I were able to procure identification and travel documents where the Australian government could not.[98]

Carrier-contracted escort services In those cases where the airline or shipping company which brought an unauthorised arrival to Australia has been required under section 217 to remove the person, DIMIA contracts for ACM to take the person to the port of departure and to transfer the person into the custody of an escort organised by the airline or shipping

---

[93]   DIMA, *Protecting the Border*, above n 90, chapter 5.

[94]   SLCRC, above n 8, para 10.11.

[95]   DIMA, *Protecting the Border*, above n 90, chapter 5.

[96]   SLCRC, above n 8, para 10.11.

[97]   Ibid.

[98]   SLCRC, *Official Committee Hansard: Reference Inquiry into the Operation of Australia's Refugee and Humanitarian Program* (Canberra, Commonwealth of Australia, 5 July 1999), p L&C 51 (Mr Metcalfe, DIMA).

company.[99] Both airlines and shipping companies may well obtain the escort services under contract from another company. For example, P & I has been for many years a popular choice of airlines and shipping companies when an escort to Africa is required.[100] According to the SLCRC's *A Sanctuary Under Review* report, airlines may need to contract such specialist services where, for example, removal involves 'guarding of an individual while in transit between countries, transfers to other airlines, and the obtaining of documentation'.[101]

Manner of removal Section 189 of the Migration Act requires that non-citizens in Australia be detained while in, or suspected of seeking to be in, Australia's migration zone unlawfully.[102] Unlawful non-citizens must, therefore, be detained during that part of the removal process that takes place within the migration zone. Detention is defined to include 'taking such action and using such force as are reasonably necessary' to take or keep in immigration detention.[103] 'Immigration detention' in turn is defined to include:

being in the company of, and restrained by:

(i)   an officer; or

(ii) in relation to a particular detainee – another person directed by the Secretary [of DIMA] to accompany and restrain the detainee.[104]

The Air Navigation Regulations 1947, made pursuant to the Air Navigation Act 1920, provide that a person being removed from Australia pursuant to the Migration Act must not be allowed to board or remain upon

---

[99] SLCRC, *Official Committee Hansard: Consideration of Additional Estimates* (Canberra, Commonwealth of Australia, 20 February 2001), p L&C 223 (Ms Goodwin, DIMA).

[100] SLCRC, above n 98.

[101] SLCRC, above n 8, para 10.10.

[102] The Migration Amendment (Excision from Migration Zone) (Consequential Provisions) Act 2001 amended section 189 so that detention of unlawful non-citizens in, or suspected of seeking to be in, an 'excised offshore place' (see above n 1) is permitted rather than required.

[103] Migration Act, section 5.

[104] Ibid. Where DIMA contracts the escort services of a person who is not an 'officer' within the meaning of the Migration Act, the escort is provided with a written direction to accompany and restrain the person in question: SLCRC, above n 8, para 10.39.

a civil aircraft, unless the person is escorted or the Secretary of the Department of Transport has authorised carriage in writing.[105] According to DIMIA, there is a further statutorily authorised requirement that escorts be trained in 'appropriate methods of restraint in case there are security incidents on board' and be equipped to do so.[106] These domestic provisions are intended to implement Australia's obligation under the Civil Aviation Convention[107] to comply with international standards and procedures adopted by the International Civil Aviation Organisation.[108]

The Minister for Immigration has informed parliament that:

> Every effort is made by my Department to ensure that removal procedures are not unnecessarily stressful for the individuals concerned and that removals occur under conditions of maximum dignity for the removees. That objective can be undermined when removees choose to resort to dangerous or unacceptable behaviour.
>
> In a relatively small number of cases removees behave aggressively, threaten self-harm or by their actions impose a danger to the travelling public. These behaviours are generally intended to prevent a removal occurring and are addressed with appropriately graduated responses which can include the lawful application of physical restraints.[109]

In the course of its Inquiry into the Operation of Australia's Refugee and Humanitarian Program, the SLCRC was advised by DIMA that 'reasonable force' had been necessary to effect only 12 of the 1718 removals/deportations carried out in 1998–99.[110]

According to DIMIA, chemical *restraint* is not used in the removal process.[111] However, removees, who are of 'medical or psychiatric concern', are assessed by a medical practitioner prior to removal.[112] If that person prescribes medication for the removee, a suitably trained medical or

---

[105]   Air Navigation Regulations 1947 (Cth), reg 33; DIMA, *MSI 54*, above n 50, para 4.6.

[106]   SLCRC, above n 8, para 10.10 quoting evidence given by DIMA.

[107]   Convention on International Civil Aviation, 7 December 1944, Australian Treaty Series 1957 No 5. This treaty entered into force for Australia and generally on 4 April 1947.

[108]   SLCRC, above n 8, para 10.10.

[109]   Parliament of Australia, *Hansard*, House of Representatives, 10 October 2000, p 21208 (Mr Ruddock).

[110]   SLCRC, above n 8, para 10.5.

paramedical attendant is contracted to accompany the removee for the purpose of administering the medication as prescribed.[113]

Despite the foregoing official statements about DIMIA policy and practice, there are, from time to time, allegations made of the use of involuntary sedation, dangerous methods of restraint such as taping of mouth, binding of hand and feet and excessive force on the ground in Australia, on board aircraft or on the ground in transit countries in the course of effecting removals. For example, allegations along these lines made on 13 March 2000 by the ABC's *Four Corners* program forced the Minister for Immigration to order a departmental inquiry into the forcible removal from Australia of three rejected Algerian asylum seekers.[114]

Thus far we have been dealing with removals for which DIMIA has accepted responsibility. What about those situations where a carrier has been made responsible for the removal under section 217 of the Migration Act? The attempted removal of Mr SE from Australia was such a situation. British Airways was required to remove Mr SE, who had entered Australia as an unauthorised arrival on a British Airways flight. British Airways contracted P & I to escort Mr SE all the way through to his destination. On 30 October 1998, Mr SE's lawyers applied to the High Court for an order nisi for prohibition and certiorari and an interlocutory injunction restraining

---

[111] Id, para 10.70.

[112] Ibid.

[113] Ibid.

[114] M Saunders, 'Illegals "Drugged then Deported"', *The Australian*, 14 March 2000, p 6; ABC Four Corners, transcript of broadcast, 13 March 2000, http://www.abc.net.au/4corners/stories/s110015.htm. The findings of the departmental inquiry have not been made public.

The UN Human Rights Commission's Special Rapporteur on Torture has taken an interest in an attempt made in December 1999 to remove a family of rejected Libyan asylum seekers from Australia. The attempt, which allegedly involved the verbal and physical abuse of the adult removees, was unsuccessful because the physical condition of one of the removees led to a refusal by the airline to carry them: Special Rapporteur, *For the Record 2000: The UN Human Rights System, Australia Thematic Reports* (Human Rights Internet & Netherlands Institute of Human Rights, 2000), http://www.hri.ca/fortherecord2000/vol6/australiatr.htm.

Allegations of the use of involuntary sedation in the removal process were made to the SLCRC in the course of its Inquiry into the Operation of Australia's Refugee and Humanitarian Program. In its report the Committee stated that it had 'not been in a position to thoroughly evaluate the allegations that have been made about sedation, or the evidence provided to refute such allegations': SLCRC, above n 8, para 10.71.

removal pending the hearing and determination of the order nisi. The ground of relevance to the present context was that the proposed removal of Mr SE was unlawful because there was no legislative authority for 'the detention in custody of a non-citizen by a private contractor, where the detention is for the purpose of removing the non-citizen from Australia and delivering him or her to his or her country of nationality'.[115] In dismissing the application, Hayne J said:

> If the airline, or those engaged by the airline, were to seek to exercise some restraint over the applicant, beyond the confinements that are the consequences of being in an aircraft in flight and of being in the transit area of an international airport with no papers permitting entry to the country concerned, there is nothing in the material to suggest that this additional restraint would be imposed by or on behalf of the first respondent or at his direction. It would be entirely a matter for the airline and those whom it has engaged and would be done with no authority – actual or pretended – given by the first respondent. There is, in my view, no factual basis established for the grant of an order nisi for prohibition or the grant of an injunction restraining removal on the basis that the first respondent proposes removal of the applicant by a means which includes extra-territorial custodial restraint or his detention in custody by a private contractor.[116]

Given this judicial pronouncement it is not surprising that the Australian government's formal position is that:

> [w]here a particular carrier is responsible for removing an illegal arrival (because that carrier brought the person to Australia) the procedures adopted are a contractual matter between the carrier and the removal service provider it engages.[117]

Evaluation

Article 9 ICCPR Article 9(1) of the ICCPR states:

> everyone has the right to liberty and security of person. No one shall be subjected to arbitrary arrest or detention. No one shall be deprived of his liberty

---

[115] *Re MIMA; Ex Parte SE* (1998) 158 ALR 735 at 736.

[116] Id, pp 738–9.

[117] Parliament of Australia, *Hansard*, Senate, 8 February 2001, p 21753 (Senator Ellison).

except on such grounds and in accordance with such procedure established by law.

The Article 9(1) right can be derogated from only '[i]n time of public emergency which threatens the life of the nation and the existence of which is officially proclaimed' and then only to the extent 'strictly required by the exigencies of the situation'.[118]

According to the UNHRC, to escape characterisation as 'arbitrary', detention must be permitted by domestic law and must also be a necessary and proportionate means of achieving a legitimate end.[119] Detention of removees during that part of the removal process that takes place within Australian territory is permitted by Australian law. It is accepted that such detention is also a necessary and proportionate means of achieving the legitimate goal of immigration control.

Detention of removees, which continues after they have left Australian territory, is a different matter altogether. The statutory power of detention given in section 189 does not even purport to have extra-territorial application. Possibly a power to detain can be read into the statutory power to remove in order to render the latter power effective, but the power to remove appears to be spent the moment that the removee is outside Australia's territorial limits.[120]

---

[118] ICCPR, Article 4(1).

[119] *A v Australia* (Communication 560/1993, UN CCPR/C/59/D/560/1993, 1997), para 9.2; Human Rights and Equal Opportunity Commission, *Those Who've Come Across the Seas: Detention of Unauthorised Arrivals* (Sydney, AGPS, 1998), http://www.hreoc.gov.au/pdf/human_rights/asylum_seekers/h5_2_2.pdf, p 47.

[120] *Re MIMA; Ex parte SE* (High Court transcript, M99/1998, 9 November 1998). In *Ruddock v Vadarlis* (2001) 110 FCR 491, French J (with whom Beamount J agreed) held that the executive power of the Commonwealth conferred by the Australian Constitution, section 61, included power to prevent the entry of non-citizens which had not been displaced by statute. However, French J explicitly stated (p 543, para 193) that this finding did not 'involve any conclusion about whether the Executive would, in the absence of statutory authority, have a power to expel non-citizens other than as an incident of the power to exclude'. *Vadarlis v MIMA* (High Court transcript, M93/2001, 27 November 2001) was a special leave application to the High Court against the orders of the Full Court of the Federal Court. The court held that the pursuit of a writ of habeus corpus was now futile because it had been 'overtaken by events', namely that the detainees had been removed from the jurisdiction and were now subject to the laws of Nauru or New Zealand. The application was accordingly dismissed.

Re MIMA; Ex parte Farah[121] deals with a case in which DIMA had responsibility for removing Mr Farah, a Somali national and rejected asylum seeker, from Australia. DIMA arranged for Mr Farah to be returned to Somalia via Johannesburg, Addis Ababa, Dubai and Djibouti and contracted P & I to escort Mr Farah from Johannesburg (where he was to spend several days in transit) to Dubai. Mr Farah's lawyers approached the High Court seeking orders nisi for prohibition and certiorari and an interlocutory injunction. The ground of relevance to the present context was that the method of removal proposed was an unreasonable or unlawful exercise of the section 198 power of removal in so far as it involved delivery of Mr Farah into the custody of a third party in South Africa. Mr Farah's lawyers were successful in convincing Hayne J to grant an order nisi on this ground and, of course, an injunction restraining removal of Mr Farah by the method that was under challenge.[122] Mr Farah's case was 'otherwise disposed of administratively' before the hearing and determination of the order nisi.[123] It is unlikely that the Minister would have won if there had been a hearing and determination of the order nisi. In fact, in *Ex parte SE*, counsel for the Minister freely conceded that:

> As a matter of law, it is not competent for the Minister for Immigration to presume to say what a citizen of Somalia can or cannot do in the transit lounge in Johannesburg.[124]

The concession was, of course, made in the context of a case in which the Minister was arguing that it was British Airways and not he that was presuming to say what a citizen of Somalia could or could not do in the transit lounge in Johannesburg.

An obvious means of ensuring the domestic lawfulness of extra-territorial detention of removees by or on behalf of Australia would be for the Commonwealth parliament to legislate to that effect. Given the extreme deference with which the High Court approaches the exercise of the

---

[121] *Re MIMA; Ex parte Farah* (High Court transcript, M44/1998, 15 June 1998).

[122] Ibid.

[123] Information provided to the court in *Ex Parte Abebe* (1998) 151 ALR 711. The Minister decided to exercise his section 48B power to allow Mr Farah to make a repeat protection visa application: information provided by Martin Clutterbuck, 8 June 2001. Mr Farah's repeat application was successful at primary stage.

[124] *Re MIMA; Ex parte SE* (High Court transcript, M99/1998, 9 November 1998).

'aliens' power, it is unlikely that such legislation would be found to be unconstitutional. It is argued, however, that the implementation of such legislation in the territory of another state, would be beyond Australia's jurisdictional competence as a matter of international law. In the words of the Permanent Court of International Justice in the *SS Lotus Case:*

> the first and foremost restriction imposed by international law upon a state is that – failing the existence of a permissive rule to the contrary – it may not exercise its power in any form in the territory of another State.[125]

Thus, extra-territorial detention of a person by or on behalf of Australia would necessarily be 'arbitrary' detention within the meaning of Article 9 of the ICCPR in the absence of consent from the state with territorial jurisdiction. In the case previously mentioned involving the removal from Australia of three Algerian men, allegations have been made that the contracted escorts (P & I) detained the men for three days in a hotel in South Africa without the knowledge let alone consent of the South African government.[126] It is argued that even where the consent of the territorial state is obtained, detention of removees will only escape characterisation as 'arbitrary' if authorised by that state's law and a necessary and proportionate means of achieving that state's goal of immigration control.[127]

The bottom line then is that Australia's present removal practices often involves subjecting removees to 'arbitrary detention' within the meaning of Article 9(1) of the ICCPR.

Article 7 ICCPR Even before the development of international human rights law as we know it today, it was acknowledged that a state could not resort to the use of 'unnecessary force or other improper treatment' when exercising its sovereign right to expel aliens.[128] That proposition holds even truer today, in light of Article 7 of the ICCPR, which provides

---

[125] *SS Lotus Case (France v Turkey)* PCIJ Ser A (1927) No 9.

[126] ABC Four Corners, above n 114.

[127] It is difficult to see how detaining a non-citizen in the territory of another state could be either a necessary or proportionate means of achieving the goal of *Australian* immigration control.

[128] *Dillon* case, Mexico–USA General Claims Tribunal (1928) quoted in G S Goodwin-Gill, 'The Limits of the Power of Expulsion in Public International Law', *British Year Book of International Law*, **47** (1974–75) p 62.

that 'No one shall be subjected to torture or to cruel, inhuman or degrading treatment or punishment'.

Article 7 is one of a handful of ICCPR provisions that are stated to be non-derogable.[129] However, the 'nature, purpose and severity of the treatment' must be taken into account in determining whether there has been a violation of Article 7 in the first place.[130] Thus, whether particular treatment of a removee in the course of effecting a removal amounts to a violation of Article 7 of the ICCPR, depends on whether that treatment amounts to a necessary and proportionate means of achieving the legitimate end of immigration control. As Gregor Noll argues:

> It must be recalled that an individual removal contributes to this goal only as a fraction of total removals. Thus, the usage of handcuffs, sedative medication and other intrusive measures in removal cases can give rise to serious legal concerns. In each individual case, the suffering and humiliation it causes must be weighed against the contribution the individual's removal would make to migration control.[131]

Even Peter van Krieken, whose general approach is that host states owe no international legal obligations to rejected asylum seekers, takes the following position in relation to forcible removal:

> As usual, one needs two to tango, meaning that if the returnee/rejectee refuses to cooperate, the sending state may have to revert to some level of force, as it indeed concerns 'enforcement' per se. Never ever, however, should such force be allowed to harm the returnee ...[132]

---

[129] ICCPR, Article 4(2).

[130] UNHRC, *General Comment 20: Replaces General Comment 7 Concerning Prohibition of Torture and Cruel Treatment or Punishment* (Geneva, UNHRC, 1992), para 4. See further Joseph et al, above n 77, paras 9.24–9.26.

[131] Noll, above n 3.

[132] P van Krieken, 'Return and Responsibility', *International Migration* **38(4)** (2000) p 38, n 21.

There are well-documented cases of death or other serious injury being inflicted during the course of forcibly removing individuals from some European countries. Austria,[133] Belgium,[134] Germany,[135] Switzerland[136] and the United Kingdom[137] have attracted adverse comment from UN and non-government human rights bodies as a result of such incidents. As well as expressing general concern about the excessive use of force in the course

---

[133] The Special Rapporteur on Extra-judicial, Summary or Arbitrary Execution questioned Austria about the 1999 death during deportation of a bound and gagged Nigerian national and the Committee Against Torture also expressed concern about the death: Special Rapporteur, *For the Record 2000: The UN Human Rights System, Austria Thematic Reports* (Human Rights Internet & Netherlands Institute of Human Rights, 2000), http://www.hri.ca/fortherecord2000/vol6/austriatr.htm; UN Committee Against Torture (UNCAT), *Concluding Observations of the Committee Against Torture: Austria* (Geneva, UNHCR, A/55/44, 12 November 1999), para 49.

[134] The UNHRC criticised Belgium over the 1998 death of a Nigerian national, who had a cushion placed over her face in the course of an attempt at forcible removal: Amnesty International, *Belgium: Correspondence with the Government Concerning the Alleged Ill-treatment of Detained Asylum seekers* (Geneva, Amnesty International, AI Index EUR 14/001/1999, 1 June 1999).

[135] The 1994 death during deportation from Germany of a Nigerian national, who was tied, gagged and sedated, was investigated by the United Nation's Special Rapporteur on Extrajudicial, Summary or Arbitrary Executions: G Noll, 'Wanted – A Policy for Unwanted Returnees', *On the Record UNHCR* **2(6) Part 2** (3 November 1998), http://www.advocacynet.org/news_102.html. More recently, the Special Rapportuer on Extrajudicial, Summary or Arbitrary Executions has questioned Germany about the death in the course of forcible deportation of a Sudanese asylum seeker: Special Rapporteur, *For the Record 2000: The UN Human Rights System, Germany Thematic Reports* (Human Rights Internet & Netherlands Institute of Human Rights, 2000), http://www.hri.ca/fortherecord2000/vol6/germanytr.htm.

[136] In June 2001 three police officers and a doctor went on trial in Switzerland for the negligent manslaughter of a Palestinian man, who was bound, gagged and sedated, in an attempt to forcibly deport him from Switzerland in March 1999: Amnesty International, *Racism and the Administration of Justice* (Geneva, Amnesty International, AI Index ACT 40/020/2001, 2001), p 106.

[137] In July 1993 a Jamaican woman died as a result of being gagged during an attempt to forcibly deport her from the United Kingdom: Amnesty International, *United Kingdom: Cruel, Inhuman or Degrading Treatment During Forcible Deportation* (Geneva, Amnesty International, AI Index EUR 45/05/94) http://www.amnesty.org/ailib/aipub/1994/EUR/450594.EUR.txt. See also UNHRC, *Concluding Observations of the Human Rights Committee: United Kingdom of Great Britain and Northern Ireland* (Geneva, UNHRC, A/50/40, 3 October 1995), paras 408–35.

of forcible removals, these bodies have expressed particular disapproval of the use of mouth restraints, which appears to have been the cause of most of the deaths. Use of mouth restraints is now banned in all of those countries with first-hand experience of the possible tragic consequences.[138] As mentioned above, in the Australian context, too, allegations have been made of involuntary sedation, dangerous methods of restraint and excessive force being used to effect forcible removal. When asked by the SLCRC what protocols were in place for handling allegations of assault made against escorts contracted by DIMA, a departmental officer responded:

> If the department receives a complaint, either through a third party organisation such as the Ombudsman, HREOC or direct to us, then we arrange for them to be investigated as appropriate. On occasion that may be an investigation by our own internal investigation section or, depending on the nature of the claim, and certainly if there are criminal matters alleged, it would be referred to the police.[139]

However, the officer was quick to point out that only about five or six complaints had been made.[140] Unfortunately, this fact does not necessarily indicate that mistreatment of removees is not a significant problem. The potential complainants have, after all, been removed from Australia to places and situations that may make communication with Australia quite difficult.[141] In *A Sanctuary Under Review*, the SLCRC commented:

---

[138] UNHRC, *Summary record of the 1434th meeting: United Kingdom of Great Britain and Northern Ireland* (Geneva, UNHRC, CCPR/C/SR.1434, 27 July 1995), para 54 (UK delegation); Noll, above n 135; Amnesty International, *Racism and the Administration of Justice*, above n 136, p 106; Amnesty International, *Belgium: Correspondence with the Government* above n 134. In Austria, a ban was in place at the time of the incident described in n 133 above, but was not generally observed: UNCAT, *Summary Record of the First Part of the 395th Meeting: Austria* (Geneva, UNHRC, CAT/C/SR.395, 15 November 1999), para 27 (Mr Yakovlev, Alternate Country Rapporteur).

[139] SLCRC, *Official Committee Hansard: Reference Inquiry into the Operation of Australia's Refugee and Humanitarian Program* (Canberra, Commonwealth of Australia, 16 September 1999), p L&C 602–3 (Mr Metcalfe, DIMA).

[140] Ibid, p L&C 602 (Mr Metcalfe, DIMA).

[141] SLCRC, *Official Committee Hansard: Reference Inquiry into the Operation of Australia's Refugee and Humanitarian Program* (Canberra, Commonwealth of Australia, 29 July 1999), p L&C 379 (Mr Beckmann, RILC).

Although the department has established guidelines concerning the treatment of people being removed, and such guidelines appear to adhere to principles in the ICCPR, the lack of accountability and monitoring processes in the management of contracted services may render such guidelines very limited in effect.[142]

The bottom line here is that it is not possible to state with any confidence that Australia's present removal practice never involves 'cruel, inhuman or degrading treatment' of removees within the meaning of Article 7 of the ICCPR.

State responsibility Australia has undertaken 'to respect and to ensure to all individuals within its territory and subject to its jurisdiction' the rights recognised in the ICCPR.[143] If the human rights of removees are violated *by anyone* during any part of the removal process taking place within Australia's territorial limits, Australia can be held responsible for failure 'to ensure to all individuals within its territory' the rights recognised in the ICCPR.[144] Furthermore, the UNHRC's interpretation of Article 2(1) as well as the general doctrine of state responsibility support the proposition that an individual is subject to a state's jurisdiction:

in circumstances in which they can be said to be under the effective control of that state or ... affected by those acting on behalf of the state more generally, wherever this occurs.[145]

When, though, is the conduct of a natural person in any particular case, in fact, attributable to a state so as to render the state responsible for that conduct?

It is a firmly established rule of state responsibility, that the conduct of persons acting in their capacity as state officials is attributable to the state

---

[142] SLCRC, above n 8, para 10.82.

[143] ICCPR, Article 2(1).

[144] See G Townsend, 'State Responsibility for Acts of De Facto Agents', *Arizona Journal of International & Comparative Law* **14** (1997) p 635.

[145] E Lauterpacht and D Bethlehem, 'The Scope and Content of the Principle of Non-Refoulement', Background Paper for the Global Consultations on International Protection, 20 June 2001, para 67. See also Joseph et al, above n 77, paras 4.05 and 4.07; M Gibney, K Tomasevski and J Vedsted-Hansen, 'Transnational State Responsibility for Violations of Human Rights', *Harvard Human Rights Journal* **12** (1999) p 267; G S Goodwin-Gill, *The Refugee in International Law* (Oxford and New York, Clarendon Press, 2nd ed 1996), pp 141–2, 147.

in question. It is also firmly established that the conduct of persons, who appear to be acting in their capacity as state officials,[146] is attributable to the state even if, in terms of the state's domestic law, they are actually acting outside their competence. Australia is, therefore, responsible for the conduct of DIMIA officers, police officers, Australian Protective Services officers and all other Commonwealth, territory or state government officials in executing removal both within and outside Australian territory, even if they are acting ultra vires in terms of Australian law.

According to Article 8 of the Draft Articles on State Responsibility adopted by the International Law Commission at its meetings on 31 May and 3 August 2001:

> 8. The conduct of a person or group of persons shall be considered an act of a State under international law if the person or group of persons is in fact acting on the instructions of, or under the direction or control of, that State in carrying out the conduct.

This suggested rule has considerable support in the international case law and would apply to make Australia responsible, as a matter of international law, for the conduct both within and outside Australian territory of the employees or subcontractors of private escort companies contracted by it to effect removals.[147]

Australia is also, it is argued, responsible for the conduct both within and outside Australian territory of persons employed or contracted by airlines and shipping companies to carry out the removal obligations imposed on them by notice under section 217 of the Migration Act. As Debbie Mortimer, counsel for the applicant, submitted in *Re MIMA; Ex parte SE*:

> the notion of removal ... is an exercise of a power that resides in a nation State because it is a nation State. No carrier has that power. What the carrier has is a statutory obligation to transport... The carrier is simply the vehicle by which

---

[146] Under international law, the Commonwealth of Australia is held responsible for the conduct not only of Commonwealth officials but also of the officials of the component units of the Australian federation.

[147] UNHRC, *Concluding Observations of the Human Rights Committee: United Kingdom of Great Britain and Northern Ireland* (Geneva, UNHRC, A/50/40, 3 October 1995), paras 408–35 in which the Human Rights Committee made this point in relation to activities contracted out by the UK government.

the Minister exercises the power to remove so that so long as that power of removal continues, the carrier is no more than a vehicle.[148]

Counsel was here trying to convince the court to attribute to the Minister the manner of executing removal proposed by British Airways and its contractors. As mentioned above, she did not succeed. Hayne J accepted the Australian government's position that, as a matter of domestic law, 'removal' from Australia is complete the moment that the removee is outside Australia's territorial limits.[149] His Honour found that nothing that might occur thereafter could be attributed to the Minister because there was no evidence to suggest any of the arrangements for escort or supervision were 'made at the behest of [the Minister] or his Department'.[150]

What DIMIA has learned from *SE's case* is that it can keep out of domestic legal trouble by ensuring that it has no apparent involvement in the removal arrangements made by carriers on whom a section 217 notice is served. For example, MSI 283 informs DIMIA officers that a section 217 notice 'does not need to state a country of destination', because 'the law gives the carrier responsibility to make appropriate arrangements for the removal of the person' including the responsibility to arrange for some other country to accept the person being removed.[151]

Australia cannot, however, evade *international* responsibility quite so easily. Whatever the domestic law definition of 'removal', as a matter of practical reality, a person is removed from Australia *to somewhere*.[152] As a matter of practical reality, the carrier will need to obtain travel documents, make sure it does not get into legal trouble in any transit countries by being the means by which a removee from Australia manages to enter one of those countries, and so on. It is argued that Australia bears international responsibility not just for what the carrier does in effecting technical

---

[148] *Re MIMA; Ex parte SE* (High Court transcript, M99/1998, 9 November 1998).

[149] See submissions by counsel for the Minister in *Re MIMA; Ex parte SE,* M99/1998 (High Court transcript, 30 October 1998). See also submissions by counsel for the Minister in *Re MIMA; Ex parte Farah,* M44/1998 (High Court transcript, 15 June 1998).

[150] *Re MIMA; Ex parte SE* (1998) 158 ALR 735 at 738.

[151] DIMA, *MSI 283: Carrier Obligations and Offences* (Canberra, DIMA, 17 May 2000), para 9.4.2.

[152] That somewhere will usually be the removee's country of nationality, because in most cases, the country of nationality will be the only country with an obligation to accept the removee.

'removal', but also for what the carrier does (or its agents do) throughout the whole practical process of removal.

A particularly tricky question is that of responsibility for the treatment of removees on board a civil aircraft.[153] Article 6 of the Tokyo Convention,[154] implemented in Australian law by the Crimes Aviation Act 1991, section 29, provides that:

1. The aircraft commander may, when he has reasonable grounds to believe that a person has committed, or is about to commit, on board the aircraft, an offence or act contemplated in Article 1 paragraph 1,[155] impose upon such person reasonable measures including restraint which are necessary;

    (a) to protect the safety of the aircraft, or of persons or property therein; or

    (b) to maintain good order and discipline on board; or

    (c) to enable him to deliver such person to competent authorities or to disembark him in accordance with the provisions of this Chapter.

The captain's authority extends to authorising others on board to assist.[156] In light of the authority given to the captain, the SLCRC has queried whether DIMIA could play an official role in overseeing the treatment of removees aboard civil aircraft.[157] It is argued that regardless of the answer to the SLCRC's query, the authority given to the captain cannot be interpreted as relieving Australia of *responsibility* for the treatment of removees aboard aircraft. It is certainly the case that by reason of the authority given to the captain, the captain (and the airline company) can be

---

[153] The treaty discussed below does not apply to state aircraft, i.e. military, customs and police service aircraft.

[154] Convention on Offences and Certain Other Acts Committed on Board Aircraft (Tokyo, 14 September 1963) Australian Treaty Series 1970, No 14. Entry into force generally: 4 December 1969. Entry into force for Australia: 20 September 1970.

[155] Article 1(1) provides:

This Convention shall apply in respect of:

(a) offences against penal law;

(b) acts which, whether or not they are offences, may or do jeopardize the safety of the aircraft or of persons or property therein or which jeopardize good order and discipline on board.

[156] Tokyo Convention, Article 6(2).

[157] SLCRC, above n 8, para 10.66.

held responsible for the treatment of removees aboard the aircraft. In fact, in some European countries death or injury suffered by removees has led to criminal proceedings being instituted against the captain of the aircraft.[158] However, it is also undoubtedly the case that human rights treaty bodies have held the removing state responsible for ill treatment of removees by their (usually police) escorts while on board aircraft.[159] The only question on which there may be doubt is whether the removing state can be held responsible for the ill-treatment of a removee on board an aircraft where it has invoked a provision such as section 217 of the Migration Act and purported to wash its hands of further involvement. It is suggested that the question should be answered in the affirmative. This is on the basis, already canvassed above, that the removal is taking place at the order of the state and in exercise of the power of the state.

Pragmatic Solutions

In 1998, the Executive Committee of the High Commissioner's Programme (Ex Com) noted that 'effecting the return of individuals not in need of international protection to their countries of origin' was something easier said than done.[160] It further noted that some states faced with the problem of returning rejected asylum seekers had put in place 'comprehensive

---

[158] Deportation Alliance, 'Pilots' Assosiacion [sic] steps up against deportations', 16 February 2001, http://www.deportation-alliance.com. The Tokyo Convention, Article 10 provides:

> For actions taken *in accordance with this Convention*, neither the aircraft commander, any other member of the crew, any passenger, the owner or operator of the aircraft, nor the person on whose behalf the flight was performed shall be held responsible in any proceeding on account of the treatment undergone by the person against whom the actions were taken. (Emphasis added.)

The key words are those italicised. Article 6 allows 'reasonable measures' to be taken in defined circumstances. It does not give carte blanche. Where the bounds of Article 6 are exceeded, criminal jurisdiction can and should be invoked by the state of registration of the aircraft or the territorial state: Article 3.

[159] See above n 131–135.

[160] Ex Com Standing Committee, *Composite Flows and the Relationship to Refugee Outflows, Including Return of Persons not in need of International Protection, as well as Facilitation of Return in its Global Dimension* (Geneva, UNHCR, UN Doc EC/48/SC/CRP.29, 25 May 1998), para 14.

voluntary return programmes based on a philosophy of incentives rather than coercion' and stated that these programs deserved 'a careful "lessons learned" analysis'.[161]

The United Nations High Commissioner for Refugees (UNHCR) is open to cooperating with governments in implementing comprehensive voluntary return programs provided always that its involvement is within a protection framework and within its guidelines on the return of rejected asylum seekers in humane and safe conditions.[162] The International Organisation for Migration (IOM)[163] is also open to involvement in the implementation of voluntary return programs. In fact, the IOM presently offers member governments three different packages of services (called 'return programmes') to assist return of irregular migrants including unsuccessful asylum seekers.[164]

According to a key IOM document, 'IOM divides return into three chronological stages: pre-departure, transportation and post-arrival'.[165] At the pre-departure stage, IOM offers various services including information and counselling.[166] The Swedish experience suggests that this may be the key to procuring voluntary departure by rejected asylum seekers. According to Anna Wessel of the Swedish Migration Board, Sweden returns 80 per cent of its rejected asylum seekers but rarely has to resort to coercive measures.[167] She attributes this to the fact that asylum seekers are treated with respect for their human dignity, and respond accordingly.[168] Translated into practical terms, this involves, inter alia, motivational counselling of each asylum seeker by a caseworker throughout the asylum

---

[161] Ibid, para 15. For discussion of EU experimentation with voluntary return programs see G Noll, *Negotiating Asylum: The EU Acquis, Extraterritorial Protection and the Common Market of Deflection* (The Hague, Martinus Nijhoff Publishers, 2000), pp 246 and 248.

[162] Ex Com Standing Committee, above n 160, para 15.

[163] IOM is the inter-governmental body responsible for migration issues.

[164] IOM, *IOM Return Policy and Programmes: A Contribution to Combating Irregular Migration* (IOM, MC/INF/236, 5 November 1997), http://www.iom.int/iom/Publiciations/entry.htm, para 11.

[165] Id, para 15.

[166] Id, para 16.

[167] P Mares, 'How Sweden Deals with Its Influx', *The Age*, 11 January 2001, p 11.

[168] Ibid.

process with a view to thoroughly preparing that person to deal with all possible outcomes including having to leave Sweden following rejection.[169]

At the third stage (post-arrival), IOM provides another critical service: re-integration assistance. In its sales pitch for its return programs, IOM argues:

> In most cases, assisted return is likely to be a more durable solution than forced return. Where reasonable reintegration assistance is provided, it bridges the gap between return and initial housing and employment, thus considerably enhancing the chances of a successful and lasting reintegration. Assisted return is often a more realistic solution than deportation, given the latter's costs, logistics, lack of internal cooperation and political repercussions in the country and abroad. In these situations, IOM-assisted return programmes have proved to be a useful complement to forced return, thereby maximizing returns overall.[170]

It should be noted, however, that not all assessments of the usefulness of assisted return programs are quite as positive as that of the IOM.[171] In addition, Peter van Krieken makes a valid point when he suggests that in order to succeed in achieving voluntary returns a state must not only offer inducements but limit alternatives so that rejectees are necessarily led to draw the conclusion that 'return is the only viable "way out"'.[172]

In the Australian case, the alternatives have already been limited. The only alternative to return that Australia offers is immigration detention.[173] On the inducement front, Australia says that it is working with the IOM 'to

---

[169] Ibid. Sweden also provides incentives for voluntary repatriation in the form of financial assistance to cover costs of resettlement: G Mitchell, 'Asylum Seekers in Sweden: An Integrated Approach to Reception, Detention, Determination, Integration and Return', Paper presented to the Australian Fabian Society, August 2001, http://www.fabian.org.au/NEW%20PAPERS/Protocol.html.

[170] IOM, above n 164, para 19. States that choose to provide reintegration assistance need, of course, to strike a balance between assistance so parsimonious that it makes no real contribution to sustainable return and assistance so generous that it becomes in itself a migration pull factor. European states are very awake to the latter danger.

[171] See, for example, van Krieken, above n 132, p 33.

[172] Ibid.

[173] Where return is not a realistic option, indefinite immigration detention pending return itself raises human rights issues. It is assumed throughout this chapter that the cases being dealt with are those in which the only obstacle to return is the will of the rejectee.

encourage and assist unauthorised arrivals, who are found not to be owed protection obligations by Australia, to voluntarily return home'.[174]

Some human rights non-governmental organisations (NGOs) are wary of the IOM, believing it to be more concerned with implementing the agendas of its member governments than with observing human rights principles.[175] This is a good reason for subjecting Australian government–IOM return programs to intense scrutiny, but not, it is suggested, a reason for opposing them before they have been given a fair chance to prove their worth in trial runs.

Conclusion

A point that has been made many times is that the good sense of maintaining an expensive process for the determination of asylum claims is called into question unless those found not to be in need of international protection are, in practice, removed.[176] It is, however, important never to lose sight of the fact that 'persons not in need of international protection' are still human beings whose human dignity must be respected in all circumstances. According to Gregor Noll, European Union member states have 'largely failed to address' the human rights issues arising from removal of rejected asylum seekers.[177] This chapter has demonstrated that, unfortunately, the same can be said of Australia. The trialing of voluntary return programs is, however, a step in the right direction.

---

[174] DIMA, *Summary of Initiatives* (Canberra, DIMA, 2001), para 16. The only further detail made readily available is that the 2000–01 Commonwealth budget included an allocation of $2 million to develop a pilot program to provide 'targeted reintegration assistance for unauthorised arrivals returned to their previous country of asylum or origin': DIMA, *Protecting the Border*, above n 90, chapter 2.

[175] E Schenkenberg van Mierop, 'Editorial: Migration, Inc.', *TALK BACK – The Newsletter of the International Council of Voluntary Agencies,* 3(2) (2001), http://www.icva.ch.

[176] See, for example, Ex Com Standing Committee, above n 160, para 14; Millbank, above n 12; J Harding, *The Uninvited: Refugees at the Rich Man's Gate* (London, Profile and the London Review of Books, 2000), pp 57–8.

[177] Noll, above n 161, p 250.

9 The Role of the United Nations High Commissioner for Refugees and the Refugee Definition

JOSE ALVIN C GONZAGA*

Introduction

The 50th anniversary of the 1951 Refugees Convention offers an opportunity to re-examine the definition[1] of 'refugee' and the role of the United Nations High Commissioner for Refugees (UNHCR). It is also timely since in the last few years, the Convention has come under increasing criticism. On one hand, some states are questioning its relevance in the context of the present migration challenges. On the other, many refugee advocacy organisations are expressing concern that its scope is too narrow as its provisions do not sufficiently cover other categories of persons who need international protection.

---

* The views expressed in this paper are the personal views of the author, and not necessarily shared by the United Nations or by the UNHCR.

[1] The term 'refugee' under the 1951 Convention and the 1967 Protocol applies to any person who, 'owing to well-founded fear of being persecuted for reasons of race, religion, nationality, membership of a particular social group or political opinion, is outside the country of his nationality and is unable or, owing to such fear, is unwilling to avail himself/herself the protection of that country or who, not having a nationality and being outside the country of his former habitual residence as a result of such events, is unable or owing to such fear, is unwilling to return to it'. The human rights focus of this definition is clear. It should be read broadly with the exclusion and cessation clauses in Article 1C–F. The exclusion clauses describe circumstances in which an individual may not be entitled to benefit from international protection, notwithstanding that he/she meets the criteria for recognition as a refugee, because of breach of basic human rights standards. The cessation clauses describe circumstances in which protection by continuing recognition of refugee status is no longer warranted because of the lack of risk of human rights abuse.

Despite these criticisms, the UNHCR maintains that the Convention remains relevant as a statement of the fundamental rights of refugees. It is the universal international instrument that has protected tens of millions of refugees, in all parts of the world, over the last half century. Even at present, the UNHCR is responsible for 21.8 million 'persons of concern', approximately 12 million of whom are refugees in the legal sense. Erika Feller, the UNHCR's Director of International Protection has stated that:

> the Convention has already a legal and political significance that goes well beyond its specific terms: *legal* in that it provides the basic standards on which principled action can be founded; *political* in that it provides a truly universal framework within which states can cooperate and share the burden resulting from forced displacements; and *ethical* in that it is a unique declaration by 140 state parties[2] of their commitment to uphold and protect the rights of some of the world's most vulnerable and disadvantaged.[3]

The Main Basis of the Current Criticisms

The growing disillusionment among states about the relevance of the Convention is directly linked to the immigration challenges that they are facing, mainly brought about by or as an effect of globalisation. These challenges, in the form of increased irregular migration and people smuggling, are further complicated by being mixed with refugee-related issues. These include: large and protracted refugee producing conditions and situations, high costs of refugee status determination systems and the cost of hosting refugees, as well as real or perceived abuses of the system. Thus, many states now argue that the Convention no longer provides a

---

[2]   The significance of the Convention is not only limited to signatory states. There have been a number of states, which despite not having acceded to the Convention, have established refugee status determination processes and used the definition of 'refugee' in the Convention. One example is the Comprehensive Plan of Action (CPA) approved by the International Conference on Indo-Chinese Refugees held at Geneva, Switzerland, June 1989 to address the influx of the Vietnamese and Laotians asylum seekers. See Migration Act 1958 (Cth), sections 91A–D.

[3]   E Feller, 'The Convention at 50: The Way Ahead for Refugee Protection,' *Forced Migration Review*, **10** (April 2001) p 6. (Emphasis added.)

suitable legal framework to address these complexities. Instead, as a response, they have adopted even harsher measures to curb or refuse admission to their territory[4] and have introduced even more restrictions on the application of the Convention.[5]

Due to these measures, refugee advocacy groups are concerned that there are more persons in need of international protection who are either not recognised as refugees or only given minimalist treatment. In addition, they have realised that the UNHCR has been involved in providing assistance and protection to categories of persons who are not 'refugees' in the Convention sense, such as internally displaced persons (IDPs), on an ad hoc basis. These groups would like to see a United Nations (UN) body, possibly the UNHCR, respond to the needs of these persons with a more concrete and permanent involvement.[6] They suggest that the UNHCR's mandate should be expanded to recognise the practice. Thus, they urge a re-examination of the Convention, with the purpose of expanding the coverage of the 1951 Convention definition. In this sort of environment there is strong pressure to reform the Convention from both state parties and the advocacy groups. These are the challenges that the Convention is facing today.

In this chapter I discuss issues about the refugee definition and gaps in the protection which the 1951 Convention provides.[7] I will cite both state and UNHCR approaches to address these issues and gaps, the UNHCR's position on states' approaches and the weaknesses or dilemmas of

---

[4] See P Mathew, 'Safe for Whom? The Safe Third Country Concept Finds a Home in Australia', chapter 6 in this book.

[5] See M Crock, 'The Refugees Convention at 50: Mid-life Crisis or Terminal Inadequacy? An Australian Perspective', chapter 3 in this book.

[6] Another 'category' of persons that the refugee definition is silent upon but who may need international protection or for whom international protection is being advocated to be extended, is the family members of persons recognised as refugees (based on the principle of family re-unification). Some countries do not apply this principle. Editor's note: see below n 21.

[7] Editor's note: contrast E Feller, 'Statement by the Director, UNHCR Department of International Protection, to the 18th Meeting of the UNHCR Standing Committee', 5 July 2000, *International Journal of Refugee Law* **12** (2000) p 401 at p 405 where these are referred to as the middle and outer circles of issues about the Refugees Convention. The inner circle represents the core values of 'universality, impartiality and a fundamental humanitarian spirit': id, p 403.

these approaches, taking into account the UNHCR's experiences over the last 50 years.

The Refugee Definition – Interpretive Issues

Sophisticated and Costly Procedures to Determine the Refugee Claims

One of the main criticisms by the states of the Refugees Convention is the requirement under the refugee definition in Article 1A to examine asylum seekers' claims of persecution on an individual basis. Some states, especially in advanced or First World countries, have set up sophisticated procedural mechanisms to determine refugee status, which include not only administrative but a couple of layers of judicial examination. Due to the high number of asylum seekers, these states are now contending that their procedures are becoming inadequate because of the considerable time, expense and effort. For example, a recent estimate of the annual amount spent by states on refugee status procedures is US$10 billion for half a million asylum seekers in western Europe as compared to the annual budget of the UNHCR of US$1 billion for 21.8 million persons of concern. On a per capita basis, US$20 000 is spent per claimant while the UNHCR spends US$50 per person under its care.[8] Therefore, the amount spent by some countries to process asylum claims equals or exceeds the entire budget of the UNHCR.[9]

Meanwhile, advocacy groups have criticised these procedural mechanisms because they place refugees in a vulnerable situation while they are waiting for the final outcome of their refugee status determination. As an example, during this period, the asylum seekers are not able to regularise their stay in the country of first asylum or avail themselves of the benefit of local settlement or other durable solutions (such as resettlement in a third country). Thus, for advocacy groups also, the existing refugee status determination procedural mechanisms do not reflect the needs and reality of the current situation.

---

[8] Editor's note: contrast the discussion in R Illingworth, 'Durable Solutions: Refugee Status Determination and the Framework of International Protection', chapter 4 in this book. There it is suggested that each place in the Humanitarian Program costs the Australian public $21 000.

[9] G Van Kessel, 'Global Migration and Asylum', *Forced Migration Review Issue* **10** (10 April 2001) p 12.

In response to the arrival of thousands of asylum seekers, especially in industrialised First World countries, for fear that their asylum system would be overwhelmed, states have recently adopted and legislated complementary and/or temporary forms of Convention protection. This type of response places the UNHCR in a dilemma because the protection that is provided by these forms is often a less satisfactory alternative to the Convention-based protection. It also results in varying standards of treatment for asylum seekers and refugees.[10] From the standpoint of the UNHCR, these forms should only be considered as additional or complementary protection devices, but should not serve as substitutes for the Convention based protection regime.

Inconsistent Interpretations of the Refugees Convention

Another criticism of the refugee definition is that it has been subject to different and inconsistent interpretations, especially recently due to a tendency of some states to interpret it restrictively. This they do by

---

[10] Complementary forms of protection should be distinguished from temporary forms of protection. The latter is a specific provisional protection response to situations of mass influx providing immediate emergency protection from refoulement, while the former is offered after a status determination providing a defined status. Temporary forms of protection involve a group assessment of international protection needs based on the circumstances in the country of origin, whereas complementary protection measures applies to individuals whose protection needs have been specifically examined: UNHCR *Complementary Forms of Protection* (UN Doc EC/50/SC/CRP18, April 2001), in *International Journal of Refugee Law* **12(3)** (July 2000) p 401–6. The temporary forms of protection have also created issues that need to be clarified. These include; the determination of the scale of mass influx; establishing the standards of treatment; defining the status of the beneficiaries; and setting the duration of the 'temporariness'. The traditional response by the UNHCR to mass influx has been to use prima facie determination or acceptance on a group basis. However, there are some dilemmas with this approach. (1) In cases when the camp populations are mixed with non-refugees, the government becomes doubtful whether to continue treating these persons as refugees. A current example of this is Pakistan, which was a hospitable country for refugees, but lately has considered the recent Afghan arrivals as prima facie economic migrants instead of refugees. (2) In cases when refugees who faced protection problems in host countries need to be resettled to third countries. In these cases, the resettlement countries' criteria do not assure that they would accept refugees in the context of this 'extended definition'. These dilemmas have put into question the continuing viability of the 'prima facie' approach: UNHCR, *Protection of Refugees in Mass Influx Situations: Overall Protection Framework* (Geneva, UNHCR, UN Doc EC/GC01/4, 19 February 2001), p 2.

focusing more on the letter rather than spirit or purpose of the Refugees Convention, to minimise their responsibility instead of ensuring protection to legitimate beneficiaries. There are a number of issues upon which states vary the refugee definition in Article 1A of the 1951 Convention or have a restrictive interpretation of it. Below are some of the current and most common examples.

Some of the Common and Current Examples of Inconsistent Interpretations

Persons who flee from conflict situations Some states argue that the 1951 Convention does not provide protection for such persons. They argue that for an asylum seeker to be 'persecuted' within the meaning of the Convention, he or she must be singled out or in some way 'individually targeted'. Thus, for persons who are fleeing from conflict situations, these states argue they are 'victims of indiscriminate violence' rather than refugees, although the conflict they flee may be rooted in ethnic, religious or political differences. These states therefore argue that the Convention is not a suitable legal framework for addressing refugee problems as often these occur in the context of internal war or other armed conflicts. They argue that these asylum seekers do not fit within the five grounds under the refugee definition upon which the well-foundedness of their fear of persecution can be based, that is, 'race, nationality, political opinion, religion and membership in a particular social group'.

These arguments are not consistent with the UNHCR position that persons who flee as specific victims of conflicts that are rooted in ethnic, religious or political differences should qualify as 1951 Convention refugees.[11] Also, even in war or conflict situations, persons may be forced to flee on account of a well-founded fear of persecution for Convention reasons. War and conflict are frequently the means chosen by persecutors to repress or eliminate specific groups, targeted on account of their ethnicity or other affiliations.[12]

---

[11] See UNHCR note, *Interpreting Article 1 of the 1951 Convention Relating to the Status of Refugees*, (Geneva, UNHCR, April 2001), para 21, www.unhcr.ch/prexcom/standocs/english/gc01_18e.pdf.

[12] Ibid. In the same document it mentioned that the UNHCR equally recognised that there are persons who flee the indiscriminate effects of violence associated with conflict with no element of persecution. Such persons might not meet the Convention definition, but may still require international protection on other grounds.

Gender related persecution On this ground there are also varying interpretations. There are some states that do not accept this as a ground of persecution because of the lack of express reference to 'gender' in the Convention definition. But there are others which argue that this should be construed within the context of 'membership of a particular social group'.

The UNHCR position is that it considers violence with a basis in gender to be persecutory in Convention terms as with any other violence when the harm inflicted is sufficiently serious and can be linked to a Convention ground. It does not matter that the Convention is silent on gender as a ground for persecution, just as it does not matter that the crime is gender-specific, with women as its victims.[13] Thus, the UNHCR opinion is that there is no need to add sex or gender as a ground to the Convention, if the refugee definition is properly interpreted.

Fear of persecution by non-state agents This is also an issue on which some of the states have applied the refugee definition strictly given that the 1951 Refugees Convention does not define persecution or say anything about perpetrators of persecution. Thus, these states do not recognise as refugees those persons who flee persecution committed by those who do not represent the state, such as rebel groups, despite the fact that the state is unable to protect them.

The states' interpretation on this issue is not in line with the UNHCR's viewpoint. The UNHCR maintains the position that the Convention applies to any person who has a well-founded fear of persecution regardless of who is responsible because it does not say that a state must be responsible for the persecution. The UNHCR observes that any group that holds substantial power in a country can persecute.[14] An example of such a situation is Somalia, in which the government did not hold a firm control over its territory or people. Instead, it had fiefdoms, where armed bands and warlords controlled different stretches of land.[15]

---

[13] E Feller, 'Challenges to the 1951 Convention in its 50th Anniversary Year', Speech, Seminar on International Protection Within One Single Asylum Procedure, Norrkoping, Sweden, 23–24 April 2001, p 2.

[14] UNHCR, *The State of World Refugees*, (New York, Oxford University Press, 2000), p 163.

[15] Editor's note: see S Kneebone, 'Moving Beyond the State: Refugees, Accountability and Protection', chapter 11 in this book.

With regard to proper interpretation of the 1951 Convention in general, the UNHCR maintains that the aim of the drafters of the Convention was to incorporate human rights values in the identification and treatment of refugees. This principle should be used as a guide in its interpretation. This is consistent with well established international law rules for interpreting treaties, which have been codified under the 1969 Vienna Convention of the Law of Treaties.[16] According to the latter, a treaty, such as the 1951 Convention, should be interpreted in good faith in accordance with the ordinary meaning to be given to the terms of the treaty in their context in light of its object and purpose. It also states that the Preamble of the treaty is a source of such object and purpose. The Preamble of the Refugees Convention, if read closely, concludes that the object and purpose of the 1951 Convention is to ensure the protection of the specific rights of the refugees and to encourage international cooperation for that purpose, and the UNHCR is given a special role in that regard. The Preamble also contains strong human rights language, referring to the international community's affirmation of the principle of human beings' enjoyment of fundamental rights and freedoms without discrimination, such as those set out in the Universal Declaration of Human Rights.[17]

In order to promote and harmonise the proper interpretation of the definition, the UNHCR has been actively advising governments under its supervisory role set out in Article 35 of the Convention and under its statutory mandate.[18]

States' Approaches

It is sometimes argued that the Refugees Convention is weakened by the use of the use of complementary forms of protection or by adopting regional instruments. The UNHCR responds that these forms of protection are not a substitute for Convention protection and that the Refugees

---

[16] Adopted by a Diplomatic Conference of states on 23 May 1969 and entered into force on 27 January 1980.

[17] Adopted and proclaimed by United Nations General Assembly resolution 217A (III) on 10 December 1948.

[18] The UNHCR was established by the General Assembly of the United Nations in 1950. Its basic functions are set out in the 1950 Statute: G S Goodwin-Gill, *The Refugee in International Law* (Oxford, Clarendon Press, 2nd ed, 1996), pp 7–14, 212.

Convention remains the paramount instrument. Because the Convention contains basic human rights standards, it is the primary instrument.

Complementary forms of protection In some states where asylum seekers are not recognised as refugees, because their claims are based on grounds which are not recognised by that state as being the basis for refugee protection, due to restrictive interpretation of the Convention (such as those who were fleeing the conflict), these states nevertheless allow them to remain on some other basis. In those cases, when it would not be possible or advisable to return them to their country of origin for a variety of reasons, some states resort to the use of complementary forms of protection in order to regularise the stay of these persons, through either an administrative or legislative mechanism. For example, in Australia the Minister has an administrative discretion under section 417 of the Migration Act to substitute a more favourable decision for that of the Refugee Review Tribunal.[19] In the United Kingdom there is provision for 'exceptional leave to remain'. The European countries have similar provisions creating complementary statuses.[20]

In these instances, the UNHCR urges that in the implementation of these measures, states should provide guarantees of basic civil, political, social and economic rights, and harmonise them with the terms of treatment of asylum seekers or refugees. This includes provisions which respect the fundamental principle of family unity.[21] As previously stated, the UNHCR views the complementary forms of protection as supplements but not substitutes for the Convention protection regime.

Regional instruments Another approach adopted by some states to address the possible gaps arising from conflicting interpretations of the Refugees Convention definition is to enter into regional agreements and instruments. The following are the examples of regional instruments that have been created so far:

---

[19] This power is discussed in Crock, above n 5.

[20] J van Selm-Thorburn, *Refugee Protection in Europe: Lessons of the Yugoslav Crisis* (The Hague, Kluwer Law International, 1998), part 3, 'Temporary Protection in Four European States', pp 173–240.

[21] Editor's note: contrast the provisions of the Temporary Visa subclass 785 which was created by amendment to the regulations under the Migration Act 1958 (Cth) in 1999. Under the terms of this visa no family unification is allowed.

- Organisation of African States' Convention Governing the Specific Aspects of Refugee Problems in Africa of 1969 (OAU Convention), which extends the definition in Article 1A of the 1951 Convention to 'every person who was compelled to leave his country of origin on account of external aggression, occupation, foreign domination or events seriously disturbing public order'. Thus, persons fleeing civil disturbances, violence and war are entitled to claim the status of refugee in states which are parties to the OAU Convention, irrespective of whether or not they can establish a well founded fear of persecution;[22]

- 1984 Cartagena Declaration, in which the Latin American states agreed to extend the definition to include 'those who have fled their country because their lives, safety or freedom have been threatened by generalised violence, foreign aggression, internal conflicts, massive violations of human rights or other circumstances which have seriously disturbed public order'. Although the Declaration is not legally binding on states, it has repeatedly been endorsed by the General Assembly of the Organisation of American States. Most states in Central and Latin America are party to the 1951 Convention or its Protocol, and most apply the Declaration's broader definition of a refugee as a matter of practice;[23]

- 1966 Bangkok Principles Concerning Treatment of Refugees adopted by the Asian African Legal Consultative Committee, which is a regional but non-binding instrument on refugee matters;

- Council of Europe. Under the Declaration on Territorial Asylum adopted by the Committee of Ministers in 1977, it was declared that the member states and parties to the 1951 Refugees Convention reaffirmed the right to grant asylum to any person who comes within the Article 1A definition, as well as to any other person they consider worthy of receiving asylum for humanitarian reasons.[24] Moreover, in its Parliamentary Assembly's Recommendation 773 in

---

[22] UNHCR, above n 14, p 56.

[23] Id, p 123.

[24] 'Declaration of Territorial Asylum' in UNHCR, *Collections of International Instruments and Other Legal Texts Concerning Refugees and Displaced Persons* (Geneva, UNHCR, Vol II, 1977), p 270.

1976 the Committee of Ministers expressed their concern in regard to the situation of 'de facto' refugees, that is persons who are either not formally recognised as Convention refugees, (although they meet the criteria) or who are unable or unwilling for other valid reasons to return to their country of origin.[25] To date, this recommendation is only partially implemented.

In general, the UNHCR views these regional instruments as complementary to the 1951 Refugees Convention. To a certain extent, these instruments may have beneficial effects as they cover perceived gaps, where the Convention is interpreted restrictively as omitting grounds of persecution. To a certain degree, the UNHCR was involved in the development of these instruments by cooperating with the regional bodies that adopted these instruments. However, the dilemma for the UNHCR is that these regional instruments (or other efforts to develop regionally specific legal frameworks) may make the Convention redundant in some parts of the world and its universal applicability may thus be put into question. Also, it is concerned that there is a possibility that these instruments are inconsistent with the Refugees Convention. But so far there has been no conflict of authority nor have any other legal incompatibilities arisen between the UNHCR and a regional organisation with regard to the respective instruments.[26]

Gaps in Refugee Protection

UNHCR Mandate Extended to Persons in Need of International Protection

One of the apparent gaps, which concerns advocacy organisations, is that the refugee definition in Article 1A of the Refugees Convention does not cover categories of persons such as IDPs, other than those who satisfy the legal definition, who are equally in need of protection. Thus, they want to ensure that the Convention includes these categories. But it is important to note that this gap was recognised from the outset of the Convention. It must

---

[25] Id, recommendation 773 (1976), 'On de Facto Refugees', p 398.

[26] V Turk, 'The role of UNHCR in the Development of International Refugee Law' in F Nicholson and P Twomey (eds), *Refugee Rights and Realities, Evolving International Concepts* (Cambridge, Cambridge University Press, 2000), p 167.

be recalled that for this reason, the Conference of Plenipotentiaries, which adopted the 1951 Convention, recommended in the Final Act that states should apply the Convention beyond its strictly contractual scope, to other refugees within their territory.[27] This declaration clearly indicates that there would be persons fleeing persecution and in need of international protection for reasons beyond those for which the Convention definition provided.

Moreover, it becomes clear that this gap in the definition is illusory if it is compared with the actual protection and assistance provided by the UNHCR in accordance with its extended mandate. For the past 50 years, the UNHCR has been called upon by the UN Secretary General, General Assembly or competent principal organs of the UN to provide international protection and assistance to different categories of persons who do not strictly come within the refugee definition under the Refugees Convention. Obviously, the international community recognises that these categories of persons are in need of international protection.[28] Otherwise, they would not have extended the mandate of the UNHCR. These categories of persons are discussed in the following sections.

Internally Displaced Persons (IDPs)

Under the Guiding Principles on Internal Displacement formulated by the Representative of the Secretary General of the United Nations on IDPs are:

> persons or groups of persons who have been forced or obliged to flee or leave their homes or habitual residence, in particular as a result of or in order to avoid the effects of armed conflict, situations of generalised violence, violations of human rights or natural or human-made disasters, and who have not crossed an internationally recognised state border.[29]

Obviously, IDPs do not fall within the refugee definition under the Convention. However, except for the fact that they have not crossed an

---

[27] Goodwin-Gill, above n 18, p 19. This recommendation may be invoked to support extension of the Convention to groups or individuals who do not fully satisfy the definition requirements. Goodman-Gill points out that states generally claim the rights to grant asylum to others, for example, for 'humanitarian reasons'.

[28] Turk, above n 26, p 153.

[29] F Deng, *Guiding Principles on Internal Displacement, Report of the Representative of the Secretary General* (Geneva, UN Doc E/CN4/1998/53/Add 2, 11 February 1998).

international boundary, they are in a similar situation to refugees because the conditions that led them to flee are usually the same as those that led refugees to flee: that is, persecution, gross human rights violations, and similar causes. Thus, they too may need international protection and assistance. This is especially true in areas of conflict, where state protection is weak or non-existent. Currently, the UNHCR is involved in operations with a total of around 5.2 million IDPs. Examples of these operations are in the Former Yugoslavia, and Sri Lanka. In the 1999 report of the Representative of the UN Secretary General on Internally Displaced Persons, it was stated that there are 25 million people who have been affected by internal displacement.[30]

The reference to 'displaced persons' dates at least from 1972, when the Economic and Social Council of the United Nations (ECOSOC) acted both to promote the voluntary repatriation of refugees to Sudan, including measures of rehabilitation and assistance, and also extended the benefit of such measures to 'persons displaced within the country.'[31] Since then, the UNHCR has periodically become involved in enhancing protection and assistance to IDPs through special operations, undertaken at the request of the Secretary-General or General Assembly, on a 'good offices' basis.[32] The UNHCR has established parameters of operational involvement with IDPs. Under these parameters the UNHCR will only be involved with IDPs operations if:

- it is ensured that its involvement does not compromise its humanitarian mandate;
- its involvement improves the situation of the IDPs while upholding the right to seek asylum (as its activities may be misinterpreted as obviating the need for international protection);
- political efforts to resolve the displacements are underway or being clearly contemplated; and,
- its experience and expertise are relevant to the situation.

---

[30] F Deng, *Specific Groups and Individuals: Mass Exoduses and Displaced Persons (Internally displaced persons)*, Report of the Representative of the Secretary General, submitted pursuant to Commission on Human Rights Resolution 1998/50 (UN Doc E/CN4/1999/79, 1999).

[31] Goodwin Gill, above n 18, p 11.

[32] Turk, above n 26, p 158.

In addition, its involvement also requires:

- a specific request or authorisation from the UN Secretary General or other competent organ of the UN;
- the consent of the state concerned, or other relevant entity in the conflict;
- access to the affected population and adequate security for the UNHCR and implementing partners to operate effectively;
- clear lines of responsibility and accountability with the ability to intervene directly with parties concerned, particularly on protection matters; and,
- adequate resources and capacity to carry out activities.[33]

The UNHCR has faced dilemmas in its involvement with IDPs. In theory, in keeping with the traditional notions of sovereignty, IDPs should be under their state's protection. Under the terms of its mandate the UNHCR is not supposed to provide a substitute to such protection if the persons remain within the territorial jurisdiction of their state. Moreover, due to this sovereignty issue the international community is not as ready to respond to the problems of IDPs, as it is in the refugee situations. Presently, there are still many countries that are reluctant even to have international humanitarian intervention for IDPs. For example, resettlement countries are reluctant to provide placements for displaced persons even when the only protection solution for them is either their evacuation or resettlement, because they are not 'refugees' since they have not crossed an international boundary.

On the other hand, there are also instances in which a state has gone beyond the refugee definition to respond to the needs of displaced persons. Among them is the US Refugee Act of 1980, where the geographically based definition is abandoned by offering resettlement opportunities to those who might qualify as Convention refugees, except for the fact that they have not yet left their country. Another example is the issuance of the Temporary Safe Haven Visas by the government of Australia to facilitate the emergency evacuation of East Timorese from the United Nations

---

[33] UNHCR, *Internally Displaced Persons: The Role of the United Nations High Commissioner for Refugees* (Geneva, UNHCR, UN Doc EC/50/SC/INF2, 6 March 2000), pp 8–9.

Assistance Mission in East Timor (UNAMET) compound in Dili during the violence that followed the popular consultation in 2000.

Asylum Seekers

The UNHCR defines an asylum seeker as an individual whose claim for refugee status has yet to be determined by the authorities, but whose claim to asylum entitles him or her to a certain protective status on the basis that he or she could be a refugee. This term is also applied in large-scale influxes of mixed groups where individual refugee status determination is not undertaken because it is impractical. Clearly, asylum seekers form part of the UNHCR's competence ratione personae.[34] One of the main concerns of advocacy groups is that asylum seekers are placed in vulnerable situations while awaiting processing, especially those who have valid refugee claims, since they may not be able to avail themselves of the rights to which they are entitled under the 1951 Convention.[35]

The term 'asylum seekers' has also been particularly useful to cover those who are refugees in the international sense, but find themselves in countries, especially in Asia, which are not parties to the Refugees Convention and who wish to avoid the potentially political term 'refugees'. The UNHCR obviously has competence to look after the protection and assistance needs of these asylum seekers on the basis that they may be recognised as refugees. It must be noted that the General Assembly has employed the category of asylum seeker in general resolutions relating to the UNHCR since 1981. At present the UNHCR is responsible for some 896 000 asylum seekers.

Returnees

The UNHCR defines a returnee as a former refugee, who returns to his or her country of origin in an organised fashion when the circumstances that caused him or her to flee no longer exist. The Executive Committee of the Programme of the United Nations High Commissioner for Refugees (Ex Com) Conclusion 40 recognises the UNHCR's legitimate concerns for

---

[34] Turk, above n 26, p 157.

[35] For example, the Refugees Convention provides the right to employment (Articles 17 and 18), freedom of movement and travel documents (Articles 26 and 28), education (Article 22), housing (Article 21).

the consequences of return. The UNHCR's mandate with regard to voluntary repatriation has been refined and extended from an initial premise that the UNHCR's responsibility ended when returnees crossed the border into their country of origin, to a substantive involvement in securing, protecting and providing assistance to returnees in the country.[36] Obviously, it is clear that the need for international protection does not end after the refugees cross the border and return. There is a need for the international community to monitor these returns to ensure that these are conducted in a dignified manner and that the returnees are safe upon their arrival and able to re-establish their lives. This need was not anticipated and addressed in the refugee definition under the 1951 Refugees Convention. At present, the UNHCR is responsible for some 793 000 returnees. In addition, the UNHCR also is looking after some 369 000 returned IDPs.

Other 'Persons of Concern'

In some countries where its involvement was primarily of a humanitarian and preventive nature, the UNHCR has exercised its 'good offices' function to extend its protection and assistance to local residents, for example, war-affected civilians and besieged populations. This function was extended especially in circumstances where it was neither feasible nor reasonable to treat these persons differently from other categories of concern to the UNHCR.[37]

Moreover, the UNHCR has some responsibility for stateless persons. Under the 1961 Convention on the Reduction of Statelessness,[38] the UNHCR has been referred to as the body to which persons claiming to be stateless may apply for assistance in presenting their claims to the appropriate authorities. Stateless persons are referred to as those whose nationality status cannot be established, or whose nationality is doubtful, undetermined or unknown. Concerning stateless persons, however, the

---

[36]   Turk, above n 26, p 158.

[37]   Id, p 159.

[38]   Convention on the Reduction of Statelessness, adopted on 30 August 1961 by a conference of plenipotentiaries which met in 1959 and reconvened in 1961 in pursuance of General Assembly resolution 896 (IX) of 4 December 1954, entry into force 13 December 1975, in accordance with Article 18.

UNHCR's responsibility is already stipulated in separate instruments, such as the Convention on the Reduction of Statelessness.

Conclusion

Based on the above discussions, it is recognised that the refugee definition under the Convention is being challenged. In sum, these challenges include:

- sophisticated and costly procedures to determine refugee claims based on the definition in Article 1A of the Convention. Thus, some states are now contending that their procedures are becoming inadequate to respond to the number of current arrival of asylum seekers. States are instead offering complementary or temporary forms of protection or applying a restrictive or varied interpretation of the definition;
- complementary forms of protection are providing less rights and guarantees to asylum seekers or refugees in comparison to those stated in the Refugees Convention. The UNHCR views these forms of protection as a complement rather than a substitute to the Convention-based protection regime. The UNHCR is concerned that these forms of protection should be harmonised and standardised with Convention protection;
- the UNHCR is also concerned that there are inconsistent or restrictive uses of the refugee definition in Article 1A of the Convention. This may leave some beneficiaries with legitimate claims as refugees without some form of protection. The UNHCR is concerned that interpretation of the refugee definition should be harmonised among the states;
- the existing regional specific frameworks which address perceived gaps in the Convention definition complement the 1951 Convention. However, the UNHCR is concerned that these instruments may make the existence of the Convention redundant in some parts of the world and may undermine its international applicability. There is also a real, if unintended, possibility that these instruments could be inconsistent with the Convention;
- the definition does not cover other categories of persons to whom the UNHCR's competence has been extended, such as IDPs, asylum

seekers and returnees in contrast to Convention refugees, the persons for whom states have explicitly accepted responsibility under the 1951 Convention. With this discrepancy, there is a need for states to recognise the legitimate concern of the UNHCR for these persons and to share in their responsibilities.

Obviously, there are gaps in the definition and the existing approaches either by the states or the UNHCR to cover these gaps have also resulted in dilemmas. Currently, in addressing these gaps, the UNHCR is undertaking Global Consultations, an initiative, which aims to reaffirm the centrality of the Convention but not to reopen or renegotiate it. Specifically, to work towards the revitalisation of the Convention regime, which would preserve its centrality but would buttress it with more enlightened migration policies and additional protections.[39] Further, the UNHCR is convinced that despite these gaps and challenges, the Convention has to remain the foundation of refugee protection. The UNHCR is concerned that if the Convention is reopened for the purpose of reforming it, the likelihood that it will be replaced by anything approaching its value is remote.[40]

---

[39] Editor's note: see L Curran, 'Global Solutions', chapter 12 in this book.

[40] Ibid; Feller, above n 13, pp 2–3.

10 New Uses of the Refugees Convention: Sexuality and Refugee Status

KRISTEN WALKER*

Introduction

In the past decade administrative decision makers and courts in most western refugee-receiving nations have begun to recognise a new kind of refugee claim based on sexual orientation. This development follows the increasing recognition of international human rights claims by lesbians and gay men in areas such as privacy, non-discrimination and respect for family life.[1] In this chapter I examine the basis for refugee claims by lesbians and gay men under the refugee definition in Article 1A(2) of the Convention Relating to the Status of Refugees (the Refugees Convention). I also consider whether the refugee definition might extend to permit claims for refugee status based on other aspects of sexuality, such as prostitution and sex outside marriage.

I will begin by outlining the judicial and administrative developments that have resulted in the recognition of gay and lesbian claims for refugee status in western refugee receiving countries such as Australia, the United States (US), the United Kingdom, Canada and New Zealand. Under 'The rationale for recognising gay and lesbian refugee claims' I will consider the

---

* Part of this chapter is based on an earlier article on the subject: K Walker, 'Sexuality and Refugee Status in Australia', *International Journal of Refugee Law* 12 (2000) p 175.

[1] See for example, the jurisprudence of the European Convention on Human Rights, discussed in K Walker, 'Moving Gaily Forward? Lesbian, Gay And Transgender Human Rights In Europe', *Melbourne Journal of International Law*, 2 (2001) p 122. The decision of the UN Human Rights Committee in *Toonen v Australia* (Communication 488/1992, UN Doc CCPR/C/50/D/488/1992, 4 April 1992) is also an important recognition of lesbian and gay rights claims: see, for example, K Walker, 'International Human Rights Law and Sexuality: Strategies for Domestic Litigation', *New York City Law Review* 3 (1998) p 115.

underlying basis for the recognition of such claims. Finally, in 'Recognition of refugee claims based on other sexuality issues' I will raise the question of whether the application of the refugee definition to include lesbians and gay men could be extended to include other aspects of sexuality, such as sex outside marriage and prostitution.

The Judicial and Administrative Recognition of Refugee Claims Based on Sexual Orientation

The Refugees Convention defines a refugee in Article 1A(2). According to that article, a person is a refugee when he or she:

[o]wing to a well-founded fear of persecution for reasons of race, religion, nationality, membership of a particular social group or political opinion, is outside the country of his nationality and is unable or, owing to such fear, unwilling to avail himself of the protection of that country ...

Lesbians and gay men may be able to make refugee claims on several grounds under this definition. Some individuals may fear persecution on the basis of race or religion, for example, independently of their sexual preference or behaviour, but my focus here is on how such claims may be made where persecution is feared because of sexual orientation. Into what category might such persecution fall? There are several possibilities: religion,[2] political opinion[3] or membership of a particular social group.

---

[2] Religious persecution may occur where a religious state persecutes a person for sexual practices that violate religious laws or beliefs: *Minister for Immigration and Multicultural Affairs (MIMA) v Darboy* [1998] 931 FCA (6 August 1998) at 7–8.

[3] Persecution on the basis of political opinion may occur either where a person is persecuted for political activities around sexual issues, for example campaigns for law reform, or, more broadly, if the decision-maker accepts that merely being queer is viewed by the state as a challenge to state policies or as a sign of political disloyalty: E Ramanathan, 'Queer Cases: A Comparative Analysis of Global Sexual Orientation-Based Asylum Jurisprudence', *Georgetown Immigration Law Journal* 11 (1996) p 1 at p 6.

There is a Canadian case where a transsexual person succeeded in a refugee claim because her transsexualism would be perceived as being a 'defiant demonstration of political opposition to the current regime' and thus she had a well-founded fear of persecution on the basis of political opinion: see Ramanathan, id, p 29. A similar approach was taken in the UK to a gay Syrian applicant for refugee status in *Gelab v Immigration Officer, Heathrow* (Special Adjudicator at Hatton Cross, HX/75712/94,

Of these, membership of a particular social group has emerged as the most commonly accepted basis for gay and lesbian claims to refugee status, and it is on this ground that I will focus.[4] I will consider the position of the United Nations High Commissioner for Refugees (UNHCR) on the question and then turn to the approach adopted in the jurisdictions referred to above.

UNHCR

The UNHCR, the UN body charged with providing international protection to refugees and supervising the application of the 1951 Convention and 1967 Protocol, has recognised that gay or lesbian identity may form the basis for a claim of refugee status. In 1996, it stated:

> It is the policy of UNHCR that persons facing attack, inhumane treatment, or serious discrimination because of their homosexuality, and whose governments are unable or unwilling to protect them, should be recognised as refugees.[5]

---

23 August 1995), although this was ultimately not the basis for the Special Adjudicator's decision.

[4] This ground has been the subject of various articles: see N Bamforth, 'Protected Social Groups, The Refugees Convention and Judicial Review: The *Vraciu Case*', *Public Law* (1995) p 382; B F Henes, 'The Origin and Consequences of Recognizing Homosexuals as a 'Particular Social Group' for Refugee Purposes', *Temple International and Comparative Law Journal* 8 (1994) p 377; S Goldberg, 'Give Me Liberty or Give Me Death: Political Asylum and the Global Persecution of Lesbians and Gay Men', *Cornell International Law Journal* 26 (1993) p 605; S Grider, 'Sexual Orientation as Grounds for Asylum in the United States', *Harvard International Law Journal* 35 (1994) p 213; D McGhee, 'Persecution and Social Group Status: Homosexual Refugees in the 1990s', *Journal of Refugee Studies* 14 (2001) p 20; B McGoldrick, 'United States Immigration Policy and Sexual Minorities: Is Asylum for Homosexuals A Possibility?', *Georgetown Immigration Law Journal* 8 (1994) p 201; J Millbank, 'A Well-Founded Fear of Persecution or Just a Queer Feeling? Refugee Status and Sexual Orientation in Australia', *Alternative Law Journal* 20 (1995) p 261; J S Park, 'Pink Asylum: Political Asylum Eligibility of Gay Men and Lesbians Under US Immigration Policy', *UCLA Law Review* 42 (1995) p 1115; E Vagelos, 'The Social Group that Dare Not Speak Its Name: Should Homosexuals Constitute a Particular Social Group for the Purposes of Obtaining Refugee Status? Comment on *Re Inaudi*', *Fordham International Law Journal* 17 (1993) p 229; Ramanathan, above n 3. On the concept of particular social group generally, see M E Fullerton, 'A Comparative Look at Refugee Status Based on Persecution Due to Membership in a Particular Social Group', *Cornell International Law Journal* 26 (1993) p 505.

[5] UNHCR, *Protecting Refugees: Questions and Answers* (Geneva, UNHCR, 1996), p 12.

This provides a starting point for the consideration of the issue, but the UNHCR's pronouncements are not binding on domestic courts, although under Australian law they may be of assistance in deciding whether a person is a refugee[6] and in interpreting the terms of the Refugees Convention and Protocol.[7] In any event, it is particularly important to examine exactly how refugee receiving countries have treated lesbian and gay claimants for refugee status.

Australia[8]

Lesbians and gay men have been recognised as refugees by the Refugee Review Tribunal (RRT) on the basis that lesbians and gay men may form a 'particular social group' in the applicant's country of origin. In doing so, the RRT has, over the years, relied upon two Australian cases that dealt generally with the concept of 'membership of a particular social group': *Morato v Minister for Immigration, Local Government and Ethnic Affairs*[9] (in the Federal Court) and *Applicant A v Minister for Immigration and Ethnic Affairs*[10] (in the High Court). In *Morato*, Lockhart J held that for a person to be a member of a particular social group, it is necessary that the person 'belongs to or is identified with a recognisable or cognisable group within society that shares some experience in common'.[11] This has been applied by the RRT to include 'homosexuals' as a particular social group within the meaning of the Refugees Convention.[12]

The RRT's approach was implicitly affirmed by the High Court in *Applicant A* in several dicta comments. There, McHugh J stated that:

---

[6]   *Chan v Minister for Immigration and Ethnic Affairs* (1989) 169 CLR 379 at 392.

[7]   *Applicant A v Minister for Immigration and Ethnic Affairs* (1997) 190 CLR 225 at 302.

[8]   In Australia, the definition of refugee in Article 1A(2) is incorporated into Australian law by section 36(2) of the Migration Act 1958 (Cth), which provides that a criterion for a protection visa is that the person applying for the visa is a person to whom the Minister consider Australia owes protection obligations under the Refugees Convention.

[9]   (1992) 39 FCR 401.

[10]   (1997) 190 CLR 225.

[11]   (1992) 39 FCR 401 at 416.

[12]   See, for example, RRT N93/00846 (8 March 1994); RRT N93/02240 (21 February 1994).

[I]f the homosexual members of a particular society are perceived in that society to have characteristics or attributes that unite them as a group and distinguish them from society as a whole, they will qualify for refugee status.[13]

Kirby J observed that:

the following categories have been upheld as particular social groups, the membership of which gave rise to a well-founded fear of persecution: ... homosexual and bisexual men and women in countries where their sexual conduct, even with adults and in private, is illegal.[14]

There have since been many cases where the Federal Court has recognised – both implicitly and explicitly – that gay men and lesbians may constitute a particular social group for the purposes of the Refugees Convention.[15]

Notably, the Australian courts have on some occasions referred to lesbians and gay men as if they form a universal social group, while on other occasions judges have indicated that it must be clear that gay men and lesbians constitute a distinct social group within the society they are seeking to leave. The latter approach is technically correct under refugee law and will not generally be difficult to prove in the case of lesbians and gay men. It may be argued, however, that given the impact of globalisation on lesbian and gay identity there is currently no country in which lesbians and gay men are not perceived as a separate group within society.[16]

---

[13] 190 CLR 225 at 265.

[14] Id, p 303–4.

[15] *MIMA v Guo Ping Gui* [1999] FCA 1496 (29 October 1999) (explicit); *MMM v MIMA* [1998] 90 FCR 324 (implicit); *Bhattachan v MIMA* [1999] FCA 547 (27 April 1999) (implicit); *F v MIMA* [1999] FCA 947 (9 July 1999) (explicit); *Hossain v MIMA* [1999] 59 ALD 453 (implicit).

[16] See K Walker, 'Capitalism, Gay Identity and International Law', *Australasian Gay and Lesbian Law Journal* **9** (2000) p 58; D Altman, 'On Global Queering', *Australian Humanities Review* (July 1996), http://www.lib.latrobe.edu.au/AHR/archive/Issue-July-1996/altman.html, and the responses thereto.

The United States[17]

In a series of decisions, US Immigration Judges and the Board of Immigration Appeals (BIA) have accepted that 'homosexuals' constitute a particular social group for the purposes of US asylum law.[18] The first such case was *Matter of Toboso-Alfonso*[19] concerning a gay Cuban man. There, the BIA stated that:

> The [Immigration and Naturalization] Service argues that 'socially deviated behavior, ie homosexual activity is not a basis for finding a social group within the contemplation of the Act' and that such a conclusion: 'would be tantamount to awarding discretionary relief to those involved in behavior that is not only socially deviant in nature, but in violation of the laws or regulations of the country as well.' The applicant's testimony and evidence, however, do not reflect that it was specific activities that resulted in the governmental actions against him in Cuba, it was his having the status of being a homosexual.[20]

The BIA concluded that:

> [T]he Service did not challenge the immigration judge's finding that homosexuality is an 'immutable' characteristic. Nor is there any evidence or argument that, once registered by the Cuban government as a homosexual, that that characterization is subject to change. This being the case, we do not find the Service's challenge to the immigration judge's finding that this applicant was a member of a particular social group in Cuba adequately supported by the arguments set forth on appeal.[21]

In 1994 the *Toboso-Alfonso* decision was elevated to the status of precedent by Attorney-General Janet Reno.[22] There have since been several decisions in the US where gay men have been recognised as a 'particular

---

[17] The US is a party to the 1967 Protocol but not the Refugees Convention. The Protocol is implemented in domestic law by the Refugee Act (Pub L No 96-212, 94 Stat 102 (1980)).

[18] See Ramanathan, above n 3.

[19] Board of Immigration Appeals, Case A23-220-644, 12 March 1990.

[20] *Matter of Toboso-Alfonso*, 20 I & N Dec 819, 822 (1990).

[21] Id, pp 822–3.

[22] Memorandum from US Attorney-General J Reno to M M Dunne, Acting Chair, Board of Immigration Appeals, 16 June 1994.

social group',[23] culminating in a recent decision of the 9th Circuit Court of Appeals that recognised 'gay men with female sexual identities' in Mexico as a particular social group.[24]

Canada[25]

In Canada several quasi-judicial decisions have recognised that homosexuals may form a particular social group[26] and this has been confirmed in obiter dicta by the Supreme Court of Canada. In *Ward v Attorney-General (Canada)*, the court stated:

> The meaning assigned to particular social group in the [Immigration] Act should take into account the general underlying themes of the defence of human rights and anti-discrimination that form the basis for the international refugee protection initiative. [There are] three possible categories:
>
> 1. groups defined by an innate or unchangeable characteristic;
>
> 2. groups whose members voluntarily associate for reasons so fundamental to their human dignity that they should not be forced to forsake the association; and
>
> 3. groups associated by a former voluntary status, unalterable due to its historic permanence.
>
> *The first category would embrace individuals fearing persecution on such bases as gender, linguistic background and sexual orientation ...*[27]

This has subsequently been applied in Canada by the Federal Court[28] and by the Immigration and Refugee Board.[29]

---

23 See, *Matter of Tenorio* (Immigration Judge, San Francisco, Case A72-093-558, 26 July 1993), extracted in K Musalo, J Moore and R Boswell, *Refugee Law and Policy: Cases and Materials* (Durham, North Carolina, Carolina Academic Press, 1997), p 713.

24 *Hernandez-Montiel v INS* 225 F.3d 1084 (2000). The specific framing of the particular social group in that case was a result of evidence that in Latin America, including Mexico, men who engage in male to male sex are divided into masculine and feminine sub-groups. It might have been possible for Hernandez-Montiel to have brought his claim on the basis of what we in the west might call (trans)gender identity, but the case was not argued in that way.

25 The refugee definition in article 1A(2) of the Refugees Convention is incorporated into Canadian law by section 2(1) of the Immigration Act 1976 (Can).

26 See, *In Re Inaudi* (Immigration and Refugee Board Case T91-04459, 9 April 1992).

27 [1993] 2 SCR 689 at 739 (emphasis added).

New Zealand [30]

Ward has also been applied by the Refugee Status Appeal Authority (RSAA) in New Zealand. In *Re GJ*,[31] the RSAA canvassed jurisprudence from the US, the UK, Canada, the Netherlands, Denmark, Germany and Australia. The RSAA concluded that:

> Homosexuals in Iran are a cognisable social group united by a shared internal characteristic namely, their sexual orientation. We also find that homosexuality is either an innate or unchangeable characteristic, or a characteristic so fundamental to identity or human dignity that it ought not be required to be changed.[32]

The United Kingdom[33]

The United Kingdom has recently, after some years of conflicting and unsatisfactory decisions,[34] brought its approach to refugee claims on the

---

28 See, *Rojas v Minister of Citizenship & Immigration* (1999) Fed Ct Trial LEXIS 40; *Gomez v Minister of Citizenship & Immigration* (1998) Fed Ct Trial LEXIS 677; *Muzychka v Minister of Citizenship & Immigration* (1997) Fed Ct Trial LEXIS 1338.

29 See, Immigration and Refugee Board Case M92-08129, 24 February 1994; Immigration and Refugee Board Case T94-06899, 23 January 1995.

30 The refugee definition in Article 1A(2) of the Refugees Convention is incorporated into New Zealand law by section 35 of the Immigration Act 1987 (NZ).

31 *Re GJ* (NZ Refugee Status Appeals Authority, Refugee Appeal 1312/93, 30 August 1995).

32 Id, p 58.

33 The refugee definition in Article 1A(2) of the Refugees Convention is incorporated into English law by section 8(2) of the Asylum and Immigration Appeals Act 1993.

34 Until the House of Lords' decision in *Islam v Secretary of State for the Home Department* [1999] 2 All ER 545 there had been only one judicial decision that had dealt with the issue of sexual orientation and refugee status: *R v Secretary of State for the Home Department; Ex parte Binbasi* [1989] Imm AR 595 (QB Div). There, the Home Secretary argued that homosexuals did not constitute a particular social group. The court found it unnecessary to decide the question, as it concluded that there was no persecution of 'homosexuals who are not active' and thus Mr Binbasi could avoid persecution by 'self-restraint'.
At the administrative level, the UK cases were mixed, although they tended against accepting that homosexuals constitute a particular social group: *Golchin v Secretary of State for the Home Department* (IAT, Appeal TH/17184/89, Unreported, 17 January 1991); *Jacques v Secretary of State for the Home Department* (IAT, Appeal

basis of sexual orientation into line with the approach of the US, Canada New Zealand and Australia. In *Islam v Secretary of State for the Home Department*,[35] a case concerning gender and refugee status, three Law Lords accepted that homosexuals constitute a particular social group for the purposes of refugee law. Lord Steyn stated:

> Following the New Zealand judgment in *Re GJ* [1998] 1 NLR 387 I regard it as established that depending on the evidence homosexuals may in some countries qualify as members of a particular social group.[36]

Lord Hoffman quoted the passage from *Ward*, above, with approval,[37] and Lord Millett also accepted that homosexuals may constitute a particular social group.[38] These judicial pronouncements on the question are obiter, but are nonetheless significant.

Other States

Although comprehensive survey of state practice on the issue is beyond the scope of this chapter, it is worth noting that many European nations have also recognised gay and lesbian claims of refugee status.[39]

HX/70684/94, Unreported, 22 November 1994. Compare *Vraciu v Secretary of State for the Home Department* (IAT Appeal HX/70517/94(11559), Unreported, 21 November 1994); *Gelab v Secretary of State for the Home Department* (Special Adjudicator at Hatton Cross, HX/75712/94, 23 August 1995). For a more detailed analysis of the UK cases, see McGhee, above n 4.

[35]   [1999] 2 All ER 545. See G S Goodwin-Gill, 'Judicial Reasoning and 'Social Group' After *Islam* and *Shah*', *International Journal of Refugee Law* 11 (1999) p 537; M Vidal, '"Membership of a Particular Social Group" and the Effect of *Islam* and *Shah*', *International Journal of Refugee Law* 11 (1999) p 528.

[36]   Id, p 557.

[37]   Id, p 563.

[38]   Id, p 574.

[39]   ILGA-Europe, *Equality for Lesbians and Gay Men: A Relevant Issue in the Civil and Social Dialogue* (Brussels, ILGA-Europe, 1998), pp 23, 32–3 (Austria), p 36 (Belgium), p 43 (Finland), p 57 (Greece), p 63 (Ireland), p 75 (The Netherlands), p 84 (Sweden).

Conclusion

There is now general consensus in the common law world – and in most western refugee-receiving countries – that gay men and lesbians can constitute a particular social group within the meaning of the Refugees Convention and Protocol. However, the question then arises whether this recognition might extend to persons persecuted because of other aspects of sexuality, such as their occupation as a sex worker or their engagement in sex outside marriage. This clearly does not follow automatically from the recognition of gay and lesbian refugee claims. Rather, it is necessary to examine the basis for those claims in the Refugees Convention and consider whether the rationale for recognising gay and lesbian claims also extends to the recognition of claims based on other aspects of sexuality.

Before turning to this task, it should be noted that the recognition of gay men and lesbians as legitimate subjects of refugee law is not the end of the practical and legal problems that are confronted by refugee claimants. In particular, the way in which decision makers and courts have approached the question of persecution has been crucial in denying many claims for refugee status based on sexuality. An analysis of those problems is beyond the scope of this chapter, but has been undertaken elsewhere.[40]

The Rationale for Recognising Gay and Lesbian Refugee Claims

It is clear from the survey of the jurisprudence that the recognition of lesbian and gay refugee claims is a new development in refugee law. At the time the Refugees Convention was drafted, same-sex sexual activity was illegal in 'many, perhaps most, countries'.[41] It is thus safe to say that the drafters of and signatories to the Refugees Convention would not have contemplated refugee claims on the basis of sexual orientation. This is so notwithstanding that refugee law was in large part influenced by the atrocities of the Nazi regime in Germany before and during World War II when lesbians and gay men had been incarcerated in concentration camps by the Nazi regime. In the 1940s and 1950s, lesbians and gay men were simply sexual deviants – not individuals deserving of equal respect and

---

[40]   See K Walker, 'Sexuality and Refugee Status in Australia', *International Journal of Refugee Law* **12** (2000) p 175.

[41]   *Applicant A*, above n 10, p 294 (Kirby J).

basic human rights. Indeed, many western countries at that time still considered lesbians and gay men to be mentally ill and subjected them to involuntary detention, electric shocks to the genitals, nausea inducing drugs and sometimes lobotomies.[42] In the US 'sexual deviation' was a lawful basis for refusing an alien entry to the country until 1990.[43]

However, as Kirby J said in *Applicant A:*

> nowadays, a different content and application of the phrase ['particular social group'] affords the protection of the Convention deriving from a larger understanding of the 'persecution' and the identity of the 'particular social group' in question.[44]

What, then, is the basis for this new approach to membership in a particular social group that recognises lesbians and gay men as constituting a particular social group?

This question turns, in part, on the way in which one approaches the meaning of 'membership of a particular social group', for it is this ground

---

[42] See W Dynes and S Donaldson, 'Introduction' in W Dynes and S Donaldson (eds), *Studies in Homosexuality Vol XI: Homosexuality and Psychology, Psychiatry and Counselling* (New York, Garland Publishing, 1992) vii; M Stephen, 'Heterosexual Bias in Psychological Research on Lesbianism and Male Homosexuality', *American Psychologist* **32** (1977) p 629, reprinted in Dynes and Donaldson, ibid.

[43] From 1952 to 1965, lesbians and gay men were excluded from entry into the US on the basis that they were 'afflicted with psychopathic personality' – one part of the 'medical exclusion' clause (s 212) of the Immigration Act 1917. In 1965 the Act was amended to include 'sexual deviation' as a basis for exclusion, in response to a federal court holding that the term 'psychopathic personality' was too vague to be constitutionally applied to homosexuals generally: *Fleuti v Rosenberg* 302 F 2d 652, 658. Shortly afterwards, the Supreme Court, in *Boutilier v Immigration & Naturalization Service* 387 US 118 (1967), affirmed the application of the medical exclusion provisions to homosexuals.

Eventually, in 1990, the medical exclusion provisions were substantially rewritten, omitting 'sexual deviation' and designating mental health as a ground for exclusion only when the alien posed some threat to the life, health or property of others. See generally, R Foss, 'The Demise of the Homosexual Exclusion: New Possibilities for Gay and Lesbian Immigration', *Harvard Civil Rights–Civil Liberties Law Rev* **29** (1994) p 439; J L Carro, 'From Constitutional Psychopathic Inferiority to AIDS: What is in the Future for Homosexual Aliens?', *Yale Law and Policy Review* **7** (1989) p 201; W Eskridge, 'Challenging the Apartheid of the Closet: Establishing Conditions for Lesbian and Gay Intimacy, Nomos and Citizenship, 1961–1981', *Hofstra Law Review* **25** (1997) p 817; S Legomsky, *Immigration and Refugee Law and Policy* (Foundation Press, 2nd ed, 1997), pp 138–9.

[44] *Applicant A*, above n 10, pp 382–3.

of persecution that provides the textual basis for the recognition of gay and lesbian claims. It is not my intention in this chapter to examine extensively the various possible approaches to the meaning of that phrase; however, it is useful to outline briefly three contrasting possible approaches to that phrase to assist with our understanding of why lesbians and gay men are now recognised as refugees. Furthermore, it should be more generally noted that, in so far as new uses of the Refugees Convention are possible, 'membership of a particular social group' is a particularly useful vehicle for new claims, as can be observed in relation to claims by women[45] and by 'black children' in China.[46]

Membership of a Particular Social Group

The phrase 'membership of a particular social group' has proved particularly difficult to define both in practice and in academic writing. The history of the Refugees Convention, while useful in understanding much of the Convention, is remarkably opaque on the question of what might constitute a particular social group. The phrase was introduced as an amendment to the initial draft by the Swedish delegate, who stated only that '[s]uch cases existed, and it would be as well to mention them'.[47]

Other than this oblique comment, there was no debate or discussion of the phrase. It was accepted unanimously and the delegates seemed more concerned with the temporal and geographical limitations in the refugee definition than they did with the categories of persecution.[48] We may thus disregard the drafting history of the phrase 'membership of a particular social group' in our inquiry into the interpretation of that phrase.

Academic and judicial approaches to the meaning of 'particular social group' have varied from narrow to moderate to broad. Some have argued that no definition is possible, and that the meaning of 'particular social group' must simply be determined on a case-by-case basis. At issue is how

---

[45]   See *Islam*, above n 34.

[46]   See *Chen Shi Hai v MIMA* (2000) 201 CLR 293. A 'black child' is a child born to parents in China who already had one or more children, in violation of the 'one child policy'.

[47]   Comments of Mr Petren (Sweden), UN Doc A/CONF.2/SR.19, p 14.

[48]   Comments of Mr Robinson (Israel), UN Doc A/Conf.2/SR.22, p 6. See also M E Fullerton, 'A Comparative Look at Refugee Status Based on Persecution Due to Membership in a Particular Social Group', *Cornell International Law Journal* **26** (1993) p 505 at p 510.

to identify the group – whether the group must be based on an immutable or unchangeable characteristic or a changeable characteristic that one should not be required to change; whether a particular social group must involve voluntary association by its members; or whether a particular social group should be identified by its member's desire to exercise some fundamental human right or freedom. Also at issue is the relevance of internal identification as a group (by the group's members) and of external identification (by society or the government or, more specifically, the persecutors). Different approaches have been adopted by different courts and commentators and I will not canvass all of them here. Rather, I will set out several of the most prominent approaches before drawing my own conclusion as to the preferred approach.

At the narrow end of the spectrum is the approach adopted by the US Ninth Circuit in *Sanchez-Trujillo*: that a social group is a group primarily defined by voluntary association. The court stated:

> Of central concern is the existence of a voluntary associational relationship among the purported members, which imparts some common characteristic that is fundamental to their identity as a member of that discrete social group.

No other kind of social group is recognised under this approach – that is, voluntary association is a necessary feature of a particular social group. This approach emphasises internal self-identification as well as associational activity. It is narrow because many groups in society are defined externally – that is, by society or by other individuals, rather than by the members of the group. Further, even groups defined internally – that is, by the individuals themselves – may not engage in an associational relationship. The *Sanchez-Trujillo* approach has not found favour with academic commentators[49] or non-US courts[50] and has not been generally accepted in the US by the BIA or other circuits.[51] Most recently, is has been qualified by the 9th Circuit itself.[52] It is safe, therefore, to reject it with little discussion.

---

[49] See, for example, Fullerton, above n 4, p 555-8; T D Parish, 'Membership in a Particular Social Group Under the Refugee Act of 1980: Social Identity and the Legal Concept of the Refugee', *Columbia Law Review* 92 (1992) p 923 at pp 942–3.

[50] See, for example, Australian High Court in *Applicant A*, above n 10, p 241 (Dawson J), 306 (Kirby J); Canadian Supreme Court in *Ward*, above n 27.

[51] See Parish, above n 49, p 944.

[52] *Hernandez-Montiel*, above n 24.

At the broad end of the spectrum is Arthur Helton's approach: that 'membership of a particular social group' was included as a 'catch-all which could include all the bases for and types of persecution which an imaginative despot might conjure up.'[53]

Helton's approach would recognise as a particular social group all of the above-mentioned types of groups, whether defined in statistical, societal or associational terms. As Hathaway observes, such an approach is 'seductive' from a humanitarian perspective,[54] as it will maximise the protection offered to those who are persecuted. However, it is so broad as to essentially remove the need to demonstrate a nexus between the fear of persecution and a specific ground of persecution. In that sense it seems to go well beyond the intentions of the drafters, which were to ensure that only specific categories of persecuted persons were recognised as refugees to whom states parties would owe obligations.[55]

More moderate approaches are offered by Guy Goodwin-Gill and James Hathaway. Goodwin-Gill considers a fully comprehensive definition impossible, but suggests the central inquiry is whether the group has 'shared interests, values or background' (echoing the language of the UNHCR Handbook).[56] He suggests that:

> Attention should be given to the presence of linking and uniting factors such as ethnic, cultural, and linguistic origin; education; family background; economic activity; shared values; outlook and aspirations. Also highly relevant are the attitude to the putative social group of other groups in the same society and, in particular, the treatment accorded to it by State authorities ... The notion of social group thus possesses an element of open-endedness potentially capable of expansion in favour of a variety of different classes susceptible to persecution.[57]

Although Goodwin-Gill acknowledges the potential breadth of his approach, it does not, I suggest, make the need for a nexus between

---

[53] A Helton, 'Persecution on Account of Membership in a Social Group as a Basis for Refugee Status' *Columbia Human Rights Law Review* **15** (1983) p 39, at pp 41–2.

[54] J Hathaway, *The Law of Refugee Status* (Toronto, Butterworths, 1991), p 159.

[55] Ibid.

[56] UNHCR, *Handbook on Procedures and Criteria for the Determination of Refugee Status* (Geneva, UNHCR, 2nd ed, 1992).

[57] G S Goodwin-Gill, *The Refugee in International Law* (Oxford, Clarendon Press, 2nd ed, 1996), p 48.

persecution and a Convention ground redundant in the way that Helton's approach does. I thus characterise Goodwin-Gill's approach as a moderate one, though it may well be somewhat broader than Hathaway's. It certainly offers less certainty as to the nature of the groups that might fall within the term 'particular social group' and, for that reason, is not as attractive as Hathaway's approach, which I outline below. However, Goodwin-Gill's list of factors may be of assistance in applying the Hathaway approach.

The final approach I will outline is that adopted by Hathaway and by the Canadian Supreme Court in *Ward*. Hathaway argues that the approach to membership in a particular social group should be based on the maxim ejusdem generis – that is, the phrase 'membership of a particular social group' should be interpreted consistently with the other grounds of persecution mentioned in Article 1A(2). According to Hathaway, this approach would recognise three different categories of social group:

> (1) groups defined by an innate, unalterable characteristic; (2) groups defined by their past temporary or voluntary status, since their history or experience is not within their current power to change; and (3) existing groups defined by volition, so long as the purpose of the association is so fundamental to their human dignity that they ought not to be required to abandon it. Excluded, therefore, are groups defined by a characteristic which is changeable or from which disassociation is possible, so long as neither option requires renunciation of basic human rights.[58]

Part (1) of this test is thus analogous to race, part (2) to nationality (perhaps) and part (3) to religion and political opinion. Indeed, it is significant that two of the four other Convention grounds are not immutable characteristics but rather aspects of one's life that an individual ought not be required to change. Indeed, it is difficult, if not impossible, to *force* a person to change their religion, beliefs or political opinions, though they may *choose* to make such a change themselves at any time. In fact, such voluntary changes are a regular part of human life.

Hathaway's approach is based on the decision of the US Board of Immigration Appeals in *Matter of Acosta*, where the court said:

> Whatever the common characteristic that defines the group, it must be one that members of the group cannot change, or should not be required to change because it is fundamental to their individual identities or conscience. Only

---

[58] Hathaway, above n 54, p 161.

when this is the case does the mere fact of group membership become something comparable to the other four grounds of persecution.[59]

Hathaway's three categories of social groups were essentially adopted by the Canadian Supreme Court in *Ward*, discussed above under 'The rationale for recognising gay and lesbian refugee claims'. Subsequently, however, the author of the *Ward* judgment, La Forest J, clarified the use of the term 'association' in the third category:

> In order to avoid any confusion on this point let me state incontrovertibly that a refugee alleging membership in a particular social group does not have to be in voluntary association with other persons similar to him- or herself. Such a claimant is in no manner required to associate, ally, or consort voluntarily with kindred persons.[60]

This clarification is particularly important for claims based on sexuality, as I will discuss below.

It is my argument that Hathaway's approach, modified as indicated by La Forest J, provides a useful tripartite classification of the kinds of social groups that are appropriately recognised by the Refugees Convention. It is not so broad as to remove all limitations from Article 1A(2), which would clearly frustrate the intentions of the drafters and signatories. Nor is it so narrow as to deprive large numbers of deserving claimants of refugee status. In particular, it is important that the definition of 'particular social group' offered by Hathaway is closely linked to human rights law. That is, groups based on a changeable or voluntary characteristic are protected only where to require a person to change their identity or renounce their group membership would be a violation of their basic human rights. This is congruent with the clear commitment of the drafters and signatories to the Refugees Convention to the protection of individuals from serious violations of human rights.[61] It also allows the meaning of particular social group to develop as human rights law develops. Refugee law is, after all, one mechanism for the protection of human rights – albeit not the only or the best mechanism.

---

[59] 801 F 2d 1571.

[60] *Chan v Canada* [1995] 3 SCR 593, at 646. It should be noted that La Forest was in dissent in *Chan* – nonetheless, his clarification of his previous judgment is, I argue persuasive – and in any event, I rely on *Ward* and *Chan* not as binding precedent but as illustrations of my preferred approach to the meaning of 'particular social group'.

[61] See, for example, the Preamble to the Refugees Convention, para 1.

Lesbians and Gay Men as Particular Social Groups

The Australian jurisprudence offers relatively little express guidance on the reason for recognising lesbians and gay men as particular social groups. In the Canadian, New Zealand and US cases, the basis for this recognition is either that sexual orientation is an 'immutable characteristic' or that it is so fundamental to human dignity that it should not be required to be changed. Both these approaches draw on the moderate approach to the meaning of 'membership of a particular social group' discussed above. Using immutability as the foundation for recognition places homosexuality in Hathaway's category (1) – analogous to race; whereas using a 'fundamental to human dignity' approach places homosexuality in Hathaway's category (3) – analogous to religion or political opinion. It is my argument that the latter approach is preferable.

The Australian case law has not expressly adopted the terminology of immutability, but it is possible to discern in the reasoning of the courts and the RRT a belief that sexual orientation is something immutable. In particular, this phenomenon can be observed in cases where there is some doubt as to whether the refugee claimant is 'really' gay. This is essentially a question of whether the applicant is in fact a member of the particular social group 'homosexuals' and arises as a result of the immigration authorities' concern that false claims may be made in order to gain entry into Australia. As one RRT member put it, 'the claim of being homosexual is in many ways an easy one to make, and a difficult one to dispute'.[62] Some cases have turned solely on the applicant's credibility.[63] To date, the RRT has rejected the use of medical evidence (such as psychiatric assessment, 'penile plesythmography'[64] or an anal

---

[62] RRT N97/16114 (2 November 1998).

[63] Ibid.

[64] This involves monitoring the individual's penis during his viewing of homoerotic images to ascertain whether he is physically aroused by such images. There is considerable doubt as to the reliability of such tests: R McAnulty and H Adams, 'Voluntary Control of Penile Tumescence: Effects on Incentive and Signal Detection Task', *The Journal of Sex Research* **28** (1991) p 557; W Simon and P Schouten, 'Plesythmography in the Assessment and Treatment of Sexual Deviance: An Overview', *Archives of Sexual Behavior* **20** (1991) p 75, cited in RRT N97/16114 (2 November 1998).

examination[65]) in assessing the applicant's sexuality,[66] a positive feature of the Australian approach that can be contrasted with some other jurisdictions.[67]

In other cases, however, the RRT or court has accepted the applicant's credibility as to his sexual experiences with men, but has doubted whether, notwithstanding his sexual activities, he is really gay. For example, in case V97/06483 the applicant had had several relationships with men and one relationship with a woman. This latter relationship was described as 'unsatisfactory'. During the hearing it was put to the applicant that:

> It was quite common for sexual activity to occur between young people of the same sex when there were very strong taboos against such activity between those of opposite sexes as in Bangladesh so it did not necessarily mean the person was destined to be homosexual.[68]

The RRT went on to comment that, because of his sexual relationship with a woman, it was:

> unable to rule out the possibility that he is able to function heterosexually also, that is there is some evidence that the Applicant has a capacity for bi-sexuality.[69]

---

[65] This form of medical examination is based on the incorrect notion that all gay men engage in receptive anal sex and that no heterosexual men do so.

[66] RRT N97/16114 (2 November 1998), pp 10, 11, 14–15.

[67] In one UK case, a Home Office lawyer requested that an applicant undergo an anal examination: N La Violette, 'Sexual Orientation and the Refugee Determination Process: Questioning a Claimant About Their Membership in the Particular Social Group' in Lambda Legal Defense and Education Fund, *Asylum Based on Sexual Orientation: A Resource Guide* (New York, Lambda Legal Defense and Education Fund, 1998), p 13. It is unclear whether the test was in fact performed. In Germany, refugee claimants have been required to undergo psychological examinations to prove that their sexual orientation is irreversible: id, pp 13–14. This may be contrasted with the approach in Canada, where the Canadian Immigration and Refugee Board has received briefings on non-medical methods of assessing the veracity of a refugee's claim to be gay or lesbian: ibid. These focus on questioning a claimant about his or her personal experiences, contacts in the gay and lesbian community and experience and knowledge of discrimination and persecution.

[68] RRT V97/06483 (5 January 1998), p 6.

[69] Id, p 7.

This may be contrasted with the RRT's approach in N98/23086, where the RRT saw lack of cross-sex sexual experience as casting doubt on the applicant's sexual preference:

> I accept that the Applicant engaged in sexual activities with a group of his male school friends. However, I note that the activities he described were activities which are relatively common amongst young people involved in sexual experimentation. Further, the Applicant has had no contact whatsoever with young women his own age. His only sexual experience with a woman involved sexual intercourse with a prostitute. This was in fact his very first sexual experience. In the circumstances, I have some difficulty accepting that the Applicant has a settled homosexual orientation. However, for present purposes I accept the Applicant's claim that he is homosexual.[70]

This reasoning was described on review by Burchett J as a 'readily understandable doubt' as to the applicant's homosexuality.[71] Part of the reason for the RRT's and the court's approach here was, no doubt, the fact that the applicant was in his 'late teens': there is a general reluctance, both culturally and judicially, to accept that young people's sexuality is fixed in their teens where that sexuality deviates from the heterosexual norm.[72]

One of the problems with the immutability approach to the question of sexual identity is that it assumes individuals have one sexual identity that is fixed for life.[73] It is clear, however, from the personal histories of lesbians and gay men that many of us have had happy and fulfilling cross-sex sexual relationships both before identifying as lesbian or gay and afterwards. In this sense, sexual orientation is mutable – yet that ought not preclude its

---

[70] RRT N98/23086 (8 July 1998), p 9.

[71] *F v MIMA* [1999] FCA 947 (9 July 1999), para 11.

[72] There is, however, no such reluctance to accept a heterosexual identity for teenagers, as is evidenced by the ability of courts to permit minors to marry: Marriage Act 1961 (Cth), section 13.

[73] There is considerable debate about the aetiology of sexual preference in the sense of the sex of a person's sexual object choice, both within and outside the gay and lesbian community. Some gay men and lesbians conceive of their sexual preference as a choice, while others see it as something innate that they were born with. Notably, even those who take a social constructionist approach to sexuality acknowledge that this approach does not imply that sexual preference can be easily altered: C Vance, 'Pleasure and Danger: Towards a Politics of Sexuality' in Vance (ed), *Pleasure and Danger: Exploring Female Sexuality* (Boston, Routledge and Kegan Paul, 1982) 16; K Walker, 'The Participation of the Law in the Construction of (Homo)Sexuality', *Law in Context* 12 (1994) p 52, pp 56, 70.

recognition as forming a particular social group. A preferable approach would be to view sexual identity as something fluid, albeit for many of us something difficult or personally traumatising to change.

What should be important in the refugee context is not whether someone 'really is' gay or could 'function heterosexually', but whether they are persecuted for their adoption of a gay or lesbian identity or sexual behaviour – regardless of whether this identity or behaviour is 'fixed'. In terms of the social group analysis, it should not matter if one may move in or out of the social group. This is consistent with the moderate approach to the definition of a particular social group, in which there were three possible ways in which a particular social group might be identified – the third being groups that are defined by voluntary activity so long as group membership is 'so fundamental to their human dignity that they ought not to be required to abandon it'.[74] Again, the analogy here is with religion – the fact that a person has changed their religion does not mean that they are not eligible for refugee status,[75] though decision makers will, no doubt, be concerned that a claim to religions conversion is not simply a ploy to gain preferential immigration treatment.[76] We recognise that religion, though it may be mutable, is something so fundamental that a person should not be required to change their religion in order to avoid persecution.

Thus the characterisation of sexuality as something fundamental to human dignity that one should not be required to change, rather than as something immutable, is appropriate in its recognition of the realities of gay and lesbian lives and by analogy to the ground of religion. This approach brings gay and lesbian claims firmly within the parameters of a particular social group. Such an approach does not *preclude* a person from changing their sexual preference; it means that people should not be *required* to do so, and should be protected from persecution if such persecution occurs because of their sexuality.

The precise basis for the recognition of lesbian and gay refugee claims is important because it will impact on the way in which sexual behaviour is considered in the context of a refugee claim. Very often, a lesbian or a gay man will fear persecution because she or he has engaged in particular forms of sexual behaviour, rather than simply for her or his identity as lesbian or

---

[74] Hathaway, above n 54.

[75] See, for example, *Re Woudneh* (Federal Court of Australia, Gray J, Unreported, 16 September 1988); Hathaway, above n 54, pp 146–7.

[76] See, for example, *Khan v MIMA* [1997] 717 FCA (4 August 1997).

gay (indeed, many persons who engage in same-sex sexual behaviour do not identify as lesbian or gay). Where the basis for a refugee claim is the individual's immutable status or identity as gay or lesbian, decision makers may (and do) conclude that persecution for particular behaviour is not persecution for a convention ground (although this is not a logically necessary conclusion). However, the recognition that sexual activity is a fundamental part of human life and, in so far as the choice of a sexual partner of a particular sex is concerned, not something a person should be required to change, suggests a greater acceptance of sexual diversity and of sexual *behaviour*. It allows us to recognise the possibility that sexual behaviour is mutable, and that individuals should not be required to alter their choice about the sex of their sexual partner(s). This can be particularly important in cases where a claimant has engaged in both heterosexual and homosexual sexual behaviour, but fears persecution for the latter.

Again, the analogy with religion is useful. A person who is persecuted for her religion is very often singled out because she practices her religion – that is, she is persecuted for what she does as well as who she is. Expression is an important, if not fundamental, aspect of religion and we do not try to separate the expression of religion from an individual's inner faith – if a person is denied the opportunity to worship without fear of persecution, this amounts to persecution for a convention reason.[77] Similarly, I argue that we cannot and should not try to separate the expression of a person's sexual orientation from their identity as gay or lesbian. This 'act/identity' split fails to recognise the centrality of sexual expression and activity to gay and lesbian identity.

If it is accepted that sexual orientation is mutable, and thus falls into Hathaway's category (3), then the question is whether to force a person to change their sexual identity or behaviour would be contrary to their basic human rights. I argue that it would be, on the basis of both the right to privacy and the right to equality.

Under the right to privacy in international human rights law it is now clear that individuals have a right to engage in private consensual same-sex sexual behaviour.[78] I thus argue that, in so far as an individual engages or wishes to engage in private consensual sexual behaviour, they are

---

[77] *Re Woudneh*, above n 75.

[78] This proposition is now reasonably well accepted in international human rights law: *Toonen v Australia*, above n 1; *Dudgeon v United Kingdom* (1981) 4 EHRR 149; *Norris v Northern Ireland* (1998) 13 EHRR 186.

exercising a fundamental human right and should not be required to alter their behaviour or change their sexual preference. This approach has some appeal, as it disconnects refugee claims from rigid identity categories that may not reflect an individual's particular self-conception or her cultural context. Rather, it focuses simply on the individual's choice of sexual partner. It is problematic, however, in so far as it is narrowly framed around a right to engage in *private* sexual activity. For many lesbians and gay men living under repressive regimes, there simply is no opportunity for sexual activity in one's own home. Furthermore, lesbians and gay men may be targeted for engaging in sexual behaviour that would be unremarkable when engaged in by heterosexuals, such as holding hands or 'kissing and cuddling' in public.[79] Thus, I argue that the privacy based argument needs to be supplemented with an argument based on equality or non-discrimination.

Although the right to non-discrimination for lesbians and gay men in international human rights law is perhaps not as clear as the right to privacy, there is now significant support in international jurisprudence for understanding the non-discrimination provisions of treaties such as the International Covenant on Civil and Political Rights, the International Covenant on Economic, Social and Cultural Rights and the European Charter of Human Rights (ECHR) as encompassing discrimination on the basis of sexual orientation.[80] This allows the recognition of gay men and lesbians as a particular social group to move beyond the narrow paradigm of privacy to a broader conception based on non-discrimination. This would provide a way to counter arguments that individuals persecuted for their public expression of sexuality are not being persecuted for who they are but for what they do. To the extent that public expression of sexuality is permitted for heterosexuals, a non-discrimination argument emphasises that it must be permitted for homosexuals also – and discriminatory persecution of persons for their public expression of homosexuality is thus persecution of a person for reasons of their membership in a particular social group.

More radically, one could argue for a right to sexuality as the foundation for gay and lesbian refugee claims. This approach would have the advantage of not requiring discrimination in the treatment of gay men

---

[79] See, for example, *MIMA v Gui* [1999] FCA 1496 (29 October 1999).

[80] *Toonen v Australia,* above n 1; *Sutherland v United Kingdom* (European Commission on Human Rights, Application 25186/94, Comm Rep 1.7.97); *Da Silva Mouta v Portugal* (European Court of Human Rights, Application 33290/96, 21 December 1999).

and lesbians, which implicitly sets up a heterosexual norm against which gay and lesbian behaviour is judged. It would also allow for other kinds of claims beyond those based on sexual identity. At present, however, it is difficult to point to recognition of a right to sexuality in international law, although there are some signs that one may be emerging.[81]

Recognition of Refugee Claims Based on Other Sexuality Issues

Gay and lesbian refugee claims are new uses of the Refugees Convention. However, they are now reasonably well-accepted, as discussed above under 'The Judicial and Administrative Recognition of Refugee Claims Based on Sexual Orientation'. What of other new uses of the Convention based on sexuality? Here I refer to things such as sex outside marriage and sex work. The purpose of this chapter is not to provide an extensive analysis of such possible new claims, but to raise these issues and to provide a brief discussion of them.

Sex Outside Marriage

Sex outside marriage is already on the refugee radar screen, in that adultery, or the allegation of adultery, has been the basis for some successful claims. The most well known of these is no doubt the House of Lords case, *Islam*, discussed above.[82] *Islam* is widely considered to be a case about women and gender – and indeed it is. But it is also a case about sexuality – it is a case about the intersection of gender and sexuality, an intersection which is crucial to an understanding of the response of refugee law to claims based on non-normative heterosexual behaviour. In *Islam*, the women in question were married and had been accused of adultery. They feared punishment as a result. What was important in the case, however, was not the fact that they might be persecuted for their consensual sexual behaviour. Rather, the crucial factor was the discriminatory approach Pakistan took to *female* adultery, as opposed to male adultery. Thus the court concluded that the particular social group in this case was women,

---

[81] A Miller, 'Human Rights and Sexuality: First Steps Towards Articulating a Rights Framework for Claims to Sexual Rights and Freedoms', *American Society of International Law Proceedings* **93** (2000) p 288; R Parker, 'Sexual Rights: Concepts and Action', *Health and Human Rights* **2** (1997) p 31.

[82] Above n 34 and accompanying text.

who feared persecution on the basis of their gender – not adulterous persons, who feared persecution on the basis of their sexuality. But at the heart of this discrimination against women was the fact that the discriminatory norms and practices in question concerned women's *sexuality* – a site of great anxiety and discrimination in many cultures.

Another recent case concerning adultery is *Jabari v Turkey*,[83] a decision of the European Court of Human Rights (the European Court). This case did not directly involve the Refugees Convention (it arose under the ECHR), but it concerned an Iranian woman who had sought and been denied refugee status in Turkey. She feared persecution if she was returned to Iran – stoning to death or whipping – because she had committed adultery and argued that if Turkey returned her to Iran it would expose her to 'inhuman or degrading treatment or punishment' contrary to Article 3 of the ECHR. The European Court accepted this argument. In doing so it noted that the UNHCR had granted Ms Jabari refugee status on the basis that she belonged to the social group of 'women who have transgressed social mores', in accordance with the UNHCR guidelines on gender persecution.[84]

There have also been cases in Australia where women have succeeded in refugee claims on the basis of discriminatory norms around female sexuality.[85] Again, these have been framed in terms of a particular social group based on gender, rather than on sexuality. This development is important and welcome – but it is strikingly limited in the protection it offers: men who fear persecution because of their sexual activity outside marriage are not protected by recognising a social group based on gender. This is apparent from the lack of success of male applicants who claimed they feared persecution because they had engaged in sex outside marriage.[86]

While refugee law has not yet recognised sex outside marriage as the basis for a refugee claim aside from discriminatory gender norms, the fact is that cases concerning heterosexual sexual activity that departs from dominant social norms are beginning to appear. To date, the approach of the courts to these claims has been based on gender – but I want to

---

[83]   *Jabari v Turkey* (Application 40035/98, European Court of Human Rights, 11 July 2000).

[84]   Id, paras 18, 41.

[85]   RRT N95 09580 (7 March 1996).

[86]   RRT V97/06522 (2 September 1998); *Z v MIMA* [1998] 1578 FCA (11 December 1998); *MIMA v Darboy* [1998] 931 FCA (16 August 1998).

challenge that and suggest that 'adulterers' could, in some societies, constitute a particular social group and thus be eligible for protection under the Refugees Convention. Such an argument would be based on the fact that adultery is a voluntary activity that involves the exercise of a fundamental human right – the right to engage in consensual private sexual activity. It can be argued, I think, that adulterers are a cognisable group in some societies where adultery is singled out as a stigmatised practice – in much the same way that 'homosexuals' became a cognisable group when same-sex sexual activity was singled out as a stigmatised practice in the later 19th century. Adultery is clearly not an immutable trait – but that is not a necessary feature of a particular social group (nor of all the other Convention grounds). So, I would argue, the international community should recognise that persecuting – for example, stoning or flogging – a person because of their adultery is persecution for a Convention reason – regardless of the person's gender.

Sex Work

> Prostitutes are systematically robbed of liberty, security, fair administration of justice, respect for private and family life, freedom of expression and freedom of association. In addition, they suffer from inhuman and degrading treatment and punishment and from discrimination in employment and housing.[87]

Prostitutes – or sex workers – suffer appalling human rights abuses in many countries around the world. Recently, for example, a woman in Iran was stoned to death as punishment for having acted in a pornographic film.[88] Could a person who is persecuted because he or she engages in sex work claim refugee status under the Refugees Convention? That is, can it be argued that sex workers constitute a 'particular social group' by analogy with lesbians and gay men? I note here that I am not concerned with claims that forced prostitution constitutes a form of persecution that should give rise to a successful refugee claim.[89] Rather, I am discussing the position of

---

[87] International Committee for Prostitutes' Rights, 'Draft Statements from the 2nd World Whore's Congress' (1986) in F Delacoste and P Alexander, *Sex Work: Writings by Women in the Sex Industry* (San Francisco, Cleis Press, 2nd ed, 1998), p 316.

[88] *The Australian*, 23 June 2001.

[89] Such claims have been made in Australia but all have, to my knowledge, failed: RRT V97/06838 (6 May 1998); RRT N98/25996 (7 May 1999). The tribunal in each case rejected the claim on the basis that the persecution alleged was not for a Convention reason.

those who 'choose' to engage in sex work (albeit often for reasons of poverty) and are persecuted for that choice.

As a starting point, sex workers are defined as a group by their sexual activity: by the fact that they engage in sexual activity for money. Lesbians and gay men, too, are defined by their sexual activity: by the sex of the partner with whom they engage in sexual activity. In addition, both sex workers and lesbians and gay men are generally identifiable as a distinct group within society whether or not their sexual activity is criminalised, although the criminal law (including the past criminal law) clearly plays a role in constituting both groups.[90] As Mathew has noted:

> Perhaps laws that ban sodomy are not merely reactions to the activities of a pre-existing social group ... but one part of the process by which the excluded group 'homosexuals' and the barriers between it and the rest of society are brought into existence.[91]

We might make the same argument concerning sex workers – the historical criminalisation of sex work helped to create a stigmatised class of persons known as whores or prostitutes. Indeed, the availability of several words of negative connotation to identify sex workers supports the argument that sex workers do form a cognisable group within society.

Sex work is clearly not some immutable characteristic analogous to race falling within Hathaway's category (1). It may, in some societies, fall within category (2) – that is, it may constitute a past experience for which one is persecuted, even though the individual has left prostitution. However, of Hathaway's three categories, I am again concerned primarily with (3) – the argument that sex work is a voluntary activity involving the exercise of a fundamental human right so that a person should not be required to change their behaviour. This, I acknowledge, is controversial, in

---

[90]　I note that Dawson J observed in *Applicant A*, above n 10, p 243 that 'where a persecutory law applies to all members of society it cannot create a particular social group consisting of all those who bring themselves within its terms'; so, for example, those who committed contempt of court or traffic offences would not constitute a particular social group. This is probably correct where the only feature defining the group is the law in question, but in relation to prostitutes (and to lesbians and gay men), the criminal law is not the only factor participating in the creation of the particular social group – such groups are identifiable because of their sexual practices, not simply because those sexual practices are (or were once) against the law.

[91]　P Mathew, 'Conformity or Persecution: China's One Child Policy and Refugee Status', *University of New South Wales Law Journal* 23 (2000) p 103 at p 130.

that most societies regulate sex work to some extent. However, not all states criminalise sex work, thus we cannot conclude that there is universal condemnation of it that would preclude the fundamental human rights argument. Many societies criminalise same-sex sexual activity, yet lesbian and gay rights are now accepted, as are lesbian and gay refugee claims.

A claim by sex workers could rest, I argue, on a variety of rights: a right to work; a right to a basic standard of living; a right to engage in consensual, private sexual behaviour (though the exchange of money might remove the private element here) and a right to sexuality. I acknowledge, however, that it would no doubt be difficult to persuade a court that engaging in prostitution is something that a person should not be required to change.

Conclusion

The category 'membership of a particular social group' provides a key way in which new uses of the Refugees Convention can develop. It has to date allowed lesbians and gay men to claim the protection of the Refugees Convention. It has also been used – with differing degrees of success – by women claiming fear of persecution based on their gender. In these respects, the Refugees Convention is following developments in international human rights law that have recognised gay and lesbian rights and placed women's rights firmly on the international human rights agenda. Whether the Refugees Convention will be extended further in the area of sexuality is an open question, though we have already seen that, where gender and sexuality intersect, some states have been responsive.

A more radical proposition is that sex workers might be able to claim refugee status if they are persecuted because they are sex workers. Such a claim seems unlikely to succeed at present, particularly given that prostitutes' rights have not yet been recognised by international human rights law. Ultimately, it seems to me that the Refugees Convention follows human rights law rather than leading the way into new areas of rights protections. This helps explain why lesbian and gay claims have only recently been recognised – and suggests that more radical claims will not be successful until human rights develops further.

11 Moving Beyond the State: Refugees, Accountability and Protection

SUSAN KNEEBONE*

Refugees ... represent a failure of the state system, a 'problem' to be 'solved'.[1]

Introduction

Persecution by non-state actors currently poses one of the greatest challenges to the application of the refugee definition in the Refugees Convention. Increasingly claims for protection are based upon the actions of persons other than the state, in situations where the state is unwilling or unable to provide protection, perhaps because non-state agents have gained control, or perhaps because no state authorities exist. These scenarios, involving civil war or internal conflict, and the internal breakdown of law and order, are symptoms of a worldwide decline of state power.[2] At the same time, it has been argued that in western countries where the receiving refugees states are situated, the state is increasingly decentralised and shrinking due to the twin forces of privatisation and globalisation.[3]

* I would like to thank the following for their useful comments on earlier drafts of this chapter: Rodger Haines, Gail Hubble and Pene Mathew. Thanks also to Eddy Gisconda, Kobi Liens and Eliza Meehan, for helpful research assistance. I am responsible for any remaining errors.

[1] T Alexander Aleinikoff, 'State centred refugee law: From Resettlement to Containment', *Michigan Journal of International Law* 14 (1992) p 121.

[2] J Mertus, 'The State and the Post-Cold War Refugee Regime: New Models, New Questions', *International Journal of Refugee Law* 10 (1998) p 321. In this context note that the global number of internally displaced persons (IDPs) is estimated at 25 million persons, which is larger than the number of refugees globally.

[3] C Sampford, 'Reconceiving and Reinstitutionalising Liberal Democratic Values in a More Global World' in C Sampford and T Round (eds), *Beyond the Republic: Meeting the Global Challenges to Constitutionalism* (Australia, Federation Press, 2001) p 438;

Yet despite the decline in the state as the prime source of authority and protection, refugee protection as the above quotation implies (and indeed as its author observes) is still regarded as a matter for states. The question I ask in this chapter is whether the concept of a refugee enshrined in the 1951 Refugees Convention is tied to a model of the state that is appropriate for refugee protection in the 21st century?

The history of the drafting of the 1951 Convention demonstrates that the refugee definition is predicated upon an individualistic concept of persons fleeing the borders of hostile governments.[4] The test enshrined in the 1951 Convention concentrates upon a person's fear of persecution in their country of nationality, and the reasons for persecution, which by and large arise from the person's civil or political status. Specifically Article 1A(2) defines a refugee as:

> ... any person who ... owing to a well-founded fear of being persecuted for reasons of race, religion, nationality, membership of a particular social group or political opinion, is outside the country of his nationality and is unable or unwilling to avail himself of the protection of that country ...

There are two interlocking elements of the refugee definition set out above, which are relevant for the purposes of this discussion. The first relates to the words 'persecuted for reasons of'. These words require a nexus or causal link between the acts of persecution and the ground or grounds for claiming refugee status. The issue that this raises is what link, if any, between persecution and the state is necessary to satisfy the nexus? A 'state centred' approach[5] to the meaning of 'persecution' in the definition requires some evidence of state involvement, whether actual or constructive, to satisfy the nexus. The second element comes from the

---

D Kinley, 'The Shrinking State's Growing Responsibilities for Human Rights Protection' Paper presented to the Castan Centre for Human Rights Law Conference on Human Rights and Global Challenges, Melbourne, December 2001, http://www.law.monash.edu.au/castancentre.

4   W Kalin, 'Non-state Agents of Persecution and the Inability of the State to Protect', *Georgetown Immigration Law Journal* 15 (2001) p 415 at p 419; A Fortin, 'The Meaning of "Protection" in the Refugee Definition', *International Journal of Refugee Law* 12 (2001) p 548.

5   The term 'state centred' is used by Aleinikoff, above n 1, in discussing overall responses and solutions to the refugee problem. By extension the term can be used to describe approaches to interpretation of the definition as described in this chapter.

words 'is outside the country of his nationality and is unable or unwilling to avail himself of the protection of that country'. This raises the issue of what lack of protection is relevant. Does this mean as Shacknove argues,[6] the *internal* failure of a state to protect its citizens, or does it mean as a recent body of scholarship argues, external or 'diplomatic' protection in international law?[7] And if that view is correct of what relevance is the internal failure of a state to protect its citizens? Is its relevance limited to the reasonableness of the 'well-founded fear' of persecution? Or does it qualify the meaning of persecution?

In this chapter I demonstrate the use of a restrictive 'state centred' accountability theory as the basis of protection under the Refugees Convention. This implies the use of a 'state' concept which does not sit squarely with international law concepts.

I take two recent decisions of the High Court of Australia to illustrate my argument. The decision in *Minister for Immigration and Multicultural Affairs (MIMA) v Ibrahim (Ibrahim)*[8] concerned a person caught up in the violence of civil or clan warfare in Somalia, where no state authorities exist. In the second decision, *MIMA v Khawar (Khawar)*[9] it was held that a married woman from Pakistan who claimed that she was the victim of serious and prolonged abuse by her husband, and that the state was unwilling or unable to protect her, could potentially satisfy the test for a 'refugee' within the meaning of Article 1A(2) of the 1951 Convention. I argue through an analysis of these two decisions that a state centred accountability model embodies an inappropriate concept of the state in the context of the Refugees Convention, and that this fact needs to be recognised in order to move forward to solving the refugee problem.

State Centred Approaches to Accountability and Protection

The first of the two elements of the refugee definition comes from the words 'persecuted for reasons of'. These words require a nexus or causal link between the acts of persecution and the ground or grounds for claiming

---

6   A Shacknove, 'Who is a Refugee?' *Ethics* **95** (1985) p 274.

7   Fortin, above n 4; Kalin, above n 4, p 425; contrast N Nathwani, 'The Purpose of Asylum', *International Journal of Refugee Law* **12** (2001) p 354.

8   (2000) 204 CLR 1. Discussed below, n 88 and text.

9   (2000) 67 ALD 577. Discussed below, n 112 and text.

refugee status. A state centred approach has been used to argue that if the state is not the actual perpetrator of the acts of persecution, that 'persecution' requires at least that it be condoned or tolerated by the state. This 'accountability' view stresses the unwillingness of the state of origin to provide protection, and its implicit complicity for the acts of persecution. It is consistent with an authoritarian model of a state, with a duty to protect its members. The position is less clear and more contentious where the state has not condoned the persecution but is unable to provide protection, perhaps because non-state agents have gained control.[10] It is not clear whether responsibility extends to situations of mere inability of control by the state. The situation where no state exists is even more controversial.

The view that there must be a direct nexus between the acts of persecution and the state is supported by two arguments which rely upon notions of *national* state power. The first argument focuses upon the grounds in the refugee definition. The second is based upon a concept of state power.

The Refugees Convention definition of a refugee emphasises as stated above, grounds for protection which by and large arise from the person's civil or political status. It is sometimes said that it presupposes a public duty on the part of the state to protect the individual (private) applicant. Shacknove for example, suggests that it contains an implicit assumption that the normal basis of society is the bond of trust and loyalty between the state and its citizens.[11] Shacknove argues that neither persecution nor alienage captures what is essential about refugeehood, that it is the absence of state protection which is the essential condition of refugee status. On that view, satisfaction of the elements of the refugee test presupposes that the bond of allegiance of a citizen with the sovereign country of origin, the persecuting state, has been severed.

Consistent with this concept of the refugee, the object of conferring refugee status has been described by Hathaway as 'a response to the disfranchisement from the usual benefits of nationality'.[12] Hathaway

---

[10] Kalin, above n 4, p 416.

[11] Shacknove, above n 6.

[12] J Hathaway, *The Law of Refugee Status* (Toronto, Butterworths, 1991), p 124. This approach was specifically applied in *Hellman v Minister for Immigration and Multicultural Affairs* (*MIMA*) [2000] FCA 645 (17 May 2000) in which a US citizen claimed persecution on the basis of religion as he feared reprisals from a religious sect

suggests that the meaning of 'persecution' is concerned with determining whether there have been human rights abuses, and *additionally*, requires 'scrutiny of the state's ability and willingness effectively to respond to that risk'.[13] Hathaway's concern is with the quality of the claimant's fear and the nature of the 'municipal relationship between an individual and her state'[14] (or country of nationality). But this view can be misinterpreted (as indeed the authorities discussed in this chapter illustrate) as focussing the test of 'persecution' upon the willingness and ability of the state to protect the claimant, rather than focussing upon the well-foundedness of the claimant's fear. It is often said for example that the Convention confers 'surrogate protection' to an asylum seeker. Under this model, international law has a role 'only when the state will not or cannot comply with its classical duty to defend the interests of its citizenry'.[15]

This description of the role of the state under the Refugees Convention focuses upon the duty of a state to its citizens. That is, it focuses upon lack of internal or national protection. To suggest that the protection provided by the Convention is of a 'surrogate' nature means that an equation is made between the role of the persecuting state and that of the receiving state. Both are conceived in terms of the duty of a state to its citizens. Even though, as Hathaway points out, this protection arises from international law,[16] it carries with it the idea of the sovereign right of a state to decide who will enter its borders. It fits with a model of 'state centred refugee law' in which the states signatory to the Convention (in practice the wealthy industrialised countries) call the shots. States have control over the entrance of asylum seekers, and the law and procedures which determine whether they acquire refugee status. It raises the issue of what lack of protection is relevant to the Refugees Convention.

Recently some scholars have argued persuasively that the basis of protection encompassed in the Refugees Convention, as demonstrated by the history of the drafting of the Convention and the historical context,

---

to which his mother belonged. In rejecting that claim the Federal Court in that case relied on the fact that he is a US citizen and is not 'disenfranchised'.

[13]   Hathaway above n 12, p 125.

[14]   Ibid.

[15]   Ibid.

[16]   Hathaway, above n 12, p 124.

is external or diplomatic protection, an international law concept.[17] That is, as Fortin argues, protection is based upon the continuing responsibility of a state to its nationals when abroad, under international law. This argument stresses that refugee protection is a privilege of states which exists at the international level.[18] It moves away from the need to show lack of internal protection and the breakdown of a citizen-state relationship. It suggests that the international protection provided by the Refugees Convention is independent and complementary to the protection that states are supposed to accord to refugees in their territory.[19] Kalin for example, refers to the 'neutral character of the institution of asylum' as an international law concept. His point here is that asylum is granted by the receiving state as an aspect of territorial sovereignty, and the obligation to protect those within a sovereign territory. It does not, he argues, involve an implicit accusation against the country of origin.[20] The significance of the diplomatic protection view is that it moves the focus of interpretation of the Convention away from internal state accountability to international law concepts. That is not to say, as I shall explain, that the level of internal state protection is irrelevant.

In relation to the internal 'surrogate' protection view, it is the reliance on Shacknove's views, which involves the concept of citizenship, which concern me in this context. If, as is the case, the Refugees Convention is an instrument of international protection, it is surely the international concepts which are relevant. The basis for protection in international law is a person's presence in a territory but not citizenship as such.[21] Other provisions in the Refugees Convention link the need for protection with residence and 'nationality'.[22] For example, the non-refoulement provision in Article 33 of the Refugees Convention links the need for protection with

---

[17] For example, Kalin, above n 4; Fortin, above n 4.

[18] Nathwani, above n 7, p 359.

[19] Fortin, above n 4, p 570 citing P Weis, 'The International Protection of Refugees' *American Journal of International Law* **48** (1954) pp 218–19.

[20] Kalin, above n 4, p 423.

[21] Fortin, above n 4. As Fortin points out, Shacknove's views are consistent with those of Grahl Madsen who thought that alienage was a precondition to obtaining refugee status. But the latter was referring to diplomatic protection.

[22] For example, Articles 1C, 1E.

presence in a territory.[23] Nationality is also the right provided for by other international human rights instruments.[24] The notion of citizenship is unknown and possibly irrelevant in international law.[25]

Another critique of an accountability theory which limits persecution to acts by states, is that it fits with a model of a strong sovereign state. Persecution by non-state agents challenges this paradigm. In *R v Secretary of State; Ex parte Adan*,[26] the Court of Appeal described the accountability theory as limiting the classes of cases in which a person can claim refugee status to situations where the persecution can be attributed to the state. The court in *Adan* contrasted the protection approach of the English courts, which concentrates upon whether protection is available without enquiring into the reason for lack of protection. The Court of Appeal thought this protection theory was shared by the majority of states signatory to the Convention:

> Our courts recognise persecution by non-State agents for the purpose of the Convention in any case where the State is *unwilling or unable* to provide protection against it, and indeed *whether or not there exist* competent or effective governmental or State authorities in the country in question.[27]

An accountability approach prevails under German law. In that jurisdiction, if the source of persecution is a non-state agent, the applicant must show that it was tolerated or encouraged by the state or that the state was unwilling to provide protection. According to this approach, the Convention has no application if there is no effective state authority.

---

23 Article 33 of the Refugees Convention states that: 'No Contracting State shall expel or return ("refouler") a refugee in any manner whatsoever to the frontiers of territories where his life or freedom would be threatened on account of his race, religion, nationality, membership of a particular social group or political opinion.'

24 For example, UDHR, Article 15; International Covenant on Civil and Political Rights (ICCPR), Article 24(3), and note the distinction between nationality and the rights of citizenship in Article 25.

25 D Adler and K Rubenstein, 'International Citizenship: The Future of Nationality in a Globalised World', *Indiana Journal of Global Legal Studies* 7 (2000) pp 519–48.

26 [1999] 3 WLR 1274 at 1288–9.

27 [1999] 3 WLR 1274 at 1289 per Laws LJ. (Emphasis added.) Note that in France a variant of the accountability theory applies: see J Moore, 'Whither the Accountability Theory: Second-Class Status for Third-Party Refugees as a Threat to International Refugee Protection', *International Journal of Refugee Law* 13 (2001) p 32.

Kalin explains how this accountability theory fits with the German monopolistic view of state power and the political obligation of the state to protect its citizens from abuse of power.[28] He explains why the German concept of 'persecution' is tied to the idea of the abuse of such power. This concept of political 'persecution' is endorsed by Article 16 of the German Constitution which states: 'The politically persecuted enjoy the right of asylum'.[29] Kalin argues that this accountability theory fits with a model of state that is no longer generally appropriate – an authoritarian type state that no longer exists. He argues that this is too narrow a concept of a modern 'state' as it does not take the notion of civil society and the role of the people in shaping it, into account.[30] This is a stricter or literal version of accountability which as Kalin points out means that applications for refugee status will fail in the absence of an effective state. He argues that this theory is not consistent with the international law concept that states continue to exist even when no longer functioning.[31]

The accountability theories described above focus on the state–citizen relationship rather than on international obligations. They are consistent with a model of state centred refugee law under which the Refugees Convention confers surrogate *national* protection. This model focuses upon the accountability or responsibility of the state which is denying protection, rather than on the responsibility of the international community to confer surrogate protection. Arguably it is consistent with a concept of a strong, authoritarian state. I argue that this model is an inappropriate one in the context of international protection. Moreover, it overshadows the central or primary purpose of the Convention to confer protection from persecution. That is, it has the potential to ignore the crucial link between *fear* of persecution and lack of protection. It also avoids discussion of the fundamental concept of protection from refoulement in Article 33 of the Refugees Convention.

If we focus upon the second element of the definition of refugee, namely the words 'is outside the country of his nationality and is unable or

---

[28] Kalin, above n 4.

[29] Basic Law of the Federal Republic of Germany, 23 May 1949, Article 16 discussed in G S Goodwin-Gill, 'The Margin of Interpretation: Different or Disparate?', *International Journal of Refugee Law* 11 (1999) p 730.

[30] Kalin, above n 4, p 422.

[31] Mertus, above n 2, argues that although this is correct in principle, in reality and politically failed states depend on international support to survive.

unwilling to avail himself of the protection of that country', as an international law concept, we can conclude that a broader concept of protection is relevant. Clearly these words recognise that the need for international protection arises because there is a *'well-founded fear* of being persecuted' in the country of origin. This requires proof of a prospective fear of persecution, applying both subjective and objective tests.[32] It requires an assessment of the 'degree of probability' of persecution in the state of origin.[33] My argument is that evidence of internal state practice is relevant to the objective test, but is not relevant to the meaning of persecution.

Protection from Persecution

The external or diplomatic protection view raises the issue of the relevance of internal protection of the refugee definition. Although the definition refers to the individual being unable or unwilling to get protection, the need to show a causal link between the fear and the Convention grounds is usually cited as the reason for internal protection. For example, Kalin recognises that external or diplomatic protection is no longer a relevant or helpful concept to interpretation of the Refugees Convention.[34] So he asserts on the basis of the 'surrogacy' idea discussed above, that an inherent part of the refugee definition is to stress the loss of internal protection, and that there is a link between persecution and the role of the state. The implication of his view, that there is a link between persecution and the role of the state, is that the level of protection provided by the country of origin is relevant to the refugee definition. By contrast, Fortin's view is that local or internal protection is relevant to the examination of refugee claims:

> only to the extent that the general ability of the State to ensure law and order is an essential factor for assessing the well-foundedness of the person's fear of persecution by non-State agents.[35]

---

[32] For example, *Chan Yee Kin v MIEA* (1989) 169 CLR 379.

[33] *MIEA v Guo* (1997) 191 CLR 559.

[34] Above n 4, p 427. Nathwani, above n 7, also argues that the diplomatic protection explanation does not make sense.

[35] Fortin, above n 4, p 574.

He makes this argument on the basis that it is wrong to characterise the role of the state as a 'duty of protection' against persecution, except in that context.[36]

The Kalin view about the relevance of internal protection to the refugee definition contains two propositions. The first is that internal protection, or the role of the state, is relevant to the notion of 'persecution' in the Refugees Convention. The second proposition, which is supported by Fortin, is that the general effectiveness of state protection is relevant to determining whether the fear is 'well-founded'. The first proposition can be questioned on the basis of interpretation of the definition, and the second by reference to the non-refoulement principle.

The meaning of persecution in the Refugees Convention was left deliberately flexible. Although it is agreed that there is no exhaustive definition of what amounts to persecution,[37] it is clear from the non-refoulement obligation in Article 33 of the Convention that its primary obligation is to protect against persecution. The usual focus of such protection, says Hathaway, is against sustained or systemic violation of basic human rights in relation to one of the core entitlements recognised by the international community.[38] Goodwin-Gill defines its core meaning to include deprivation of life or physical freedom.[39] The rights which the Refugees Convention protects are mirrored in other human rights instruments.[40]

As Goodwin-Gill points out, an accountability theory (which includes Kalin's) requires reading an additional element into the refugee definition, namely that the state is a participant in the persecution.[41] But the Convention says nothing about the source of the persecution. This view is

---

[36] Ibid.

[37] G S Goodwin-Gill, *The Refugee in International Law* (Oxford, Clarendon Press, 2nd ed, 1996), p 66.

[38] Hathaway, above n 12, p 112.

[39] Goodwin-Gill, above n 37, p 68.

[40] For example, Convention Against Torture and Other Cruel, Inhuman, or Degrading Treatment or Punishment entered into force on 26 June 1987; UDHR, Article 14 (right to asylum), Articles 18 and 19 (freedom of religion and opinion); ICCPR, Article 1 (right to life), Article 7 (freedom from torture), and Article 18 (right to freedom of thought, conscience and religion).

[41] Goodwin-Gill, above n 37.

supported by the United National High Commissioner for Refugees (UNHCR) Handbook, paragraph 65 of which provides:

> Persecution is normally related to action by the authorities of a country. ... Where serious discriminatory ... acts are committed by the local populace, they can be considered as persecution if they are knowingly tolerated by the authorities, or if the authorities refuse, or prove unable, to offer effective protection. [42]

Kalin's view is supported by the decision in *Horvath v Secretary of State*,[43] where a majority of the House of Lords interpreted the meaning of 'persecution' in the case of non-state agents as requiring evidence of the failure of the 'home' state to provide protection. In that case, the applicant was a Roma citizen of Slovakia who claimed that he feared persecution by 'skinheads' against whom the Slovak police failed to provide adequate protection for Roma. The Immigration Appeal Tribunal found as a matter of evidence that there was an increasing level of police protection of Roma in Slovakia, and that the behaviour which the applicant feared could not be said to amount to persecution. The Court of Appeal upheld the decision, holding that persecution by non-state actors required both serious harm and failure of state protection.[44] This decision was confirmed by the House of Lords, with Lord Lloyd dissenting.

Lord Hope formulated the issue in the House of Lords as follows:

> does the word 'persecution' denote merely sufficiently severe ill-treatment, or does it denote sufficiently severe ill-treatment against which the state fails to afford protection?[45]

He answered the last part of that question affirmatively by relying upon the Hathaway concept of 'surrogacy' which he said was the central principle for interpreting the Refugees Convention.[46] In the case of

---

[42] UNHCR, *Handbook on Procedures and Criteria for Determining Refugee Status* (Geneva, UNHCR, 2nd ed, 1992), para 65.

[43] [2001] 1 AC 489.

[44] [2000] INLR 15.

[45] *Horvath*, above n 43, p 494. Note three separate questions were posed, but the House of Lords found it unnecessary to answer the other two.

[46] Id, p 495.

persecution by non-state actors, he said the 'bridge' or link was the failure of state protection:

> If the principle of surrogacy is applied, the criterion must be whether the alleged lack of protection is such as to indicate that the home state is unable or unwilling to discharge *its* duty to establish and operate a *system* for the protection against persecution of its own nationals.[47]

He concluded that it is the failure of the state to provide protection which converts discriminatory acts into persecution.[48] In this formulation, the claim for refugee status depends upon the insufficiency of state protection against persecution by non-state agents, rather than upon the objective reasonableness of the claimant's fear. That is, Lord Hope thought that 'the failure of state protection is central to the whole system'.[49] But there is an important difference between an individual fear of persecution and an assessment of the general level of protection provided. As the Refugee Legal Service argued:

> The question is the efficacy of protection for the individual claimant rather than a general assessment of the system of protection.[50]

Lord Clyde, who delivered the other majority opinion, agreed that the principle of surrogate protection was central to interpretation of the Convention,[51] but adopted a different approach.[52] His opinion, which is similar to Fortin's, is that generally the level of state protection is relevant to the issue of 'well-founded fear' of persecution.[53] However in cases of persecution by non-state agents, his opinion was that the principle of surrogacy required evidence of the insufficiency of 'home' state protection. Thus he expressed a view similar to that of Fortin, namely that where non-state agents are involved an 'accountability' approach applies:

---

[47] Ibid. (Emphasis in the original.)

[48] Id, p 500.

[49] Id, p 495.

[50] Id, p 493.

[51] Id, pp 508–9.

[52] H Lambert, 'The Conceptualisation of "Persecution" by the House of Lords: *Horvath v Secretary of State*', *International Journal of Refugee Law* 13 (2001) p 16.

[53] *Horvath*, above n 43, p 513.

The Convention was worked out and agreed between states and it is at the state level that it has to be understood.[54]

Yet a third approach was suggested by Lord Lloyd in his dissenting opinion. Lord Lloyd regarded persecution and the absence of state protection as two separate issues. That is, he distinguished the two elements of the refugee definition identified in this chapter, and concluded that the absence of state protection was not relevant to the meaning of 'persecution'. It was however relevant to the objective test of a 'well-founded fear' of persecution.[55] He was critical of the use of a concept of 'surrogate protection' to define 'persecution'.

It is important to note that while the House of Lords in *Horvath* thought that it was applying a 'protection' approach, in fact the majority reasoning supports a state centred accountability approach. Lord Hope's reasoning which was accepted by the other Lords in the majority is similar to Kalin's view discussed above, namely that there is a link between persecution and the role of the state. Lord Hope's reasoning slips from the notion of international protection to national surrogate protection. The concept of 'surrogacy' which he applies, does not distinguish between the reasons for the lack of protection and the granting of asylum. Lord Hope suggests a test for the nexus requirement of the first element of the refugee definition ('persecuted for reasons of') based on the inability or unwillingness of the home state to provide protection. However, the words of the refugee definition refer to the *applicant's* unwillingness 'to avail himself of the protection of that country'; that is, to the reasons for the applicant's fear. Thus, on this view, Lord Clyde's reasoning began from the correct premise, but was then derailed by confusion about the 'protection' element of the refugee definition.[56]

Horvath imposes a two part test for the refugee definition when non-state actors are involved. First it requires evidence of failure of state protection to establish 'persecution'. That is, it involves reading an extra element into the meaning of 'persecution' in the refugee definition.

---

[54] Id, p 508.

[55] On that basis, Lord Lloyd found that the applicant did not satisfy the refugee test.

[56] Lambert, above n 52, p 20, suggests that 'leading academic writing concurs that the failure or absence of State protection is fundamental to the concept of persecution'. The purpose of this chapter is to critique that view which relies too heavily on the 'surrogacy' principle.

Second, it requires an assessment of the general, systemic level of protection provided by the state.[57] As Lambert has pointed out, this second aspect has the potential to run foul of the non-refoulement obligation in the Refugees Convention as it fails to focus upon the individual.[58]

In *Horvath* the House of Lords said the meaning of 'persecution' where non-state agents are involved required evidence of state failure to afford protection. *Horvath* requires evidence of constructive state participation. It is arguably contrary to the UNHCR Handbook paragraph 65.[59] It suggests a state centred approach to the meaning of 'persecution' which runs counter to the Refugees Convention and the need for a 'well-founded fear'. Arguably, satisfaction of the latter is not only necessary but also sufficient for the refugee definition.

Generally it is recognised that persecution by non-state agents which is condoned or tolerated by the state will come within the Refugees Convention definition. The position is less clear and more contentious where the state has not condoned the persecution but is unable to provide protection, perhaps because non-state agents have gained control.[60] This is arguably covered by paragraph 65. At the other end of the spectrum, and arguably not envisaged by paragraph 65 is the situation where no state authorities exist. The two recent Australian High Court cases which are examined below are examples from each end of the spectrum.

Accountability Approaches to the Refugee Definition

As background to these two cases it is useful to summarise some approaches which have developed in the context of persecution by non-state agents, which can be associated with an accountability approach. In general these concentrate on showing that there is a nexus between the state and the acts of persecution.

---

[57] For example, *Canaj v Secretary of State; Vallaj v Special Adjudicator* [2001] EWCA 782.

[58] See above n 52, p 28. For this reason *Horvath* was not followed by the New Zealand Refugee Status Appeals Authority in Refugee Appeal 71427/99 (16 August 2000).

[59] UNHCR Handbook, above n 42.

[60] Kalin, above n 4, p 416.

The Complicity Argument

The clearest example of this is the 'complicity' test which concentrates upon the motivation of the persecutor,[61] to determine whether the persecution is related to state purposes. For example, in *MIMA v Ndege*[62] Weinberg J decided that the relevant motivation must show state complicity for it to be 'a Convention reason'. In *Ndege* a married woman from Tanzania was a victim of domestic violence. The Refugee Review Tribunal (RRT) had decided that married women in Tanzania were members of a particular social group as there was a direct nexus between such membership and the motivation for persecution. However, the RRT declined to make a finding on whether the husband was motivated by a Convention related reason, holding that the state's failure to protect women in the applicant's position was sufficient to give rise to a well-founded fear of persecution within the meaning of the definition. On judicial review, Weinberg J said this conclusion was not open as the evidence disclosed that only the husband was the source of the well-founded fear. While a state may be complicit in persecution, complicity in non-Convention related violence will not suffice. Absent a finding that the husband was motivated by a Convention reason, Weinberg J said that complicity by the state was not relevant.

The argument that state complicity is required was rejected in *Ward v Attorney-General of Canada*.[63] That case concerned a former member of the Irish National Liberation Army (INLA) who fled Ireland after he had 'turned coat' on the INLA. Ward successfully argued that he was a refugee because neither the Irish nor the United Kingdom police could promise him protection. The Supreme Court of Canada focused upon the words 'unable' and 'unwilling' in the Refugees Convention definition. It concluded that the state was not required to be involved in the persecution. It said that the words 'unable' and 'unwilling' were intended to refer to stateless persons.[64] The decision suggests that an applicant need not prove that she had unsuccessfully sought internal state protection of the country of origin.

---

[61] In *MIMA v Chen Shi Hai* (2000) 201 CLR 293 the High Court disapproved of the use of a motivation test.

[62] (2000) 59 ALD 758.

[63] [1993] 2 SCR 689.

[64] Id, p 717.

Macklin suggests that the unarticulated corollary of this decision is that persecution subsists in violation of fundamental human rights regardless of the identity of the perpetrator.[65] That is, the Supreme Court of Canada in *Ward* focused on *both* protection against fundamental human rights abuse, *and* the failure of state responsibility when the state is either unwilling or unable to protect the individual. But it did not require state complicity in the persecution in any constructive sense, as for example the House of Lord did in *Horvath*.

The Public–Private Distinction

The use of this distinction in this context implies that refugee law is concerned with 'public' issues and state protection. By contrast, 'private' issues are said not to come within the Convention.

In a number of cases, individuals with 'private' grounds have failed to show a causal connection between the persecution and the alleged 'membership of a particular social group'. For example, in *Moradgholi v MIMA*,[66] an Iranian nurse who gave evidence that her husband was executed as a counter-revolutionary and that because she was unable to obtain work officially, she was forced to work in pornography, claimed that she was a refugee. The basis of her claim was that she faced punishment under Iran's criminal laws. Her application was rejected on the basis that her claims arose from criminal laws of general application rather than Convention grounds. It was also suggested that her claim raised non-Convention issues of gender and sexuality. The implication of this decision is that her claim involved 'private' issues. A similar approach was applied in *Mehenni v MIMA*,[67] a case involving an Algerian conscientious objector, and in *Maygari v MIMA*,[68] where the applicants claimed discrimination as gypsies.[69]

---

[65] A Macklin, '*Attorney-General v Ward*: A Review Essay', *International Journal of Refugee Law* **6** (1994) p 362.

[66] [2000] FCA 13 (12 January 2000).

[67] (1999) 164 ALR 192.

[68] (1998) 50 ALD 341.

[69] See also *MIMA v Gutierrez* (2000) 59 ALD 89 about a Peruvian seaman who jumped ship to escape death threats he received after joining an international trade union.

The public–private distinction is implicit in the motivation cases where the technique is to ask whether the applicant has been persecuted, in the sense of being discriminated against, for motives linked to Convention reasons. For example in *Lama v MIMA*,[70] it was decided that persons who based their claim upon bovicide were not refugees. In *MIMA v Zamora*,[71] it was said that tourist guides were not members of a particular social group.[72] In *MIMA v Darboy*,[73] the RRT had said that the applicant, an employee of the Australian Embassy, had suffered persecution for his religion. The applicant had had an affair with a married woman in Iran and claimed that he would be punished under the criminal laws of that country. On review, Moore J remitted the case to the RRT as it had not asked whether the applicant was discriminated against by a law of particular application. The discussion in this and the other cases implies that they involved private matters. The combined effect of these arguments is to concentrate upon the link between the persecution and state responsibility.

But in an increasing number of cases it has been accepted that refugee status can be recognised in cases of domestic abuse where there is a 'private' perpetrator of the persecution, and the state is unwilling or unable to protect the individual. Apart from these 'gender' cases, refugee status is increasingly being recognised where the alleged persecution relates to a person's sexuality, or other 'private' status.[74]

A number of commentators have suggested that this trend is consistent with an accountability perspective, that reflects the role of the (public) state to accept responsibility for private actors. They suggest that it also shows that the state does not need to be an active agent of the persecution, and that it recognises state responsibility for inaction. By implication they propound a theory of state responsibility. And as others have said, it also shows the 'privatisation' of human rights.

---

[70]   (2000) 57 ALD 613.

[71]   (1998) 85 FCR 458.

[72]   Contrast *Shetty v MIMA* (2000) 59 ALD 431 regarding an Indian divorcee considered not to be a member of a particular social group.

[73]   (1999) 52 ALD 44.

[74]   K Walker, 'New Uses of the Refugees Convention: Sexuality and Refugee Status', chapter 10 in this book.

Macklin for example, compares the gender guidelines which have been developed to guide decision makers in Australia, Canada and the USA.[75] She suggests that they all derive from the basic proposition that a state owes an obligation to protect its citizens from private actors or agents of persecution.[76] Adjin-Tetty makes a similar point when she suggests that this trend is consistent with the liberal tradition that the state is responsible for privately inflicted harm in some situations.[77] She suggests that the evolution of 'the state responsibility' doctrine transcends the public\private dichotomy.[78] Under this dichotomy the 'private' or domestic is considered to be invisible, whereas the 'public' sphere is properly the domain of the state. However, I would argue that the state responsibility doctrine view is dangerously close to the accountability theory as it potentially focuses upon the protection provided by the state, rather than upon the individual's fear of persecution.

The legal issue in these cases is whether such persons have a well-founded fear of persecution as 'a member of a particular social group' within the meaning of the Convention. The leading case is *Islam v Home Department; R v Immigration Appeal Tribunal; Ex parte Shah (Shah and Islam)*[79] in which the applicants, two married women from Pakistan argued that if they were forced to return to Pakistan, they would be at risk of being beaten by their husbands, that the state would not protect them and that they were at risk of criminal prosecution for adultery for which the penalty could be flogging or stoning to death. The Secretary of State argued that they were not part of a particular social group which existed independently of persecution and that they feared persecution because of the hostility of their husbands rather than because of their membership of a particular social group. However, the House of Lords found that domestic abuse of women in Pakistan was prevalent, relying on an Amnesty International

---

[75] A Macklin, 'Cross-Border Shopping for Ideas: A Critical Review of US, Canadian and Australian Approaches to Gender-Related Aslyum Claims', *Georgetown Law Journal* 13 (1998) 25. See DIMA, *Refugee and Humanitarian Visa Applicants: Guidelines on Gender Issues for Decision Makers* (Canberra, DIMA, July 1996).

[76] Macklin, above n 75, p 48.

[77] E Adjin-Tetty, 'The Failure of State Protection Within the Context of the Convention Refugee Regime with Particular Reference to Gender-related Persecution', *Journal of International Legal Studies* 3 (1997) 53.

[78] Id, p 86.

[79] [1999] 2 AC 629.

report. It found that such abuse was either partly tolerated or sanctioned by the state of Pakistan as it did nothing to prevent it. The House of Lords gave a broad meaning to 'membership of a particular social group', saying that cohesiveness of the group was not an essential requirement. Lord Hoffmann, Lord Steyn and Lord Hope found that because in Pakistan women were discriminated against as a group in matters of fundamental (human) rights and freedoms in comparison to men, and as the state gave them no protection, women in Pakistan constituted a 'particular social group'.[80] Thus the essential reasons for this decision were *both* the basic entitlement to protection against fundamental human rights abuse which the Convention recognises, *and* the failure of state responsibility when the state is either unwilling or unable to protect the individual. But the House of Lords did not describe the issues in terms of either state complicity or the public-private divide. It focused upon the persecution leading from the status of the applicants. Like the Supreme Court of Canada in *Ward* it focused on the failure of state responsibility when the state is either unwilling or unable to protect the individual.

Civil War and Laws of 'General and Particular' Application

In the context of civil war and internal conflict, a distinction has been made between laws or acts which apply to the general populace (which are presumably not persecutory by nature) and those which single out an individual or group of individuals (and may amount to 'persecution'). The individualistic concept of refugee in the Convention definition led Hathaway to conclude that it does not apply to those affected by generalised violence arising from war and civil conflict.[81] The arguments against protection here are similar to those above, namely that unless the applicant can link the persecution specifically to the state, the Convention will not apply.

The individualised nature of the Convention definition is highlighted by paragraphs 164–6 of the UNHCR Handbook[82] which make it clear that the Convention does not apply to persons affected by general armed conflict.

---

[80] Lord Steyn and Lord Hutton also found they were 'members of a particular social group' because of other more narrowly defined characteristics such as being suspected of adultery.

[81] Hathaway, above n 12, p 186.

[82] UNHCR Handbook, above n 42.

However, paragraph 165 envisages situations where some such individuals might be able to demonstrate a well-founded fear of persecution within the context of a conflict. Paragraph 166 suggests that protection may not be available if there are no diplomatic ties between the applicant's host country and his country of origin. But it does not exclude the possibility, stating that 'every case has to be judged on its merits'.

The courts have developed a number of approaches for determining when an individual caught up in generalised violence is entitled to protection under the Refugees Convention. One such test to make the causal link is the *differential test* which requires victims of war and conflict to show that they are subject to differential victimisation based on civil or political status. The differential impact principle was formulated by Lord Lloyd in *Adan v Secretary of State for the Home Department.*[83] Lord Lloyd in that case said this required an applicant to 'be able to show fear of persecution for Convention reasons over and above the ordinary risks of clan warfare'.[84] In formulating that principle, Lord Lloyd appeared to be influenced by the argument that when a claim arises from a civil war situation, participants on both sides of the civil war would be entitled to protection unless that principle were adopted. Lord Lloyd concluded that this was not what was intended by the words 'persecution' under the Convention. That approach starts from the premise that such persons are prima facie not refugees. It requires them to demonstrate that their well-founded fear arises from their civil or political status rather than from persecution as such.

In his book, Goodwin-Gill discusses this issue in the context of the meaning of persecution. He stresses that fear of persecution and lack of protection are interrelated.[85] Goodwin-Gill discusses the difficulties of establishing refugee status for victims of civil war, but does not exclude the possibility.[86] He is critical of the Hathaway discussion which is directed at state responsibility, and emphasises that no necessary linkage between persecution and government authority is required by the Convention definition. Goodwin-Gill's view accords with the guidelines formulated by the Canadian Immigration and Refugee Board (IRB).

---

[83] [1999] 1 AC 293.

[84] Id, p 311.

[85] Goodwin-Gill, above n 37, p 67.

[86] Id, pp 72–6.

The Canadian IRB guidelines[87] begin from the general premise that there is nothing in the Refugees Convention definition which excludes its application to such persons. The guidelines reject the differential test and opt for a 'non-comparative approach' which concentrates upon the claimant's fear of persecution. They suggest that it must be asked whether the claimant's risk is of sufficient serious harm and linked to a Convention reason as opposed to general indiscriminate consequences. They require the claimant to demonstrate that he/she was targeted personally or collectively.

Where There is No State ... *Minister for Immigration v Ibrahim*

The decision of the High Court of Australia in October 2000 in *Minister for Immigration v Ibrahim*[88] concerned a person caught up in the violence of civil or clan warfare in Somalia, where there is no, or no effective, state protection. It thus involved one of those situations at the far end of the spectrum, that is where no state authorities exist. In *Ibrahim* the High Court decided by a narrow majority of four judges to three that the applicant was not entitled to refugee status. Interestingly, the majority reasoning as represented by the judgment of Gummow J, described refugee rights in terms of the responsibility of the receiving state at both the international and national levels. Statements in his judgment are consistent with an accountability theory. Although the differential impact test (discussed above), and motivation were rejected as relevant aspects of the refugee definition, the majority reasoning appears to preclude the possibility that persons who are caught up in the violence of civil war or internal conflict, where there is no, or no effective, state protection, can establish that they are refugees within the meaning of the Convention. The majority view is consistent with requiring a nexus between persecution and the state. By contrast McHugh J and the other dissenting judges focused on the link between persecution and lack of protection, and the need for protection. That is, they concentrated upon the reasonableness of the 'well-founded fear' of persecution.

Mr Ibrahim was born in Somalia in 1960 and was a member of a sub-clan of the Rahanwein clan. Until 1991 Somalia was controlled by a

---

[87] IRB Guidelines, 'Civilian Non-Combatants Fearing Persecution in Civil War Situations' (Ottawa, IRB, 1996), http://www.irb.gc.ca/legal/guideline/civilian/index_e.stm.

[88] (2000) 204 CLR 1.

dictator of the rival Darod clan. After his overthrow in 1991 civil unrest broke out between rival clans and sub-clans who formed militia groups. Since that time no central government has existed in Somalia. According to a 1996 document cited by Gummow J, 300 000 persons have been killed in Somalia since 1991 and the lives of another 1.5 million are at risk.[89]

Mr Ibrahim claimed that his house was destroyed by the militia of a sub-clan of the Darod clan which controlled the city in which he lived in June 1991. He escaped with his family, but was captured and imprisoned by a sub-clan of the Darod clan. He claimed that his wife was raped and he was forced to labour in the fields. He escaped from that situation in April 1992, and after leaving his family with relatives, he left Somalia in 1995. In 1997 he made his way to Australia by air via Thailand.

Mr Ibrahim claimed refugee status for his membership of a particular social group, namely his membership of the clan or sub-clan. His claim was rejected by the RRT on the basis that his fear of persecution arose from struggles for land and power arising from clan warfare, and not because of his 'membership of a particular social group'. The tribunal described the situation in Somalia as one of 'instability and anarchy' and concluded that Mr Ibrahim was not subject to a 'differential impact which is over and above the ordinary risks of clan warfare'. In reaching this conclusion, the tribunal applied the differential impact principle formulated by Lord Lloyd in *Adan*.[90]

The tribunal also applied a test of 'systematic persecution' as a requirement to establish the persecution which qualifies for protection under the Convention. The tribunal referred to the need to show a nexus or link between the persecution and the membership of a particular social group. It said 'unsystematic warfare without more is not *persecution*', and that fighting aimed at establishing control over land or resources 'would generally not be persecution *for reasons of membership of a particular social group*'.[91] The test of 'systematic persecution' appears to have been used in the sense of organised persecution which comes from an established authority base. That is, it resonates with the accountability theory. The proposition that the cause of the persecution related to

---

[89] Id, para [113].

[90] Above n 83, p 311.

[91] (1999) 94 FCR 259 at 263. (Emphasis in original.)

squabbles over resources suggests that the tribunal characterised Mr Ibrahim's troubles as 'private'.

Mr Ibrahim's application for judicial review in the Federal Court was unsuccessful at first instance. However on appeal, the Full Court of the Federal Court held that the tribunal had erred in law. In the High Court, it was decided by a narrow majority of four to three to restore the decision of the Federal Court at first instance.

The Full Court of the Federal Court concluded that the tribunal had erred.[92] It said the tribunal had applied the wrong test of persecution by requiring 'systematic persecution' in the sense of 'habitual behaviour according to a system, regular or methodical'.[93] They accepted however that it was correct to refer to 'systematic' in the sense of 'deliberate or premeditated or intended'[94] conduct, but they said this was not what the tribunal had done.

In the High Court the leading judgment in the majority was that of Gummow J who with the other three judges in the majority, held that the tribunal decision did not contain any errors of law. In particular, Gummow J found that the tribunal had not applied the test of 'systematic persecution' inflexibly, by excluding the possibility that a single act of persecution would suffice. While agreeing with the minority that the *Adan* differential impact 'principle' contained a 'flawed hypothesis', Gummow J thought that it had not 'distracted' the tribunal from its task, and neither had it over-stressed the 'civil war' context which he thought was an equally 'distracting' category.[95]

The important aspect of the High Court reasoning for present purposes is the discussion about persecution and state responsibility. Gummow J specifically posed the question of whether the Refugees Convention is premised upon state responsibility and whether the refugee definition was to be understood in that light. By this he meant the orthodox accountability theory because he said that if this was the case 'Somali' cases do not fit the definition because of the absence of a state.[96]

---

[92] A second reason given by the Full Court was that the RRT had failed to enquire about the motivation of the persecutors.

[93] (1999) 94 FCR 259 at 266.

[94] Ibid.

[95] (2000) 204 CLR 1 at 50–3, para [144]–[150].

[96] Id, p 44, para [132].

In his discussion of 'state responsibility', Gummow J described the Refugees Convention as an agreement between contracting states which does not confer individual general rights. He emphasised the domestic legislative context as the source of rights.[97] He said that Article 14 of the Universal Declaration on Human Rights (UDHR) (the right to seek asylum) does not confer any guarantee or individual right.[98] On that basis, he said that, 'the right of asylum is a right of States, not of the individual'.[99] In contrast to the views of Fortin discussed above, who stresses that the right to and obligation to grant asylum arises in international law from an individual's presence in a territory, Gummow J found an equivalent proposition in international customary law of the domestic law right to regulate the admission of aliens. He also discussed the circumstances in which the asylum state could expel or extradite aliens. Thus Gummow J largely viewed the Convention from the perspective of the rights of the receiving state, rather than from the need of individuals seeking protection or asylum in international law. When dealing with the rights of individuals he applied the traditional theory that international law instruments do not confer rights without express municipal incorporation.

Although Gummow J did not think the two theories, namely accountability and protection as described in *Adan* were in opposition, other statements in his judgment suggest that his views are more consistent with an accountability approach which requires a nexus between the state and the persecution. For example, Gummow J emphasised the 'limited' scope of the Convention by referring to fact that it does not apply to persons fleeing generalised violence. He summarised his views as follows:

> The Convention was adopted against a particular background of customary international law concerning the consequences of *delinquency in the exercise of State responsibility for the welfare of its nationals* and the acceptance by asylum states of responsibilities under their *municipal* laws towards those they accepted as refugees.[100]

---

[97] Id, p 34, para [107], referring to the Migration Act 1958 (Cth), sections 36 and 65. Similar views were expressed by Callinan J at para [209].

[98] Id, p 46, para [138].

[99] Id, p 45, para [137].

[100] Id, p 50, para [143]. (Emphasis added.)

Gummow J returned again to the theme of state responsibility at the end of his judgment when he referred to customary international law and the duty of a state to protect its nationals:

> The protection spoken of in the Convention definition is not that of a 'country' in an abstracted sense, divorced from the notion of a government with administrative organs.[101]

This evidences his opinion that the Refugees Convention does not apply where there is no effective state. This is contrary to Kalin's view of the international law position, namely that the state continues to exist in the absence of effective organs.

Other statements in Gummow J's judgment suggest that he regarded the Refugees Convention as a 'limited' document, other than in the sense he spoke of as set out above, that is, as an agreement between contracting states. He referred for example, to the fact that it provides neither comprehensive nor humanitarian based assistance. He also referred to the manifest lack of agreement amongst states of its interpretation [implying perhaps that states are free to interpret it as they see fit].[102] Overall, he limited the Convention to the extent to which it is incorporated into Australian law, rather than interpreting it as an instrument of human rights protection.

When Gummow J's view about state responsibility is added to the non-disapproval of the tribunal's 'systematic persecution' approach, we can see further support for a state centred accountability approach. It is also important that his conclusion on this point conflicts with a line of Federal Court decisions beginning with *Abdalla v MIMA*,[103] in which this 'systematic persecution' approach was rejected and the claims of the applicants were accepted on the basis of an individual investigation into their claims of persecution. This line of cases largely involves persons caught up in civil war situations in Somalia and Sri Lanka. *Abdalla* was followed in *Anjum v Minister for Immigration and Ethnic Affairs (MIEA)*,[104] and *MIMA v Abdi*.[105] In *Ibrahim* Gummow J expressly declined to follow *Abdi*.[106]

---

[101] Id, p 54, para [153].

[102] Id, p 49, para [140].

[103] (1998) 51 ALD 11.

[104] (1998) 52 ALD 225.

The three dissenting judgments contain slightly different reasons. Both McHugh and Gaudron JJ thought the Full Court was correct to say that the Tribunal was in error, but for different reasons. Kirby J however accepted the Full Court's reasoning as correct, in particular its rejection of the RRT's application of the 'systematic persecution' approach.[107]

Gaudron J said that persecution is not confined to conduct authorised by a state or condoned by it, although she acknowledged that this was the usual context.[108] This case, she said, involved the 'challenge of the unfamiliar'. Gaudron J said that as a matter of 'ordinary usage' persecution includes sustained 'discriminatory conduct' against individuals or a group who 'as a matter of fact, are unable to protect themselves by resort to law or by other means'. Together with McHugh J in the minority, Gaudron J stressed that the rationale of the Convention is to prevent unjustifiable and discriminatory conduct, which McHugh J also described as conduct which interferes with the basic human rights or the dignity of a person. They emphasised the link between persecution and protection, and the reasonableness of the 'well-founded fear' of persecution.

McHugh J said that the object of Convention is to provide refuge for those who have lost de jure or de facto protection.[109] He thought that protection needs arise where the country of nationality authorises or does not stop the persecution.[110] Where there is no state, he said, 'persecution' will fall within the definition just as if an existing government had failed to protect the victim. He saw no reason for reading down the definition in these circumstances.[111]

The contrast between the majority and the minority views in this case demonstrates that starting points in judicial reasoning are important. The majority view as represented by Gummow J corresponds to a 'state

---

[105] (1999) 53 ALD 558.

[106] (2000) 204 CLR 1 at para [147].

[107] Note that McHugh J thought that the Full Court's view of 'systematic persecution' was correct but he interpreted it to be consistent with his approach in the earlier decision in *Chan Yee Kin v MIEA* (1989) 169 CLR 379 in which he had formulated the approach. Gaudron J thought that 'systematic persecution' was not a relevant concept.

[108] (2000) 204 CLR 1 at 7, para [17].

[109] Id, p 22, para [68].

[110] Id, p 21, para [65].

[111] Id, p 22, para [68].

centred' accountability approach as it emphasises the responsibility of the 'delinquent' home state. Gummow J's overall view was that absent a state, the Convention has no application. Gummow J concentrated upon the rights of the receiving state in national law, rather than upon the need for protection under international law. By contrast, the minority view emphasises the link between persecution and protection, rather than a link with the state.

Persecution Condoned or Tolerated by the State ... *Minister for Immigration v Khawar*

On 11 April 2002 the High Court handed down the decision in *Khawar*,[112] in which it held that a married woman from Pakistan who claimed that she was the victim of serious and prolonged abuse by her husband, and that the police in Pakistan refused to enforce the law against such violence or otherwise offer her protection, could arguably satisfy the test for a refugee within the meaning of Article 1A(2) of the 1951 Convention. The significance of this decision for the present discussion is the contrast with the reasoning in *Ibrahim*. In particular in *Khawar* there is a joint judgment of McHugh and Gummow JJ who held opposing views in *Ibrahim*. Importantly, in their judgment in *Khawar* they reject the surrogacy/internal protection view, which I have argued is tied to a state centred approach.

This decision resulted from an appeal by the Minister from a decision of the Full Court of the Federal Court,[113] which was in turn an appeal by the Minister against a decision of a single judge of the Federal Court[114] overturning a decision of the RRT rejecting Mrs Khawar's application for a protection visa.[115] Mrs Khawar gave evidence before the RRT of four occasions on which she approached the police, alone or together with a male relative, to complain of violence by her husband. She said that the police response on each occasion was one of indifference and refusal to help. Mrs Khawar's solicitor also filed a submission about the general

---

[112] (2002) 67 ALD 577.

[113] *MIMA v Khawar* (2001) 61 ALD 321.

[114] (2000) 59 ALD 668 (Branson J).

[115] Technically it was an appeal to the RRT under the Migration Act 1958 (Cth), section 411, against a decision of a delegate of the Minister rejecting her primary application for a protection visa under section 36.

position of women in Pakistani society, detailing widespread and institutionalised discrimination that is partly tolerated and partly sanctioned by the state. The RRT however said that the acts directed at Mrs Khawar were motivated by purely personal considerations related to the circumstances of her marriage, the fact that she brought no dowry with her marriage, and the personal disapproval of her in-laws of the marriage. The RRT as Kirby J stressed in his judgment in the High Court made no findings about the substantial material produced by Mrs Khawar. In particular, the RRT did not address the issue of whether she was a 'member of a particular social group'. The High Court remitted the case to the RRT.

The Minister for Immigration argued that persecution and protection are distinct concepts, and that the absence of state protection did not convert private harm to persecution. That, as McHugh and Gummow JJ observed, was an argument for the accountability theory. It was an argument based on the *Horvath* decision in which the House of Lords said that 'persecution' must involve some state failure of protection.

There were three majority judgments. Apart from the joint judgment of McHugh and Gummow JJ, Gleeson CJ and Kirby J gave separate reasons.[116] There are interesting contrasts in their reasoning which illustrate the arguments made in this chapter.

Gleeson CJ who delivered the first judgment discussed the concept of protection, and the two senses of 'broader' (internal) and 'narrower' (diplomatic) protection. Although he thought that both views were intended in the Refugees Convention, he referred to *Horvath* with approval.[117] He appeared to accept the Kalin view that there is a link between persecution and the role of the state, which there was on the facts of this case. He described Mrs Khawar's situation as one where the persecution was condoned or tolerated by the state.[118] He also described the persecution as 'systematic discrimination' against women.[119] He accepted that the persecution could be inflicted by the combined effect of the conduct of two or more agents, as on the facts of this case where there was a non-state agent and the state. Thus although he did not apply the unsubtle

---

[116] Callinan J dissented.

[117] (2002) 67 ALD 577 at 582, [21]. Note that he cited the views of Kalin, above n 4, and Fortin, above n 4.

[118] Id, p 584, para [26] and p 585, para [31].

[119] Id, p 583, para [25] and p 584, para [26].

'complicity' theory,[120] or accept the Minister's argument, he thought that in the circumstances the state had a duty to act to protect Mrs Khawar. Later in his judgment when discussing whether Mrs Khawar was a 'member of a particular social group', he rejected the argument that the potentially large size of the class in Pakistan (abused women whose abuse is tolerated or condoned by the state) was an obstacle: 'It is power, not number, that creates the conditions in which persecution might occur.'[121]

This last statement could be read as introducing the public-private rubric into this context. On a positive note however it is significant that Gleeson CJ rejected an argument about cultural relativism.[122] He thus implicitly accepted the universality of women's rights as human rights. I would argue that overall Gleeson CJ's reasoning displays a 'state centred' stance, which is particularly evidenced by his approval of the *Horvath* decision. It is also illustrated by his reliance upon the idea of state responsibility.[123]

By contrast McHugh and Gummow JJ accepted the argument that the Refugees Convention is intended for diplomatic/external protection and thought that the surrogacy/internal protection view accepted in *Horvath* was 'apt to mislead and to distort'.[124] In an important passage they emphasised the need to establish a 'well-founded fear' of persecution in the refugee definition.[125] This they explained was the reason for accepting the external protection construction.[126] Thus they seemed to accept that the relevance of internal protection was limited to the reasonableness of the 'well-founded fear' of persecution. This reasoning embodies a construction of the Refugees Convention which supports a protection approach to the second element of the refugee definition, namely the words 'is outside the country of his nationality and is unable or unwilling to avail himself of the protection of that country'. It involves a rejection of the Minister's

---

[120] Which had been applied by the dissenting judge in the Full Federal Court decision, adopting the reasoning of Weinberg J in *Ndege*, above n 62.

[121] (2002) 67 ALD 577 at 585, para [33].

[122] Id, p 584, para [26].

[123] This concept is rejected by Fortin, above n 4.

[124] (2002) 67 ALD 577 at 592, para [68].

[125] Id, p 591, para [61].

[126] (2002) 67 ALD 577 at 594, para [73] referring to a publication by the UNHCR cited at 593–4, para [72].

argument that persecution and protection are distinct concepts, and that the absence of state protection does not convert private harm to persecution.

On the question of whether the acts amounted to persecution, their reasoning needs to be read in light of the facts – it was a case of state tolerated or condoned legislation. Their reasoning on this point, which goes to the first element of the definition, the nexus requirement, is more equivocal. McHugh and Gummow JJ described the treatment of Mrs Khawar as '*selective* or discriminatory' persecution. They distinguished the facts from previous decisions which they described as persecution arising from the enforcement of laws,[127] on the basis that *Khawar* involved a *failure* to enforce the laws.[128] They stressed that persecution requires that a person is singled out for one of the five Convention reasons, as distinct for example from a failure to enforce the laws due to lack of resources.[129] They referred to the discriminatory activity of the state in not responding to the violence of non-state actors in this case.[130] Thus they did not adopt the 'systematic discrimination' approach of Gleeson CJ, which looks for organised, authority-based acts of persecution. If their reasoning on this point is read with their emphasis on establishing a 'well-founded fear' of persecution, a sharp contrast with Gleeson CJ's reasoning is clear.

The McHugh and Gummow JJ judgment represents a significant modification on the part of Gummow J of the views he had expressed in *Ibrahim* which, I argue, supported an accountability approach. It is also important that McHugh and Gummow JJ expressed the view that the Convention imposes a limitation upon the absolute right of member states to admit whom they choose.[131] This suggests, in contrast to Gummow J's views in *Ibrahim*, that they looked at the position of the receiving (asylum) state with international law in mind. McHugh and Gummow JJ also stressed that the refugee definition must be read with the whole Convention, although it is only incorporated into national law in a limited way. In *Khawar* McHugh and Gummow JJ are very aware of the different impact of international and national law. They also clearly distinguish the

---

[127] For example, *Chen Shi Hai*, above n 61, which involved the application of China's one-child policy.

[128] (2002) 67 ALD 577 at 595, para [77].

[129] Id, p 597, para [84].

[130] Id, p 597, para [87].

[131] Id, p 592, para [68].

reasons for the lack of protection and the granting of asylum by the receiving state.

In the third judgment, Kirby J relied upon *Ward* and *Shah and Islam*, and accepted that the Minister's argument was contrary to international jurisprudence. He emphasised that on the facts the nexus requirement could be satisfied by the failure of state protection.[132] That is, Kirby J reminds us that this case is about tolerated or condoned activity, where the state is constructively implicated in the acts of persecution. It is not one of the 'hard' cases like *Ibrahim* where no state existed. Nevertheless, the contrast between Gleeson CJ's views and those of McHugh and Gummow JJ in this case, and the comparison between Gummow J's views in the two cases, illustrates the argument in this chapter.

Conclusion: The Way Forward

In this chapter I have demonstrated that a state centred refugee law accountability approach in applying the Refugee Convention definition means that the nexus requirement will be read as involving a link between the state and the persecution. Such an approach is supported by the internal 'surrogacy' concept. A 'protection' approach by contrast focuses upon the reasonableness of the 'well-founded fear' of persecution, or, as Gaudron and McHugh JJ in *Ibrahim* emphasised, upon the link between persecution and protection. The difference in result which arises from these two contrasting approaches can be seen by comparing the outcomes of *Ibrahim* and *Horvath* for example, with that of *Khawar*,[133] and by analysis of the minority and majority judgments in those cases. I have also demonstrated that in dealing with these issues, the courts conflate important distinctions, such as the reasons for the lack of protection and the granting of asylum under international and national law.

So now it is time to respond directly to the question I posed at the outset, namely, whether the concept of a refugee enshrined in the 1951 Refugees Convention is tied to a model of a state that is appropriate for refugee protection in the 21st century? The answer to that question is yes if a protection approach is accepted and no if a state centred accountability approach is applied. The latter, which relies upon an internal surrogate

---

[132] Id, p 608, para [126].

[133] The analysis of McHugh and Gummow JJ.

protection principle, is contrary to the international law view of asylum as a neutral concept. As Kalin points out asylum is granted by the receiving state as an aspect of territorial sovereignty, and the obligation to protect those within a sovereign territory. An accountability approach also conflicts with the principle of external or diplomatic protection as McHugh and Gummow JJ recognised in *Khawar*. Whereas an accountability approach fits with a model of a strong sovereign state, the protection theory does not depend upon such a basis. Although I would argue that the protection theory does not need a state, arguably it is consonant with the modern reality of the state.

A model of state centred refugee law is consistent with a traditional liberal model of international law, as comprising agreements between consenting states. Such a model does not reconcile readily with the reality of international law mechanisms. For example, it does not acknowledge the rights of individuals under international law.[134] It does not acknowledge the role of non-governmental actors in formulating international law standards.[135] The traditional international law model of consenting states arguably concentrates on the formal aspect, on the sovereign rights of states to enter into treaties and to exclude aliens, rather than on the practical reality of how standards are formulated and who is included in that process. It is difficult to reconcile with the process of globalisation and the ideal of universal human rights.

The significance of this discussion is that it illustrates that in refugee law the state represents a paradox.[136] Under a traditional international law regime the state is both the source of the problem (through the concept of state sovereignty) and the solution (through the doctrine of consensus and burden sharing arrangements). As Hathaway says, this traditional picture enables states who hold dominant positions in the international system to continue to pursue their interests in a global context.[137]

---

[134] G J Simpson, 'Imagined Consent: Democratic Liberalism in International Legal Theory', *Australian Year Book of International Law* 15 (1994) p 103.

[135] C Schreuer, 'The Waning of the Sovereign State: Towards a New Paradigm for International Law', *European Journal of International Law* 4 (1993) p 447.

[136] D Warner, 'The Refugee State and Refugee Protection' in F Nicholson and P Twomey (eds), *Refugee Rights and Realities* (Cambridge, Cambridge University Press) 1999.

[137] J Hathaway, 'A Reconsideration of the Underlying Premise of Refugee Law', *Harvard International Law Journal* 31 (1990) 129.

This conclusion has implications for the way ahead. If the state is a hindrance to recognising new categories of refugees as persons requiring protection against persecution, such as in *Ibrahim*, can we move beyond the state in seeking solutions? For example, should the mandate of the UNHCR be enlarged? Should another international body be created and charged with supervision of the internal standards applied by states?[138] In that case the consensus needed to achieve that solution should include the views of refugee organisations and refugees themselves. Or can we persuade states to think about the refugee problem in different terms? It has been suggested by several writers that the self-interest of states be appealed to: that states should recognise that a solution to the refugee problem is in their own interest, which interest coincides with international stability.[139] It has been pointed out that in any event it is only the most determined asylum seekers, skilled at representing their interests, who slip through the procedural nets created by states. In that case, there is an argument that the self interest of the individual and the state coincides.

In the meantime, as the decisions in *Ibrahim* and *Khawar* illustrate, it is important to recognise the tension that exists between the accountability and the protection approaches and to attempt to ensure that the latter is not overshadowed.

---

[138] Aleinikoff, above n 1.

[139] For example, H Adelman, 'Refugee or Asylum: A Philosophical Perspective', *Journal of Refugee Studies* 1 (1988) p 7; A Shacknove, 'From Asylum to Containment' *International Journal of Refugee Law* 5 (1993) p 516.

12 Global Solutions

LIZ CURRAN

Introduction

It is always easy to find the problems in the operation of a system but thought and considerable energy are needed to work towards finding solutions. When the problem is a global one, finding solutions is even more complex. As Crock highlights, the practical operations of the Refugees Convention often 'fly in the face of politically sacrosanct notions of sovereignty and prerogative power'.[1] Adrienne Millbank, whose paper informed many of the chapters produced by the workshop, argues that the Convention's failure to take into account states' needs is a serious problem. Millbank observes that responses of states are shaped by the domestic political environment and not by international treaties.[2] Such a view is reflected in many of the examples of human rights violations cited by the contributors to this book. It is a salutary reminder that the commitment of states to human rights protection is often conditional. It highlights the issues that can jeopardise adherence to the Refugees Convention.

The resounding view of the majority of contributors to this book is that the arguments in favour of the Convention are as compelling today as they were 50 years ago and that an international mechanism for the protection of refugees remains essential. At the Global Consultations of the Ministerial Meeting of States Parties to the 1951 Convention and/or its 1967 Protocol Relating to the Status of Refugees (Global Consultations) which was the first ministerial meeting of state parties to the Convention commencing on 12 December 2001 and which involved 80 ministers, the delegates affirmed continued support for the Convention. They stated it had 'served its role

---

[1] M Crock, 'The Refugees Convention at 50: Mid-life Crisis or Terminal Inadequacy? An Australian Perspective', chapter 3 in this book.

[2] A Millbank, *The Problem with the 1951 Convention* (Canberra, Department of the Parliamentary Library, Research Paper 5 2000–01), http://www.aph.gov.au/library/pubs/rp/2000-01/01RP05.htm, p 12.

well' and had 'continued relevance'.[3] This was despite some nations, such as the United Kingdom and Australia, arguing that the Convention was outmoded.

The global problem of refugees and displaced people requires humanitarian solutions which are flexible, able to take into account a range of considerations and capable of adapting to the complexities of a situation. This chapter will seek to outline a number of possible global solutions. It is hoped that these will provide ideas and suggest innovations that enhance discussion and debate and ensure that responses can be refined, fairer and overcome many of the difficulties articulated in the chapters of this book.

I would like to emphasise the new context in which this debate takes place. The Global Consultations were held in the wake of the terrorist attacks on 11 September 2001. At them the delegates recognised that caution should be exercised to ensure that state obligations to provide protection to refugees not be sacrificed in this context.[4] Such caution is timely in view of the devastation which can be left through bombing, landmines and action based on fear rather than reason and evidence. Civil unrest in Israel, Palestine, and Afghanistan and mooted extensions of the response against terrorism in Iraq, Somalia, North Korea and beyond are likely to lead to even higher levels of displacement of people, and thought should go into the likely long term after effects of such actions.

At the workshop in June 2001 from which the chapters for this book are derived, Paris Aristotle, the Chairperson of the Foundation for the Survivors of Torture, stressed the critical importance of full and responsible debate as a component of civil society. He noted that debate should be founded upon facts and understanding rather than upon paranoia, disinformation and the taking advantage of people's fear of 'other' through the demonising of people seeking refuge. It is my view that until some of the hysteria and fear of 'other' can be dispelled very little progress will be made in ensuring adequate protection is offered to those most in need. In addition, until nation states respect and adhere to human rights benchmarks, they will have little success in controlling their borders.

Aristotle observed that in Australia for instance, the richness of its people derives from a long history of different nationalities, many of them

---

[3]   Ministerial Meeting of States Parties to the 1951 Convention and/or its 1967 Protocol Relating to the Status of Refugees, *Global Consultations on International Protection*, (Geneva, UNHCR, 12 December 2001), pp 1–2 (Global Consultations).

[4]   Id, p 4.

initially refugees, arriving on our shores. He states that it is easy to forget that what is occurring today, as people flee from human rights abuse, is nothing different from previous decades. It commenced when the first boat people came to Australia from England followed by the Irish, Jewish people, Eastern Europeans, Indo-Chinese, Vietnamese, Former Yugoslavians, Chinese and the recent arrivals from Afghanistan and Iraq, all seeking to escape persecutory regimes. This has all occurred both before and since the foundation of the Convention half a century ago. Sadly, as Aristotle observes, memories can be short and one ethnic group can find itself so easily pitted against another, although they have a common past experience of persecution. The Australian situation is not unique as recent experiences in North America and Europe indicate.

Western nations have the resources and economic wealth to assist countries struggling under the burden of mass refugee influx, poverty and potential upheaval. There is consensus among the contributors to this book that citizens need to be better informed, in order to understand the links between world conflict and refugee movement towards domestic borders. This is needed to balance the more limited attention to sovereignty issues, which gives rise to policy-making in a vacuum. Australia, as part architect of many Conventions and the United Nations Declaration on Human Rights has an important leadership role to play both in the domestic and world stage. But as the *Tampa* incident discussed in the introduction[5] demonstrated, the nature of that leadership is questionable.

The *Tampa* incident also pointed to another associated issue or problem which some of the contributors to this book noted. This is the fact that the Convention lacks a central body for effective independent oversight and interpretation, to hold nation states to account when they do not abide by Convention requirements. The Australian government clearly agreed with Millbank's questionable view that the Convention confers no rights on refugees unless and until they reach a signatory country and are admitted.[6] The current context points to the gap between the Convention and its implementation by sovereign states. It suggests the need to oversee its implementation if the states do not themselves adhere to its standards.

---

[5]   L Curran and S Kneebone, 'Overview', chapter 1 in this book.

[6]   Millbank, above n 2, p 3. It is arguably a breach of Executive Committee of the High Commissioner's Programme (Ex Com) Conclusion 8, 'Determination of Refugee Status', 12 October 1977, http://www.unhcr.ch, not to provide processing facilities.

With those preliminary comments in mind I now turn to discuss some potential solutions.

Research to Inform Policy-making

First, I would suggest that there is room for more active and inclusive discussion to occur not just between the key decision makers (states and governments) and their own bureaucracies or supporters, but also with non-governmental organisations (NGOs) such as the Red Cross, Care International, the United Nations High Commissioner for Refugees (UNHCR) and academics, who can provide some reflective and qualitative research to better inform policy making and practice. There is a critical need for more research, information and analysis on the causes and ramifications of international movements.[7]

Further, many of the issues raised in this book require further exploration, research and follow-up. For instance, Taylor highlights the need to track the consequences of removal for asylum seekers.[8] What happens to the asylum seekers when 'safe third country' provisions are activated? Does the 'safe third country' resettle them? How safe are they? Such considerations would become a valuable tool in measuring whether countries are meeting the non-refoulement requirements in Article 33 of the Convention.

Also, why and to what extent do people roam stateless? What measures can be put in place to reduce such displacement and what obligations or standards could be enacted to ensure nation states are less inclined to expel and mistreat minorities? Do the asylum seekers face or experience persecution upon their return to their nation state particularly where a nation that they received temporary protection in has determined it is safe for them to return? Are they discriminated against? Are there fatalities? Currently, many of these questions are not answered.[9]

---

[7] Global Consultations, Chairperson's Report on Roundtable 3, *Upholding Refugee Protection in the Face of Contemporary Challenges Involving Mixed Flows* (Geneva, UNHCR, 2001), p 1.

[8] S Taylor, 'The Human Rights of Rejected Asylum Seekers Being Removed from Australia', chapter 8 in this book.

[9] 'Australia denies blame for asylum seeker's death', *The Age*, 10 October 2002, p 3.

Global Solutions

Public Participation in the Debates

The public needs to be better informed about the causal links between the flight of people and world events, about the terrible effects of flight upon individuals and populations, and the reasons behind the arrival of refugees on domestic shores. According to the report of the Chairperson of the Global Consultations, enlightened leadership, along with a recognition by leaders that they must uphold the basic values underpinning the Convention, is needed.[10] Gibney notes in his chapter, that it was when people were better informed during the Kosovo crisis, that the public were more supportive of policies designed to help these people.[11]

To accommodate discussion and exchange, forums need to be established where frank discussion can occur. There is a need for internal dialogue and transparency within the domestic sphere as a basis of, and to inform, international dialogue. At the workshop, Piper and Gonzaga stated that it is imperative that NGOs and academics are actively involved in these dialogues, so that the human rights framework which underpins the 1951 Convention is not marginalised or forgotten.

Australia and other nations, as international citizens, should also consider the impact of their own policies upon the policy-formation of other nations, where the latter struggle with their human rights obligations due to resource constraints and limited international support. In addition to the focus on the meetings of world ministers, the resolutions of meetings of the Executive Committee of the High Commissioner's Programme (Ex Com) should not be seen as an outcomes but rather as part of an ongoing process encouraging the formulation of ideas. These involve two weeks of meetings and a much broader range of ideas could be encouraged and developed. The actual engagement of refugees or former refugees in the process both before and at Ex Com would provide some insight for those people who make policy decisions which affect these people and others like them.

Rodger Haines QC, a commentator from New Zealand at the workshop, observed that there is immense value in involving NGOs in discussions and

---

[10] Chairperson's Report on Roundtable 3, above n 7, p 3.

[11] M Gibney, 'The State of Asylum: Democratisation, Judicialisation and Evolution of Refugee Policy', chapter 2 in this book.

dialogue in a collaborative way, to enhance the development and relevance of policy. As it is often NGOs who are dealing directly with the very people that the Convention is designed to assist, much can be gained from including them in discussions. Concern was raised by some of the workshop participants in question sessions about the manner in which many NGOs are sidelined. It was noted that the lessons from the experience of both NGOs and asylum seekers can ensure that policies are humane and relevant.

These suggestions are echoed by Gibney who highlights the need for a multilayered approach to ensure greater responsiveness involving improved public awareness and the development of a human rights culture.[12] He argues this development should be reflected in political life. Only then can governments respond to the electorate with policies that are more inclusive. Gibney suggests the need for the reordering of citizen preferences by increasing the awareness of why there is a movement of people around the world. He argues for a greater voice and hearing by political elites of the experiences of these people and the connection of their circumstances to the world situation and not just domestic effects.

Neville J Roach, the former Chairman of the Council for Multicultural Australia, who recently resigned from this post as a result of personal concerns over the Australian government's handling of asylum seeker issues, has made a number of similar observations.[13] In particular, Roach called for more responsibility in public commentary on asylum seekers when that commentary is designed to create hysteria, fear and negative perceptions. Like Crock,[14] he suggested that playing to 'protectionist and racist elements' in the community should be resisted and that the international flight of people should be acknowledged as a worldwide phenomenon. At the Global Consultations delegates noted that national campaigns against racism and xenophobia are required.[15] Roach also called on the media to be more responsible particularly where sensationalism puts national cohesion at risk.

---

[12] Gibney, above n 11.

[13] 'Show Mercy', *The Bulletin*, 12 February 2002, pp 31–2.

[14] Crock, above n 1.

[15] Global Consultations, above n 3, para 23.

Accountability Issues and Mechanisms

Independent Oversight

Many of the contributors to this book have highlighted the lack of independent oversight and a lack of enforcement of the key requirements of the Convention and other human rights instruments which pertain to persecuted and displaced people. There is arguably a need for independent mechanisms to ascertain whether the processes for seeking refuge and ongoing protection comply with the Convention and its aims. Some further ideas about the possibility for independent oversight will be discussed later in this chapter.

The legality of processes upon arrival, which lead to persons being 'screened out' without adequate processing, was raised by Crock.[16] The measures and processes adopted by states at the entry stage need to be scrutinised by an independent body to determine whether they accord with human rights standards. This proposal is likely to provoke considerable controversy. However, unless some level of consistency and objective oversight and benchmarking occurs then political motivations will often hinder the adherence to the Convention's raison d'etre, that is the protection of persons who have a well founded fear of persecution. As I have pointed out elsewhere,[17] the fact of whether a person arrives by boat, by air, with or without a valid visa, can lead to disparities and discrimination in the processing at the point of entry.

Mode of Removal

In her chapter, Taylor highlights that the mode of removal of asylum seekers also needs consideration.[18] She questions the legal capacity of the Commonwealth of Australia to detain persons who are outside its jurisdiction. What measures are adopted in the process of removal to ensure that human rights are observed, both during and after removal, and what is

---

[16] Crock, above n 14.

[17] L Curran 'Hordes or Human Beings? – A Discussion of some of the Problems Surrounding Australia's response to Asylum Seekers and Possible Solutions to those Problems', Discussion Paper Number 8, Catholic Commission for Justice Development and Peace, Melbourne Archdiocese, March 2000, p 22.

[18] Taylor, above n 8.

the legal liability of services that are contracted to carry out removal? For instance can they medicate to ensure compliance?

Regional Protection

The need for a regional protection mechanism in the Asia-Pacific region was raised at the workshop. Already in Europe the European Union (EU) and the European Court exist. These require member states to have minimum human rights mechanisms which are enforceable. The Asia-Pacific region has been slow to discuss or develop such mechanisms. Efforts so far with Indonesia and Thailand have tended to have a narrow focus on the prevention of people smugglers. An Asia-Pacific regional mechanism is needed which, in an humanitarian context, can examine better methods of burden sharing which could be supported by the international community.

The UNHCR

The role of the UNHCR is another focus for change. Haines and Poynder argue for a broader role for the UNHCR in the monitoring and implementation of the Convention.[19] Gonzaga states his personal view that the UNHCR has an unenviable role as it requires state cooperation regarding the intake of refugees while the UNHCR's continued presence in states depends upon them assisting it.[20] This often constrains the UNHCR in any advocacy role it could or should undertake. This again highlights, as stated earlier, the need for a reinvigoration and commitment of resources of nation states to the work of the UNHCR. The delegate ministers at the Global Consultations also observed that it is critical that state parties cooperate with the UNHCR and use its expertise in protection issues.

The delegates proposed that the UNHCR's Ex Com should establish a Sub-Committee on International Protection, empowering it to ask the UNHCR for frank views on serious protection problems and to call on states to take concrete actions. It would involve experts and NGOs.[21]

---

[19] N Poynder, '"Mind the Gap": Seeking Alternative Protection Under the Convention Against Torture and the International Covenant on Civil and Political Rights', chapter 7 in this book.

[20] J A Gonzaga, 'The Role of the United Nations High Commissioner for Refugees and the Refugee Definition', chapter 9 in this book.

[21] Global Consultations, above n 3, p 3.

Hathaway has a different view and urges caution before such an approach is adopted.[22] Hathaway notes the support for the establishment of an advisory committee by state ministers at the Global Consultations but warns that its establishment alone will still avoid the critical question of the oversight of the Convention itself. Merely because such a body may be capable of operation, he notes, does not mean such a body will ensure the objectivity and inclusiveness required.

Hathaway urges caution in rushing to accept a 'quick fix' and in making compromises which will not resolve issues of accountability. His view is that the UNHCR has taken on a role which is broader than that envisaged by the drafters of 1951 Convention and that the UNHCR is not necessarily the most appropriate mechanism to provide 'arms length' oversight. He observes that Article 35 of the Convention does not preclude a mechanism other than the UNHCR from being charged with the responsibility for oversight of the Convention.[23] Nevertheless on the issue of procedures, in the absence of references to administrative practices in the Convention, considerable guidance can be found in the UNHCR guidelines themselves, something which is often ignored in state practice.[24]

The question remains, what form might an alternative mechanism to the UNHCR take? While not providing a definitive answer, Hathaway points to the implementation in the 1970s of a range of United Nations Human Rights Committees which are external to states. He observes that unless there is:

> some good principle why refugee law should be immune from this general commitment, it is high time to reverse the historical aberration by bringing the committee supervision of refugee law into line with the practice of human rights law more generally.[25]

Hathaway recognises that often states parties (and others) need 'persuading, cajoling and indeed shaming' and notes that this has been

---

[22] J Hathaway, 'Taking Oversight to Refugee Law Seriously', Speech, Global Consultations on International Protection, Ministerial Meeting of States Parties, 12–13 December 2001.

[23] Id, p 10.

[24] For example, UNHCR, *Handbook on Procedures and Criteria for the Determination of Refugee Status* (Geneva, UNHCR, 2nd ed, 1992).

[25] Hathaway, above n 22, p 5.

'critical to the success of the international human rights'.[26] Hathaway does not overlook the role of the Department of International Protection in assisting governments' draft policies and legislation nor that of Ex Com, but sees a need for additional oversight. He argues that:

> it is vital that we not see important laudable efforts to devise an advisory committee structure to advise the High Commissioner on the exercise of his protection mandate as either consistent with, or as a substitute for a genuine program of independent, impartial, transparent, and socially accountable supervision of the Refugee Convention.[27]

Overseas Migration Facilities

The Global Consultations on 13 December 2001 called for quality decision making which is fair, efficient and which has enforceable results, including the return of those not found to be in need of international protection. However it was noted that these processes should not lose sight of the needs of individuals.[28] The expansion of legal migration programs could, it was observed, offer new opportunities for those forced to seek asylum.

Millbank suggests that the problem of illegal arrivals and people smuggling should be addressed by posting more migration officers overseas, including in refugee camps in the Middle East.[29] In addition, I believe that staffing levels at assessment posts are insufficient and the outposts are often too distant from trouble spots. Addressing these staffing and resource issues would increase the number of access points for people seeking asylum who are in desperate straits and reduce the need for people to use the smuggling operations. Even where overseas posts do exist, the backlog of applications lodged can be high and staff commonly report allegations of corruption and short staffing.[30]

Refugee camp safety is also an issue. In March 2002 UN investigators undertook an inquiry into allegations of the sexual abuse of young girls in refugee camps in Guinea, Liberia and Sierra Leone in exchange for food

---

[26] Id, p 8.

[27] Id, p 4.

[28] Global Consultations, Chairperson's Report on Roundtable Three, above n 7, p 1.

[29] Millbank, above n 2, p 15.

[30] For more discussion see Curran, above n 17.

and aid. The UNHCR and Save the Children in the United Kingdom released a report on 26 February 2002 alleging that almost 70 aid workers from 40 agencies had been pushing young children into sex. The report also observed that UN Peacekeepers from several countries had exploited children in the refugee camps.[31] When overseas posts are better staffed and resourced, less remote from regions of tension and have more integrity, then perhaps more refugees in imminent danger will be able to access offshore programs. But until then, many will face incredible danger to escape from significant threat of persecution. It is therefore not surprising that so many people are unable to take advantage of the 'offshore program' and arrive in Australia by boat, notwithstanding the personal cost involved.

As Millbank observes, the EU has concluded that asylum-driven migration can only be controlled through providing for development to source countries and through forging agreements with their governments on aid, trade and training and temporary migration opportunities.[32] The difficulty arises when aid or interest in development occur only because there is some trade or political benefit and not because there is a genuine need for repatriation. Such short-sighted activities can create further instability.

Revitalising the Refugees Convention

The need to strengthen and revitalise the Convention is an important way to mark the 50th anniversary of the Convention. Questions can be asked such as, how do we ensure better monitoring and compliance around the world? How can all states be encouraged to be involved? How can the world community and its component parts work more effectively to protect those who fall through the gaps, and to commit more resources, especially the wealthy states?

Millbank suggests redefining the notion of refugee to encompass all displaced persons, with a focus on groups rather than individuals.[33]

---

[31] UNHCR and Save the Children-UK, *Sexual Violence & Exploitation: The Experience of Refugee Children in Guinea, Liberia and Sierra Leone* (UNHCR and Save the Children–UK, February 2002); Save the Children, 'Extensive Abuse of West African Refugee Children Reported', Press Release, 27 February 2002, http://www.savethechildren.org.uk/pressrels/270202.html.

[32] Millbank, above n 2, p 14.

[33] Id, p 16.

She argues that this would strengthen a world response by refocusing the Convention on the provision of humanitarian assistance rather than on individual persecution. While governments which are keen to limit their commitment may find this option attractive, the danger is that too much discretion would be left for governments to determine the scope of the group. The risk is that the danger faced by particular individuals may be ignored.

Walker and Mathew have highlighted that there are dangers inherent in treating people only as groups or in providing solace for only limited time periods. Mathew argues that safe haven categories can overlook the protection of individuals within a group, who by reason of their specific vulnerability or political associations or family links, can be more at risk than others in the group. There is also a danger that governments may seek to send people home after conflicts appear to be over but before the country is safe. This is highlighted by the Australian government's commitment to returning people who had fled Afghanistan after the Taliban fell, even though the UNHCR warned it was not safe for people to return as various clans and splinter groups were causing trouble and land mines had not been cleared.

The Convention in Changing World Circumstances

By the end of the Cold War in 1989 there was an expectation about peace and universal cooperation. Since 1989 there have been an increasing number of countries experiencing internal conflicts, border conflicts and ethnic cleansing. In the *UN Development Report* the UN Development Program counted only three wars between states from 1989–92, but there were 79 instances of intrastate conflict.[34] These intra-state conflicts are often more complex and multi layered. The continued oversight of the changing nature of world conflict needs to be addressed and factored in to world protection responses. The constraints which apply under the four Geneva Conventions to international conflict, which is narrowly defined, need to be addressed so that intrastate conflicts can avail themselves of the

---

[34] UN, *UN Development Report* (New York, Oxford University Press, 1994). See also S P Malik and A M Dorman, 'United Nations and Military Intervention: A Study in the Politics of Contradiction', in A M Dorman and T G Otte (eds), *Military Intervention: from Gunboat Diplomacy to Humanitarian Intervention* (England, Dartmouth, 1994), chapter 6.

greater humanitarian and human rights responses and standards in times of conflict. In the past in Somalia and currently in relation to the holding of suspected terrorists from al-Qa'ida in Cuba by the United States of America, resistance has been shown to the application of the Four Geneva Conventions in a broader context, and to signing on to the Optional Protocols of those Conventions. This no doubt will remain a continuing issue. Improved frameworks are therefore needed to deal with the changing nature of world conflict. Increasingly new developments are changing the nature of conflicts.[35] The development of biological and chemical warfare and technologies will present new challenges to the task of offering protection to those who are persecuted or have their human rights abused.

Conclusion

At the Global Consultations the UNHCR stressed that burden sharing was a key to finding solutions for refugees, and that a positive culture of respect for refugees was also critical.[36]

In addition, in the Declaration of the Global Consultations the delegates asked all states to respond 'promptly, predictably and adequately to funding appeals issued by the UNHCR'[37] and 'to recognise the valuable contributions made by non-government organisations'.[38] A reinforced, better-funded UN would be able to make a speedier response and put in place preventative measures so that countries could avoid being faced with major humanitarian crises. Some effort is being made to resolve disputes but often this can be undermined by vested interests in countries with strategic economic or military objectives. A standby world fund should be

---

[35] A number of countries have however signed on to the Optional Protocols to the Geneva Conventions which enable application of Geneva Conventions standards to intrastate conflict. Australia is a signatory; the United States is not.

[36] Global Consultations, above n 3, pp 1–2

[37] Global Consultations, Ministerial Meeting of States parties to the 1951 Convention and/or its 1967 Protocol Relating to the Status of Refugees, *Declaration* (Geneva, UNHCR, 13 December 2001), reaffirming the commitment of States Parties, Operative Paragraphs, para 10.

[38] Id, para 11.

established to deal with mass influxes with regional allocations as suggested at the Global Consultations.[39]

It is critical that tracking of what happens to asylum seekers when they are returned to their countries be conducted to monitor what occurs upon their return. It is difficult to assess risk to asylum seekers and Convention compliance unless such research is undertaken. It was noted at the Global Consultations on 12 December 2001 that the principle of non-refoulement was now considered to be a principle of customary international law and not merely a Convention requirement.[40] A new and effective global reception and assessment system which is free from corruption and quick in resolving issues but adheres to due process, and respectful partnerships with nations struggling to control their populations is needed as a matter of urgency. Currently the problems caused by corruption are often overlooked or tolerated.

The UNHCR needs to develop a fearless and independent role in ensuring that states bear their responsibilities equitably and in accordance with the spirit of human rights provisions, ensuring a more rigorous implementation of the Refugees Convention requirements.

In August 2000 Mr Ruddock, the Minister for Immigration in Australia, announced the government was reviewing the interpretation and implementation of the Refugees Convention in Australia.[41] Then in March 2001 he described the international system as open to exploitation and manipulation.[42] In April 2001 the United Kingdom's Home Secretary Jack Straw, criticised the Convention as 'too broad for conditions in the 21st Century' and 'no longer an adequate guide to policy'.

Withdrawal from the Convention is not a practical solution for governments who find the Convention problematic.[43] It makes it more

---

[39] Global Consultations, Chairperson's Report on Roundtable 2, *International Cooperation to Protect Masses in Flight* (Geneva, UNHCR, 13 December 2002), p 3.

[40] Id, p 3.

[41] P Ruddock, 'Australian Government Measures to Reform UN Refugee Bodies', Media Release MPS 088/2000, 29 August 2000, http://www.minister.immi.gov.au/media_releases/media00/r00088.htm; Millbank, above n 2, p 6.

[42] This was the rationale for the Migration Legislation Amendment Act (No 6) 2001 (Cth). See the second reading speech by Senator Robert Hill, Parliament of Australia *Hansard* Senate, 24 September 2001, p 27603.

[43] Millbank, above n 2, p 18.

difficult to retain influence and reshape the development of the international framework.

Strategic, centrally coordinated approaches are needed. It is important that it is recognised that the refugee issue is a worldwide phenomenon. Communication and cooperation between nation states, governments, the non-government sector and the voluntary sector who have extended themselves admirably over the past years will be critical if sound policy approaches and successful integration of refugees are to occur.

Australia and other developed nations with resources need to adopt a comprehensive approach which, rather than responding to the immediate symptoms, addresses some of the causes of dispossession, including ways to prevent forced migration through early intervention and the bolstering of the humanitarian role of the United Nations so that it can work more effectively in reducing the causes of turmoil, unrest, repression, wars, violation of human rights, famine and so on.[44] In an age which prides itself on technological advances there is scope to track refugee movements, gather research on causes and preventative measures and to make more of a concerted effort to implement the necessary changes. To continue to adopt electorally popular short-term solutions will do little to address the humanitarian issues and refugee flow in the long term.

No review of the Convention will be a good review if it is undertaken in a vacuum of the considerations which cause people to take flight, their experiences during flight, and the impact upon border countries. The challenge for policy makers is to ensure that frameworks operate in a way that promotes human rights, fairness, transparency and adherence to due process at all levels, notwithstanding increased complexities. Other international instruments can be used as guides where confusion arises so that government agencies err in favor of human rights rather than merely convenience, pragmatics or policy making in a vacuum. At the Global Consultations on 12 December 2001, the President of Latvia, Ms Vaira Vike-Freiberga, a former refugee, lamented the tendency to think of refugees in bureaucratic language rather than 'lending a helping hand' and retaining a 'human perspective'.[45]

---

[44] For further discussion see C De Jong, 'The Legal Framework: The Convention Relating to the Status of Refugees and the Development of Law Half a Century Later', *International Journal of Refugee Law*, **10** (1998) p 688 at p 694.

[45] Global Consultations, Chairperson's Report on Roundtable 2, above n 39, p 2.

Index

boat arrivals 94–5, 134–6
and CAT 179, 187–90, 192
detention centres 49–50
gay and lesbian claims 254–5
history, immigrants 314–15
human rights 88, 174, 191–2
and ICCPR 184–7, 192, 212, 225
Minister for Immigration, role 60
MRT 200–1
people smuggling 98–9, 100–1
RCOA 30, 139–40
refugees
  exclusion law 133–72
  funding 100
  illegal 140–1
  protection 84–9, 152–71
  reception arrangements 101–3
  resettlement 58, 92–3
  smuggling 98–9
  status, determination 59–70
Refugees Convention 2–3, 8, 12, 17
  courts, role 61–4
  future 84–9
  implementation 3, 48, 53–4, 59–84,
  177–9
  interpretation 103–5, 148–52,
  176–7
  judicial review 73–9, 178
RRT 70–3, 74, 78, 79, 154, 164, 166–7,
168, 195, 197, 267–9, 293, 300, 305–
6
safe third country concept 7, 152–72
SLCRC 64–8, 72, 83, 199, 203, 205,
214, 215, 224–5
Temporary Safe Haven Visas 246–7
TPV system 14–15, 82–3, 102, 105,
142, 156–7, 210–11
see also Pacific Solution; *Tampa*
incident
Australian Human Rights and Equal
Opportunities Commission 170

Austria, asylum policies 19

Bangkok Principles Concerning
  Treatment of Refugees (1966) 242
BIA (Board of Immigration Appeals),
  US 256
Blair, Tony, on the Refugees Conven-
  tion 17, 19–20
boat arrivals
  Australia 94–5, 134–6
  Canada 129–30
border control
  and asylum seekers 10–11
  and the *Tampa* incident 10
'Bracero' labour, deportation from US
  37
British Refugee Council, UK 30

Canada
  boat arrivals 129–30
  and CAT 109–10, 114–16, 121–4, 126
  Charter of Rights 109, 120–1, 123
  gay and lesbian claims 257
  IRB guidelines 298–9
  refugee law 109–32
    and criminality 110–12, 113–16
  refugees
    ineligibility 8–9, 113–16, 126–9
    protection 111–12
  Refugees Convention 8–9, 124–5,
    128
Cartagena Declaration (1984), refugees
  242
CAT (Convention Against Torture)
  Australia 179, 187–90, 192
  Canada 109–10, 114–16, 121–4, 126
  complaints procedures 180–4, 187–90
  ratification 179
  and refoulement 39
  and the Refugees Convention 109–10,
  175